THE BETRAYAL
OF THE
Duchess

ALSO BY MAURICE SAMUELS

The Spectacular Past

Inventing the Israelite

The Right to Difference

THE BETRAYAL
OF THE

Duchess

THE SCANDAL THAT UNMADE THE BOURBON
MONARCHY AND MADE FRANCE MODERN

———— • ————

MAURICE SAMUELS

BASIC BOOKS
New York

Basic Books
Hachette Book Group
1290 Avenue of the Americas, New York, NY 10104
www.basicbooks.com

Printed in the United States of America

First Edition: April 2020

Published by Basic Books, an imprint of Perseus Books, LLC, a subsidiary of Hachette Book Group, Inc. The Basic Books name and logo is a trademark of the Hachette Book Group.

The Hachette Speakers Bureau provides a wide range of authors for speaking events. To find out more, go to www.hachettespeakersbureau.com or call (866) 376-6591.

The publisher is not responsible for websites (or their content) that are not owned by the publisher.

Additional copyright/credit information is on page 329. Family tree and map by Patti Isaacs.

Print book interior design by Trish Wilkinson.

Library of Congress Cataloging-in-Publication Data

Names: Samuels, Maurice, author.
Title: The betrayal of the Duchess : the scandal that unmade the Bourbon monarchy and made France modern / Maurice Samuels.
Description: First edition. | New York : Basic Books, 2020. | Includes bibliographical references and index.
Identifiers: LCCN 2019041779 | ISBN 9781541645455 (hardcover) | ISBN 9781541645462 (ebook)
Subjects: LCSH: Berry, Marie-Caroline de Bourbon-Sicile, duchesse de, 1798–1870. | France—History—Restoration, 1814–1830—Biography. | France—History—Wars of the Vendée, 1793–1832. | Deutz, Simon, 1802–1844. | Antisemitism—France—History—19th century.
Classification: LCC DC260.B5 S36 2020 | DDC 944.04/6092 [B]—dc23
LC record available at https://lccn.loc.gov/2019041779

ISBNs: 978-1-5416-4545-5 (hardcover), 978-1-5416-4546-2 (ebook)

LSC-C

10 9 8 7 6 5 4 3 2 1

For my friends

Contents

If in the course of centuries to come, historical novels are still in fashion, a new Walter Scott will have a difficult time finding a more poetic subject than the expedition of Madame la duchesse de Berry in France during the years 1832 and 1833.

—ADÈLE D'OSMOND, COMTESSE DE BOIGNE, *MEMOIRS*

Twenty years ago, everyone would have known even the most minor details that we are about to recount. Today everyone has forgotten them. History moves so quickly in France!

—ALEXANDRE DUMAS, *MY MEMOIRS*

BOURBON FAMILY TREE

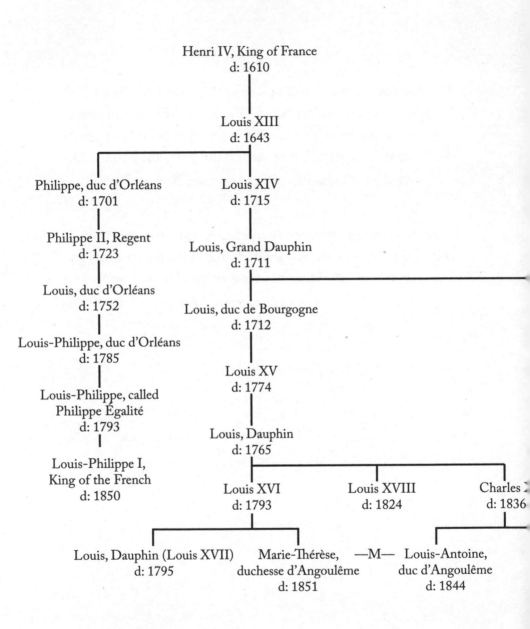

Henri IV, King of France
d: 1610

Louis XIII
d: 1643

Philippe, duc d'Orléans
d: 1701

Louis XIV
d: 1715

Philippe II, Regent
d: 1723

Louis, Grand Dauphin
d: 1711

Louis, duc d'Orléans
d: 1752

Louis, duc de Bourgogne
d: 1712

Louis-Philippe, duc d'Orléans
d: 1785

Louis XV
d: 1774

Louis-Philippe, called
Philippe Égalité
d: 1793

Louis, Dauphin
d: 1765

Louis-Philippe I,
King of the French
d: 1850

Louis XVI
d: 1793

Louis XVIII
d: 1824

Charles
d: 1836

Louis, Dauphin (Louis XVII)
d: 1795

Marie-Thérèse,
duchesse d'Angoulême
d: 1851

—M—

Louis-Antoine,
duc d'Angoulême
d: 1844

Philip V, King of Spain
d: 1746

Charles III, King of Spain
d: 1788

Ferdinand IV, King of Naples
(after 1815: Ferdinand I, King of the Two Sicilies)
d: 1825

Francis I,   Marie-Amélie, —M— Louis-Philippe I
King of the Two Sicilies   Queen of the French
d: 1830   d: 1866

Charles Ferdinand, —M— Marie-Caroline,
duc de Berry   duchesse de Berry
d: 1820   d: 1870

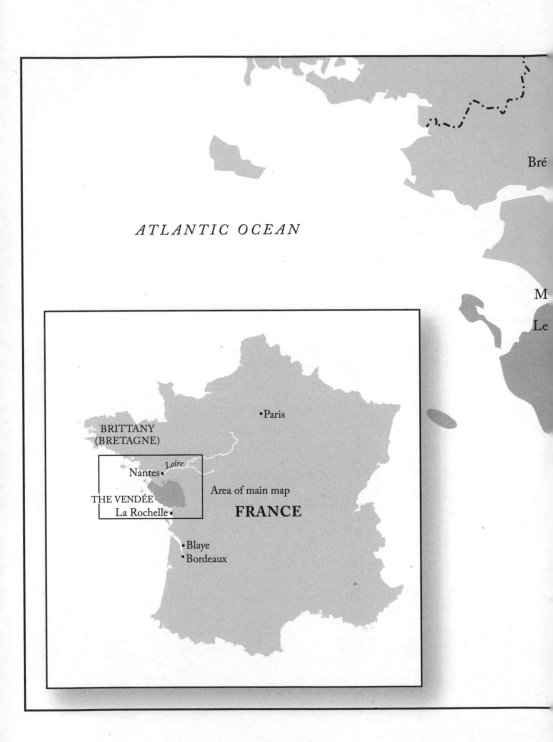

ATLANTIC OCEAN

Bré

M

Le

•Paris

BRITTANY
(BRETAGNE)

Loire

Nantes•

THE VENDÉE
La Rochelle•

Area of main map

FRANCE

•Blaye
•Bordeaux

Map of the Vendée

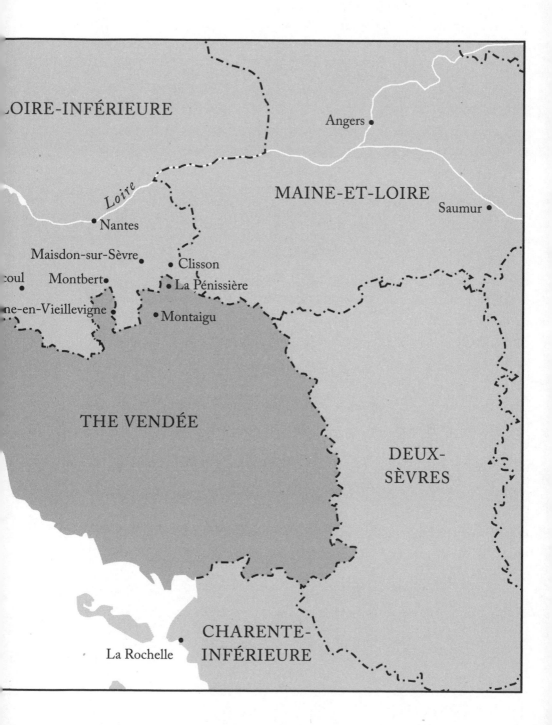

LOIRE-INFÉRIEURE

Angers

MAINE-ET-LOIRE

Saumur

Loire

Nantes

Maisdon-sur-Sèvre

Clisson

coul

Montbert

La Pénissière

ne-en-Vieillevigne

Montaigu

THE VENDÉE

DEUX-
SÈVRES

La Rochelle

CHARENTE-
INFÉRIEURE

Introduction

A T HALF PAST five on the evening of November 6, 1832, police raided a house in a quiet residential enclave of Nantes, the largest city in France's western region. Shoving past frightened servants, they moved methodically from room to room, overturning beds and rifling through wardrobes as twelve hundred soldiers—two entire army regiments—filed into the dark cobblestone streets below to make sure that nobody could escape out the back. They were searching for the duchesse de Berry, the most wanted woman in France.

The mother of the heir to the throne, she had been forced into exile with the rest of the Bourbon royal family after the Revolution of 1830, only to return two years later to launch a bloody civil war. Her dream was to reconquer the kingdom for her eleven-year-old son. All through the spring she had commanded a guerrilla army in a series of battles against the government, but by the early summer she was on the run. And now, after six months of evading capture, the luck of the four-foot-seven duchess was coming to an end.

The police had been tipped off by the duchess's confidant, a seductive yet volatile man named Simon Deutz. He had pledged undying loyalty to her cause, then turned against her once it appeared that her campaign would fail. For a large cash reward, he had agreed to lead the police to her hiding place in Nantes. But when the agents forced their way into the house, the duchess was nowhere to be found.

Just minutes before, she had slipped into a secret closet behind the fireplace in the attic. Created during the Reign of Terror to save priests from the guillotine, the closet was so small that the duchess and her three accomplices could barely stand up straight and there was not an inch of space between them. Praying for a miracle, she tried not to move while the agents sounded the walls and knocked holes in the roof. She could hear the police commissioner cursing on the other side of the thin partition as he ordered his men to reduce the house to rubble in their efforts to find her.

After sixteen hours, the agents were about to give up the search when one of the soldiers standing guard in the room decided to light a fire. As the secret compartment filled with smoke and the walls glowed red with heat, the duchess did her best to endure the torment. Eventually, though, the trapdoor to the fireplace opened, and out crawled the tiny, soot-covered rebel. Straightening her scorched dress and shielding her eyes from the light, she declared in the most regal manner she could summon: "I am the duchesse de Berry. You are French soldiers. I entrust myself to your honor!"

THOUGH LARGELY FORGOTTEN today, the betrayal of the duchess shocked the world at the time. It made international headlines and engrossed the public for months, all the more so when it emerged that the arrested duchess was pregnant, despite not having had a husband for over a decade. The case fascinated the leading writers of the day: François-René de Chateaubriand and Victor Hugo both wrote significant works about it, while Alexandre Dumas *père*, the author of *The Three Musketeers*, returned to the events surrounding the betrayal in a novel, a historical chronicle, his own memoirs, and a memoir that he ghostwrote for the general charged with suppressing the duchess's revolt.

Beyond its many obvious attractions—a glamorous heroine, a quixotic military campaign, an illicit romance, and a dramatic double-cross—the scandal had major repercussions for French history. It ended the hopes for another Bourbon restoration and helped stabilize the monarchy of Louis-Philippe, who had claimed the throne in 1830 but whose grip on it was still tenuous. But the case also had another, and perhaps even more far-reaching, effect: Simon Deutz had been born a Jew, and his betrayal of the duchess provoked modern France's first major outpouring of antisemitic hatred.[1]

Historians often date the rise of modern antisemitism in France to the decade leading up to the Dreyfus Affair of the 1890s. This notorious case, in which a Jewish army officer was falsely accused of treason, is considered a turning point in world history, the moment at which Theodor Herzl, the founder of the Zionist movement, claimed to have concluded that antisemitism made the dream of Jewish integration in Europe impossible. Yet the first real warning bell—the first signal that modernity would not necessarily be good for the Jews—had actually sounded some sixty years earlier, following the betrayal of the duchesse de Berry.[2]

In 1832 the modern era was just beginning. Charles Darwin's *HMS Beagle* arrived in South America that year on the trip that would lay the foundation for his theory of evolution. A young lawyer named Abraham Lincoln was about to enter Illinois politics, and the start of Queen Victoria's long reign was a mere five years in the future. Recent innovations such as the telegraph were shrinking the world while also speeding it up. Railroads would soon carry passengers between distant cities faster than anyone thought possible.

The changes associated with the birth of modernity gave rise to a great deal of social and political strife, and nowhere more so than in France. By 1832, the country had been fighting over the legacy of the French Revolution for fifty years. France was also in the throes of an industrial revolution that was no less momentous. The period's unrest was perhaps most vividly captured by Victor Hugo in his epic novel *Les Misérables*. Set largely in 1832, the novel's plot unfolds against the backdrop of a failed political uprising, as idealistic young students and starving workers fight to create a republic but are brutally repressed by the soldiers of King Louis-Philippe. What Hugo barely mentions is that at the same moment leftist firebrands were dying on the barricades, the French government was also attempting to suppress the right-wing revolt of the duchesse de Berry.[3]

Louis-Philippe—from the Bourbons' rival dynasty, the Orléans—had claimed the throne from the duchess's son during the Revolution of 1830, and she wanted it back. She believed in the Bourbons' divine right to rule, but she also believed that only France's traditional monarchs—and their ally the Catholic Church—could restore stability to a country fractured by revolutionary upheaval. By fighting to bring about yet another Bourbon restoration, the duchess seemed to promise a return to a simpler, better world—a world of religious duties and feudal privileges in which everyone knew their place. This was the key to the force she exerted on those who were engaged in the century-long battle against the French Revolution and the political and economic modernization that it unleashed. Like her idol Joan of Arc, the duchess proposed her own heroic persona as an antidote to the troubles of her time.[4]

Her betrayal by Simon Deutz turned her into a martyr instead. In the aftermath of her arrest a legend took shape among the duchess's supporters in which the betrayal became a symbol for the evils that had been ushered in by the French Revolution. This legend was powerful because it told a simple story: a Jew had betrayed the mother of France's rightful king. The story transformed resistance to modernity into a passion play with the Jew as villain and, in so doing, helped make antisemitism a key feature of right-wing ideology in France.[5]

Hatred of Jews, of course, predates modernity. Antisemites have always attempted to define who they were by turning the Jew into the embodiment of what they were not. The biblical figure of Judas, the betrayer of Christ, reflects the way that ancient Christians already saw the Jew as corrupt and treacherous. But by the time of the Dreyfus Affair at the end of the nineteenth century, antisemitism had come to mean much more. The Right had turned the Jew into a symbol of everything they were fighting against, from industrialization to cosmopolitanism, secularism to revolution. The betrayal of the duchesse de Berry marks a key stage in this transition, the moment at which modern stereotypes of the Jew crystallized in the popular imagination. Simon Deutz represents a bridge between old and new forms of antisemitism. He is the missing link between Judas and Dreyfus.[6]

THIS BOOK IS rooted in history, anchored in a specific time and place. But it also has contemporary relevance. With deindustrialization now taking place in much of the West and globalization concentrating wealth ever more intensely, our own moment is experiencing a transformation similar in scale to that of France in the 1830s. And some of those who feel displaced by changes still blame the disruption on Jews and other minorities.

That certain protesters—in France, the United States, and around the world—have turned antisemitic should come as no surprise. Opponents of modernity have projected their fears and anxieties about change onto Jews since the beginning of the nineteenth century. Nor should the antisemitism of radical Islamist movements startle us: they too are at war with modernity, much like the conservative Catholics in the duchess's time. The specifics have changed, but many of the fundamental features that govern how antisemitic hatred operates have not. People still tell stories about Jewish treachery. They still consume paranoid plots to assuage their fears and explain their failures. The discourse of modern antisemitism still performs much the same function for reactionaries and populists today as it did in the 1830s. Resurrecting the forgotten story of Simon Deutz's betrayal of the duchesse de Berry sheds light on this discourse by revealing how it first took shape.

But why does it need resurrecting? If it had such a profound effect on the formation of right-wing ideology and on the development of antisemitism, why has the betrayal of the duchess faded from memory? Historians have perhaps been reluctant to examine the betrayal in recent years because of its unsettling nature. Unlike Dreyfus, who was a model victim, or at least a blameless one, Deutz was actually guilty of betrayal. Even more disturbingly, the duchess's uncommon heroism and alluring wit risk eliciting sympathy for her reactionary politics. The story lacks the clear moral guideposts that make the Dreyfus Affair such a satisfying tale of justice triumphing over prejudice. It offers no "J'Accuse!" moment, no cause for righteous indignation. But this moral ambiguity should not deter us from studying the case; on the contrary, the betrayal of the duchess merits attention precisely because of its ambiguity. It is in the gray areas, the shadows, that history has the most to teach us.

PART ONE

The Duchess

CHAPTER 1

The Volcano's Edge

N APLES CURLS INVITINGLY around its bay, the ocher buildings of the city glittering gold against the deep blue of the water. The culmination of the grand tour in the eighteenth century, this capital of southern Italy lured visitors from colder climes with a mix of sunshine, lush natural beauty, antiquarian curiosity, and more than a hint of danger. The threat came not just from the *lazzaroni*, the rough urban street dwellers thought to lie in wait for unsuspecting tourists, but also from Mount Vesuvius, the giant volcano towering a thousand feet above the city and visible from every point in the dense metropolis, the streets of which were paved with its hardened lava. "Vede Napoli e poi mori" ("See Naples and die"), proclaimed the proverb that visitors interpreted literally as they watched white smoke puff from the volcano's giant crater. The volcano was particularly active in the late eighteenth century, when seismic pressures of a political nature were also building.

Maria Carolina Luisa di Borbone, the future duchesse de Berry, was born at the royal palace of Caserta, just north of Naples, on November 5, 1798. Her great-grandfather, the first Bourbon king of

Naples and Sicily, had constructed the enormous palace on a site slightly to the north of the city to shield it as much as possible from the danger of Vesuvius. Modeled on France's palace of Versailles, Caserta spread out over more than two million square feet and contained twelve hundred rooms: a grander building could not be found in Italy. Such neoclassical splendor was meant to convey the power and prestige of the Bourbon kingdom in Italy, but by the time of Carolina's birth, the foundations of the kingdom had begun to shake.[1]

The future duchess's grandfather, King Ferdinand, was known as the *Re Lazzaroni*, the Lazzaroni King, because he was beloved by the urban ruffians. Interested only in hunting and fishing, he left the running of the government to his wife, Maria Carolina of Habsburg, a determined woman who, despite her various public responsibilities, bore him no fewer than eighteen children over the course of their long marriage. The first surviving male of this large brood was the future King Francis I, the duchess's father. Another child was Maria Amalia, the duchess's aunt, who would marry Louis-Philippe d'Orléans and become Marie-Amélie, queen of the French, after the Revolution of 1830.[2]

By the time of the future duchess's birth in 1798, all European monarchies were feeling the aftershocks of the French Revolution as its leading general, Napoleon Bonaparte, spread revolutionary fervor to the lands he conquered. And nowhere was royalist fear more palpable than in the Kingdom of Naples, where the queen had lost her sister, Marie Antoinette, to the guillotine in France and where the monarchs' absolutist policies had ignited a liberal opposition. British admiral Horatio Nelson had little trouble enlisting the Neapolitan Bourbons in the fight to beat back Napoleon's forces in Italy.

After Napoleon conquered Rome in 1798, the queen of Naples and Sicily decided to take no chances. With the help of the British, the Bourbons began moving their treasure from the Royal Palace of Naples onto Nelson's ships waiting in the harbor. The plan was to transport the entire court and its riches to the island of Sicily, the other capital of the twin kingdom, which the British fleet could protect more easily from French invasion. Once they had been loaded with jewels, gold, paintings, clothing, and cash, the ships moved into deeper waters, out of range of enemy fire, as they waited for the royal family to flee. The transfer of the treasure took place in secret, over the course of several nights, so as not to alert the anxious Neapolitans.[3]

On the evening of December 21, 1798, the king and queen attended a reception held at the Turkish Embassy. At the height of the festivities, the monarchs slipped out, making their way incognito on foot through the dark streets of the city as their carriages remained in front of the embassy to make it look like they were still at the event. Once back at their palace, they were met by the rest of the royal household. By torchlight, the party passed through tunnels that ran under the palace, directly into the port where British sailors would row them out to the waiting ships.[4]

During this operation, the future duchesse de Berry was a baby, not yet two months old. Her parents were double first cousins and had been married in 1790. They christened their first child, born in 1797, Maria Carolina Luisa in honor of her grandmother, the queen, and called her Carolina. She joined the other members of the royal family on the first rowboat heading toward the British ship, the *Vanguard*. It was a terrifying journey out into open water.[5]

A storm delayed their departure for Sicily for two agonizing days. When they did finally set sail, at 7 p.m. on the night of December 23, 1798, the choppy seas made for a gruesome voyage. Most of the passengers were prostrate with seasickness for the entire forty-eight hours that it took to travel to Palermo. The misery was intense. One six-year-old prince began having convulsions shortly after setting sail, and he died later that night of exhaustion. Baby Carolina, however, survived the journey.[6]

Palermo was the other capital of the twin kingdom, but it was not one that the royal family had often visited. They took up residence at the barren and poorly heated Colli Palace amid a snowstorm, which was unusual for Sicily, and let the other two thousand Neapolitan refugees find whatever accommodations they could. "Palermo is in full ferment and I expect grave events," the queen wrote to a friend. "Having neither troops nor arms, lacking everything, I am ready for anything and quite desperate. Here the priests are completely corrupted, the people savage, the nobility more than uncertain and of questionable loyalty. . . . The dangers we run here are immense and real. You may imagine what I suffer. Before forty days [have passed], revolution will have broken out here. It will be appalling and terribly violent." The queen also worried about her family's health: "My daughters are all ill. As for my daughter-in-law [Carolina's mother], she is dying of consumption." King Ferdinand did not share his wife's despair. Having brought his dogs along on the journey, he quickly arranged for a hunt.[7]

With the help of the invading French army and without the royals in residence, republicans in Naples established the Parthenopean Republic on January 21, 1799. Meanwhile, the exiled Bourbons dispatched an army to reconquer their kingdom. Led by a priest, their forces landed in Calabria and began a march toward Naples, peasants flocking to this growing "army of the faith" as it moved through the countryside. The Neapolitan republicans realized that the tide had turned against them. With Nelson blockading the port, the French withdrawing their military support, and the *lazzaroni* in revolt, they sought terms for surrender, hoping to obtain safe passage out of the city in exchange for agreeing to a restoration of the Bourbons.[8]

But Nelson was urged toward ruthlessness in letters from the vengeful queen in Palermo. The fate of her beheaded sister, Marie Antoinette, never far from her mind, Maria Carolina wrote the following on June 25, 1799: "It is . . . impossible for me to deal tenderly with this rebellious rabble. . . . We must make an example of the leading representatives. . . . The same applies to the women who have distinguished themselves during the revolution, and without pity." Nelson arrested over eight hundred of the city's republicans, executed hundreds without a trial, and hanged one of their leaders from the yardarm of his ship, refusing him confession and leaving his body to dangle in the wind. The British admiral received a hero's welcome in Palermo from the king and queen.[9]

The future duchesse de Berry's first months were thus spent in an atmosphere of counterrevolutionary fervor. To say she imbibed reactionary royalism and hatred of the French Revolution with her mother's—or grandmother's—milk would hardly be an exaggeration; all around her, the embittered Neapolitan Bourbons plotted revenge on their enemies and made plans to reimpose absolutist rule. The royal family would remain for another year and a half in Palermo, and when they returned to their former capital on January 25, 1801, Carolina was displayed in front of a jubilant crowd of *lazzaroni* from a balcony of the Neapolitan palace.[10]

This first restoration of the Neapolitan Bourbons did not last long. Ferdinand and Maria Carolina joined the next allied coalition against Napoleon, and in February 1806 the royal family, including young Carolina, was forced to flee to Sicily once again after France conquered Naples. The French succeeded, where the Parthenopean Republic had not, in undoing the feudal structure of the Neapolitan Bourbon regime. They imposed the Napoleonic Code in legal matters, dismantled many of the privileges of the church and nobles, opened schools for the poor, built roads, and illuminated the dangerous streets with oil lamps. Many notable French intellectuals visited Naples during the eight years of French rule, including the writer and statesman Chateaubriand, who observed from up close an eruption of Vesuvius in 1804.[11]

Carolina, meanwhile, grew up in Sicily surrounded by furious royalists waiting for Napoleon's downfall in order to retake their kingdom. No one was more furious than her grandmother, who spent her days dashing off letters, taking opium, and complaining to anyone who would listen about the misfortunes that had befallen her family. Otherwise occupied, the queen did not pay much attention to the education of her precociously bright granddaughter, nor unfortunately did her parents. Carolina's mother had died of tuberculosis in 1801, and the little girl's father and new stepmother—a Bourbon *infanta* from Spain—devoted their attention to their rapidly expanding brood. Carolina was raised largely by her governess, the comtesse de la Tour-en-Voivre, a French aristocrat whose husband was an admiral in the service of the king of Naples. A cultivated woman, the countess tried without much success to impart the rudiments of French, Italian, and Spanish, as well as a bit of history, geography, and literature, to the willful girl. The unusual circumstances in which Carolina grew up meant that the future duchess enjoyed far more liberty than was usually accorded to royal princesses.[12]

As a young woman, Carolina was not a conventional beauty, but most people who met her found her attractive. She was what the French call a *jolie laide*. Small of stature, she was extremely near-sighted and used an opera glass whenever she needed to see something at a distance. Her eyes protruded, her left eye wandered, and her reddish-pink lids were often enflamed. Her teeth were uneven, and she possessed the pendulous lower lip that ran in the Habsburg family. However, what was most notable about her was her coloring: she would later tell her doctor that until the age of twenty-three she was so blonde as to seem almost albino. Her light hair and translucent skin made her a special object of curiosity for the Sicilians. A very pale girl growing up in a land of very hot sun, Carolina was out of place in Sicily, but she spoke the local dialect fluently.[13]

The island of Sicily lies just off the toe of Italy's boot, like a giant rock kicked almost to the coast of Africa. It has always been a cross-roads of cultures: a place where North meets South and East meets West. Early-nineteenth-century guidebooks described Sicily as a land of poverty and superstition, of burning streets, ornate fountains, and cool, dark churches smelling of must and incense. "The Sicilians are known for being extremely jealous and vindictive," warned one French guidebook from the period, which recalled the time in 1282 when church bells announcing the start of vesper services gave the signal for people all over Sicily to slit the throats of their French over-lords. In addition to mastering the dialect, Carolina would grow up to be hot tempered and bold, given to making split-second decisions and trusting her instincts. She was deeply loyal to those she trusted and vengeful to those who crossed her. Most of all, she nursed a hatred for the forces of revolution that had thrust her and her family from their home in Naples.[14]

Fuming at the loss of her power and the inefficacy of her husband, Carolina's grandmother decided to return to her native Vienna. Soon after, war broke out again between the coalition of European monarchs and Napoleon, who in 1804 had crowned himself emperor, officially putting an end to the French Revolution. However, the Russian invasion of 1812 had badly damaged Napoleon's army, and he was unprepared for the next great attack by the coalition forces. When the queen of Naples and Sicily arrived in Vienna in 1814, news of Napoleon's defeat preceded her. She immediately began negotiating for the return of her husband's Neapolitan throne, but she died of a stroke before the Congress of Vienna made the restoration a reality.[15]

Because of the political uncertainty in Naples, Carolina did not accompany her grandfather when he entered the city—triumphantly, on horseback—in June 1815 to reclaim his kingdom. Even after the situation had stabilized, an outbreak of bubonic plague on the Italian peninsula kept the seventeen-year-old princess in Palermo during the fall and winter of 1815–1816. As the newly restored Ferdinand tried to undo the liberalizing measures put in place by the French, Carolina pursued her familiar pleasures, occupying her time with music, drawing, and whatever lessons in history and French that her governess could force upon the refractory pupil. It would be her last moment to enjoy the innocent pursuits of childhood. In January 1816 she received word that the French ambassador had made a marriage proposal on behalf of the recently installed French king's nephew, the duc de Berry. Carolina's father let her know that the decision whether to accept him was hers to make.

Like their Neapolitan cousins, the fortunes of the French Bourbon royal family had taken a marked turn for the better after Napoleon's defeat. Two of the younger brothers of the last French king, Louis XVI, had escaped the French Revolution with their heads intact: Louis and Charles. They had spent the twenty-five years since the French Revolution shuttling among various European capitals, urging the allied monarchies to oppose first the Revolutionary republic and then the Napoleonic Empire. After Napoleon's exile to the island of Elba in 1814, they made their triumphant return to Paris but in the "baggage" of the allied soldiers who occupied the capital, as their critics would put it. Propped up by the other European monarchies, the older of the two remaining brothers became King Louis XVIII.[16]

The newly restored French Bourbons immediately set about eliminating the traces of the French Revolution. Although it proved too difficult to return all the land that had been confiscated from nobles who had been executed or forced to flee, Louis XVIII ordered an enormous government indemnification—the so-called "billion of the emigrés"—which ensured that the aristocracy would recover its dominant economic position. The Place de la Concorde, which had been called the Place de la Révolution while it housed the guillotine, was renamed Place Louis XV and then, in 1826, Place Louis XVI, after the guillotine's most famous victim.

Yet for all the symbolic effort to scrub away the recent past, Louis XVIII was a realist. He knew he could never completely set back the clock, and he accepted a constitution, called *la Charte* (the Charter of 1814), which placed some limits on his power. This effort to placate the liberals and former revolutionaries angered the *ultras* in his entourage, so named because they were ultra-royalist—which is to say more royalist than the king himself. It was said that the Restoration *ultras* had "learned nothing and forgotten nothing" from the French Revolution. Among these diehards was the king's younger brother Charles, the next in line for the throne, and the king's niece Marie-Thérèse, the duchesse d'Angoulême, whose permanent mourning for her parents, Louis XVI and Marie Antoinette, helped set the Restoration's tone of nostalgia for the Old Regime.[17]

No sooner had the French Bourbons settled back into the Tuileries Palace than they were forced out once again by Napoleon's surprise return from Elba in March 1815. The escaped emperor marched on Paris, and much of the French army rallied to him. Louis XVIII and the Bourbon royal family scuttled off to exile once again as the allied powers prepared for yet another war. For a period known as the Hundred Days, Napoleon put back in place the imperial administration that the Bourbons had begun to dismantle. Then came Napoleon's ultimate defeat at Waterloo and the second restoration of the Bourbons. This time the allies took no chances. They sent Napoleon to the distant island of Saint Helena, in the middle of the Atlantic Ocean, and guarded him day and night until his death in 1821. The Bourbons again returned to power thanks to the intervention of foreign powers.

Once back on his unsteady throne, Louis XVIII realized that he needed to address what was perhaps the greatest threat to his regime: the looming crisis of succession. Childless and a widower, the gout-ridden monarch was also morbidly obese; people called him the legless king, *le roi sans jambes*, because he was so fat he could barely walk. Knowing that the sixty-year-old ruler could not produce an heir and that he was unlikely to live a great many more years, royalists pinned their hope for the perpetuation of the monarchy on the family of his brother, Charles.

More conservative and less intelligent than Louis—he would be known as the headless king, *le roi sans tête*—Charles had at least managed to have children. But his older son, the duc d'Angoulême, the second in line to the throne, suffered from extreme shyness exacerbated by facial tics. He had married his first cousin Marie-Thérèse, the dour orphan of Louis XVI and Marie Antoinette, and the already fifteen-year-long union of these two pious souls had produced no offspring. All eyes turned to his younger brother, Charles Ferdinand, the duc de Berry, who at nearly forty had still not married.

If the duc de Berry did not produce a legitimate male heir, the French Bourbon bloodline would come to an end and the throne would pass to the Bourbons' cousin, Louis-Philippe d'Orléans. Louis XVIII had allowed Louis-Philippe to recover the fortune he left behind when he fled the Revolution. This included the Palais-Royal, the vast residence situated across from the Louvre, which the commercial instincts of Louis-Philippe's father—called Philippe Égalité (Philippe Equality) because he had supported the French Revolution—had turned into the capital's first shopping mall and premier entertainment destination. Beneath its covered arcades clustered bookshops, cafés, theaters, and casinos, along with a good portion of the city's prostitutes. All this was highly profitable and burnished the Orléans' image with everyday Parisians who felt snubbed by the Bourbons' hauteur and put off by their reactionary politics.[18]

Fortunately for the Bourbons, the duc de Berry had already displayed ample proof of his virility. During his long years of exile, Charles Ferdinand fought in various armies, including the Russian, against revolutionary France. In 1801 he settled in London, where, according to gossip in the large French émigré community, he accumulated "debts and scandal." His debauchery subsided a bit after he began an affair with Amy Brown, the beautiful dark-haired daughter of a Protestant pastor. They had two daughters together, whom he would later acknowledge as his own. When Charles Ferdinand returned to Paris in 1814, he brought his English family with him, setting them up in an apartment on the rue Neuve-des-Mathurins, where he regularly visited.[19]

Amy Brown was not the duke's only concubine. The Paris police, who were assigned to protect him, would report regularly to Louis XVIII about his nephew's movements between various women's apartments. In 1815 the duke installed a dancer from the Opera on the rue de Valois. Other liaisons, and possibly other offspring, followed. The royal family decided it was time to channel all this fecundity into more legitimate ends.[20]

During the Revolution, as a penniless émigré, the duke had not been such an appealing marriage prospect. His quest for a royal bride even led him to Sicily in 1799, when his future wife was a baby. Young Carolina's mother noted in a letter how much she enjoyed meeting the "charming prince" and how "attached" the whole Neapolitan royal family grew to him. This did not stop them from denying him permission to marry Amalia, who a few years later married Louis-Philippe, also an exile. Although his father had voted for the execution of Louis XVI, Louis-Philippe had at least escaped France with some semblance of his fortune intact.[21]

Needless to say, the situation changed after the restoration of the Bourbons. Despite his reputation as a playboy, as third in line to the

French throne the duc de Berry now became one of the world's most eligible bachelors. The Russian Emperor Alexander tried to make a match with his sister. The duke agreed, but Louis XVIII felt that the Russian royal house was not sufficiently ancient in lineage to provide a mother to future French monarchs. According to one of the period's most astute memoirists, the comtesse de Boigne, the duchesse d'Anouglême also feared having an independent-minded sister-in-law whom she could not control.[22]

Carolina of Naples was the perfect choice of bride for the duc de Berry. A distant cousin of the duke, she was also a Bourbon and thus met the king's standards of royal pedigree. Young and poorly educated, she also fulfilled the duchesse d'Angoulême's desire for an ignorant sister-in-law to dominate. Furthermore, the newly restored Neapolitan monarchy was an important strategic ally for France as the various powers jockeyed for primacy in post-Napoleonic Europe. Louis XVIII thus dispatched one of his most important ministers, the comte de Blacas, to Naples ostensibly as a diplomatic ambassador but really as a matrimonial one. Blacas soon learned that the Austrians were also sizing up Carolina as a marriage prospect, so he cut short his mission and proposed the marriage on his second interview with the king of Naples.[23]

Despite eagerness on both sides, a few obstacles remained, including the question of Carolina's assent to the marriage. Even if rumors of the duke's promiscuous past had not reached her, what could Carolina have felt for a man she had never met? At the same time the prospect of marrying the nephew of the king of France must have excited her ambitions. No doubt she also realized that if the duc de Berry were to outlive his father and older brother, she would become queen of France and that if she had a son, he would become king. She soon indicated her willingness to accept the proposal.

Blacas still needed to meet the princess to make sure she was presentable, but he was delayed in traveling to Sicily by the outbreak of bubonic plague on the Italian peninsula. When he eventually arrived, he deemed Carolina worthy enough to commission a portrait to send to the duke. The result was not very promising. Blacas found himself obliged to package the unflattering portrait of the wan, thin young girl with his own opinions on the princess's charms, and he blamed whatever limitations were revealed in the portrait on the lack of artistic talent available in Palermo. "It would be difficult for a painter who is ignorant of the first principles of drawing and who is unable to render a likeness to flatter his subject," the count wrote. He continued:

> The health of the young princess is very good; her face, without being regularly pretty, is agreeable; she has talents and a taste for music; her character is very sweet and very timid, which makes her seem a bit awkward, especially since, as the prince [her father] never consented to providing her with a dancing instructor, she lacks the grace that it would be easy to give her. As for her teeth, it appears nobody has paid any attention to them, and I am assured that they will be fine once some care has been taken.

Blacas perhaps thought it wise not to call attention to Carolina's extreme nearsightedness and wandering left eye, the features that the sharp-tongued courtiers would latch onto as soon as descriptions of the princess began to arrive in Paris. However, as Jean Lucas-Dubreton notes, a defective eye counted much less than the princess's general health to a court obsessed with the production of a male heir. The duc de Berry, in any event, was sufficiently reassured by Blacas to proceed with the proposal.[24]

Pictures of the duke from the era, which Carolina studied intently, show a man with receding blond hair, coiffed in the carefully messy Romantic fashion of the day, and thick sideburns like muttonchops on each cheek. He had a small, almost pug nose; heavy eyebrows; a full, sensual mouth; and a round, slightly dimpled chin. His blue-green eyes bore a devilish glint. This was clearly someone who liked his pleasures. Most observers found him handsome.[25]

Once the wedding date was set, Carolina and her father returned from Palermo to Naples. All the church bells in the city rang, their chimes merging with cannon fire from the fort and from the ships

Charles Ferdinand, duc de Berry

in the harbor, celebrating her arrival. Crowds swarmed to catch a glimpse of the princess who would soon leave for the court of France. Carolina had not seen Naples since 1806, when she was eight years old. And knowing she would not see it again for many years to come, she set off on a sightseeing tour over the course of the next month. The comte de Blacas accompanied her, and the future duchess came to value Blacas as a precious source of information about the French court. Blacas was especially effusive in his praise of the duchesse d'Angoulême, whom all the members of the French royal family seemed to think would provide a good role model for the inexperienced girl, who would now go by *Caroline.*

At this early moment Caroline seemed willing to place herself under the older woman's wing or at least felt the necessity of appearing to do so. In a letter to her future sister-in-law, expertly crafted to ingratiate herself, the young fiancée wrote, "I have the truest friendship for you, which I long to express to you in person, my very dearest sister. I hope that it will merit yours for me, which I value infinitely and will do all in my power to increase." If the prospect of submitting to the will of the stern, pious, thirty-seven-year-old orphan of the Revolution chilled the blood in her veins just a bit, she wisely did not let it show.[26]

While Caroline negotiated her relations with her future in-laws, the diplomats negotiated her marriage contract. Dated April 15, 1816, it contained eleven articles. First, it stipulated payment for the special religious dispensation required by the pope because the bride and groom were distant cousins. As for a dowry, the king of the Two Sicilies (as the kingdom was now called) provided his granddaughter with 120,000 Neapolitan ducats, which was the equivalent of 500,000 French francs (roughly 3–4 million dollars today). She would also receive the inheritance she was entitled to from her deceased mother, with interest. In addition, His Sicilian Majesty gave her jewelry valued at 500,000 ducats, and the French king gave her precious stones worth 300,000 francs. In case of the death of her husband, her in-laws would provide her with an annual income of 100,000 francs, "with the right to live anywhere she pleases, whether in France, the lands of her grand-father, or in any other state outside the states of His Very Christian Royal Highness."[27]

Although the couple had still not met, they were married by proxy in Naples on April 24. Such long-distance ceremonies were relatively common among royalty at the time because they allowed the bride to be officially married before traveling to meet her husband. The ceremony was followed by an elaborate dinner at the home of the French ambassador to Naples and then by a command performance at the Teatro del Fondo. At the end of the performance a magic lantern projected an image of King Louis XVIII blessing the couple.

In Paris, preparations began for the arrival of the princess. The duchesse d'Angoulême took it upon herself to determine how her sister-in-law's house would be organized: like herself, she would have six ladies-in-waiting, chosen from among the highest of the nobility, and the comte de Mesnard would serve as her *premier écuyer*, her first equerry or squire. The forty-seven-year-old Charles de Mesnard had had an illustrious military career before following the royal family into exile during the French Revolution. Her future in-laws saw him as a stabilizing force, capable of monitoring the young duchess and making sure she stayed in line; they would later come to regret their mistake.

Back in Naples, Caroline's departure was delayed for a few days because of illness. But she finally embarked on May 14, 1816, aboard the *Christine*, which entered the Gulf of Naples as an enormous crowd of well-wishers stood on shore to wave good-bye. The comte de Blacas decided that three French warships would accompany the Neapolitan vessel both as a sign of respect and as a means of protection, for Barbary pirates still roamed that part of the Mediterranean.

To the annoyance of the welcome party waiting in Marseille, the municipal authorities quarantined the vessels arriving from Naples because of the plague. The duchess spent ten days waiting until it was determined that she did not bear the signs of the dreaded disease. Her first meetings with the French courtiers who had come to greet her thus took place through a protective screen. Along with giving the teenager lessons on how to comport herself at court and training her in the exact etiquette required during her meeting with the king, the French delegation did its best to entertain the isolated duchess, diverting her with military parades and jousting competitions that she could watch from her ship.[28]

If the young duchess did not grow bored in quarantine, however, it was more thanks to the letters that she exchanged with her still-unmet husband than any of the official entertainments that her hosts provided. Whereas the missives the couple had exchanged up to this point had an official tone and may have been composed for them by their advisers, the letters they sent while Caroline was in quarantine slowly begin to reveal genuine feeling and even a growing passion.

In one letter the duke informs his bride that he has chosen as her ladies-in-waiting women whose virtue and sweet temper he can personally vouch for. He then concludes in a bantering tone: "You were in great danger at sea when you approached that awful island of Elba, the origin of all our troubles last year. I was trembling, but I was happy to learn that you did not display the least fright. The blood of Henri IV and of Louis XIV does not lie." (The last sentence was a reference to their shared Bourbon ancestors. The founder of the Bourbon dynasty in the sixteenth century, Henri IV, was still known as "the good King Henry"; Louis XIV, the "Sun King," had reigned over France at the height of its glory in the seventeenth century. Both were symbols of royal authority and prestige whom their descendants looked to as a model.) In another letter the duke makes a reference to their age difference, this time underscoring his hopes for their romantic compatibility: "I'm worried about my thirty-eight years; I know that at seventeen, I found those who were approaching forty quite old. I'm afraid that you won't find me handsome since the painters in Paris are not like those in Palermo: they flatter." This was a rather risqué comment for the duke: the romantic desires of royal and aristocratic spouses, especially the bride, were not normally acknowledged.

She attempted to respond in the same bantering, self-deprecating tone: "I feel that I am lacking a great deal, but really a great deal, to be what I would want to be in order to please you, and to live up to the overly flattering idea that they have given you of Caroline." One can almost feel the duke growing more interested as he realizes his wife was not the timid schoolgirl he had feared she would be, despite the pink paper with garlands of flowers along the border on which her letters were written.[29]

Not seeing himself rebuffed in his first attempt to play the lover, the playboy pushed the boundaries of propriety much further in a later letter: "Your nice letter managed to completely turn my head and if you continue like this, they will need to lock me up. . . . I burn with the desire to see you, my Caroline, because you will understand me better in person than you read me!" Even more shocking than the frank display of sexual appetite is the duke's shift to the informal mode of address: he uses *tu* rather than the formal *vous*. It marks an intimacy that most upper-class couples often spent their whole lives together without displaying. And it accompanies an even more bold display of desire on the eve of her departure for Paris: "My heart races, and I think it will race even more when my lips press your pretty cheeks." At the end of the letter, however, he returns to Earth; she must remember not to use *tu* when addressing him in front of the king. Such a breach of etiquette would be unthinkable.[30]

Finally, on May 30, 1816, the diamond-clad bride made her official entry into France, carried from her quarantine in a golden boat that was rowed by twenty-four sailors adorned in white satin and that had white flags bearing the fleur-de-lis, symbol of the Bourbon monarchy, flapping in the wind. From this point forward, the French etiquette experts choreographed every detail of her journey to mimic the royal weddings of the Old Regime, yet another attempt by the Bourbons to pretend that the Revolution had never taken place.

The duchess entered the City Hall of Marseille through the right door, under the flag of her Neapolitan homeland. Once inside, the duchess symbolically said good-bye to her governess and the other friends from her childhood who had accompanied her on the journey (they would all accompany her to Paris). She exited through the right door of the building, over which flew the white flag of France, on the arm of the duchesse de Reggio, her new lady-in-waiting. She had now officially become French.[31]

AFTER CELEBRATIONS IN Marseille, she began her slow journey to Paris, stopping in towns along the way—Toulon, Lyon, Nemours— to be feted by the local dignitaries. All along the route, she saw crowds of cheering peasants, dressed in their Sunday best and straining to catch a glimpse of the very blonde princess inside her gleaming carriage.[32]

Finally came the day she had both anticipated and feared: her arrival at the forest of Fontainebleau, outside Paris, where she would meet her husband, and his uncle the king, in a clearing. Two tents made of golden fabric glittered in the June sun. A hundred Swiss guards arranged in battle formation linked the two carriages, which arrived at the same time, one bearing the bride and one bearing the groom, a red carpet running between them. Royal tradition dictated that the foreign bride should descend from the carriage and walk halfway along the carpet, while the king led the royal family to the midpoint from the other direction, a much longer walk than the obese monarch was accustomed to taking. "Madame, here is your husband," the king said when he saw his new niece, gesturing to the duc de Berry. "I am your father."

The next day, she made her first entry into Paris, marveling at the crowds celebrating her arrival. On June 17 Caroline and Charles Ferdinand met again in Notre Dame Cathedral, the symbolic and geographic center of Paris, for a royal wedding in the classic French style. The church was decked in yards of blue velvet, on which glittered golden fleurs-de-lis, blue and gold being the Bourbons' heraldic colors. The groom wore a white satin coat and a golden doublet, along with a hat with white feathers, in the style of their common ancestor, Henri IV. The bride wore a jewel-encrusted white dress with an enormous train.

That night they held a traditional *grand couvert* wedding feast in the Galerie Diane at the Tuileries Palace. At a long table sat assembled the royal family: they were the only ones allowed to sit; the other noble guests, arrayed in full court dress despite the suffocating heat, had to remain standing at attention (with the exception of women holding the rank of duchess, who were allowed to perch on stools). Each time the king wished to take a drink, the royal cupbearer would loudly signal the event. Otherwise, silence reigned. Perhaps most disconcertingly for the duchesse de Berry, who was accustomed to much less ceremony at her grandfather's court in Palermo, the common people filed along an elevated walkway to gape at the royal family, as if looking at figures in a wax museum or animals at the zoo. A tradition inherited from prerevolutionary Versailles, the elaborate choreography of the *grand couvert* was meant to convey the majesty of the monarchy and to remind the postrevolutionary public of the glory of the Old Regime. To the young duchess, it must have been a stark reminder that her every movement would now be on display.[33]

CHAPTER 2

A Parisian Education

T HE RITUALS OF the French court seemed bizarre and alienating to the young bride, but the city of Paris beckoned: a
place of excitement, alive with possibility. There were ave-
nues grander than she had ever seen, lined with glittering cafés and
glass-covered arcades where exclusive boutiques lured a discerning
clientele. But there were also streets so narrow that the houses on
either side almost touched in the middle, where no light could penetrate and starving families huddled in freezing sixth-floor attics.
Crowds thronged the streets, and carriages scraped along the cobblestones. The noise was infernal, and so was the stench of horses and
soot. If people didn't move quickly, they got run over. Or splattered
with the muck that, in the absence of a proper sewer system, ran
down the center of every thoroughfare like a black river of rot.

In 1816 Paris had begun the remarkable growth spurt that would
transform it from a quaint medieval city into a global metropolis.
After losing 100,000 residents—a fifth of its population—to emigration and the guillotine during the French Revolution, it had gained
160,000 since 1800 and would double in size, to more than a million

inhabitants, by 1850. A city of migrants, like the duchess, all a little out of place and all struggling to figure out how things worked. It is not a coincidence that so many of Honoré de Balzac's novels, set during the early years of the Restoration, center on young men who come to Paris to make their fortune. Tens of thousands of newcomers, like the shrewd Eugène de Rastignac in *Old Goriot* or the handsome and talented Lucien de Rubempré in *Lost Illusions*, moved to Paris every year. Some, like Rastignac, made it big: they quickly assimilated the codes of the city, shedding their innocence along the way like the unfashionable clothes they had brought with them from the provinces. Others, like Lucien, succumbed, done in by a lack of will or the pangs of conscience. Scholars call these works "novels of education" (bildungsromans) because their protagonists learn how to navigate the maze of the city and master the challenges of the modern world.[1]

Like one of Balzac's ambitious young men, the duchess threw herself headlong into the Parisian whirlwind. Her home was the Élysée Palace, located at the foot of the capital's most famous street, the Champs-Élysées. Built in the early eighteenth century, the Élysée was confiscated from its noble owner during the French Revolution and turned into a gambling parlor. After the fall of Napoleon, Russian Cossack soldiers camped there during their occupation of the city before Louis XVIII returned the palace to its original owner, who then promptly sold it to the duc de Berry. The duke spent a fortune—316,000 francs—preparing it for his seventeen-year-old wife: a crimson drawing room, her bedroom hung with tented silk, enormous vases of fresh flowers everywhere. The linens alone cost 103,800 francs, roughly 700,000 dollars in today's money.[2]

Whereas the rest of the royal family largely stayed cloistered at the Tuileries Palace—the king not necessarily by his own choice but because he could not walk—the duchess explored Paris. She became a frequent patron of the city's most expensive clothing shops, whose owners were only too happy to dress the youngest and most glamorous member of the royal family. Like her great-aunt Marie Antoinette, the duchess eagerly embraced her role as fashion icon and set numerous trends, including the vogue for tall, ostrich-feather head adornments—cleverly intended to add inches to her modest height—and higher hemlines to show off her famously tiny feet.[3] Louis XVIII encouraged the duchesse de Berry's lavish expenditures, which not only spurred the luxury trade—then as now one of France's leading industries—but also added a much needed layer of gloss to the Bourbons' stodgy image.[4]

Establishing their home away from the rest of the royal family meant freedom for the Berrys: freedom for the duchess to get to know the city, but also freedom for the duke to visit his many mistresses. Rumors of her husband's liaisons soon reached the duchess. "Madame la duchesse de Berry was extremely jealous," the comtesse de Boigne writes, reporting how the duke enlisted her ladies-in-waiting to distract his wife from the "indiscreet reports that troubled their *ménage*."[5] When these diversionary tactics failed, the duke prevailed upon the Neapolitan ambassador to explain Parisian customs. The ambassador assured her that "all men had mistresses, that their wives knew it and were perfectly content with the situation." The duchesse de Berry was not one of those wives but reluctantly accepted what she could not change. She was coming to understand the Restoration's ambivalent posture toward sexual mores. Dominated by aristocrats who had come of age at the permissive end of the Old Regime, the period was in some ways reactionary, with its showy religious piety, but in others quite liberal, or at least *libertine*.[6]

The first months of the duchess's marriage flew by in a blur of social engagements, recorded in her journal. She went fox hunting on August 15, following the hunters in a carriage through the Sèvres woods. On October 19 she organized a party at the Élysée in honor of her father-in-law's birthday, at which actors from the Variétés, one of the main Parisian theaters, performed a play written for the occasion. That same week she helped to host the dukes of Kent and Cambridge, sons of King George III, with gala dinners, parties at the British ambassador's residence, and a hunt at the royal château of Rambouillet, thirty miles southwest of Paris. On October 16 she partook for the first time in one of the mournful rituals relished by the royal family: the anniversary of the death of Marie Antoinette, mother of the duchesse d'Angoulême. While the martyred queen's edifying last letter was read out in churches throughout France, a private mass was held for the royal family in a chapel newly erected in the very rooms occupied by Marie Antoinette in the Conciergerie prison in Paris.[7]

The duchess also devoted much of her time during the early days of her marriage to making up for the rather large gaps in her studies. According to the comtesse de Boigne, who no doubt exaggerated slightly, "Madame la duchesse de Berry arrived in France completely ignorant of everything. She barely knew how to read." Thanks to the best masters and to her natural intelligence, she made quick progress, especially in improving her French and in the subjects she liked, such as music and art. Flower painting was all the rage during the Restoration, especially for women, and the duchess received instruction from the most-renowned practitioners.[8]

But, according to Boigne, "If they tried to show her how to scratch a keyboard and scribble on a piece of paper, nobody attempted to instruct her how to do her job, which was to be a princess." Observers noted that she would frequently yawn in church and arrive late for dinner at the Tuileries, delayed by some excursion in town or in the country. As she fumbled to take her place at the table, the king would greet her in stony silence, pointing to his pocket watch with great solemnity but with the barest hint of a smile crossing his lips. Her husband also found her childish temperament amusing. Only the duchesse d'Angoulême, whom the duc de Berry had vaunted as a role model in his letters to his future bride, attempted to correct her behavior. The first order of business was to summon an etiquette expert to teach her how to behave. But the duchesse d'Angoulême's efforts to dominate the younger woman backfired; the duchesse de Berry began by fearing her sister-in-law and soon came to hate her.[9]

Marie-Thérèse, duchesse d'Angoulême, was thin and angular, with dark hair, angry eyes, and a beaky nose. She was the physical opposite of her sister-in-law, despite their shared Bourbon and Habsburg genes. Her years in prison as a child, and the murder of her entire immediate family by the revolutionaries, had left her little inclined to liberalism of any sort. Nicknamed the "New Antigone" in reference to the daughter of Oedipus, who lived at her uncle's court after the death of her family, Marie-Thérèse was forced to marry her stuttering first cousin during their exile from France and found herself childless at thirty-eight, stymied in the one thing she longed most to do: give France an heir to carry on the Bourbon line. This duty now fell to the young blonde princess from Naples, whom Marie-Thérèse considered "silly, frivolous and ill educated."[10]

As the only female member of the royal family prior to the arrival of the duchesse de Berry, the "New Antigone" set the tone for the Tuileries, frowning upon all amusement as sacrilegious because the palace had seen so much suffering by her family. Permissible evening entertainments consisted of hushed rounds of *loto*—a bingo-like game—and the occasional hand of whist. Marie-Thérèse's ladies-in-waiting had to wear simple white dresses, like nuns. The men of the royal family treated the duchesse d'Angoulême with reverence and publicly celebrated her virtues. In private, however, the king complained about her stringency and pressured her to appear festively adorned, in jewels and elaborate gowns, at public events. The duc de Berry at first tried to support the efforts of his sister-in-law to mold his wife in her image but then found it easier to side with his wife, particularly if it meant that she turned a blind eye to his infidelities.[11]

The unified public face of the royal family masked not only disagreements concerning style but also deep political divisions. Louis XVIII understood that if the monarchy was to survive, it needed to adapt to the changed circumstances of post–Revolutionary France. He accepted the *Charte*, the constitution limiting his powers, and pursued policies of reconciliation with various liberal factions, including those granted noble titles by Napoleon and those who had served the imperial administration. The king's nephew, the duc d'Angoulême, husband of Marie-Thérèse, had returned from exile in London enamored of English-style parliamentary democracy and supported Louis XVIII's moderate policies, although his natural reticence prevented him from playing a major political role. Charles, the brother of the king and father of the duc d'Angoulême and the duc de Berry, had drawn very different lessons from his own time abroad. The leader of the *ultras*, the extreme monarchists who accused even the king himself of not being sufficiently royalist, Charles had become a devout Catholic in recent years. His reactionary views were shared, naturally enough, by the "New Antigone."

During her early years in France, the duchesse de Berry stayed neutral in these disputes, even though her husband sided with his father and the *ultras* against his brother and his uncle, Louis XVIII. She also tried to act as a bridge to the Orléans family. Despite Louis-Philippe's efforts to repair the rupture with the Bourbons, the wound opened by his father, who had voted for the execution of Louis XVI, did not close easily, especially given the power wielded at court by the late king's daughter. Louis XVIII insisted on humiliating Louis-Philippe by not according him the title of royal highness, which he reserved for the immediate family members of monarchs. At ceremonial occasions, when both doors would open to allow all the royal highnesses to enter a room—including Louis-Philippe's wife, Marie-Amélie, the daughter of the Bourbon king of Naples—one door would swing shut when Louis-Philippe passed through, signaling his lower status.[12]

Stung by this sign of disrespect, Louis-Philippe remained something of a fifth column within the extended royal family. Historian Munro Price suggests that Louis-Philippe may have conspired with Napoleon during the Hundred Days and it was an open secret that he hoped that the throne would revert to himself or one of his descendants once the elder branch of the royal family went extinct. This seemed increasingly likely. If partisans of the Bourbons had high hopes that the evident attraction that existed between the Berrys would yield a male heir, the duchess soon came to learn that having a son was not as easy as it seemed; two miscarriages came back-to-back, followed by the birth in 1819 of a healthy child, the princess Louise. But according to Salic law, a girl could not inherit the throne. Sensing the disappointment of the royal family clustered around her delivery bed, the duchess is supposed to have remarked with characteristic optimism, "After the girl comes the boy," and cheerfully welcomed the crowds that quickly surrounded her to celebrate the princess's birth.[13]

The following year, the forty-two-year-old duchesse d'Angoulême believed that she too had finally become pregnant and announced the good news, even posing for a portrait clutching her breast in imitation of the famous 1594 painting of the pregnant Gabrielle d'Estrées, mistress of Henri IV. However, the humiliated Marie-Thérèse soon realized that she had mistaken the signs of menopause for pregnancy. All hopes for the Bourbon succession now lay in the womb of the duchesse de Berry.[14]

Not everyone was anxious for a Bourbon heir. The capital's bourgeois elites, snubbed by the Bourbons, sided with Louis-Philippe, whereas much of Paris's working-class population remained fiercely loyal to the memory of Napoleon and called for the restoration of his exiled son. Meanwhile, a determined group of republicans hoped another revolution might bring back a real democracy. This latter faction elected to the Chamber of Deputies the Abbé Grégoire, a radical priest from Lorraine who had declared during the French Revolution, "Kings form a class of purulent beings who have always been the leprosy of the government and the scum of the human race." Because the *Charte* granted freedom of the press, Louis XVIII could do little to silence his increasingly vocal opponents, much to the frustration of the *ultras*.[15]

As the only Bourbon male capable of producing an heir, the duc de Berry began to receive anonymous letters containing death threats. Rumors circulated of a conspiracy to assassinate him. Refusing the safety precautions recommended by his advisers, the duke expressly prevented the police from arresting protesters who attempted to bar his passage and continued his busy schedule of visits to his various mistresses. This nonchalance did not prevent the duke from playfully joking to his wife about her future widowhood.[16]

On the night of February 12, 1820, the duke and duchess attended a masked ball. After the duchess complained of a mild indisposition, the duke ordered her not to dance. She nevertheless made a splendid appearance dressed as a queen from the Middle Ages, draped in a cherry-red, ermine-lined velvet cape and coiffed in a black velvet hat topped with red and white ostrich feathers. The next night, a Sunday, the duke and duchess debated whether to attend still more balls or go to the Opera, where three productions were on the bill: *Le Carnaval de Venise*, *Le Rossignol*, and *Les Noces de Gamache*. Feeling under the weather, and also a bit superstitious—it was February 13—the duchess at first thought they should go home after the customary dinner with the royal family at the Tuileries, a plan approved by her doctor. But at 8 p.m., the royal carriage pulled up in front of the entrance of the Opera, which was then located on the rue Richelieu between the rue de Louvois and the rue Rameau, across from the National Library.

The usher opened the door to their loge, decked in blue taffeta with gold trim, and the duchess took her seat on a red plush chair next to the madame de Béthisy, her lady-in-waiting, and the comte de Mesnard, just in time for *Le Rossignol*. At the intermission, the duke and duchess paid a visit to Louis-Philippe and Marie-Amélie in their box, and the crowd, seeing the amicable relations between the two branches of the royal family, applauded. When the duchess returned to her loge, she began to yawn, and the duke urged her to go home to rest. At first she resisted, hoping to see the ballet in *Les Noces de Gamache*, but the duke eventually accompanied her to their waiting carriage. (He, of course, had an ulterior motive in being so solicitous to his wife: he planned to signal to his dancer girlfriend that he would visit her that night.[17])

What happened next would forever haunt the nightmares of Bourbon loyalists. As the duke moved from the carriage back to the Opera entrance, a young man pushed his way toward him, grabbed the duke by the shoulder, and stuck a knife into his side. At the sound of her husband's cry, the duchess jumped out of the carriage and flung herself at his feet. The comte de Mesnard and a footman lifted the duke into the lobby of the Opera, where he collapsed onto a banquette after pulling out the dagger himself. Blood shot everywhere, drenching the duchess's white dress. As the duke lay dying in the vestibule, the performance continued inside. Eventually, doctors arrived, but the duke knew he could not be saved. Word spread through the hall. The Orléans family rushed in; Madame Adélaïde, sister of Louis-Philippe, fainted when she saw the blood-splattered duke and had to be carried away. Singers in costume and ballerinas in tutus—including, it was said, some of the duke's mistresses—crowded around for a glimpse of the dying prince. Louis Joly of the Paris police, assigned to guard the duke, arrested a saddle maker with Bonapartist sympathies named Louis-Pierre Louvel. Questioned that night, Louvel claimed that he had wanted to avenge Napoleon and had acted alone.[18]

Over the course of the next few hours, as members of the royal family, including the king himself, made their way to the Opera to bid him a tearful farewell, the duke begged for mercy for his assassin. (The king refused his request, and Louvel would be executed the following June.) Charles Ferdinand also asked his wife to take care of his two daughters by Amy Brown, who hurried with their mother to the Opera to receive the duke's final blessing. Despite her jealousy, the duchess would remain true to her oath; she made sure that both girls received noble titles and made advantageous marriages.

Never taken very seriously as a political figure during his lifetime, the playboy duke made as heroic an exit as anyone could have hoped. News reports the next day all recounted the edifying deathbed scene: the duke surrounded by his family, performing a last act of Christian charity by begging for the life of his assassin. How different it would have been if Louvel had struck a few hours later when the duke was on his way to visit his mistress! Following his assassination, he became a royalist martyr.

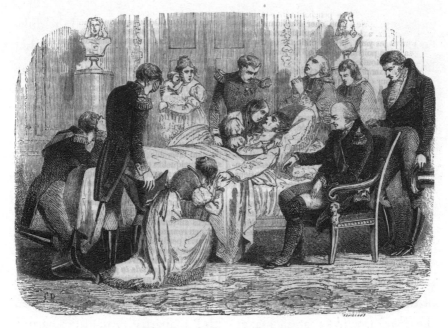

The duc de Berry's deathbed

The assassination turned the duchess into a different kind of celebrity. Engravings of the duchess in a heroic posture, clutching her dying husband, her white dress stained red with blood, would be seen for months to come in shop windows throughout France, just as newspapers would endlessly recount her stoic devotion on her husband's gruesome deathbed. She was no longer the flighty little princess yawning in church; she had become the grieving widow, symbol of royalist suffering.

If the French public was floored by news of the assassination, it was even more surprised by what came next, the kind of coup de théâtre more likely to be delivered on the Opera's stage than in its lobby: the duchess announced that she was two months' pregnant. The slight indisposition she had complained about in preceding days was morning sickness. Louvel's knife had not ended the Bourbon line after all. For royalists, this "miraculous" pregnancy seemed like confirmation of the divine destiny of the Bourbons. To their opponents,

it seemed a trick. When the duchess's waistline expanded in the following months, libelous tracts insisted that she had quickly found a
lover to substitute for her husband or that she had put stuffing under
her dress and would pass someone else's baby off as her own when the
time for delivery came.[19]

Whatever joy and hope she may have felt because of the pregnancy, the twenty-one-year-old widow's sense of loss was very real.
She wrote to her half sister, "All I do is cry," and described the pang
of acute sorrow at the sight of her daughter Louise's smile because
it reminded her of the husband she had lost after only four years of
marriage. She also described her sense of duty to maintain her good
health for the sake of the unborn child: "If God, in his mercy, will
grant me a son, that will be my consolation." To her uncle, the emperor of Austria, she wrote, "If something can, in this awful moment,
sustain my courage, it is the heroic and Christian end of the man to
whom I was united and who, in his solemn and heart-wrenching
farewell, commanded me to live for our daughter and for the pledge
of his love that I bear in my womb."[20]

To make matters worse, the king forced her to give up her home
at the Élysée Palace and to reside at the Tuileries. Built in the
sixteenth century at the base of the Tuileries gardens, next to the
Louvre, the palace (which was burned to the ground during the Paris
Commune in 1871) had housed many French monarchs, including
Henri IV and Napoleon. The duke's bachelor quarters in the Marsan
wing of the palace were hastily readied for the duchess, little Louise,
and their retinue. Already a gloomy place, thanks to the duchesse
d'Angoulême, the Tuileries had become even more somber following the duke's death. The walls of the duchess's new apartment had
been hung with black cloth, which also covered all the moldings and
mirrors. Only the duchess's bedroom was spared, where the cloth
was gray instead.[21]

The Tuileries palace was not only depressing; it was also unsani-
tary. More than eight hundred people lived there—royals, courtiers, servants—and it had not been renovated for decades. There were

kitchens on every floor and no toilets or drainage pipes. According to the comtesse de Boigne, the presence of "all kinds of filth" was so "pestilential" that one almost asphyxiated when climbing up from the magnificent staterooms on the main floor to the warren of dark apartments above. It was in this setting that the duchess spent the first months of her widowhood, reliving the happy days of her marriage and praying for a son. Even now, the antiroyalists who had murdered her husband did not leave her in peace, and firecrackers were set off under her window to frighten her into a miscarriage.[22]

The king had planned for the royal birth to take place in the presence of witnesses to dispel any doubts about the pregnancy. On September 28, 1820, the duchess had seemed perfectly fine during the day, giving no indication that the end of her pregnancy was at hand. Around 11 p.m., she said good night to her ladies-in-waiting. Then, at 2 a.m., she had a burst of pain and called out. After a second burst, she delivered the baby just as Madame Lemoine, one of the governesses, arrived in her room.

"It's Henri," she proclaimed, as her flustered ladies-in-waiting rushed to her side. Despite her jubilation and exhaustion, the duchess maintained enough presence of mind to demand that the ladies summon witnesses not connected to the royal family to testify to the birth of the boy, whom everyone would soon call the "miracle child." Madame de Gontaut dashed into the hallway, still dressed in her nightgown, and grabbed the first people she came upon: two soldiers, one belonging to the National Guard and the other to the Royal Guardsmen. "Approach, gentlemen," the duchesse de Berry said, baring herself for all to see. "You are witnesses that it is a prince and that he is still attached to me." Disconcerted by this royal spectacle, the two soldiers awkwardly nodded their assent. Once they and several other witnesses, including the duc d'Albuféra, were in place, Dr. Deneux snipped the umbilical cord.[23]

Soon the royal family arrived, including the limping king. "God be praised, you have had a son!" he declared with joy as he made his way to the duchess. And then he handed her a bouquet of diamonds.

"This is for you and this is for me," he said as he took the newborn into his arms. Despite her own frustrations at not producing the heir herself, the duchesse d'Angoulême was also overjoyed; she would be the child's godmother. Louis-Philippe, who crowded into the airless room along with Marie-Amélie and his sister Adélaïde, was less enthusiastic. Taking the duc d'Albuféra aside, he made him swear on his honor that the baby really belonged to the duchess. When the gentleman recounted what he had seen, Louis-Philippe offered his congratulations to his niece, reluctantly accepting that his own progeny would most likely never rule.[24]

That day, twenty-four cannon shots announced the birth of the future Henri V, who would take the provisional title of duc de Bordeaux, and all the bells in Paris rang out. The city erupted into choruses of "Vive le roi! Vive le duc de Bordeaux! Vive la duchesse de Berry!" Soldiers fired off round after round, lighting up the sky. The delighted duchess had her bed pushed to the window so she could drink in the celebration and show herself to the crowd of people below. It is said that during that night Parisians consumed two hundred thousand bottles of Bordeaux in honor of the new duke, their future king.[25]

IN THE DECADE that followed, as the Bourbons sought vengeance on their political enemies for the assassination of the duc de Berry and their absolutist tendencies grew more pronounced, the duchess began to play a more public role. As the mother of the third in line to the throne, she held a much stronger position within the royal family than she had previously: even the childless duchesse d'Angoulême reluctantly had to accord her consideration. When Louis XVIII finally died in 1824—his body covered in pustulant sores, his toes falling off from gangrene—and his brother became Charles X, the duchesse de Berry attempted to assert her authority in her father-in-law's court by claiming the title of "Madame" or "Madame Royale," which had been vacated by the duchesse d'Angoulême, now styled the Dauphine (as wife of the heir presumptive, the Dauphin). Technically, as a widow, Caroline was not entitled to this honorific style, but those in her service and those wanting to curry favor with her began calling the duchess "Madame," which the royal family firmly opposed. Whenever the duchesse d'Angoulême heard someone use the title, she would ask, "Are you referring to the duchesse de Berry?"[26]

The duchess attempted to strengthen her hand further by positioning herself between *cour et ville*, court and city. The reticence of the royal family members and their *ultra* exclusivity meant that they circulated among their subjects very rarely. Only the highest aristocrats belonging to the oldest noble families had the privilege of attending those mournful parties of *loto* and whist at the Tuileries, and many among the elite felt excluded, including the large numbers of lesser and Napoleonic nobility and especially the rising ranks of the bourgeoisie: the bankers, businessmen, and professionals whose economic power had only continued to increase after the French Revolution even as their share of political power had decreased dramatically. More liberal than his *ultra* cousins, Louis-Philippe knew that the future lay with the bourgeoisie and welcomed them to his parties at the Palais-Royal, preparing the ground for his political future should another revolution come to pass. Among the Bourbons, only the duchesse de Berry attended these events and cultivated relations with a relatively broad constituency.[27]

She was also the only member of the royal family to be seen in the city itself. According to one widely repeated if possibly apocryphal story, when the first omnibus began operating in Paris, she bet her father-in-law ten thousand francs that she would be among the first to ride it. Dressed as a working girl, in a simple gray dress, she was immediately recognized as she stepped onto the bus because of her famously tiny feet. "It's Madame's foot!" the conductor supposedly cried, and all traffic ground to a halt. Even if the story is not authentic, it conveys the sense that people had of the duchess as a mobile figure, someone out among them, a kind of "people's princess."[28]

The duchess was everywhere in the 1820s, patronizing the leading Romantic artists, writers, and composers, such as Delacroix, Scribe, and Rossini. Boutiques, such as that of the great fashion designer Leroy, vied for her attention, and newspapers dedicated to fashion, such as the *Journal des dames et des modes* and later *La Mode*, which was created with her patronage, chronicled her outfits and hairstyles. "She was everywhere joyous," wrote one journalist in a retrospective account, "animated, and alert, taking everything in, protecting every industry, intelligent and good, and alive, and a spendthrift, making an assault on the boutiques and throwing money along the way with a royal profusion." She continued to be at the vanguard of fashion trends, such as the *coiffure à la girafe*, a very high hairdo, named in

Duchess with giraffe hairstyle,
portrait by Alexandre-Jean Dubois-Drahonet (1827)

Fashion plate from *La Mode* (1829, plate VI)

honor of the animal sent as a gift in 1827 to Charles X by the viceroy of Egypt, the first of its species in France, which the duchess went to see on several occasions. She attended the theater so frequently that the proprietors of the Gymnase renamed their theater in her honor, calling it, of course, the *Théâtre de Madame*.[29]

The duchess circulated outside of Paris as well. In the early years of her marriage she and the duke had purchased the château of Rosny, a sumptuous brick and limestone castle built at the end of the sixteenth century and located a few hours by carriage to the northwest of Paris. This became her refuge from the tedium of life at the Tuileries and

Parisian politics. Her first task was to construct an elaborate tomb for the duke on the grounds of the château. Although her husband's body had been interred at the Cathedral of Saint-Denis, the traditional resting place of French monarchs, the duchess had his heart removed and placed it in the special monument that she constructed on her property.

In addition to this macabre relic, Rosny housed her increasingly impressive collections of paintings and furniture. Advised by an art expert, the duchess purchased paintings by leading Romantic artists of the day, such as Ary Scheffer and the celebrated flower painter Redouté, who gave her lessons. She particularly favored works by contemporary women artists, such as Marguerite Gérard and Pauline Auzou. The catalog of the auction of her objets d'art in 1865 gives a sense of the splendor of Rosny's contents and of her taste, which ran toward the monumental: voluminous Aubusson carpets, heavy Gobelins tapestries, beds with gilt-bronze columns, intricate Louis XIII clocks, lots of marquetry tables and precious porcelain. The château also had a rich library, featuring eighty-six precious manuscripts and hundreds of beautifully bound books on all subjects, from ancient history to theology. Most of these were probably collected by the duke, and we cannot assume that the duchess read them, but it is a good bet that the volumes of Romantic poetry and especially the historical novels by Walter Scott came from her personal collection.[30]

During the hot summer months she decamped to Dieppe, a resort town on the Normandy coast, which she popularized. Prior to the arrival of the duchess in 1824, bathing in the ocean was viewed mainly as therapy for the mentally ill. Crowds gathered the first time the duchess took a dip, carried in the arms of an *aide-baigneur* because it was considered unseemly—and dangerous—for women to convey themselves into the ocean alone. Soon Dieppe became a vacation destination, and large hotels sprung up to cater to the fashionable clientele who followed the duchess's lead.

She took other trips around France as well, including in 1828 to the Vendée, the province in western France that had been the scene

Portrait of the duchess by Thomas Lawrence (1825)

of a brutally repressed counterrevolutionary insurrection in the 1790s. There the duchess felt all around her the warmth of devotion to the Bourbons and received promises that should another revolution break out, she could always count on the brave Vendéen noble leaders, and their devoutly Catholic peasant soldiers, to come to her aid. The memory of this voyage would be decisive in motivating her fight for the throne a few years later.[31]

One painting of the duchess from this period gives an indication of how far she had come since leaving that quarantine boat in Marseille a decade before, a scrawny and disoriented adolescent, and

perhaps also a sense of what lay in store for her. Painted in 1825 by
the English portraitist Thomas Lawrence, it shows a woman in full
bloom, wearing a white satin dress—white being the color of the
Bourbon banner—with pink roses attached to her bodice and a large
white pearl like a teardrop between her breasts. She has a slight smile
on her lips and a left eye that wanders slightly, as if on the lookout
for excitement. On her head she wears another of her signature fashion statements that would soon be copied around town: a *toque à la
Walter Scott*, a tartan hat in homage to her favorite Scottish author,
whose romantic historical novels, many of them centered on female
heroines, made her dream of the chivalrous past.

It was perhaps after having read Scott's *The Abbot* that the duchess decided, in 1829, to throw a legendary "Mary Stuart"–themed
costume ball at the Tulieries: one of the most famous social events
of the Restoration, and one of the last. Scott's novel, published in
1820 and translated into French the same year, describes an episode
in the life of the sixteenth-century Scottish monarch who was briefly
queen of France before being imprisoned for eighteen years by her
cousin Elizabeth I and then beheaded. The duchess assigned each
of her guests a historical role to play, and those noble guests descended from members of sixteenth-century aristocrats came dressed
as their august ancestors. The role of Mary Stuart went, of course, to
the duchess. No expense was spared for the Renaissance costumes,
which were designed by the celebrated artist Eugène Lamy. When
the duchess appeared, wearing an ermine-trimmed blue velvet gown
over a white satin skirt, all eyes were drawn to the real crown jewels glittering on her forehead. Unsurprisingly, the duchesse d'Angoulême disapproved of dressing up as a queen famous for having
been decapitated. But the duchesse de Berry didn't care. She danced
the quadrille that night with little regard for her sister-in-law's feelings or whatever bad omen that her historical playacting portended.[32]

Sixteen months later, another revolution broke out.

It was precipitated by the *ultras* pushing their reactionary policies
too far. Right from the moment of his coronation in 1824—which

was held at Reims Cathedral and modeled on the traditional coronations of the Old Regime—Charles X began undermining the *Charte* and undoing his brother's liberalizing reforms. He made public displays of sacrilege—such as profanation of the host—a capital crime. He replaced the popular prime minister with a right-wing one. Then, in July of 1830, he issued a series of four ordinances, which limited freedom of the press, among other antiliberal measures. The next day, Parisians took to the streets, urged on by the very newspapers that the king had attempted to silence. Barricades, constructed of torn-up paving stones and furniture thrown from apartments above, blocked the streets and provided the revolutionaries cover from which to shoot at the government's soldiers.

From the comfortable remove of his château in Saint-Cloud, outside the city, Charles X ignored the uprising, assuming that it would soon blow over. He had seen riots before and believed that the best thing to do was ignore them. Meanwhile, Louis-Philippe donned a tricolor *boutonnière*, symbolically aligning himself with the revolutionaries as his father had done in 1789. Urged on by a group of bourgeois moderates who saw him as a compromise between monarchy and republic, he slowly made his way from his country estate in Neuilly to Paris. After years of humiliation at the hands of his Bourbon cousins, the duc d'Orléans dared to think that his time might finally have come.

PART TWO

The Convert

CHAPTER 3

A Modern Jew

W HEN NEWSPAPERS BEGAN to publish details about the
man who betrayed the duchesse de Berry in the days
following her arrest in 1832, they got almost everything
wrong. Some claimed that Simon Deutz had been born in Italy, when
he was really from Germany. Reporters who knew he was from Germany identified the city of his birth as Cologne, when he was really
born in Koblenz. They said his uncle was the chief rabbi of France,
when it was really his father. They added or subtracted years to his
age. Some reports even got his name wrong or spelled it incorrectly.
But they were all right about one thing: Simon Deutz had been born
a Jew.

As they digested this bit of information with their morning café
au lait, French readers could be forgiven for expressing shock. It was
not that it was so difficult to believe that a Jew could betray the duchess; the story of Judas, recounted with the rest of Christ's Passion in
every Catholic church during Holy Week, made the French all too
aware of the potential perfidy of the Jews. No, their astonishment

would have arisen from the idea that a Jew was ever able to become the confidant of a Bourbon princess.

How such a thing became possible is bound up with the enormous changes ushered in by the French Revolution, which opened vast new opportunities for French Jews at the very moment that Simon Deutz entered the world. But if the French Revolution made it *possible* for Deutz to interact with the duchess, it didn't make it *likely*. Deutz's story remains exceptional, the result of a very specific set of drives, desires, talents, and insecurities, as well as a certain amount of happenstance.

Deutz came from a family of religiously observant Jews in the Rhineland region of western Germany. His surname suggests that the male line of the family originated in the town of Deutz, which is now a part of the city of Cologne. Little is known about the Deutz part of the family tree, but quite a lot is known about another branch on his father's side, the Wallichs, who since the Middle Ages had been one of Germany's leading Jewish families of scholars, rabbis, and physicians. Joseph ben Meir Wallich, one of the more celebrated members of the family, obtained his medical degree in Padua in 1600, and the Holy Roman Emperor appointed him "Jew doctor" of Worms, although he would later have to defend himself against a charge of poisoning brought by non-Jewish colleagues, jealous of his success.[1]

Simon's father, whose Hebrew name was Menachem Mendel Deutz but who would go by Emmanuel, was born in Koblenz in 1763. Destined for the rabbinate, he studied at the yeshiva (rabbinical seminary) in the town of Mainz, some sixty miles away, before moving back to Koblenz to take up his rabbinical position. As a rabbi, Emmanuel Deutz occupied the highest social position within the local Jewish community, but he was still a stigmatized figure in broader society because Jews in German lands, as in all of Europe, suffered discrimination and had few privileges. Yet this was about to change: when Emmanuel Deutz married Simon's mother, Judith Bermann, in 1789, the Revolution had just broken out in France. If it weren't for this political event, Emmanuel would almost surely have spent his entire career in Koblenz, following in the footsteps of his rabbinical ancestors. But Rabbi Deutz found himself caught up in the changes that were transforming the lives of his fellow Jews, and he would come to play an active role in implementing them.

Koblenz (spelled Coblenz or Coblentz before 1926) is an ancient town along the Rhine in the Palatinate region. Jews had lived in Koblenz since at least the year 1100, although they were expelled during the Middle Ages. Despite popular hostility, a handful of Jewish families were allowed to resettle there in the early sixteenth century under highly restrictive conditions. They were barred from all but a small number of occupations, forbidden from wearing bright or costly clothing, and forced to live in a ghetto. When French revolutionary soldiers tore down Koblenz's "Jews' gate" in 1794, the roughly three hundred Jews living in the town rejoiced. Simon's parents might well have been part of the jubilant crowd that day.

That the French came to be seen as the liberators of Germany's Jews is ironic: France had been exceedingly hostile to Jews through much of its history. Although France was a leading center of European Jewish life in the early Middle Ages—Rashi, one of the most acclaimed Talmudic scholars, was born in northern France in 1040—French kings would periodically expel the Jews, confiscate their assets, and then invite them back, only to do it all again a few years later. Charles VI definitively expelled them in 1394, and, technically, Jews were not allowed to reside in France again until the French Revolution came some four hundred years later.

Nevertheless, several small Jewish communities had formed in French territory: around five thousand Sephardim (Jews of Spanish origin) had fled the Inquisition to settle in and around Bordeaux, although they had to appear to be Christian until 1723; between thirty and forty thousand Ashkenazim (Jews of German origin) were allowed to remain in the eastern provinces of Alsace and Lorraine when this region became part of France in 1648; and several thousand Jews lived in the southern region of Provence, which belonged to the pope until the French Revolution. Although the Sephardic Jews of

Bordeaux had achieved a level of economic and cultural integration into French society, they were still technically considered foreigners. The Ashkenazic Jews of Alsace and Lorraine faced greater restrictions, which increased their isolation from the Christian population; forbidden to live in most towns or cities, to own land, or to engage in most trades or professions, they mainly worked as small-scale merchants or moneylenders, spoke Yiddish rather than French, and practiced a highly observant brand of folk-inflected Judaism. They were largely impoverished, living on both the literal and figurative margins of French society. As for the Jews in the Papal States of Provence, they were physically locked into ghettos known as *carrières* until the French Revolution set them free.[2]

The French Revolution radically transformed the legal status of France's Jews. After debating the issue on something like thirty separate occasions, the revolutionaries granted full civil rights to Jews in two separate decrees, 1790 for the Sephardic Jews and the Jews of Provence, and 1791 for the Ashkenazic Jews of Alsace and Lorraine. The revolutionaries made this gesture as a way of demonstrating their fidelity to the universalist principles they had proclaimed in *The Declaration of the Rights of Man and the Citizen* (1789), which stated that all men had equal rights. This was in line with the principles that the revolutionaries in America had proclaimed a few years earlier, although it was even more radical and inclusive. According to the French revolutionaries, there could be no more privileges based on blood or ancestry, no more restrictions based on race or religion. Overnight, the numerous laws governing where French Jews could live or what they could do simply fell away. The French Revolution had made the Jews the equals of their fellow Frenchmen.[3]

The same event that the family of the duchesse de Berry viewed with horror in Naples was hailed as a salvation by Jews the world over. For the millions of Jews who faced grievous discrimination in other countries, the French Revolution represented a radical turning point and a beacon of hope. It signaled that they too might one day gain equality, that they might eventually escape from segregation and become full-fledged members of European society. For the first time in European history, Jews faced no legal restrictions on their upward mobility. They were free to reinvent themselves, to follow their dreams and desires. Of course, there had always been Jews who tried to leave Judaism behind through conversion. But after the French Revolution, Jews could climb the social and economic ladder *while remaining Jews*. Or they could simply decide that religion played no role in their lives whatsoever, a decision had never been an option under the Old Regime.

Jews outside of France soon benefited from these freedoms. As Napoleon began conquering neighboring countries in the 1790s, he brought revolutionary liberties with him. This meant emancipation for some of the Jews living in the German principalities that formed part of the Holy Roman Empire, as well as for the Jews in much of Italy. By the time Simon Deutz was born, in 1802, the Jews of Koblenz had gained legal equality.

When Napoleon put an end to the French Revolution and established the empire in 1804, he began reorganizing almost every aspect of French national life. From government administration to the educational system to inheritance laws, he left few remnants of the Old Regime in place. No detail seemed too small for Napoleon, now styling himself emperor, to take in hand as he attempted to rationalize the laws of the nation and bring every aspect of existence under state control, not even France's small and marginalized communities of Jews. Napoleon had grown concerned about Jewish moneylending practices in Alsace after receiving complaints from local administrators there. He also worried that fifteen years after their emancipation, France's Jews still had not integrated, that they retained their distinctive religious customs and continued to follow their seemingly arcane religious laws. They remained, according to their critics, a people apart, a "nation within the nation," and continued to inspire neighbors' distrust.[4]

Rather than ending animosity toward the Jews, as their defenders had hoped, emancipation had in fact generated a new kind of hatred.

Whereas before the French Revolution, the Jews had been denounced as the most backward of peoples, mired in religious superstition, they were beginning to be seen as epitomizing what was bad about the new world that the revolutionaries had inaugurated. The small handful of Jewish bankers, who began to make an economic mark during the Napoleonic Empire, became lightning rods for this backlash. In 1806 the counterrevolutionary aristocrat Louis de Bonald called for the Jews to be expelled from France.[5]

In response to these complaints, Napoleon decided it was time for Jews to declare their allegiance to France once and for all, to make plain that the practice of Judaism was not in conflict with the demands of French citizenship. In April 1806 he convened an Assembly of Jewish Notables, made up of leading rabbis and lay communal leaders in France and the annexed territories of Germany and Italy, and charged them with determining the limits of Jewish religious law. Led by the rabbi of Strasbourg, the assembly also included Rabbi Deutz, who journeyed to Paris for the occasion.

To guide the discussion, Napoleon's ministers submitted a series of questions. These included general queries about Jewish loyalty to France: Do the Jews born in France acknowledge France as their country? Are they bound to defend it? Are they bound to obey the laws and follow the directions of the civil code? Napoleon also included questions designed to show that Jewish law did not mandate that Jews must treat other Jews more favorably than Christians in business dealings. And he included questions pertaining to specific matters of Jewish religious law, such as whether Jews could marry non-Jews, that might hinder his ultimate goal of pushing France's Jews toward integration. The notables were clearly expected to affirm that their primary allegiance was to France.

Realizing that the decisions of the Assembly of Notables would not seem religiously binding to Jews, Napoleon decided to create a more august body, composed of representatives from throughout the empire. He dubbed it the Grand Sanhedrin, in imitation of the ancient religious court. Napoleon's Grand Sanhedrin would have seventy-one members, like its ancient antecedent, two-thirds of whom would be rabbis. A solemn call to elect delegates went out in French, Hebrew, German, and Italian. On February 12, 1807, the newly elected body convened with great pomp and ceremony at the Hôtel-de-Ville in Paris, wearing fanciful costumes specially designed for the occasion: black suits, silk capes, and three-cornered hats. Emmanuel Deutz was once again among their number.

Over the course of the next several weeks, the Grand Sanhedrin considered the questions posed by Napoleon and the provisional answers outlined by the Assembly of Notables. The delegates eventually rendered nine decisions. These included prohibitions against lending money at usurious interest rates either to Jews or Christians and exhortations for Jews to abandon peddling for the supposedly more noble occupations of agriculture and artisanal labor. They also included solemn assurances that Jews consider the land of their birth as their fatherland, that they would fight to defend it, and that they consider non-Jewish citizens as their brothers. These answers so closely followed the script laid down by Napoleon that some Jewish nationalist historians would later blame the Grand Sanhedrin for going along with Napoleon's plan for Jewish assimilation.[6]

The Grand Sanhedrin did, however, resist Napoleon on one key point. While the delegates acknowledged that marriages between Jews and non-Jews were legally binding, they specified that rabbis would not bless such unions. Given how rare it was for anyone to oppose Napoleon's will on any matter whatsoever, this moment of resistance to his desire for assimilation should not be overlooked. French Jews did not necessarily plan on just blending in, even as they welcomed the possibility of joining French society on equal terms.

The Grand Sanhedrin dissolved after concluding its business, but Napoleon was not done with the Jews. He also created the consistory system: every department (administrative region) in France containing at least two thousand Jews would have a local consistory council, elected by the wealthiest Jews in the region. There would also be a central consistory, based in Paris, with three chief rabbis. Under the supervision of the minister of religion, the central consistory would be responsible for administering all aspects of Jewish religious life in France and for making all decisions pertaining to the practice of the religion. This system would outlast the Napoleonic Empire, creating a uniquely French brand of Judaism.[7]

Emmanuel Deutz evidently made a favorable impression on Napoleon's ministers during the deliberations of the Grand Sanhedrin because in 1810 he was chosen to become one of the three *grand rabbins*—chief rabbis—of the central consistory, along with a rabbi from Alsace and one from Italy. When the Alsatian rabbi died in 1812 and the Italian rabbi moved back to Italy in 1826, they were not replaced. Deutz became the sole chief rabbi of the central consistory.

From 1826 until his death in 1842, Emmanuel Deutz was the most powerful Jewish religious authority in France. It was he who resolved all matters pertaining to religious practice at a time when Jews first began to question the multitude of laws and prohibitions governing their daily life. It was he who represented the Jewish community in dealings with the French government. And it was he who was responsible for setting the moral tone of French Judaism, a role that became increasingly difficult to perform as his children came of age and began to rebel.

When Rabbi Deutz arrived in Paris with his large family, the Jewish population of the capital was small but growing rapidly. Whereas Jews were forbidden to live in Paris during the Old Regime, and fewer than eight hundred lived there—clandestinely—at the time of the French Revolution, by 1808 there were almost three thousand. In 1831, the year before Simon betrayed the duchess, there were twelve thousand. The Jewish population thus grew even faster than the general population of Paris, which itself experienced unprecedented growth during this period. Although still small in relative numbers, the Jews of the capital became *visible* for the first time during the Napoleonic Empire and the Bourbon Restoration, especially because they tended to cluster in certain neighborhoods near the center of the city.[8]

Emmanuel Deutz

Emmanuel Deutz settled with his family at no. 3, rue Geoffroy l'Angevin, in the Marais neighborhood of Paris sometime around 1810, when Simon was eight years old. In French, *marais* means "swamp," and this area, on the right bank of the Seine, had indeed been a swamp in the early Middle Ages, when the emperor Charles the Bald donated it to a Catholic monastery. Jews lived in the Marais from the beginning. And even after their expulsion in 1394, Jews haunted the neighborhood in its street names: what is now the rue Ferdinand Duval was called the rue des Juifs (Jews' Street) until 1900. Legend has it that the rue des Ecouffes—today one of the centers of Jewish life in the Marais—got its name from the Old French word for a buzzard-like bird of prey (*escofles*), used as a slur to designate the Jewish moneylenders who made the street their home in the Middle Ages.[9]

In the early seventeenth century the Marais became fashionable. Aristocrats built luxurious mansions, *hôtels particuliers*, in the neighborhood. The serene Place des Vosges (originally called the Place Royale), built by Henri IV, attracted a wealthy elite. When the court left Paris for Versailles in the 1680s, however, the neighborhood began to decline, and aristocrats abandoned the Marais for the Faubourg Saint-Germain on the Left Bank. By the time of the French Revolution, the Marais had become shabby. Poor and working-class people crowded into the neighborhood, setting up workshops in the decrepit mansions vacated by the rich. When poor Jews began to immigrate to Paris in the late eighteenth century, they gravitated to the neighborhood less because of its ancient Jewish ties than because it was both central and affordable. In 1810, when the Deutz family arrived, 65 percent of Paris's Jews lived in the Marais, which had two synagogues: one on the rue Sainte-Avoye (now the rue du Temple), in which Rabbi Deutz officiated, and one on the rue Chaulme (now the rue des Archives).[10]

An 1809 census conducted by the newly created consistory gives a sense of the diversity of Rabbi Deutz's congregants. Many, like the Deutz family, had immigrated to Paris, drawn by the promise of freedom and by the economic opportunities of continental Europe's biggest city. Of the nearly three thousand Jews living in the capital in 1809, fewer than half were born there. Most of the newcomers came from other parts of France, mainly Alsace and Lorraine. A not insignificant minority, including the Deutz family, came from one of the German states, but there were also immigrants from Austria, Belgium, Holland, Poland, Italy, and elsewhere. Worried that the presence of too many poor foreign Jews would stir up hostility, wealthy Jewish leaders saw to it that no foreign Jew could get a permit to live in Paris without the approval of the consistory. In 1812 the consistory gave the Paris police a list of thirty Jews to be expelled from the city for insufficient means.[11]

The presence in Paris (although not in the Marais) of a small handful of wealthy banking families—such as the Rothschilds, who arrived in 1812—contributed to the stereotype that all nineteenth-century Jews were rich. This was far from the truth. In 1809 only about 12 percent of Parisian Jews had any means whatsoever. About 7 percent of the capital's Jews were in business (including commerce, industry, banking, trade); about 3 percent worked in the liberal professions (including doctors and lawyers, but also teachers, who made relatively little); and another 2 percent engaged in various other occupations (landlords, investors, soldiers, government bureaucrats) that put them above the working class. By 1840, the percentage of Parisian Jews in the bourgeoisie had risen only to 16.6 percent. This breakdown mirrored the Parisian population at large.[12]

The vast majority of Parisian Jews, therefore, were working-class or poor. Many of these impoverished Jews engaged in peddling and small-scale commerce. Some worked as artisans, especially in the clothing and jewelry trades. Women very often worked in trade as well or earned money as seamstresses, sometimes taking in piecework to do at home, making a pittance but nevertheless helping to keep their families' heads above water. Many relied on charity: in 1810 fifty Jewish households (about three hundred people, or 10 percent of the Jewish population) received bread, kosher meat, and cash assistance from the Jewish community. The number of indigent Jews actually grew in the first half of the nineteenth century, as poor immigrants continued to flood the capital. By 1840, about two thousand of the nine thousand Parisian Jews still lived in poverty.[13]

The Deutz family lived among these poor Jews. Religiously observant Jews could not ride in carriages on the Sabbath, so Rabbi Deutz needed to live in walking distance of the main synagogue on the rue Sainte-Avoye. But his decision to dwell among the poorest of his congregants also reflected his lifelong devotion to the humble and needy.[14]

His 1842 obituary in *Les Archives Israélites de France*, the recently founded Jewish newspaper, stressed this aspect of his legacy.

According to his obituary, Deutz believed that being a rabbi did not mean writing learned Talmudic commentaries but rather "giving up pride" and doing good works: "He was beloved by the lower class of Israelites, he lived among them, encouraged them in their work, engaged willingly in their intimate conversations, responded to all their religious doubts, answered their questions about religious practice, visited those struck by misfortune." Known as the "counselor and the friend of the people," Rabbi Deutz was well respected by the municipal authorities but not always by his wealthy congregants.[15]

The term *Israélite*, used in the obituary, itself reflects a certain class prejudice. Well into the nineteenth century, the word *Juif* (Jew) carried negative connotations in French. The dictionary of the Académie française, the official arbiter of the French language, defined the term in the following pejorative manner at the time: "JEW is also used, figuratively and familiarly, of he who practices usury or sells at exorbitant prices; and in general of anyone who seeks to make money through unjust and sordid means." In the nineteenth century, educated, middle-class French Jews began to call themselves *Israélites* to set themselves apart from this stereotype. It became the polite term in French for designating "members of the Mosaic religion" and remains so in some official French discourse to this day, although French Jews began to reclaim the term *Juif* in the 1960s. For one nineteenth-century writer in the *Archives Israélites*—note the title of the newspaper, which was founded in 1840—the old kind of "Jew," whose heart remained in Jerusalem, had disappeared from France. He was replaced by the modern French "Israelite," similar in all external respects to his fellow Frenchmen.[16]

Emmanuel Deutz never became that kind of Israelite. His obituary notes that he chose to live among "the still little enlightened class of our coreligionists," and it is clear that his sympathies lay with the old-fashioned "Jews." It was said that Rabbi Deutz did not speak French; he insisted on delivering sermons in Yiddish—the language spoken by the oldest and poorest of his congregants—into the 1830s. However, his obituary states that he "knew how to make himself understood in French."

Although in certain respects Emmanuel Deutz remained old-fashioned, he also believed in changing with the times. He shaved his beard early on in his career, in what the very orthodox thought constituted a violation of Jewish law. As his obituary, obviously written by a modernizer, noted, "He believed that the beard did not make the rabbi . . . and he patiently endured the clamor of . . . the bigots." On the second day of the Jewish New Year, Rosh Hashanah, when a delegation of prominent members of the community traditionally paid their respects to Napoleon, Rabbi Deutz advised them to shave. "Let them visit me," he told his orthodox critics, "and I will prove to them that the religion does not forbid it."[17]

Rabbi Deutz's decision to live among the poor Jews may have had a financial motivation as well. For although his position made him one of the most prominent members of the Paris Jewish community, he did not have anywhere near the resources of the bankers and businessmen who were elected to run the consistory. Nineteenth-century rabbi salaries were low. In 1806 communal rabbis, the lowest rank, earned a mere one thousand francs per year, barely placing them in the middle class. In 1831, when the state assumed responsibility for paying rabbis (as it had earlier for priests and pastors), their salary actually went down considerably, to a maximum of seven hundred francs per year. By comparison, the average salary for a laborer in Paris was five hundred francs per year in 1853. A skilled laborer could earn about a thousand francs annually, the minimum amount needed to support a family of four at a time when bread alone cost more than three hundred francs a year and lodging cost between one hundred and four hundred francs. When he died, in 1842, Rabbi Deutz—chief rabbi of Paris—earned six thousand francs a year, which made him solidly middle class but hardly rich.[18]

Devoted to his congregants and beset by financial worries, Rabbi Deutz did not have much time to devote to rearing his seven children: Sara, Samuel, Simon, Rose, Euphrasine, Salomon, and Mardoché (Mordechai, called Bernard). Simon's schooling seems to have been haphazard at best. He most likely attended one of the three small Jewish primary schools in Paris, which resembled traditional *hederim*, where Jewish children primarily studied the Talmud, as well as Hebrew and Aramaic. Although some of Simon's critics would later say that he could barely write French, his letters reveal a high degree of fluency, so he clearly obtained the rudiments of a secular education, even if he did not learn Latin or the other subjects studied by elite children of the day.

Several accounts of Simon's childhood exist, but they were all written by hostile critics and must be regarded with skepticism. One such account, written by a convert from Judaism who went by the name of Ignace-Xavier Morel and who claimed to have been a friend and neighbor of the Deutz family in the Marais, notes that Simon and his siblings "quickly attained the height of malice and perversity of the Jewish urchins of the rue Beaubourg." Morel further claims that one day Rabbi Deutz, too given to "indolent laziness" to maintain order in his household, was fined sixty francs because his naughty children had spilled water from a window on passersby in the street below. Although Morel is not necessarily to be trusted, Simon himself admitted to having been a troublemaker when he was young. In a letter to his father in 1828, he refers to the "more than stormy" nature of his youth.[19]

Of medium height for the time at five-foot-three, with curly black hair, a dark complexion, and brown eyes, Simon Deutz found himself adrift as he entered adolescence. Like his older brother, Samuel, he may have used his foreign birth to avoid the draft. Samuel worked with his father, copying Jewish sacred texts, and later obtained a position as a *sopher* (scribe) with the Jewish consistory. More ambitious, Simon at first envisioned following his father into the rabbinate. At the time, Paris did not offer any schools for rabbinical training, so Simon studied the Talmud in the town of Wintzenheim, in Alsace. He then studied at the yeshiva in Metz, which in 1829 would become France's first modern rabbinical school. But Simon soon grew restless. He never followed Jewish laws with any degree of rigor, despite his father's position as the head of the French Jewish community, and could not commit to becoming a rabbi.[20]

Despite his spotty education, Simon liked to read. Books provided a portal to a more exciting world, an escape from the grime of the Marais and a chaotic home life. Simon's detractors would later accuse him of reading "evil books" as a child, by which they meant works by the antireligious *philosophes* of the eighteenth century. Morel reports that Simon would devour works of an even worse variety: "filthy" novels. When his younger siblings made too much noise at home, according to a scandalized Morel, Simon would bring his book outside to read in the street. One can imagine what the Jewish housewives and poor artisans of the Marais thought as they passed the rabbi's son, his head in a book, as the life of the neighborhood buzzed around him.[21]

Simon's next choice of career followed naturally from his predilections. After possibly spending some time training as a jeweler, he decided to become a printer. His father apprenticed him to the printer Séiter, who produced prayer books and other pious reading material for the Jewish consistory. By 1823, Simon had taken a better position as a typesetter with the firm of Didot, the most prestigious printer in France. But this too did not last. According to Morel, he would show up to work drunk, and he liked to spend his time wandering around Paris, gazing at the shops and passersby—a kind of aimless meandering that the French call *flânerie*. Given his penchant for daydreaming, it's likely that Simon had a difficult time reconciling himself to the unglamorous daily grind that the printing trade required. Straddling the artisan and professional classes, the job of typesetter usually required some education, but it involved an element of manual labor as well. Although it would have brought him into contact with some of the leading writers of the day, it was in many ways a step down the social ladder from the status that his father had attained as chief rabbi. Printers got their hands dirty.[22]

In November 1822, Simon's mother died. She was only forty-nine years old, and her youngest child, Bernard, was only five. Although Emmanuel Deutz's obituary states that his first wife never provided him with "domestic happiness," her loss crushed Simon, then age twenty. He refused to accept his father's remarriage the following year to Lisbeth Moyse, who could not read or even sign her name. Simon's behavior became far more erratic beginning the year after his mother's death. A few years after that, he would turn his back on his family and his community, seeking the mentorship elsewhere: with the pope and then with the duchess.[23]

What makes a young man seek out the attention of powerful or important figures? According to Sigmund Freud, all children begin by looking up to their parents. But at some point they realize that their mother and father are not the omnipotent beings they had imagined and that they occupy a lower place on the social ladder than they had previously perceived. At the same time, children begin to feel slighted by their parents. They come to understand that they are not the exclusive object of their parents' love, a realization often brought about by the birth of siblings. The reaction to these realizations can take the form of what Freud calls a "family romance," in which children imagine that their parents are not really their parents, that they are in fact the offspring of people who belong to a much higher social sphere—celebrities or royalty perhaps—who left them to be raised by the flawed and lowly beings who constitute their current family. The child's feelings of being special, and being misunderstood, would thus have a natural explanation. According to Freud, this kind of fantasy projection is particularly common among neurotic and highly gifted people.[24]

One doesn't have to accept every aspect of Freudian theory to see the applicability of this scenario to Simon Deutz. As the third child of seven, with a father who was too busy to pay him much mind and a mother who died while he was barely out of adolescence, Simon likely felt starved for attention. And although the chief rabbi must have seemed like a very powerful figure to his son at first, contact with the outside world would have punctured this idealized image. We know from Simon's autobiography and from the testimony of those who knew him in childhood that Simon loved his parents "with a kind of passion," yet he did things to wound his father—including converting to Catholicism—that seem expressly calculated to deny his paternal authority. In many ways the pope was an all-too-poetic substitute father figure for the chief rabbi's son (the word *pope* derives from the Greek word for "father"). And for her part, the duchess was defined in the popular imagination by her role as the mother of the Bourbon heir to the throne.[25]

Simon's story is undoubtedly rooted in the specificity of his individual psychology, and it was set in motion by his very particular circumstances. On another level, though, it reads as a more extreme version of what an entire generation of Jews attempted to do, or fantasized about doing, as the world opened up to them for the first time following the French Revolution. It can even be seen as a parable of integration, the process by which Jews transformed or left their origins entirely behind. Although Simon would transform himself much more dramatically than almost any of his peers, his "family romance" typifies the identity crisis faced by so many in the nineteenth century. It is the story of the modern Jew, caught between fidelity and autonomy, tradition and invention, past and future.[26]

CHAPTER 4

Apostasy

B Y THE TIME Simon Deutz turned twenty-five years old, in 1827, he had failed at everything he had attempted. Unlike some of the more upwardly mobile French Jews of his generation, he had not attended one of the new Napoleonic *lycées*, which would have prepared him for a professional career. Both his plan to become a rabbi and his plan to become a printer had come to naught on account of his preference for idleness over hard work. He even attempted to go into business for himself selling firewood but had little more than debts to show for it.[1]

Besides laziness, Deutz seems to have contracted other bad habits on the streets of Paris. His critics would make it clear that he squandered his time and money in gambling dens and brothels. Physically at least, Deutz did not seem like the dissolute type. With olive skin, an intense gaze, and spectacles to correct his myopia, he resembled a student more than the army officer or young noble one would expect to find at such houses of ill repute. But Deutz had a problem controlling his impulses. He also possessed a driving ambition and would tell anyone who listened, "I will gain a fortune or die trying."[2]

Despite showing an early aptitude for rabbinic theology, Deutz could not obey all the laws and strictures imposed by orthodox Judaism. Jewish men had to keep their heads covered, follow kosher dietary laws, and keep the Sabbath, along with a multitude of other religious obligations governing every aspect of daily life. It was an arduous routine but one accepted willingly by those who believed in the sanctity of God's commandments, which Deutz no longer did. According to his brother-in-law David Drach, one of those who knew him best, he lost his childhood faith after reading the works of eighteenth-century *philosophes* such as Voltaire. "Sometimes [Deutz] would say that God was just a word, sometimes he would correct himself by admitting the existence of a Supreme Being," Drach wrote, referring to the deist divinity that the French Revolution substituted for the god of Judeo-Christian scripture.[3]

Drach describes Deutz as a spiritual searcher, someone intensely interested in religion, even as he rejected various forms of faith. He notes how Deutz would get carried away by whatever doctrine caught his momentary fancy: "Heaven, hell, and everything that revelation had made known to us, were not spared" by Deutz's "vagabond imagination," his "spirit in which nothing was fixed except uncertainty." According to Drach, Deutz's one constant belief was a deep dislike for Christianity, especially for those Jews who betrayed their brethren by converting. Indeed, nobody knew better than Drach just how violent Deutz's dislike could be.

David Drach was an ambitious twenty-six-year-old rabbi when he married Simon's sister, Sara Deutz, in 1817. A brilliant student, Drach had begun his rabbinical training at an early age in his native province of Alsace, and he came to Paris in order to scale the heights of the French Jewish religious establishment. When the capital's first Jewish school for boys opened in 1819, Drach served as its first teacher. He saw himself as the likely candidate to succeed Emmanuel Deutz when his father-in-law retired as chief rabbi of the central consistory.[4]

But sometime in 1821, Drach deviated from the path of orthodoxy. In his autobiographical writing, Drach hints that the roots

Portrait of David Drach by Jean-Auguste-Dominique Ingres
(c. 1840–1841)

of his disenchantment with Judaism stretched back to a childhood
sense of inferiority brought on by antisemitism, as well as to an early
fascination with Christian theology. But it is clear that a more recent series of conflicts with his bosses at the consistory were also to
blame. Unbeknownst to his family, the young rabbi made contacts
with Catholic clergy, including the dean of the Faculty of Theology
at the Sorbonne, and began the instruction necessary for conversion.
On March 29, 1823, he presented his letter of resignation to the consistory, and a few days later the archbishop of Paris baptized him and
his two daughters—Clarisse and Rosine—at Notre Dame Cathedral

in the presence of an immense crowd of witnesses. His son Auguste, barely out of infancy, had been baptized secretly a few days earlier.[5]

It would be difficult to overstate the shock and dismay of the entire Deutz family—Simon included—when news of Drach's conversion broke. His wife, Sara, was particularly distressed, and sought refuge with her newly baptized children at the home of her father. Because French law granted husbands absolute authority over the household—and did not allow divorce—Sara had very few options if she wanted her children to remain Jewish. Aided by Simon and by some of her father's influential congregants, she surreptitiously crossed the channel to England with her children, vanishing into the Jewish East End—London's equivalent of the Marais—under an assumed name. Meanwhile, Simon began a campaign of harassment directed against his brother-in-law: he smashed the windows of Drach's apartment on the rue des Singes in the Marais and broke in with some friends during the night. He also dropped hints that Sara had fled to Germany. Drach took the bait and spent the next several months moving between German cities, enlisting the help of French authorities to track Sara down. Letters exchanged between the Paris police prefect and various government ministers—including Chateaubriand, then minister of foreign affairs—throughout the winter of 1823–1824 testify to the high stakes of this drama involving the family of France's chief rabbi and one of the Catholic Church's most high-profile converts.[6]

Eventually, Drach realized he had been misled by Simon and responded with a ruse of his own. Pretending he had converted back to Judaism, Drach sent Rabbi Deutz a letter pleading to be reunited with his family. Sara eventually relented—perhaps under pressure from her father—and allowed Drach to join her and the children in London in the fall of 1824. All the while, however, he was hatching a plan to kidnap his children and bring them back to Paris to raise as Catholics. On November 9, 1824, while out for a walk in the public gardens of Tower Hill, he forced his children into a waiting carriage and sped toward Dover, managing to cross the channel before Sara could telegraph ahead to stop him.[7]

With his children safely hidden in Catholic institutions—they would never see their mother again—Drach then devoted himself to becoming a Catholic theologian. Whereas he once had tried to scale the heights of the Jewish religious establishment, he now set his sights on the Catholic one. With a sinecure as the librarian to the son of the duchesse de Berry, to whom he had been introduced by his highly placed ecclesiastical protectors, Drach began producing a series of treatises grounded in idiosyncratic interpretations of Hebrew scripture and aimed at encouraging his fellow Jews to follow him into the church. Meanwhile, Simon renewed his campaign of harassment against Drach when the latter returned to Paris, but according to police reports, hostilities between the brothers-in-law had ceased by the spring of 1825.[8]

Nobody was more surprised, however, than David Drach when Simon Deutz renewed contact with him in the late summer of 1827. Deutz's motives seem plain: he needed a job. Still, something more than desperation must have motivated him to turn to an enemy in his time of need. Perhaps he calculated that there was more to be gained from cultivating Drach than from subjecting him to fruitless persecution. Drach obliged his estranged brother-in-law by getting him a position in a Catholic printing house. But employment was not what Deutz really wanted. Like all of Deutz's attempts to follow the straight path, this new printing job lasted only a few weeks. He was clearly after something bigger.[9]

On August 20, 1827, Deutz sent a letter to Drach at the Sorbonne, where the latter was now studying for a doctorate. "Monsieur," the letter began, using the formal mode of address, "I am appealing to you [*vous*] to beg you to pull me out of a quagmire. I absolutely need 200 francs this very morning, otherwise the most disagreeable and unpleasant things might happen to me." After offering Drach some shares in an unspecified enterprise as collateral for the loan, Deutz appealed to the bond that used to unite them: "If remembering still our former friendship, you render me this important service, I will never forget it as long as I live." He instructed Drach to give the money to the bearer of the letter. Drach obliged yet again, even though two hundred francs was not an insignificant sum for the freelance theologian and part-time librarian. Two weeks later, Deutz wrote again to say that he too was considering converting to Catholicism.[10]

What drives someone to change religions? Is it genuine spirituality? Or a calculated bid for social acceptance and greater opportunities? It is impossible to know. One thing is certain, though: conversion is never a purely individual act. It is a public gesture and thus always has political and social ramifications, no matter how much the convert claims to be acting according to the dictates of his or her own conscience. The conversions of David Drach and Simon Deutz had greater ramifications than most, and they must be viewed in relation to the specific historical circumstances facing French Jews in the first half of the nineteenth century.

During the Restoration and July Monarchy (1814–1848), only about 160 Jews converted to Christianity in Paris, which amounts to fewer than five conversions per year, at a time when the Jewish population of the capital grew to almost ten thousand people. By all measures, this is a low rate of apostasy, especially as it includes Jews who converted to marry Christians. Théodore Ratisbonne, a member of a prominent Alsatian Jewish family who went on to found the Catholic Congregation of Our Lady of Zion with his brother, noted in his memoirs that when he became Catholic in 1827, conversion in France was "a rare, almost unheard-of thing." Between 1814 and 1823, it was particularly unusual: only around twenty Parisian Jews converted.[11]

The number of conversions in France was lower, in relative terms, than in the neighboring German states, despite the Jews' similar cultural backgrounds in the two countries. The difference can partly be explained by the fact that in the early decades of the nineteenth century, the Jews of France had become full and equal citizens, whereas Jews in most German states were not. The German poet Heinrich Heine, who converted in 1825 in the hope of gaining an academic post, famously said "the baptismal certificate is the ticket of admission to European culture." Because they had gained complete equality during the French Revolution, French Jews needed no such ticket to secure entry to the best schools or jobs.[12]

For certain French Jews, it was the quest for greater spirituality that led them into the arms of the church. This was the case for the Ratisbonne brothers. The older brother, Théodore, fell under the sway of several influential Catholic thinkers and received baptism along with two of his friends, also students from prominent Jewish families. Although his younger brother, Alphonse, had little Jewish education or connection to Jewish practice, he was at first outraged by his brother's defection. However, in 1842, while on a trip to Rome, Alphonse experienced a vision of the Virgin Mary at the Church of Sant'Andrea delle Fratte and also converted. "She didn't say a word to me, but I understood everything," he recounted in his widely read autobiography.[13]

If sudden accesses of religious sentiment are always a bit mysterious, in the case of Simon Deutz such a spiritual about-face was especially surprising. Not only had he threatened violence against Drach for converting just a few years before, but he was also the son of the chief rabbi of France: his conversion would cause an unprecedented scandal in the Jewish community. At a time when French Jews were just beginning to move into the mainstream of French national life, the conversion of the rabbi's son would be seen as proof that Judaism was not in fact capable of adapting to the modern world, that it was not a religion worthy of respect. Simon surely understood this. He also understood that the conversion was likely to destroy his venerable father. He could not have made the decision to embrace Catholicism lightly.

Aside from Deutz's own memoir, three accounts exist of his conversion. The first, a pamphlet published by Drach in 1828, is short and celebratory, highlighting only the most "miraculous" aspects of the Jew's entry into the church. The second, by Morel (who claimed to have been a childhood friend of Deutz but may in fact have been an alter ego created by Drach), was published after Deutz's betrayal of the duchess and is more revealing because it includes letters that

Deutz sent to Drach describing the ups as well as the downs of his religious journey. The third, by General Ferdinand Stanislas Dermoncourt (the general in charge of arresting the duchess), titled *Deutz or Deception, Ingratitude and Treason* (1836), adds still more details and anecdotes. Although Deutz's true motivations for conversion can never be known with certainty, the various reports combine to create a picture of the complex forces that set a volatile young man on a path that would change the course of history.[14]

According to Drach, it was anxiety about the future that pushed Deutz to convert. His debauchery and philosophical reflections had apparently not totally extinguished within him a belief in the immortality of the soul. Realizing that he was not currently on the path to heaven, he grew increasingly pensive. A concerned rabbi counseled him to practice his own religion more faithfully, but Deutz failed to find in Judaism "the calm and consolations that his soul required." It was at this point, according to Drach, that he turned to Christianity. The mysterious Morel even suggests that it was the loan that Drach provided him, in spite of their prior antipathy, that encouraged Deutz to convert by revealing to him the sublime virtue of Christian forgiveness. "None of my friends came to my aid," Deutz supposedly said. "It was the man whom I had persecuted without pity who opened his arms and his purse to me." The religion that inspired such generosity must be truly divine, he reasoned. Both of these explanations, of course, are self-serving: Drach wants to underscore the spiritual poverty of Judaism in comparison to Christianity; Morel wants to celebrate the moral superiority of Drach.[15]

In his own memoir, Deutz touches on his motivation for conversion only briefly, offering two possible explanations. First, he refers to a "strong desire to know the mysteries of Christianity." Given Drach's description of his "vagabond imagination," his restless adoption of different doctrines, such a religious curiosity does not seem out of character. We might in fact accept his religious explanation if Deutz did not undercut it a moment later: "Perhaps it was also the desire to avenge myself on a wretch who had betrayed the tenderness of my sister that drove me to Rome."[16]

Deutz is clearly referring to Drach, but following his brother-in-law into the church would have constituted an odd sort of retaliation against him. In fact, Drach encouraged Deutz's conversion and used it to boost his own status in Catholic circles. His pamphlet celebrating the conversion as a miracle brags about his own role in bringing it about. Deutz's "desire to avenge" thus makes little sense, unless he was planning all along to use the connections he would forge as a Catholic to do something that would embarrass Drach later on, such as betraying the duchesse de Berry. It seems more likely that the vengeance Deutz hoped to inflict on Drach was of a more mundane, vain type: Deutz knew that his own conversion would cause an even greater stir than Drach's had, and he possibly imagined he could annoy his brother-in-law by stealing the spotlight from him.[17]

In choosing to throw his lot in with the church, Deutz was in fact following an established path to career advancement during the Restoration. In Stendhal's novel *The Red and the Black* (1830), the protagonist, Julien Sorel, makes a similar calculation. Poor and provincial, Julien is approximately the same age as Simon Deutz in the late 1820s, when the novel is set. Like Deutz, Julien had watched the Napoleonic epic play out as a child, but by the time he comes of age, religious devotion had replaced military valor as the surest path to success, hence the title of the novel, in which red corresponds to the soldier's uniform and black to the priest's cassock. Julien chooses black: he resolves to become a priest and to feign religious devotion in order to advance in Restoration society. The novel follows him through his years in a seminary, where everyone is scheming to get ahead, and finally to Paris, where he uses his church connections to secure a place as the secretary to a powerful, right-wing aristocrat, whose daughter he eventually seduces. Stendhal's novel was published several years after Deutz's conversion, so it did not serve as an explicit model. But in retrospect, Julien's path seems almost like a blueprint for Simon's: Stendhal clearly understood the ambitions driving the young men of his era.[18]

Certainly, Deutz hoped to improve his material circumstances by embracing Catholicism. He was at a crossroads in his life, out of a job and pursued by menacing creditors. He had burned any number of bridges—with the Jewish religious establishment, with various Parisian printing houses. Perhaps he reasoned that only a bold move such as conversion would be sufficient to change his luck once and for all. And he had seen that Drach had used his conversion to leave behind the Jewish quarter of the Marais for a much more exalted sphere. The duchesse de Berry had become his patron, which must have seemed like an impossibly dazzling connection to the rabbi's son. Simon Deutz wanted above all to make a fortune. And in the reactionary world of Restoration France, the church seemed like his best bet to make this happen. Was it a good enough bet to sacrifice his familial ties? Was it good enough to justify turning his back on his community? Deutz was willing to make the wager.

CROSSING THE SEINE from the Marais to the Sorbonne, a short geographic distance but a world away, Deutz informed his brother-in-law of his desire "to instruct himself in the dogmas of the church." He hadn't yet committed to convert because he had not yet attained the religious knowledge necessary to make such a momentous decision. However, he made it clear that he was eager to learn more. And Drach was only too happy to put him in touch with the same church leaders who had aided his own conversion, including the archbishop of Paris, Hyacinthe-Louis de Quélen. "The illustrious pontiff deigned to converse at length with that interesting Israelite, who left edified by the unction of his words," Drach informs us in the pompous style that characterizes all his writing. Deutz was much more to the point, supposedly telling Drach that he was surprised to discover that not all priests were "jokers," as he had been led to believe by "our irreligious journalistic hacks."[19]

Inspired by his conversation with the archbishop, Deutz then expressed the desire to wade even deeper into the waters of Catholicism: he wanted to meet the Jesuits. Founded in sixteenth-century Spain by the Basque nobleman Ignatius de Loyola as a religious congregation focused on missionary work, the Society of Jesus dedicated itself mainly to educational and cultural pursuits in Europe. Almost from the time of their founding, however, the Jesuits aroused suspicion as political intriguers and were banished from much of Europe over the course of the eighteenth century, including from France in 1764. After the fall of Napoleon, Pope Pius VII officially restored the Jesuits throughout Catholic Europe, and they began to play a significant role in the effort to re-Christianize France led by conservatives in the nineteenth century.

According to Drach, Deutz had been brainwashed by the "forces of revolution" to believe that the Jesuits were pulling the strings of all the governments of Europe and were guilty of fomenting the most dangerous schemes to rob France of liberty. So it was a sign either of a complete turn in his thinking or of a budding hypocrisy that after his initial conversation with the Jesuits, Deutz declared to Drach that he was "charmed by the sage and edifying speeches of these holy religious men." On his next visit to the Jesuits, he entered a chapel with Drach and immediately fell to his knees, begging God to enlighten him. According to Drach, he declared afterward how happy he felt while praying. "It is surprising," he said, "but you know how much I always abhorred Jesus Christ, and I now experienced an extreme pleasure in praying to him." It was at that moment, according to Drach, that Deutz made the decision to convert.[20]

Convinced by his brother-in-law's performance, Drach allowed his two daughters to visit Deutz, who had not seen his nieces since their kidnapping in 1823. Apparently, the two young girls had never stopped saying prayers for the conversion of their mother and uncle. Drach recounts the touching scene of reunion, as the innocent girls—who were now preparing to become nuns—lavished caresses on Deutz and expressed how happy they were that he was no longer a "pagan."[21]

One major stumbling block, however, lay in the path of Deutz's conversion: the French Jewish community. It would not be easy for him to face his family and friends if he admitted that he was planning to convert. Rabbi Deutz's wealthy congregants had helped Sara flee France after Drach's conversion. They were even more likely now to help the rabbi keep his son from betraying their faith. In order to evade such obstacles it was decided that Deutz would complete his religious instruction in Rome.

Archbishop Quélen helped pave the way for Deutz's departure. Impressed by his rapid spiritual progress, Quélen must have realized that the conversion of the chief rabbi's son would not fail to be remarked upon favorably by his superiors in Rome. Like everyone else concerned, the archbishop had something to gain from Deutz's conversion. He thus recommended Deutz to Cardinal Cappellari, who at that time was the prefect of the Propaganda Fide (the Sacred Congregation for the Propagation of the Faith), the Vatican's missionary arm, and would later become Pope Gregory XVI. "Son of a rabbi, I knew my conversion would have a major impact in the Christian world," Deutz boasts in his memoir. For once, he was not exaggerating.[22]

The conversion of the Jews had always been desired by the church. Prophesied by the New Testament (Romans 11:25–26: "a hardening has come upon part of Israel, until the full number of the Gentiles come in, and so all Israel will be saved"), the eventual repentance of the Jews would be the ultimate "consolation" for their initial obstinacy, which Catholics believed had been responsible for the crucifixion of Christ. In the context of nineteenth-century France, conversion played a key role in the Right's ongoing battle against the forces of revolution: it was proof of Catholicism's power and appeal. It was also a way of striking back at Jews, who were seen as the prime beneficiaries of the French Revolution and as allies of the liberals. As Drach would later put it, conversion of the Jews offered encouragement to devout Catholics who were "dismayed by the new trials to which our holy religion has been subjected," by which he meant the French Revolution and its aftermath. Every Jew welcomed into the fold seemed like a miracle proving Catholicism's ability to win back the hearts and minds of the French people.[23]

During the 1820s Rome increased its missionary efforts in Europe. Every issue of ecclesiastical newspapers such as *L'Ami de la religion et du roi* (*The Friend of Religion and of the King*) in the 1820s contained accounts of nonbelievers won over to the church. Conversions of high-status Jews, as well as those with extensive knowledge of Jewish religious texts, were the most prized since they were perceived as the best advertisements for Catholicism and as the most demoralizing to the Jews. Because France had very few conversions during this period—which made the prospect of converting the son of France's chief rabbi especially attractive to the church's missionaries—the bulk of the conversions described in the French Catholic press took place in neighboring countries. This one from Italy was typical: "Salomon-Léon-Vita Ascoli, 64 years of age, father of a large family, and one of the most respected Jews on account of his age, his Biblical knowledge, his study of Hebrew, and his attachment to the synagogue, has finally, after a long resistance, given himself up to grace. . . . Last December 15, he was baptized in Ancona, and provided a very consoling spectacle." As was this one from Germany: "A touching ceremony took place, two weeks ago, in Mülheim, on the Rhine; a Protestant minister, two other Protestants, and an entire Jewish family publically abjured their error, and were entered into the bosom of the Catholic Church. The zeal and the science of R. P. [Reverend Father] Joseph Haus, Franciscan, contributed greatly to these conversions." The point of these conversion narratives was not, or not only, to exhort other Jews to follow their example. Very few Jews, it can be assumed, were reading the Catholic press. The goal was above all to reinforce the faith of Catholics.[24]

With his writings on conversion, Drach had begun to carve out an important niche for himself as a theologian. In late 1827 he had already published two in his series of *Letters of a Converted Rabbi to the Israelites His Brothers on the Motives for His Conversion*, aimed at exhorting his fellow Jews to embrace Christianity. These writings earned him the notice of top-ranking Catholic officials such as Luigi Fortis, the superior-general of the Jesuits, who wrote Drach a note on September 20, 1827, thanking him for sending his recently published writings. Fortis apologizes for not having finished the books but insists that he has read enough to be convinced of the "important service" that Drach has rendered the church. "May the holy zeal with which you are endowed be crowned with the happiest success!" Fortis proclaims. "May you be an instrument of mercy in relation to your brothers in the flesh and contribute to ripping off the veil that the apostle said has been placed on their hearts for a certain time, and that will be lifted when they search for Him whom they had the misfortune not to recognize." This letter was written just as Simon Deutz was preparing to leave for Rome. Drach must have seen it as a sign from God and also as a foretaste of the benefits that would accrue not only to Deutz but to himself as well once the veil was definitively removed from the heart of the rabbi's son.[25]

In his account of the conversion, Dermoncourt includes an antisemitic aside, commenting that Drach, "still a bit of a Jew," was especially happy to see Deutz go to Rome because it meant "that his purse would no longer be exposed to such frequent contributions." On the eve of his departure, Deutz requested another four hundred francs for the journey. Drach gave him two hundred francs before he left Paris and arranged for him to collect the remainder as Deutz passed through Lyon on his way to Italy, drawn from royalties owed to Drach by a Lyon publishing house. Yet even this sum did not entirely satisfy the potential convert. After all, he could not present himself in Rome without any decent clothes.[26]

Drach received a letter on September 21, 1827, as Deutz was about to set forth, containing the following request: "My brother, I am forced to importune you once again. Yesterday, I told you that I had no linen whatsoever. You responded that you would see what you could do. I therefore remind you that if it is possible I require multiple undershirts and socks, handkerchiefs, etc. and perhaps a few razors if you have some you can spare." After helping himself to "the better part" of Drach's wardrobe, including "some of the choicest items," the would-be convert also requested introductions to church leaders in Rome. The valediction of the letter was calculated to remind Drach of what he had to gain in exchange for his underclothes:

"I embrace you with all my heart and I hope with the help of God to soon be your brother in everything," meaning also in Christ. He signed off: "Simon Deutz *fils* [son]," perhaps to underscore his importance as the rabbi's son, as if Drach needed reminding. Shortly after Deutz's departure, on September 23 Drach returned to his rooms at the Sorbonne to find a bill for the cost of Deutz's passport.[27]

Following a moment of religious wavering in Lyon, Deutz proceeded on his journey through Turin and Modena, and down the Italian peninsula to Rome. His letter to Drach informing him of his arrival in the Holy City marveled at the ease of the journey: Deutz was used to encountering trouble everywhere he went. It must be "the finger of God" guiding him: "This is the first enterprise in my life in which I have not encountered, thanks to the Lord, any sort of unpleasant occurrence."[28]

On the contrary, many of the most important church leaders seemed only too delighted to help with the conversion of the son of France's chief rabbi. On October 25, Fortis, the superior-general of the Jesuits, wrote to Monsignor Angelo Mai requesting free accommodations for Deutz in Rome. The chief librarian at the Vatican and a future cardinal, Mai was a busy scholar who had discovered many important manuscripts from antiquity. He nevertheless flew into action to help Deutz secure lodging with the Franciscans in their residence attached to the recently restored Church of the Twelve Holy Apostles. On November 21 the Propaganda Fide granted "the French Israelite *Signore* Deutz" a monthly allowance of 25 scudi (equal to 135 francs) to maintain him while he studied for his conversion.[29]

In the first of his letters to Drach from Rome, dated November 1, Deutz cannot get over his good fortune at being received so warmly by so many important people. Ever on the lookout for alternative father figures, Deutz sought out Father Gioacchino Ventura di Raulica, a former Jesuit and one of the most eloquent philosophers within the Catholic Church. Ventura opened his large library to Deutz and introduced him to the writing of his friend Hugues-Félicité Robert de Lamennais, which quickly exerted a strong intellectual hold on the aspiring convert. Although he would later turn toward republican politics and a form of Christian Socialism, which led to his imprisonment as well as his defection from the church, Lamennais was known in the late 1820s as a staunch opponent of Cartesian rationalism and ultramontane supporter of the authority of the papacy (ultramontane Catholics were conservatives who placed special emphasis on papal power). His four-volume *Essay on Indifference in Matters of Religion*, published just a few years before Deutz arrived in Rome, argued for restoring to the Roman Catholic Church the power it had held before the French Revolution. The work had a big influence on religious and political life in France during the Restoration and earned Lamennais the favorable attention of the pope. In his first letter from Rome, Deutz laments not being the author of a famous work himself so that he could enter into correspondence with the ultramontane writer. In his second letter, dated November 8, Deutz describes settling into the library of the Collegio Romano, the headquarters of the Jesuit educational empire, in order to examine the Hebrew Bible for hidden references to Jesus as the Messiah, drawing on the writing of Drach to guide his search.[30]

On January 9, 1828, Ventura wrote a long letter to Drach informing him about the spiritual progress of his "estimable brother-in-law," whose difficult personality had begun to reveal itself. "First of all," Ventura writes, "I won't dissimulate that for a few days Monsieur Simon seemed to waver in his resolution to embrace Christianity." His hesitation derived less from the intellectual habits of Judaism than from the "the vivacity of an independent character long accustomed to a great latitude in thinking." Apparently, Deutz was having trouble accepting the brand of ultramontane Catholicism, predicated on complete spiritual submission, which Ventura had adopted from Lamennais. But just as the good priest was about to abandon hope, God came to their aid, and "His grace alone triumphed over all resistance."

Eventually, Ventura reports, a great tranquility settled over Deutz, who gave all indications of having submitted to authority: "Nothing is more edifying than his speeches and his docility. . . . He seems to

have finally understood the most difficult, but also the most important lesson, namely that it is necessary to make oneself small and to
imitate the simplicity and the candor of a child in order to enter into
the kingdom of heaven." Given his later actions, it seems unlikely
that Deutz experienced a complete change of character while studying with Ventura. More probably, he figured out how to become the
kind of hypocrite in vogue during this era, the kind that Stendhal
would paint in *The Red and the Black*.[31]

But no matter how humble he tried to appear, controversy followed Deutz. During the four months of his catechumenate, as he
studied Latin and Italian and immersed himself in the arcana of Roman Catholic theology, he became the object of a bitter tug-of-war
between intellectual factions within the Vatican. On the one side was
Father Ventura, disciple of Lamennais, and on the other were the
Cartesian rationalists, represented by Monsignor Pietro Ostini. Ostini's faction began spreading rumors that Ventura had caused Deutz
to reconsider his conversion by revealing the existence of this schism
within Catholic teaching. Various cardinals got involved, proof of the
intense interest that the Vatican hierarchy took in securing Deutz's
abjuration. Eventually, the pope himself intervened, making Ostini
Deutz's new spiritual adviser. Two years later, Lamennais would report to Ventura that news of this episode had reached him in France.[32]

A January 17 letter from Deutz to Drach announced that he was
now meeting three or four times a week with Ostini. He did not
conceal that he "experienced several stormy days" and was even on
the point of returning to Paris without having been baptized. This,
he now recognized, was the last gasp of Judaism expiring within him.
Thankfully, God had opened his eyes, and he would soon know the
joy of approaching the Holy Table: "Ah, how happy I will be!"[33]

The day of his conversion finally arrived. After Deutz wrote a letter of apology to Drach for persecuting him and his children, Ostini deemed him worthy of receiving baptism. The ceremony, held
on February 3, 1828, was full of pomp and created a sensation in
Rome, according to Dermoncourt. A prominent French cardinal did the honors at San Pietro in Vincoli, the church that houses

Michelangelo's famous statue of Moses. It was an appropriate setting for a conversion, an act intended to demonstrate how Judaism could be incorporated into—and superseded by—Christianity.[34]

Monsignor Ostini followed the baptism with confirmation. "Never did I experience such a strong emotion, nor one so sweet, as when I received the body, the blood, the soul and the divinity of Our Lord Jesus Christ in the form of bread," Deutz wrote to Drach. The cardinal then delivered a speech underlining the duties that Deutz would have to fulfill as a Christian. "I hope, with the grace of God, to be able to fulfill them all," the convert proclaimed, "even at the cost of my life, if God deigns to send me such a trial." The baptismal waters had clearly washed away neither his grandiosity nor his taste for adventure.[35]

In becoming Catholic, Deutz ceased to be Simon, adopting the Catholic name of Hyacinthe, perhaps in homage to Hyacinthe-Louis de Quélen, the archbishop of Paris, who had helped set him on his new path. No doubt he did not want to waste the opportunity to curry favor with some important personage, as he was very aware of how much he had to gain from converting. Yet there is evidence that his motivations were not wholly mercenary. The letter that he supposedly wrote to his father, in Hebrew, a few days after the ceremony, describes his new sense of security and ease:

> I am now a Catholic, thanks be to God, for the last four days. It was time. I had fallen into the depth of the abyss of incredulity. . . . Yes, it was time, since the waters had penetrated my very soul. Now I am so calm, so happy! I had not been so for a long time, as you know very well. May God deign to perpetuate that grace. My youth was, alas!, of a most stormy nature. I used to tell you often that our faith did not offer any consolation because my heart felt the need for a religion of love.

He continued by expressing his intention to study theology in order to become a priest. Knowing how much his actions would wound the rabbi, Deutz concludes with a touching—if rather mystifying, given the circumstances—expression of filial devotion: "Please know that I have never respected you as much as I do now, and that henceforth nothing will stop me from proving that I am your devoted and submissive son."[36]

If Deutz needed proof that Judaism was a religion of love, he need have looked no further than his father's response to his conversion. Although no act could have hurt the aged rabbi more, he did not renounce his son. This could not have been easy for the father, whose job it was to set an example of proper religious conduct for France's Jews. Drach ensured that all of France witnessed the rabbi's humiliation by publishing a *Relation of the Conversion of M. Hyacinthe Deutz, Baptized in Rome on February 3, 1828: Preceded by Several Considerations on the Return of Israel to the Church of God.* In this pamphlet Drach asserts that Deutz's conversion "caused a great sensation in the Synagogue, and will bear, we cannot doubt, salutary fruits," meaning more defections from Judaism.[37]

News of the conversion soon spread. Théodore Ratisbonne, who was then residing in Italy, wrote to Drach to congratulate him. Having met Simon Deutz in synagogue, Ratisbonne says he would have thought his conversion as impossible as Abraham raising up children from stones, a reference to a passage from the New Testament (Luke 3:8). The future founder of a Catholic missionary organization that specifically sought to convert Jews, Ratisbonne said that he well understood the joy of incorporating a lost lamb into the church's flock: "May our entire nation finally understand this mystery," he wrote, referring to the Jews.[38]

Following his conversion, the twenty-five-year-old Hyacinthe Deutz seems to have experienced a brief respite from the demons that had pursued him throughout his youth. "I am so happy in Rome," he wrote to Drach. "I lead a monk-like existence and I am very content." Lodged for free and still receiving his monthly allowance of 25 scudi from the Vatican, Deutz found a measure of calm for the first and probably only time in his life. With the help of Ventura, he worked for a while on a translation of a 1773 treatise called *On the Vain Expectation of the Jews for their Messiah King*, an attack on the basis of Jewish faith. "I think this is a work that will do our former coreligionists a lot of good," he wrote to Drach, although the translation was never published. On March 13, which he described as the "second most beautiful day" of his life, after his baptism, he met Pope Leo XII.[39]

But Deutz's Roman holiday was not to last. According to Morel, after only a few months Deutz began to grow restless, and the "violent passions" that he had repressed since his conversion returned with a vengeance. Unable to tolerate the monastic life, he began cavorting with French artists residing in Rome. Apparently, even these freethinkers were scandalized by his licentiousness and by the scorn he expressed for religion, which they deemed not very becoming in someone who was still on the Vatican payroll. Rumors of his behavior reached Drach in Paris.[40]

It was around this time that Deutz took up a surprising new project: pleading for the Jews of Rome, the last Jews in Western Europe to be emancipated. Present in the capital since ancient times, the Jews of Rome were confined to a squalid, overcrowded ghetto in the Sant'Angelo *rione*, a flood-prone quarter near the Tiber River. Like the Jews in much of medieval Europe, they were banned from almost all forms of economic activity, except trading in old rags; forced to wear identifying insignia; and forbidden from riding in carriages or from making contact with Christians. The popes intended the poverty and isolation of the Jews to stand as a sign of God's disgrace for having refused to accept Christ. Briefly freed by Napoleon, the Roman Jews found themselves once more subject to humiliating restrictions after the pope reasserted control of the Holy City in 1800. A Christian visitor to the ghetto as late as 1853 described the misery he saw everywhere around him: "What most horrifies the spectator in the ghetto is the narrowness and filth of these tortuous streets and alleys and the narrow houses which reach high above them. In them Jewish families live as in a Roman columbarium, stacked one over the other in rows." This writer notes that whereas the Romans preserve the marble statues of antiquity in beautiful palaces, "the only living remains of ancient Rome, human beings with long-enduring hearts, live in wretched filth."[41]

The fact that Deutz makes so much of his advocacy efforts later, in his memoir, is surely a function of his desire to show that he was always a liberal at heart—despite appearances to the contrary—and that his betrayal of the duchess grew out of a long-standing political commitment to liberty. But Deutz surely had other motivations for helping the Roman Jews. It is certainly possible that having experienced the benefits of Jewish emancipation in France, he was genuinely concerned by the plight of his former coreligionists in Rome: "Their state of misery and servitude moved me deeply. My position allowed me to believe, without too much presumption, that I could bring them some relief." However, it is also possible that he wanted to express his independence after having submitted to church authority long enough to receive baptism. At the time, this advocacy struck Drach as a bad sign: consorting with Jews, and especially visiting the synagogue, were expressly forbidden to new converts. The Vatican seems to have viewed Deutz's pet project with more indulgence, and the pope created a commission to study the question of Jewish emancipation in Rome. Headed by Cardinal Cappellari, a friend of Deutz but no friend to the Jews, the commission read Deutz's report and decided to take no action.[42]

Frustrated by this setback, Deutz found himself at loose ends. In his memoir he claims that he was offered the directorship of the Vatican's printing house but refused. The Vatican Archives tell a different story. On April 12, 1830, Cappellari submitted a request to the Office of the General Treasurer, asking for a job in the Vatican printing office for Deutz so that he would not be forced to return to Paris, which would be seen as a "triumph for the Jews." More requests were made on June 9 and 12, including by his friend Monsignor Mai, who emphasized that Deutz required occupation and distraction so that he would not spend all day in "internal struggle" and would not be forced to seek financial help from his father. It was obvious that

Deutz was blackmailing the church authorities with threats of reverting to Judaism. On June 14 the treasurer responded definitively that he could not employ Deutz, perhaps because Deutz's "turbulent character" gave the directors of the printing office enough pause to justify refusing the requests of his powerful protectors.[43]

These failures must have seemed all too familiar: the bad luck that had pursued Deutz through his youth had caught up to him once again. Despite what he threatened, the prospect of returning to Paris and throwing himself on the mercy of his father could not have seemed very appealing: the shame of admitting defeat and subjecting himself to the smug scorn of his father's congregants was enough to keep him away.

He grasped instead at another idea that promised to take him far away from the scene of his failure: he would travel to New York to open a Catholic bookstore. With an advance on his stipend from the Vatican and a pack of books that would get him started, Hyacinthe Deutz set sail for the New World in July. At the exact same moment, the Old World received yet another political shock in the form of the Revolution of 1830, which abruptly ended the reign of the French Bourbons and struck a blow to the temporal power of the Catholic Church in France. Liberalism was once again in vogue.[44]

Deutz's wager on conversion had not proven such a good bet after all.

PART THREE

The Campaign

CHAPTER 5

Exile

CHARLES X, THE French king, assumed that the Parisian uprising that broke out on July 26, 1830, would dissipate as quickly as it had started. The day before, he had issued ordinances suspending freedom of the press and dissolving the newly elected Chamber of Deputies, which moved his regime a giant step closer to the absolute monarchy desired by France's *ultras*. And now, as revolutionaries erected barricades in central Paris, the seventy-two-year-old king went about his regular routine at the Château of Saint-Cloud, three miles to the west of the city, where the Bourbons spent the summer. Daily horseback rides and endless games of whist with the duc de Maillé and other devoted courtiers dominated the royal agenda.[1]

The duchesse de Berry was more alarmed. At first she had supported the king's decision to curtail liberties: "At last, you reign! My son will owe you his crown," she had proclaimed. Then she pointed a telescope at Paris, from an upstairs window of the château, and began to regret her enthusiasm; she saw the revolutionary tricolor flag flying from the towers of Notre Dame Cathedral and plumes of smoke rising into the sky. Perhaps the king had gone too far. When reports arrived of troops fraternizing with the rioters, the duchess pleaded with her father-in-law to put an end to the uprising.[2]

The king preferred to watch and wait. He refused, on principle, to have any sort of negotiation with subjects in revolt. And attempting to quell the riot with force carried its own risks. Moreover, the king had found religion: he believed that all would proceed according to God's plan. Even the sound of cannon fire rumbling in the distance did not make him look up from his card game, although it did reportedly cause him to misplay a hand. On the night of July 28, the king went to bed confident that the insurrection would end the following day.[3]

It only picked up steam. When word came of an angry mob of revolutionaries marching toward Saint-Cloud, Charles X ordered the court to evacuate to the Trianon Palace at Versailles. Memories of the Reign of Terror loomed like ghosts. Only the duchesse de Berry, too young to have experienced the French Revolution, wanted to confront the rebels. Appearing before her father-in-law dressed in a man's riding outfit, with two pistols hanging from her belt, she begged the king to let her go to the Vendée, the bastion of royalism in the far west of France, to raise a counterrevolutionary army. The king told her that she had read one too many Walter Scott novels. The duchess reluctantly abandoned her plan, but not without making her displeasure known. "What misfortune to be a woman," she declared in frustration at the inaction of the king and the incompetence of his ministers.[4]

The royal family spent only one night at the Trianon before fleeing yet again, this time to Rambouillet, a turreted château abutting a large hunting preserve, at what they believed was a safe thirty-mile distance from the capital. When word reached the Bourbons that General Lafayette had embraced their cousin, Louis-Philippe, on the balcony of the Hôtel-de-Ville, and that the latter was going to be offered the throne by the revolutionaries, the duchess made a final plea to the king to let her appear with her son at the Chamber of Deputies in Paris. Surely the sight of the prince whose birth Parisians had celebrated with such jubilation only a decade before would remind the deputies of their love for the elder branch of the royal family. The king refused to consider exposing his grandson to such danger but hoped that if both he and the duc d'Angoulême abdicated in favor of Henri, the Bourbon monarchy might yet be saved.[5]

On August 2, 1830, Charles X signed the abdication decree before passing the quill to the duc d'Angoulême, who hesitated a minute— the entire duration of his reign—before reluctantly adding his name to the proclamation. The nearly ten-year-old Henri V was now the king of France, and the thirty-one-year-old duchesse de Berry was the queen mother.

She had little time to savor the moment. When word came that the people were now advancing on Rambouillet, Charles X panicked: not wanting to repeat the mistake of his late brother, Louis XVI, who had waited too long to leave France during the first revolution in the hope of retaining his throne, he decided to flee the country. Charles X had, after all, been forced to flee France twice before and both times had made a triumphant return to the capital. This would be the third exile for her in-laws, but it was the first for the duchesse de Berry, and she could not accept that fate had dangled the crown in front of her only to yank it away. She reluctantly took her place in the long line of horses and carriages heading toward the Normandy coast. Onlookers saw tears of frustration in her eyes.[6]

Although Charles X had ceased to reign, he nevertheless wanted to leave France in royal fashion. This meant that the procession of the Bourbon family, their servants, and followers—numbering several hundred people, with a caravan of nearly eighty vehicles—would proceed as slowly as possible to Cherbourg, where boats waited to carry them to England. Guarded by troops sent by the new authorities in Paris to prevent any last-ditch counterrevolutionary maneuver—such as making a break for the Vendée, as the duchess longed to do— the mournful *cortège* wound its way through the French countryside, stopping in numerous small villages along the way. Not everyone was sad to see the royal family go: according to Chateaubriand, the procession of the Bourbons excited very little curiosity in the public. Not even the peasants tilling their fields along the road expressed much interest as their carriages passed by. "In this exhausted country, the most significant events are now little more than dramas produced for our entertainment," he wrote. "They divert the spectator so long as the curtain is raised, and when it falls, they leave only a futile memory." Once he had made his decision to go, even Charles X seemed to lose interest in his fate: when they passed through the village of Dreux, he was warned that he would have to withstand the sight of the revolutionary tricolor flag flying from all the windows. "I am indifferent," the now former king replied.[7]

The duchesse de Berry was anything but indifferent. The prospect of leaving behind the pleasures of Paris and her château at Rosny, with all the art and antiques she had collected over the preceding decade, was bad enough. Having to flee France with her impotent, morose in-laws was too much to bear. She now found herself constantly in the company of the duchesse d'Angoulême, who became even more dour as she relived the trauma that marked her childhood, when she had been arrested during the flight to Varennes with her parents and narrowly escaped execution. Whenever she could, the duchesse de Berry descended from the carriage and walked along the road with her two dogs, Lala and Fouliche, who craved physical exertion and fresh air almost as much as she did.

The meager accommodations during the excruciatingly slow journey did not improve her mood. Forced to stop at a depressing little roadside inn and to eat off of dirty plates in the company of hostile strangers, the duchess watched as young Henri, in her mind the legitimate king of France, played with chickens in the dusty courtyard alongside his sister, Louise. When word came that Louis-Philippe would allow Henri to be king if Louis-Philippe himself were regent and the boy returned to Paris alone, the duchess angrily refused the offer. Although it might preserve the Bourbon monarchy, it would mean separation from her son. And more importantly, it would mean no political role for herself.[8]

The duchess did have one consolation on the journey: Louis, comte de Rosambo, whom she affectionately called Ludovic. The son-in-law of the comte de Mesnard, Ludovic was considered one of the handsomest men of the day, and the evident favor that the duchess showed the younger man during the trip to Cherbourg, including multiple occasions on which she sought his company alone, did not pass unnoticed by the other members of the royal retinue. Word of the duchess's indiscretions soon reached Paris. According to the comtesse de Boigne, only "the agitations of the moment" could justify such a shocking breach of etiquette.[9]

Having left almost everything behind when she fled, the duchess resorted to mending her clothes herself during the journey. The royal family lacked even basic necessities, which they purchased along the way, despite the precarious state of their finances. Altogether, they possessed barely 40,000 francs—far from enough to feed and lodge themselves and their courtiers in exile. Finally, on August 15, one of the duchess's former servants met her in Valognes with some clothes that her aunt, Louis-Philippe's wife, Marie-Amélie, allowed her to take from her apartment in the Pavillon de Marsan at the Tuileries. In a magnanimous gesture to his ousted cousins, Louis-Philippe, who on August 9 had become king of the French—he thought the title sounded more democratic than king of France—allowed James de Rothschild, a prominent Jewish banker in Paris, to provide the former king with 600,000 francs as an advance on the sale of his property.[10]

As the royal family left Rambouillet, one of their bereft followers— a young priest, whose "mouth was as big as his head," according to the royal governess, Mme de Gontaut—had shouted in a voice like thunder, "*À la Vendée!*" To the Vendée! His cry echoed the entreaties that the duchess had made to the king to let her go to the western province and stir up a counterrevolution. Her triumphant journey through the wild countryside of the Bourbon stronghold, just two years before, had convinced her of the feasibility of her plan. She had visited the places where the heroes of the war against the French Revolution had fallen in 1793, learned there to shoot a gun and wield a sword in case she ever needed to fight to protect her son's birthright.[11]

The duchess recounted to Mesnard how during her trip, the Vendéen nobleman and prominent military officer Louis de Bourmont had sung the refrain of a popular song promising the province's fidelity should the Bourbons ever need it:

> But if ever an abhorrent sect
> Were again to break the sceptre of our kings,
> Ah! Remember us, return to the Vendée
> Bring Henri, we will defend his rights.

And now, as her in-laws resigned themselves to exile, the duchess found her hopes returning to the Vendée, where she believed that the nobles were loyal to the Bourbon cause and the peasants were sufficiently under the sway of their priests to fight for the principle of divine-right monarchy. If she could find a way to take Bourmont and his compatriots up on their offer of support, perhaps the cause of the Bourbons was not irrevocably lost. Madame de Gontaut remarked that whereas there was something sad and final about the way Charles X and the duchesse d'Angoulême thanked the troops for their service as they prepared to depart, the message of the duchesse de Berry was far more hopeful: she "electrified" the soldiers by promising that she and her son would be back soon. "We will see each other again," she told them, recalling the promise she had made to the Vendéens in 1828. "If you take up arms, I will join you."[12]

In Cherbourg a conflict arose over how the Bourbons would get to England. In a fit of pique, Charles X refused to sail on a French boat bearing the tricolor flag and demanded a British vessel to carry him into exile. But although the British were willing to take the Bourbons in, they feared antagonizing Louis-Philippe's new government by ferrying the deposed king across the channel. Finally, a compromise was reached: the royals would sail on an American boat, the *Great Britain*, escorted by a French cutter, *Le Rôdeur* (*The Prowler*), which had received orders from Louis-Philippe to fire if the king's vessel deviated from its route to Portsmouth. The duchess must have felt a glimmer of rueful recognition when she saw that the ship preventing her from making a break for the Vendée was the same one she had used for pleasure cruises during her stays in Dieppe.[13]

She boarded the boat wearing a riding outfit: an *amazone* of pale-yellow Nankeen cotton. According to observers, she was sobbing. At one point during the crossing, despair gave way to wild paranoia; having overheard the captain speak of St. Helens—a fort on the Isle of Wight, near Portsmouth, where the ship could dock—she became convinced they were being taken to St. Helena, the lonely rock in the middle of the Atlantic where the British had kept Napoleon imprisoned during the final years of his life. The examination of a map reassured her, and soon she began to emerge from the deep melancholy she had felt since the outbreak of the revolution several weeks before. Brooding was not her style. Sitting on deck in a man's hat to shield her pale complexion from the strong summer sun, she joked with the captain, Jules Dumont d'Urville—famous as the commander of the *Astrolabe*, which had made an important scientific voyage to the Pacific in 1826—that with her terrible seasickness, she could never be an explorer.[14]

From the moment she set foot on British soil, the duchess began to take steps to distance herself from the grim resignation and down-at-the-heels hauteur of her in-laws. Their first place of refuge was Lulworth, near the cliffs of Dover in Dorset, a seventeenth-century castle designed to look medieval, rented from an English Catholic cardinal, Thomas Weld. This castle was not unfamiliar to the French royals: they had stayed there briefly after fleeing the first revolution. By 1830, however, it had fallen into disrepair; the roof leaked, forcing the ex-king and his entourage to sleep under strategically placed umbrellas.[15]

The duchess refused the bedroom offered to her by her father-in-law, preferring quarters as far away as possible from the rest of the royal family. Mesnard recounts that Charles X flew into a rage at this sign of independence. "I demand to be master in my own home!" the ex-king declared, provoking the duchess to retort that if he had shown such authority a few weeks before, he might have saved his crown. She worked off her anger on horseback but returned to join the rest of the family at dinner. They ate the first bitter meal of exile with iron utensils, their silver service having been left behind in France.[16]

Harassed by his creditors—Charles X had not bothered to pay off all the debts he contracted during his last exile in England—the former king spent his time hiding in the castle, justifying his actions (or inactions) to anyone who would listen and blaming the Revolution of 1830 on a plot hatched by Louis-Philippe and his bourgeois supporters. Meanwhile, the duchess began to hatch her own plot to escape from the tomb-like atmosphere of Lulworth. Emboldened by her first assertion of independence in the choice of bedroom, she started to take trips away from the family, including jaunts to Bath and Cheltenham. On September 15, 1830, she helped inaugurate the Liverpool and Manchester railway, riding in the first car of the train. Although she attempted to travel incognito, her every movement was reported by the press back in France.[17]

On October 16, 1830, the family moved—partly to escape Charles X's creditors—to a much more remote new residence: Holyrood, near Edinburgh in Scotland, where the recently crowned William IV agreed to house them in a wing of the royal castle. Charles X remembered Holyrood from his former exile—he had lived in the sixteenth-century palace from 1796 to 1803—and, like Lulworth, it had seen better days. Partly a ruin, the castle was still undergoing hasty renovations to make it habitable when the Bourbons arrived. A poem by Victor Hugo from 1840 gives a sense of the gloom that clung to the place like desiccated ivy: "Holyrood! Holyrood! O fatal abbey, / Where the hard, bitter, commanding law of destiny, / Inscribes itself on every side!" One French courtier, who fled with the royal family, described Holyrood as "the most lugubrious and sad" palace he had ever seen. Despite her fascination with the work of Walter Scott—she would meet the celebrated author while in Edinburgh—and with Mary, Queen of Scots, who had lived in Holyrood, the duchess hated the castle and the dreariness of Scotland. This time, she refused to stay in the castle altogether. Despite her precarious financial situation, she rented her own lodging in Regent Terrace in Edinburgh and soon began to absent herself from Scotland for long stretches.[18]

The duchesse d'Angoulême, whom Chateaubriand would refer to privately as "that relic-eater in Edinburgh," did not look kindly on the duchesse de Berry's travels, which she considered highly inappropriate for a family that was supposed to be in mourning for the loss of its throne. The duchesse de Berry's relations with her in-laws deteriorated rapidly. She was already seeing less and less of her son, whose education the former king had now entrusted to the baron de Damas, a staunch Bourbon loyalist.[19]

In addition to visits to London, where she was squired about town by the duke of Wellington, the duchess spent a part of the fall and winter of 1831 in the spa town of Bath, where she rented a modest house for herself and two servants. In her inimitable way, the comtesse de Boigne reports hearing rumors that the duchess went to Bath in order to give birth secretly to a daughter, possibly the fruit of her liaison with Ludovic, rumors that Boigne claims she did not believe at the time but nevertheless repeats. It would have been difficult to hide a pregnancy, given the level of interest that the duchess attracted everywhere she went. The fashion journal *La Mode*, still loyal to her despite the change in regime, reported on her every move. One dispatch from Bath describes making a pilgrimage to the house where the duchess was staying and the journalist's joy in catching a glimpse of the mother of his king on her balcony.[20]

If these royalist newspapers and their readers found the travels of the duchess so absorbing, it was because they began to see her as their natural leader in their struggle to topple Louis-Philippe. This was not so far-fetched a plan. For although Louis-Philippe had seemed to take the throne amid popular acclaim, the July Monarchy—as his regime was known because the revolution that brought it to power took place in July—actually rested on very weak foundations. To those on the Right, the reactionary Catholics and die-hard Bourbon loyalists,

Louis-Philippe lacked the claim to legitimacy of the elder branch of the royal family. His monarchy had been imposed by revolutionaries and thus was inherently fraudulent; he had usurped the crown. Meanwhile, those on the Left also thought he had stolen the crown, but by co-opting the revolution from the republicans who had done all the fighting.

Louis-Philippe was the compromise candidate imposed by the nouveau riche bourgeoisie, those professionals and businessmen who had felt excluded from power under the Restoration but who also feared the reforms that a republic would bring, such as giving the right to vote to poor workers. Although these classically liberal centrists—known derisively as the *juste milieu* (happy medium)—were economically powerful, they were not numerous enough to provide the new "citizen king," as Louis-Philippe dubbed himself, with a strong base of support. During the early years of his reign Louis-Philippe thus felt besieged from his two flanks and in very real fear of another revolution from both the Left and the Right. As one right-wing observer put it at the time, the very rapidity of the revolution that put the July Monarchy in place gave hope to those who sought to topple it: anything made so quickly could be unmade with equal rapidity.[21]

But even though they sensed an opportunity, the supporters of the Bourbons, who at this point called themselves simply "royalists," were divided over how to take advantage of the precarious political situation. The early days of the July Monarchy saw the defenders of the former monarchy in disarray as the government they had supported crumbled virtually overnight. Confused and betrayed, these loyalists disappeared from the political stage quickly, as Louis-Philippe began installing his own supporters in various ministries. A caricature from the time showed an elegant but slightly befuddled gentleman bowing to a lower-class worker and asking, "My dear sir, might you tell me what has become of the royalists?"[22]

In addition to being politically adrift, the supporters of the Bourbons were divided among themselves. Should they accept invitations to the Palais-Royal, the residence of the Orléans, and thereby confer legitimacy on Louis-Philippe? Or should they snub the usurper?

Some acquiesced to the new political reality and normalized the regime by referring to Louis-Philippe and Marie-Amélie as "king" and "queen." Other members of the high nobility—the so-called "opposition of the Faubourg Saint-Germain"—closed their salons to the "Philippistes," and some retired to their country houses, a kind of internal exile, as they plotted their next move.[23]

One faction of the royalists was angry at Charles X and wanted nothing more to do with such an inept king. They blamed him for failing to grasp the tenor of the times and for provoking the July Revolution (as the Revolution of 1830 was also called). They felt that he should have waited until his monarchy rested on more solid ground before seeking to reimpose absolutism. Some of these disillusioned royalists still hoped for another Bourbon restoration and saw the duchess as the member of the royal family most capable of bringing it about. Their dreams were fueled by Napoleon's dramatic, if short-lived, return from Elba in 1815 during the Hundred Days. Those who actively sought another restoration of the Bourbons began to call themselves "legitimists" to distinguish themselves from the supporters of the supposedly illegitimate monarchy of Louis-Philippe. The legitimists were referred to by their enemies as "Carlists."[24]

Political tensions rose to the surface on February 14, 1831, at a service held in the Church of St. Germain l'Auxerrois, directly across from the Louvre Palace in central Paris. This was the first time that the anniversary mass, said yearly in commemoration of the assassination of the duc de Berry eleven years earlier, had been held since the July Revolution. The service began in calm solemnity. However, when word got out that the worshippers had displayed a portrait of young Henri V, an angry crowd of Philippistes broke into the church and started smashing everything they saw. The rioters then moved on to the residence of the archbishop of Paris—a notorious legitimist, known to have organized the commemoration—and sacked the place, tossing his precious library into the Seine.

The tide of public sentiment soon turned against the citizen king, who was seen as incapable of controlling his supporters. Louis-Philippe reacted by shuffling his prime ministers: one wealthy banker,

Jacques Laffitte, was replaced by another, Casimir-Pierre Périer. The latter had more experience in politics and projected power and authority. Whereas Laffitte had led the "party of movement," Périer promised a new "party of order." He also promised to crack down on the conspiracies forming on both the Right and the Left.[25]

Yet, as Louis-Philippe took more decisive measures to solidify his regime, opposition increased. Measures such as putting the former ministers of Charles X on trial and abolishing hereditary peerages incensed the Bourbon loyalists. Even many of those who had begun by going to parties held at the Palais-Royal now turned against the regime during the early months of 1831.[26]

But legitimists were divided over the best manner of restoring the Bourbons. One group opposed any kind of coup d'état, believing that only parliamentary action could bring about a legal change of government and that the July Monarchy was sure to collapse of its own accord. Others sought a repeat of 1814 and 1815, when the return of the Bourbons had followed an invasion of France by the allied armies. Still others sought to foment a homegrown insurrection in Provence and the Vendée, the two most conservative regions of France. These proponents of civil war saw the duchesse de Berry as the natural leader of such a revolt.

During her years in France the duchess had never taken a particularly strong interest in politics. She had left partisan wrangling to her in-laws, preferring to amuse herself with the capital's many pleasures: art, theater, and shopping. At Rosny she had expressly forbade political discussions, which she found boring. Her political transformation began after her husband's assassination, but it was completed by the July Revolution. She now eagerly participated in plotting to bring down Louis-Philippe, relishing her role as the movement's leader and quickly learning the ins and outs of political conspiracy. She was an avid pupil, according to one observer, "seeming to intuit by perspicacity the knowledge she lacked through experience, raising . . . her intelligence to the height of every subject and her courage to the level of every danger." One of her advisers marveled at the "vivacity" of her intelligence as she absorbed all the topics in political economy she had previously ignored: "War, finances, administration, diplomacy, she understood everything and her opinions were almost always correct, wise, and noble," even as she maintained the appearance of being a "frivolous woman," concerned with her dogs and other trifles.[27]

At her small home in Bath, the duchess began to plot not just an insurrection that she hoped would bring about the end of the July Monarchy but also the new government that she would create once her son had reclaimed the throne. Learning from the mistakes of Charles X, she envisioned making liberal reforms, such as democratizing the army and extending the vote more broadly. Among the many obstacles that lay in her path, the most pressing was the question of her own authority to lead such an insurrection and the eventual government that might result from its success. She needed Charles X to agree to make her regent until Henri was old enough to govern on his own. On this point, the ex-king demurred. Horrified by the way his daughter-in-law flouted etiquette and challenged his authority, he had sought as much as possible to keep his grandson away from her bad influence.[28]

The boy's tutor, the baron de Damas, urged Charles X to avoid granting the duchess any powers whatsoever, and at first the ex-king complied by writing, in December 1830, another decree of abdication in which he himself would serve as regent for his grandson until the latter reached majority. The duchess would become regent only in the case of Charles X's death. Under pressure from Mesnard and other advisers, however, the ex-king then changed his mind yet again and agreed to appoint the duchess regent even during his lifetime, but only in the event of her being physically present in French territory. However, in order to restrain the duchess and keep her from launching a hasty civil war, Charles X also appointed the duc de Blacas as her prime minister. Although the duchess did not like how much power Blacas would hold in her eventual government, she accepted the regency decree as a victory: it gave tacit consent to her plan for insurrection.[29]

Although the ex-king and Blacas urged caution, other advisers gave the duchess opposite advice. Along with Louis de Bourmont, the Vendéen nobleman who had sung the song of fidelity to the duchess during her 1828 visit, the most vociferous proponent of immediate action was Ferdinand de Bertier, the founder of the Knights of the Faith (Chevaliers de la Foi), an ultraroyalist secret society. The son of the intendant of the Bastille, whose lynching in July 1789 had helped spark the French Revolution, Bertier slipped out of France to meet with the duchess in Bath and then returned to monitor the situation on the ground in the Vendée and Provence. In a series of letters to the duchess, he argued that the legitimists must capitalize on the popular resentment against the government and strike before Louis-Philippe had time to assemble sufficient forces to put down the revolt. "What do we have to gain by waiting?" he asked in a letter dated January 21, 1831. "In France, it is always necessary to take advantage of the first moment of enthusiasm," he wrote in another dispatch, dated May 1831. "If hot heads have the time to reflect, they cool off and it is then often difficult to restore their initial zeal."[30]

Caught between the caution of Charles X and the desire for haste urged by Bourmont and Bertier, the duchess hesitated. Initially telling Bertier she would land in Nice between May 25 and 30, 1831, which would have signaled the beginning of the insurrection, she postponed her journey until June 17. Instead of setting sail for France directly, she then decided to embark on a long voyage by way of Rotterdam, through the Rhineland and Bavaria, and down to Italy. Blacas had convinced her that she should first try to gain the support of foreign powers, such as King William I of the Netherlands, before launching her expedition in France.[31]

Hoping to elude the agents of Louis-Philippe, who were monitoring her every movement, she registered at various foreign inns under a pseudonym: the comtesse de Sagana, the name of her favorite Italian wine. Her disguise did not run very deep. With Lala and Fouliche in tow, she was flanked by her regular and highly recognizable council of male advisers, including Mesnard and Blacas, charged by

Charles X with the impossible mission of preventing her from doing anything too impetuous. They also traveled under false identities but succeeded in fooling no one. Reports immediately made their way back to Paris of this strange group of voyagers traveling through Holland and Switzerland and into Piedmont bearing Italian, German, and English passports but still speaking exclusively in French.[32]

The initial plan of the duchess was to plot her invasion of France from the town of Sestri, a little village near Genoa in the kingdom of Piedmont-Sardinia, ruled by her friend Charles Albert. A religious zealot, the king of Sardinia starved himself, wore a hair shirt, and slept alone on a narrow iron cot but nevertheless managed to carry on a dizzying series of extramarital affairs with various aristocratic ladies, including wives of ambassadors to his kingdom. He had violently opposed the July Revolution in France but then buckled under the pressure exerted by Louis-Philippe, who had heard rumors of the duchess's plans for civil war. In a long letter to the duchess, Charles Albert explained that the other European powers, including his own, feared inciting revolution in their lands if they led a war of aggression against France but that they were prepared to attack if Louis-Philippe gave them the slightest provocation. In the meantime, he invited the duchess to vacate his territory as soon as possible and promised her a large loan if she would do so.[33]

The mysterious comtesse de Sagana and her entourage then journeyed through Tuscany, stopping in Massa and Lucca. In a letter addressed to her childhood friend Suzette, with whom she had been raised in Naples and Sicily, the duchess wrote: "You can imagine the pleasure I felt in seeing once again the *sponde* [shores, in Italian] of the fatherland and hearing the sweet maternal language after sixteen years of vicissitudes." Pretending that she had come merely as a cure for her rheumatism, which had been aggravated by her stay in Scotland, she made no mention of the real purpose of her voyage: "I have come here to roam beautiful Italy, to smell warm air and take the baths which I greatly needed after having breathed so much cold and umid [*sic*] air." Her French was usually peppered with such Italianisms and spelling mistakes.[34]

Soon the Tuscan authorities had enough of the French conspirators and sent them packing. There followed a short stay in Rome, where the duchess met with Pope Gregory XVI, and then a journey to her native Naples, which she had last seen when she set sail for France in 1816. Her father had died the previous year, and her half brother, Ferdinand II, was now on the throne. Although she spent four weeks in the city, she was too preoccupied to enjoy the homecoming. A letter from the duchess to one of her advisers in France, intercepted by Louis-Philippe's ambassador to Naples, revealed that she was seeking money and a base from which to launch her invasion of France. Sensitive to pressure from the French authorities, Ferdinand II made it clear that despite their ties of blood, he could not support her endeavors.[35]

Of all the states on the Italian peninsula, only one was willing to harbor the renegade duchess: Modena. Its reigning duke, Francis IV, was a tyrannical reactionary who had opposed the July Revolution in France and was not afraid to manifest his hostility to Louis-Philippe, just as he had been unafraid to hang the leader of a democratic revolt in his kingdom earlier that year. He allowed the duchess to reside in the picturesque Tuscan town of Massa di Carrara, about three miles from the Tyrrhenian Sea.

At first, she stayed in the local inn until Francis IV invited her to live in the Ducal Palace, a large, red-hued edifice built over the course of many centuries, located on the Piazza Aranci, in the center of the town. Adorned with priceless frescoes and surrounded by fragrant orange trees, the palace of Massa called to mind the homes she had known in her youth in Naples and Sicily. The duke of Modena made sure she would be treated like a queen and ordered his military officers to stand guard at her door. Finally in command of her destiny—and more importantly, finally away from her in-laws—the duchess wasted little time savoring the pleasures of this temporary new abode. There was work to be done if she hoped to regain her son's throne.

CHAPTER 6

The Meeting

I N THE SPRING of 1831, Simon Deutz, now calling himself Hyacinthe de Gonzague, found himself in New York City with no money and no prospects. Like every other professional opportunity he had sought over the course of his life, the plan to launch a Catholic bookstore in the New World had come to nothing. After a year of traveling between Boston, Montreal, New York, and Washington, all he had to show for it was an offer made by the Jesuits to teach French at Georgetown College. But he had not crossed the Atlantic to become a teacher: his dreams had always been on a grander scale.[1]

Deutz found New York particularly inhospitable. There was no Jesuit institution in the city, so he had to find his own lodging, perhaps in one of the seedy boardinghouses that catered to single men in the Five Points area of lower Manhattan, which had the highest murder rate of any slum in the world. For what Deutz could afford to pay, the accommodations would have been far from luxurious: dirty sheets, bad food, and no privacy. In some of the lower-grade establishments, travelers risked having their throats slit in the middle of the night.

And although the Catholic population of New York was expanding rapidly—growing from just 15,000 in 1815 to more than 200,000 in 1842—the bulk of the newcomers were uneducated immigrants from Ireland, so there was not much of a market for the highbrow works of theology that Deutz hoped to sell. Moreover, with only three Catholic churches serving the whole city, Deutz could not count on much help from the local clergy.[2]

In March, having spent the last of the 300 piastres (about 1,600 francs) that the Vatican gave him as an advance on his yearly stipend, he wrote to David Drach in Rome, begging for help: "Don't leave me in this mire!" he implored his brother-in-law. Tormented by stomach troubles and other ailments, Deutz followed this up with an even more plaintive letter in June: "I have suffered a great deal during this time in the United States, and if Providence does not come to my aid, I don't know what will become of me." He also sought help from his father, most likely promising to become Jewish again if the rabbi paid for his passage home.[3]

There were reasons why Deutz wanted to return to Europe as soon as possible. Since his departure from Rome a year previously, two major events had altered his calculations for his future. First, the July Revolution in France had ousted the Bourbons, and with their departure, the reactionary elements within the Catholic Church lost influence. Deutz could thus no longer hope for favors from the French government on account of his conversion. But he also realized that he might now have something to gain by helping Bourbon loyalists regain the throne.

The second major change had happened in Rome. After a fifty-day enclave, Cardinal Cappellari, Deutz's primary protector at the Vatican, had become Pope Gregory XVI on February 2, 1831. The archconservative Cappellari had deigned to call Deutz his "friend" during the three years the French convert spent in Rome, and although the new pope had no use for the report that Deutz wrote in favor of the Roman Jews, Deutz had reason to hope that Cappellari would further his other ambitions. Deutz would later claim that his time in the

United States, the "land of tolerance and liberty," had renewed his ardor to fight for the emancipation of the Roman Jews, but it seems more likely that he hoped to profit personally from his connection with the new pope. Deutz thus decided he would return to Rome but not right away; he would first test the waters in England, where the Bourbons and their allies had fled. With 1,500 francs, obtained from the Society of the Priests of Saint-Sulpice in Montreal—on whom he had made a favorable impression during the time he spent in Canada—he booked passage to London in September 1831.[4]

When Deutz arrived in London in November, he most likely stayed with his sister in the East End. After Drach absconded with their children to Paris, Sara had given birth to a boy named Lionel, whom she had conceived during the short period of rapprochement with her husband and was now raising as a Jew. She and Simon had always been close, and she would have rejoiced in seeing her younger brother again even if she did not approve of his conversion. To placate his sister, Simon may have promised that he would return to Judaism.[5]

The East End was a gritty neighborhood. Near the docks along the Thames, it was the first place that poor immigrants settled when they arrived. Although it was not yet the vast Jewish enclave it would become by the end of the century, when it welcomed tens of thousands of Jewish immigrants from Russia and Poland, the East End already housed the capital's poorest Jews. A contemporary account describes the area as consisting of old houses with "narrow, dark, and ill-paved" streets, "inhabited by sailors and other workmen who are employed in the construction of ships and by a great part of the Jews." Leman Street, where Sara lived when she first arrived in 1823, was a short walk from the Great Synagogue, the main house of worship for Ashkenazi Jews like her. Unlike French Jews, the Jews of England, who numbered about forty thousand in the mid-1800s, did not yet have full equality under the law, although restrictions on their activities would erode over the decades. In 1832, the year after Simon's arrival, Jews were finally able to establish businesses and engage in retail trade as "freemen" in the area of central London known as "The City," and in 1833 they were allowed to join the bar. A Jew was elected sheriff of London in 1835. And in 1858 the banking scion Lionel de Rothschild was permitted to become a member of Parliament without having to swear a Christian oath.[6]

Although Simon may well have lodged with his sister in the Jewish East End, he focused his attentions on a very different neighborhood and social milieu: the community of French émigrés in the aristocratic West End. Many of these exiles already knew London well from their prior emigration during the French Revolution, and after 1830 they gravitated to the same area north of Oxford Street they had known in the 1790s, when the future Charles X lived on Baker Street and his Orléans cousin Louis-Philippe lived on nearby George Street.[7]

The central meeting point of the legitimist social world was the Chapel of St. Louis, the French Chapel Royal, a small stucco building with three bay windows in front and cast-iron columns inside, built in 1799 on Carton Street (a mews adjoining Portman Square) in Marylebone. This is where both Louis XVIII and Charles X had celebrated their marriages while in exile, and despite being frequented by legitimists, it was also the church where exiled members of the Bonaparte family worshipped in the 1830s. (Like Deutz, the little chapel vacillated religiously; it would later become a synagogue.)[8]

As the first crisp notes of fall could be felt in the air, Deutz made his way to the tonier part of town to attend mass at the French chapel, hoping to meet the legitimist exiles. Always skilled at cozying up to the clergy, Deutz quickly secured the patronage of the Abbé Delaporte, almoner of St. Louis. According to the author Alexandre Dumas, Deutz made sure to pray with extreme fervor to attract the attention of another of the French churchgoers, Eugène, marquis de Montmorency-Laval. A very devout aristocrat whom Deutz had met in Rome, Montmorency now renewed the acquaintance with an invitation to dinner. It was the chance that Deutz had been waiting for.[9]

When Deutz said he was planning to travel to Italy, Montmorency asked if he would accompany the comtesse de Bourmont and her daughters, Juliette and Ernestine, as far as Geneva. Madame de Bourmont's husband was Louis de Bourmont, the Vendéen noble-man who had performed the song about the region's fidelity to the Bourbons during the duchess's trip there. He was one of France's leading military figures. After emigrating during the French Revolution and fighting with the counterrevolutionary army, Bourmont later returned to France and joined Napoleon's forces in time for the Russian campaign. However, during the battle of Waterloo he betrayed Napoleon by defecting to the Prussian side, an act of treason for which he was later rewarded by the Bourbons. Charles X made him minister of war and then *maréchal* of France, and he was leading the invasion of Algeria when the July Revolution broke out in 1830. After refusing to pledge loyalty to Louis-Philippe, "the traitor of Waterloo" was sacked from the army. Bourmont then decided to join the duchess's conspiracy, and his vast military experience made him one of the key members of her cabal. Deutz was happy to do an agreeable favor for the wife of such an important man.[10]

After just a few weeks back in Europe, he had already managed to gain access to the highest levels of the aristocracy and to the nucleus of legitimist intrigue, even if he had not yet been initiated into their secret plans. The Bourmont ladies were apparently pleased by his company because they made a favorable report to the conspirators in Massa: this charming convert was someone they could trust. Deutz deposited his charges in Geneva in late December 1831 and then stopped for a few days in Turin, lodging with the Jesuits. There he received a visit from another important personage: Augustin-Louis Cauchy, a famous mathematician who had resigned his teaching positions in Paris in protest after the July Revolution. Cauchy invited Deutz to accompany him to Massa, where if things went well, he would be presented to the duchesse de Berry. His path was now definitively on the ascent.

ALTHOUGH THE DUKE of Modena had allowed the duchess to lodge in the palace of Massa, she continued to hold court at the local inn, where her many advisers were staying and where they all took their meals around a large table, served by the inn's proprietor. The humble inn had certainly never seen such an illustrious clientele, composed exclusively of French exiles: grand aristocrats, important diplomats, famous politicians, and their wives. It was so full of former French army officers that the duchess jokingly dubbed it *la caserne*, the barracks. *Madame*, as her acolytes called her, presided over the spirited conversations at dinner, which would grow heated as they calculated the chances of pulling off a civil war. The assembled group loudly debated plans for the insurrection despite the fact that Louis-Philippe was known to have sent spies to watch the duchess's every move.[11]

The duchess was in her element. According to one legitimist journalist from the time, she felt relieved to have shed the trappings of luxury that had cluttered her former life and relished the opportunity to focus on matters of political importance. Forced by the July Monarchy government to sell her château at Rosny, she discovered that she greatly preferred the simple life—*simple* being a relative term for someone dwelling in a ducal palace—of the Tuscan seaside town to the stultifying ceremony of the Tuileries. Although she would come to lament having left her children in the care of her in-laws in Scotland, she made the most of her freedom. Like the heroines in her favorite Walter Scott novels, the thirty-three-year-old duchess began to see herself leading an army of men and shaping the destiny of nations.[12]

The advisers in her entourage all eagerly endorsed this new image of the duchess, encouraging their distaff leader's dream of launching a civil war in the Vendée. Her chief supporter was the comte de Mesnard, the sixty-two-year-old former military officer who had been assigned to restrain the duchess's youthful enthusiasm when she first arrived in France and who now deferred to her superior intelligence and impressive force of will. The inner circle also consisted of the maréchal de Bourmont; Florian, baron de Kergorlay, a former member of the Chamber of Deputies; Emmanuel, comte de Brissac, a squadron chief who had served as an aide to the duc de Berry;

Emmanuel, vicomte de Saint-Priest, a godson of Marie Antoinette, who had served as Charles X's ambassador to Madrid; and Amédée de Pérusse, duc d'Escars (or des Cars), a military officer from one of France's oldest noble families.

As was her wont, the duchess supplemented these venerable gray-beards with several handsome and entertaining young men, including Mesnard's son-in-law, Ludovic de Rosambo, who had amused her on the painful journey out of France; and Paul de Lavenne, comte de Choulot, a thirty-seven-year-old who shared her love of hunting, drawing, and gardens, and whom she affectionately nicknamed "Paolo." The two sons of the maréchal de Bourmont, Charles and Adolphe, were also in Massa with her. The presence of these young men in the duchess's inner circle would cause Parisians to gossip about the "scandal" of the life she was leading in Italy. Women also participated in the discussions at the local inn: the marquise de Podenas and the vicomtesse de Saint-Priest were among the members of the duchess's entourage most intent on pushing her to launch a civil war.[13]

Among the various members of the duchess's inner circle, Casimir de Blacas sounded the one discordant note. An aloof sixty-year-old former diplomat who had gained an enormous fortune and the title of duke through service to the Bourbons during the Restoration, Blacas felt intensely loyal to Charles X but not to his headstrong daughter-in-law. According to the regency decree that Charles X had signed at Holyrood, which made Blacas the duchess's prime minister, it was Blacas who would actually run the government should the duchess succeed in restoring her son's throne. This obviously did not sit well with the duchess, and conflicts soon arose.[14]

Although Blacas claimed to be attempting to secure aid for her insurrection from various European courts, in reality he saw his role as attempting to hinder, or at least delay, the duchess's plan for invading France. Blacas had nothing but scorn for the fantastic schemes of the duchess and her advisers and for their lack of political knowledge. In his memoir, Mesnard reports having heard Blacas complain that as soon as he attempted to have a serious political conversation with any of the duchess's other advisers, it was as if he were "speaking Hebrew," apparently something that no real French person could be imagined doing. "They would open wide their eyes and their ears and appeared not to understand a single word I was saying," Blacas lamented. Frustrated by his obfuscations and enraged by his aloof manner, the duchess eventually managed to convince Blacas to accept a mission to return to Charles X in Scotland. It was the first victory of her campaign.[15]

The departure of Blacas eliminated a major obstacle to her command, but it did not resolve all the dilemmas she faced. Over the course of the winter of 1831–1832, she debated the best way to launch an insurrection. Should she rely entirely on an uprising of indigenous French legitimists in the Midi (the French term for the southern region of Provence) and the Vendée, which might well get crushed by the government's superior forces? Or should she first entice foreign powers to invade France in order to engage Louis-Philippe's army near the frontiers so that she could attack from the interior? The risks of a foreign invasion were as great as the rewards; she did not want her son to return to France in the "baggage" of the allies as her in-laws had done first in 1814 and then again after Napoleon's Hundred Days in 1815. Those first and second Bourbon restorations never overcame the impression that they had been imposed from the outside. To create a stable government, her son's monarchy needed to result from French popular demand, or at least it needed to be *seen* as having done so. (The would-be Henri V later named his horse "Voeu populaire": Popular Demand.)[16]

One other, more devious possibility presented itself to the duchess: a foreign invasion that she would *pretend* to oppose. If she could persuade the various foreign powers who hated the July Monarchy to attack France, they could engage Louis-Philippe's army while she appeared as a savior, riding to the rescue of the fatherland at the head of her legitimist battalions. Henri V would be proclaimed king without compromise. "If a foreign war happens to break out at the same time as the interior action that we are planning," Mensard wrote, "we will throw ourselves, armed, at the border, and we will save France!" It was a bold plan and one that depended on expert diplomatic maneuvering. The duchess thus set to work over the course of the winter of 1831–1832, writing letters to her well-placed contacts in the different foreign capitals. She had reason to hope for success: the emperor of Austria, after all, was her uncle, and her half sister was married to the king of Spain.[17]

After the July Revolution, the other monarchies feared that what had taken place in France could spread, unleashing a wave of revolutionary fervor across Europe. "Wasn't the fall of one throne the signal for the others to fall as well?" asked one royalist observer. The terrain was especially ripe for revolution in Poland and the Italian peninsula, where parties of local nationalists hoped to free themselves from their long-standing occupations by foreign powers. Russia and Austria, the main occupiers, were thus keenly attuned to what was happening in France, and the duchess rightly sensed that they wanted to see her antirevolutionary insurrection succeed. She was seconded in her maneuvering by Charles Albert, the king of Sardinia, who had refused to let her stay in his kingdom for fear of angering Louis-Philippe but who nevertheless loaned her large sums of money—as much as 780,000 francs—to begin arming the legitimists in the Midi and the Vendée. However, the duchess never quite grasped the competing desires of these foreign powers, who saw her as a pawn in a much larger game of political maneuvering.[18]

As the winter wore on, the foreign powers began to realize that they had less to fear from the July Monarchy than they had first thought. Louis-Philippe did nothing to help the patriots in Poland and Italy. Nor did he intervene decisively in Belgium. After the southern provinces of Holland erupted in revolt in August 1830—an aftershock of the July Revolution in France—and declared an independent Belgian state, the other European powers feared that France would seek to extend its sphere of influence by supporting or even annexing the largely French-speaking region.

When the Belgian revolutionaries offered the newly created crown to Louis-Philippe's second son, the duc de Nemours, nationalists in France pushed him to accept even if it meant going to war with the other European powers. Instead, Louis-Philippe sought a compromise. He prevented the king of Holland from reconquering the Belgian territories, yet he refused the crown on his son's behalf. In a canny diplomatic partnership with England, he allowed the Belgian crown to go to Leopold of Saxe-Coburg-Saalfeld, who then married Louis-Philippe's daughter Louise, founding the present-day Belgian royal family. French nationalists were outraged, but the other European powers were relieved.[19]

A foreign invasion of France that the duchess could turn to her own advantage thus became less and less likely over the course of the winter. Although the duchess kept firing off dispatches pleading for money and supplies to the various European crowned heads, she gradually came to realize that the French legitimists would have to initiate the insurrection themselves. Another dilemma now arose: the timing of the invasion that would signal the start of the campaign. Was it already too late? Had she let the right moment pass?[20]

Whereas Ferdinand de Bertier, who had gone to the Vendée to gauge popular sentiment, pleaded with her in the spring of 1831 to strike while antigovernment sentiment was reaching a peak, he now grew much more cautious, even pessimistic, about her chances for success. Already in July 1831, he wrote to Emmanuel de Brissac that "the situation is . . . much less good than it was five weeks ago." Bertier began to lose faith after the maréchal de Bourmont announced to the leaders of the insurrection in the Midi and the Vendée that the duchess would arrive on September 20, 1831, but then moved the agreed-upon signal to start the campaign back to October 2 before postponing the date again indefinitely. In a letter to the duchess in mid-December 1831, he cautioned that their supporters in Paris had grown "discouraged by too long a wait" and that "all the orders and counter-orders given the prior month had a negative effect" on the morale of the men waiting to take up arms.[21]

The marquis de Coislin, a legitimist deputy from Brittany who had at first encouraged the duchess to launch her invasion, began to share Bertier's reservations. In a long letter to the duchess, probably also from December 1831, Coislin warned that the insurrectionary forces in the Vendée lacked sufficient arms and gunpowder to conduct a successful war against the July Monarchy. He cautioned her in the strongest terms to reconsider the whole enterprise: "Madame should not let her head be turned by those words, flattering but false, that are repeated ceaselessly: everything for France! There will be nothing [for France] if she listens to her advisers; and if she makes us take up arms, a month later there will be no more Vendée; the [Bourbon] monarchy's last resource will be annihilated; all the leaders will be arrested or dead and the region will be entirely devastated." Coislin believed that the legitimists' only hope lay in a foreign invasion that would draw the government's army to France's frontiers, leaving the western provinces under-defended. To take up arms in their current position, without aid from abroad, would result in "the total destruction of the royalist party." The duchess seems either not to have understood his warning or to have deliberately ignored it. Her blithe response thanked Coislin for his devotion to her son's cause and reiterated that she was counting on his support.[22]

The duchess now began to plot in earnest, appointing a "secret government" of men in Paris to advise her in her quest to reconquer the throne. In February 1832 Chateaubriand received word that he had been named to this grand council and took it upon himself to offer a few words of caution. In a letter accepting his new role, which he later published, the writer described the political situation in France—in which the centrist or *juste milieu* supporters of Louis-Philippe had robbed the nation of its dignity—but advised the duchess to proceed with careful consideration before embarking upon civil war. He cautioned her that "the departments of the West and of the Midi . . . will never conspire. . . . Admirable as a legitimist reserve, they will be insufficient as an avant-garde force and will never successfully take the offensive." He also warned her against "placing her hope in the foreigner," adding that he assumed she would rather not have Henri V reign at all than to see him brought to power by a European coalition. He concluded with yet another warning couched in flattery: "France, since the Revolution, has oft changed charioteers, yet has never seen a woman at the helm of state. God wills that the reins of this indomitable people . . . be placed in the hands of a young princess; she will know how to wield them with both strength and grace."[23]

The duchess most likely did not receive this message. If she did, she would have disregarded it; too many people were pushing her in the opposite direction. Indeed, letters arrived all winter from supporters in France, begging her to launch her campaign. As one letter warned her, "Europe has its eyes on you. Either you come to France or a republic will be proclaimed and then there will be an invasion and war, the consequences of which nobody can predict." Félicie de La Rochejacquelein, a noblewoman from the Vendée who had taught the duchess to ride and shoot during her trip to the western region in 1828, now wrote letter after letter telling the duchess that the time had come to put those lessons to use, imploring, "This is what is worthy of you, Madame, even if you should succumb!" La Rochejacquelein knew her audience well. Appeals to the duchess's taste for danger in service of an exalted mission were precisely what would motivate her to undertake the impossible escapade. Even the duchess's brother-in-law, the awkward and stuttering duc d'Angoulême, braving the disapproval of his wife, wrote to pledge his support: "Go forward, my sister, and let heaven watch over your enterprise. As soon as you have set foot in the Vendée I will be at your side, as your first and most devoted servant."[24]

Seeing a member of the royal family acknowledge her superiority and defer to her leadership could not have failed to gratify the duchess. She also took pride in defying gender stereotypes. One of the most paradoxical aspects of the duchesse de Berry is that even while she was fighting for the principle of tradition, her own actions were anything but traditional. True, her role as mother of the Bourbon heir gave cover for her boldness: Mesnard and her other

propagandists made sure that everyone knew she was acting to protect the interests of her son. But she never tried to hide her own
ambitions to equal the great heroines of French history: Joan of Arc,
the peasant girl who had fought to save France from the British, and
Jeanne d'Albret, the duchess's own ancestor who had commanded
the Huguenots during the Wars of Religion. In fact, she seemed to
relish the gender-bending aspect of her new role. When one of her
young followers in Massa threatened to cut off his mustache if the
duchess did not launch her civil war soon, she supposedly replied that
she would grow one.[25]

With Blacas gone, the other members of her court in Massa
formed a united front pushing the duchess toward action, each one
dreaming of the exalted role that he would play in the newly restored
monarchy under the regency of the duchess. According to General
Dermoncourt, who led the government's effort to capture the duchess
and whose account of the affair was ghostwritten by Alexandre Dumas, her advisers exaggerated the feasibility of the undertaking and
strove to keep from her any conflicting points of view. They depicted
the Midi as ready to explode in revolt against the July Monarchy
and the Vendée as possessing an organized army of legitimist war-
riors ready to take up arms as soon as she gave the signal. "Madame
was thus completely misled about where things stood," Dermoncourt
writes. The combination of her "adventurous and animated character"
and the self-interest of her advisers meant there was no turning back
from an enterprise that she herself referred to as her *"folle équipée,"*
her crazy escapade.[26]

Ultimately, though, the choice to act was hers alone, and she did
not make it lightly. For someone as impetuous as the duchess, the
long delay and constant postponements over the course of the winter
of 1831–1832 indicated serious deliberation. As the first signs of spring
appeared, she began taking arduous walks through the countryside in
order to harden herself for the rigors of a military campaign. She also
used these hikes to clear her head and to sound her own counsel. On
the one hand, she knew that she faced grave danger, both for herself
and for the men who would be fighting in her name. If she lost, it

would mean a disaster for the legitimists and the end of her son's political future. But ultimately her instinct told her to have faith in the justice of her cause and in the fidelity of the French people, who would surely rally to her in admiration for her *beau geste* (her beautiful gesture). According to Mesnard, she knew deep down that "she was beloved by the people, and the French people cannot resist courage and heroism. They understand all that is generous!" She resolved to trust her instinct. She would act.[27]

The only remaining question was when. Thanks to the constant flow of letters—written in secret code and invisible ink—between Massa and the duchess's correspondents in Paris, the Midi, and the Vendée, she kept abreast of political developments in France, waiting for the right moment to launch her invasion. Louis-Philippe's popularity continued to decline. When the government sent twenty thousand troops to crush a strike by desperate silk workers in Lyon in November 1831, killing hundreds, the opposition on the Left grew even more strident than the opposition on the Right.

But it was really the government's actions in the Vendée that gave the duchess the most reason to hope. At first, Louis-Philippe had sent an army to the Vendée to give the impression that he was too busy with internal revolts to intervene in Belgium, Italy, or Poland. As Dermoncourt put it, "A little civil war in the Vendée gave just the right impression." Soon, however, the ruthless repression of the Vendéens by the government's forces threatened to turn a little civil war into a big one: "In the West, the soldiers acted like they were in a conquered territory," terrorizing the peasants under the guise of rooting out pockets of resistance. Even if the whole region was not quite a powder keg waiting for a match, as some of the duchess's advisers wanted her to believe—the July Monarchy actually enjoyed a certain amount of support among the bourgeoisie in the West, especially in the cities—the situation was highly volatile.[28]

WHEN SIMON DEUTZ arrived in Massa in late January or early February 1832, he did not know quite what to expect. He was on the lookout for a way to improve his fortunes and had begun to ingratiate himself with the legitimists as a means to do so. Although he claims in his memoir that he had no idea that the duchess was planning a civil war, this was surely not the case. The duchess's conspiracy was common knowledge, even to her enemies in France, and was reported on in the press. It seems likely that Deutz already reasoned that if he could succeed in meeting the duchess—getting her to take him under her wing—the fortune that he had dreamed of since childhood might follow. Perhaps she would even grant him a noble title in recompense for having helped her campaign.

Before he could hope to penetrate the duchess's conspiracy, he first needed to ingratiate himself with her ministers: Mesnard, Bourmont, Kergorlay, Saint-Priest, and Choulot. This was not an easy task, given his middle-class Jewish background. He managed to secure a room at the inn where they were all staying, a necessary first move, and he made their acquaintance in due course. However, according to his memoir, they did not reveal the plans for their conspiracy during this first trip: "I saw all of them, but without being admitted to their discussions or initiated into their secret projects."[29]

The aristocratic advisers did, however, agree to present him to the duchess: the moment that Deutz had been waiting for. The rabbi's son finally found himself in the presence of royalty. Even if his fantasy for the future did not come to pass, even if he never managed to befriend the duchess or become her confidant, this alone was an enormous accomplishment. It was something he could only have dimly imagined when he first decided to leave the humble Jewish world of the Marais behind or during his days of lonely misery in New York only a few months before.

Although their first meeting was short, Deutz makes clear in his memoir that it gratified his ego enormously. He tells us that the duchess received him with kindness and thanked him for having escorted the Bourmont ladies to Geneva. She then bestowed upon him "more flattering words," but, according to Deutz's retrospective account, she did not raise the subject of politics and did not tell him about her plans for civil war. He nevertheless seems to have found a way to mention that he would soon be undertaking a business trip on behalf of the Jesuits to Spain and Portugal. This was a total fabrication; nothing drew him to the Iberian peninsula. But knowing, as he surely did, that the duchess would be looking to the rulers of these countries for support for her campaign, he cleverly suggested a way that he might be useful to her in the future.[30]

What did the duchess think of this first meeting, which was so momentous for Deutz? Not much, apparently. Mesnard reports that "this little incident [meeting Deutz] was without importance" to Madame. Of course, she had no way of knowing how very important indeed it would seem to her in retrospect.[31]

After the meeting with the duchess, Deutz headed to Rome. As usual, he descended upon the Jesuits at the Collegio Romano. While in Rome, he saw Drach, who had left France after the Revolution of 1830 to take up a position as the librarian of the Propaganda Fide, the Church's chief missionary congregation. Simon was happy to be reunited with his brother-in-law: fresh from his meeting in Massa, he felt proud that he had succeeded, by his charm and wits alone, in turning his situation around. Whereas only a year prior, down and out in America, he had written Drach desperate letters begging for help, he was now able to relay to Drach the compliments of the duchesse de Berry.[32]

Deutz also saw his old friend Cappellari, now Pope Gregory XVI, and was gratified to note that his friend's "elevation had not altered his kindness toward me." According to Deutz, they spent an hour walking in the gardens of the Vatican, and the holy father opened his heart to the convert. "If I had a son," the pontiff supposedly told him, "I could not love him as much as I love you." Despite this tender confidence, the pope also made it clear that he still did not support Deutz's project to help the Jews of Rome. As usual, there is a self-serving aspect to Deutz's version of events. Deutz wants to show in his memoir that he cultivated the pope not for his own self-interest but on behalf of his less fortunate former coreligionists. He also wants to show that he only agreed to work for the duchess because the pope definitively spurned his efforts to help the Roman Jews. Deutz surely felt that portraying himself as a crusader for liberty would make more believable his claim, constantly advanced in his memoir, that he had never really been a legitimist but rather always supported liberal causes. In reality, Deutz doesn't seem to have held any political beliefs at all; instead, he adopted whatever opinion he thought most advantageous in the moment.[33]

Shortly after his walk with the pope, Deutz received a note from the maréchal de Bourmont, sending him the regards of his wife and daughters and inviting him back to Massa to meet with the duchess a second time. Deutz's plan had worked: the duchess wanted him to deliver some secret letters during his upcoming trip to Spain and Portugal. "She will be charmed to see you," Bourmont wrote. "She will probably ask you to be so kind as to accept several commissions on her behalf."[34]

According to Deutz, he shared this letter with the pope, who shocked him by openly recommending that he join the duchess's conspiracy against Louis-Philippe, something that Deutz claimed to know nothing about: "For him [the pope], it was a struggle between two principles, legitimacy in combat with usurpation; to reestablish the one by overturning the other was to serve the cause of religion." Whether or not the pope really spoke so openly about his support for a civil war to overthrow the French government, Deutz soon departed for Massa, where the pope had paved the way for him with a glowing recommendation: "The holy father had spoken of me to MADAME in very obliging terms, and had painted me as an intelligent and active man, courageous and dedicated," someone they could consider a precious conquest for the legitimist cause. A better reference would have been hard to find.[35]

In a handwritten confession titled "Devant Dieu" ("Before God"), composed immediately after the arrest of the duchess, Deutz provides some insight into his state of mind at the time of his fateful second journey to Massa: "Whether from a childish or a genuine capacity for premonition, as far back as I remember, I have always been convinced that I would accomplish a great action in the name of Liberty, and what is more, all my friends, and I have had them among the crowned heads of Europe and in the most honorable conditions of Society, would constantly repeat to me: 'You were born for great things.'" Deutz's grandiosity, which had met with such humiliating insults throughout his adolescence and early adulthood, had finally found its true calling, but whether this was to betray the duchess or to serve her, it is impossible to say. "It seemed to me as if Providence had thrown the Carlists into my arms," he wrote, referring to the legitimists by their derisive nickname, thus implying his plan was to act as a double agent. He claims that he was acting for the sake of "liberty" when he joined the duchess's conspiracy, yet it is clear that this concept had very little meaning to him other than as a mirror for his ego. "I let myself be borne along by my destiny," he writes, "without a fixed goal other than to do anything for France [*tout faire pour la France*]." It seems likely that when he arrived in Massa a second time, Deutz was more than willing to help the legitimists in their war against liberty, if it meant improving his own status.[36]

According to Bertier, Deutz went out of his way to make himself agreeable to the duchess's coterie during this second stay in Massa. He joined them for excursions to see the nearby marble quarries and spent a great deal of time with the ladies in the party. When the erudite vicomtesse de Saint-Priest engaged him in discussion about ancient Jewish civilization, he impressed her with his knowledge of the Hebrew language and of Jewish history. "He responded to all her questions, agreed with all her views, and won her over completely," according to Bertier. The aristocrat claims to have been more suspicious, finding in Deutz "a certain intelligence, but also something common and vulgar in his physiognomy and manners." Bertier also notes that although it was Lent, Deutz did not observe fast days or abstain from eating meat, which was odd for a recent convert and friend of the pope. But nothing about Deutz's behavior indicated that he was planning to betray the duchess during his time in Massa. According to Bertier, it was probably only much later, when he had been corrupted by the July Monarchy's offer of a reward, that Deutz decided to switch sides.[37]

Over the course of the next few weeks, Deutz and the duchess met on several occasions, and she initiated him into the secrets of her conspiracy. If they didn't exactly become friends, they did become close associates. She even invited him to join her table at the inn, along with all the high aristocrats and military heroes who were helping her plot her invasion, a favor almost unheard-of for a commoner, let alone one who had been born a Jew. But he had come highly recommended, not just by the pope but also by the maréchal de Bourmont, who praised his "learning, his capacities, and especially his religious sentiments and his royalist devotion." If Deutz knew anything, it was how to flatter those in power by professing to share their opinions and desires. It is noteworthy, though, that the duchess did not seem troubled by Deutz's Jewish origins. Perhaps she felt sympathy for his relatively humble circumstances. Perhaps she was also intrigued by his exotic looks: his curly black hair, brown eyes, and olive complexion so different from her own blonde hair, blue eyes, and fair skin. Most importantly, she trusted her instinct, and her instinct was to trust Deutz.[38]

The duchess gave Deutz letters for her half sisters in Spain, the Infanta Luisa Carlota and Queen Maria Christina. But the mission she charged Deutz to carry out with Dom Miguel, the king of Portugal, was more specific and more delicate. Dom Miguel, an archconservative, was a natural ally of the duchess even if he wasn't willing to risk an attack on France without provocation. The duchess nevertheless hoped he would provide her with guns and gunpowder. Appointing Deutz—under a pseudo-aristocratic *nom de guerre*, Hyacinthe de Gonzague—as her "plenipotentiary," she entrusted him with a detailed letter to Dom Miguel setting out her plans to "place herself at the head" of the insurrectionary forces in the Midi and the Vendée. She asked the Portuguese king to help her smuggle into France a secret shipment of arms packed in small crates and gunpowder in small barrels in order to avoid arousing suspicion. She also asked for a significant amount of money to be sent via a complex system of letters of exchange to a banker in Nantes so the transfer could not be traced.[39]

On April 9, 1832, the duchess wrote to Drach to thank him for a letter that his "excellent brother-in-law" had delivered to her. She complimented Deutz to Drach, although not without a hint of ambiguity, remarking that she "appreciated" him "as much as he deserves [*autant qu'il mérite*]." Drach must have felt relieved that his erratic brother-in-law had not embarrassed him in front of the duchess. He too was surely hoping for a position or some kind of favor should the duchess manage to pull off her plan for another Bourbon restoration.[40]

Deutz could barely contain his elation at being named the plenipotentiary of the duchess: "Here I was a diplomat, for better or worse, and thrown, without desiring it, almost without understanding it, into the middle of court intrigues!" But before he accepted the mission, he let it be known that he lacked the money to undertake the voyage. According to Dumas, the duchess then removed a large diamond ring from her finger—which she judged to be worth six thousand francs—and gave it to Deutz to defray the cost of the journey. It was a gesture worthy of a princess and one that reflected the total confidence she had in a man she had known for a short time but whom she trusted to serve loyally on her behalf.[41]

For his part, Mesnard claims to have shared Bertier's bad impression of Deutz. In his memoir published in 1844 but written in the present tense, like a diary, Mesnard describes the negative feelings that Deutz supposedly inspired in him in 1832: "I have little liking for these converted Jews; however, I don't let my opinion of the newcomer show. Everyone surrounding the princess showed him a proper welcome and Madame admitted him to her table. He seems entirely devoted to the cause of the Bourbons and he might well be an honest man, hence I don't want to display the antipathy I feel for him."[42]

Here is an example of the new kind of antisemitism that took hold of the French imagination following Deutz's betrayal of the duchess. Mesnard's dislike of the Jews is not religious. Whereas traditional Jew-haters saw conversion as the solution to the Jewish problem, Mesnard says he dislikes converts specifically. What displeases Mesnard is not the Jews' stubborn rejection of Christ but precisely their flexibility in religious matters, their chameleon-like capacity to shed their skin, to become something they are not, to assimilate. He continues to call these converts "Jews" as if to emphasize the indelible mark of Jewishness, its eternal or essential quality, which inspires his antipathy. For Mesnard, a "Jew" like Deutz should never be welcomed, never admitted to one's table—or, by extension, to one's country.

In early April, Deutz rode out of Massa, swelling with pride at his important mission. He was accompanied by the comte "Paolo" de Choulot, whom the duchess had dispatched on a similar mission to the Russian tsar, and Deutz may well have considered himself the aristocrat's equal. However, a mile from town they stopped in an olive grove, and Choulot forced Deutz to descend from his mount. Perhaps wondering whether someone who had abjured his religion could really be trusted, the arrogant young nobleman now ordered a frightened Deutz to take a solemn oath: "I swear to do everything in my power for the re-establishment and the maintenance of legitimacy and accord to the members of the regency, established by MADAME, the right to take my life in the event that I commit treason."[43]

Deutz conveys the gravity of the moment in his memoir and maintains that even as he swore the oath, he already planned to betray the duchess in order to save France from civil war. If that were so, it must have required great courage to hide his terror at what he was setting out to do. More likely, Deutz had no immediate plans to betray the duchess and took the oath willingly. If he felt any pang at all in that Italian olive grove, it was because he knew he was *capable* of betraying the duchess if he one day decided it was in his interest to do so.

As a student of the New Testament, did Deutz appreciate the significance of his location as he took the pledge? Did he remember that it was in another olive grove—Gethsemane, at the foot of the Mount of Olives in Jerusalem—that Jesus greeted the traitor Judas for the last time, asking the man who would betray him the famous question—*"Amice ad quid venisti?"* ("Friend, wherefore art thou come?" [Matthew 26:50])—that would echo through the ages as the motto of innocence in the face of treachery? Like Jesus, to whom the duchess would be compared by her followers after her arrest, the duchess had placed her trust in the wrong man.

CHAPTER 7

The Tightrope Walker

RUMORS BEGAN TO arrive from the East: people were dropping dead in the streets of Saint Petersburg. The morgues were overflowing in Berlin. During the last outbreak, fifteen years before, millions died in India, but the disease never reached Europe. This time was different. Anxious doctors at the Académie des sciences sent delegations to Russia and Germany to determine what preventive measures they should take, while grim health officials busied themselves with preparations back home. It was only a matter of time, they knew, before cholera arrived in Paris.[1]

March 29, 1832, was a beautiful spring day, one of the first nice days of the year. After the long Parisian winter, residents of the French capital hung up their heavy coats, like so many molting animals, and crowded the boulevards in search of sun and spectacle. Some wore masks to celebrate Mi-Carême, a Lenten carnival similar to Mardi Gras. Heinrich Heine, the great German writer who had moved to Paris the preceding year, recounts that the throngs who packed the costume balls that night danced with a feverish intensity. Suddenly, one of the merriest of the revelers, disguised as a harlequin, felt his legs grow cold. When he removed his mask, everyone gasped. His face had turned blue.[2]

Soon there was a full-fledged epidemic, one of the worst France had ever seen. More than 2 percent of the capital's residents perished—as many as 20,000 dead in a city of 800,000—in just a few months. On some ghastly days, more than a thousand people succumbed to the disease. According to the comtesse de Boigne, actors would collapse on stage in the middle of a play: healthy one minute, corpses the next. The doctors dispatched by the Académie to study the disease in Eastern Europe had not even had time to file their reports on possible cures before the city had turned into a charnel house. It was said that several of them died on their journey.[3]

The symptoms of cholera would come on suddenly: rumblings in the stomach and a feeling of oppression or constriction, followed by abundant ejections of a whitish fluid. A burning fever. Excessive thirst. Soon the pulse would slow. The skin would turn red, then blue. The tongue would grow cold. The patient would barely respond to questions. In the final phase the victim might experience a moment of perfidious calm before the end. Then the eyes filled with blood. Breathing stopped. Often, it was over within a few hours.[4]

Doctors had no idea how to guard against the disease. Groping for prophylactic aids, they warned the terrified population to beware sudden changes in temperature, to avoid sleeping outside, and to clean their rooms weekly, scouring the walls with straw. Those who hoped to avoid cholera might take warm baths but were advised to stay away from the ocean. Nobody should venture out on an empty stomach. Many types of food were prohibited, including hard-boiled eggs. People were told to avoid eating old cheese, especially at night, lest they weaken their defenses. Strong emotions were seen as a contributing factor. Fear—including of the disease itself, "choleraphobia"—was thought to bring on symptoms. In a particularly useless nod to superstition, people wore flannel belts to ward off danger.[5]

In 1832 researchers had only a limited understanding of the factors that led to disease. It would be another few decades before doctors discovered that cholera was in fact caused by the bacterium *vibrio cholerae* and that it was transmitted by water and food contaminated by human feces. Nevertheless, moralistic French health officials undertook one of the first public-hygiene campaigns, directed at the lower classes, which recommended "cleanliness in clothes and dwellings, sobriety in food, and moderation in pleasure." They also began inspecting homes and public buildings to detect the toxic vapors emanating from filth, known as *miasma*, which they thought spread the disease.[6]

They had their work cut out for them: Paris in 1832 was a very dirty place. Lacking sufficient sewers, people emptied the contents of their latrines and chamber pots into the street, where the waste mixed with the manure of thousands of horses and other animals. Stinking mud clung to boots and skirts and entered the houses of anyone unable to afford a carriage. It ran into the wells from which Parisians drew their drinking water. According to Heine, "Owing to the vast misery prevailing here, to the incredible filth, which is by no means limited to the lower classes," cholera spread more rapidly in Paris than anyplace else.[7]

Because those with means had fled the city at the first rumors of the outbreak, the poor felt targeted by the disease. And the Parisian lower classes didn't need another reason to feel aggrieved. The onset of industrialization had degraded the lives of workers in France. In the 1830s socialists began to denounce the way that impersonal factories were displacing the old workshops, where the master had known his workers. Now the relentless quest for profits drove down wages just as migrants from the countryside flooded the capital looking for work. With so many employees to choose from, factory owners could pay a pittance, and workers often spent more than half their salary just for bread. If a man fell sick and couldn't go to work for a few days, his family would starve.[8]

All these laborers looking for work needed someplace to sleep, and rents in the slums of the city center—the densely packed neighborhoods around Notre Dame Cathedral, the Tuileries Palace, and the Faubourg Saint-Antoine—rose to ever higher levels. As the rich moved to the newer and more fashionable neighborhoods in the north and west of the city, poor families tried to hang on to the places they knew, where they had ties of blood and friendship. Entire families now crowded into tiny attic rooms that became breeding grounds for disease.

In the nineteenth century the rich died at home, whereas hospitals often doubled as poorhouses or insane asylums. So when, in an effort to contain the outbreak, the Parisian health authorities began transporting cholera victims to the Hôtel-Dieu, the giant hospital in the shadow of Notre Dame Cathedral, the lower classes began to panic. Some whispered that cholera was a government conspiracy to rid the city of its poor residents.[9]

The paranoia reached a crescendo on April 2, 1832, when Henri Gisquet, the prefect of police, responded to rumors by declaring that the government had not in fact poisoned the wells or contaminated the food supply but that miscreants may have taken advantage of the chaos to do so. Intending to allay the people's fears, he stoked them. Violence ensued. Brigades of men stationed themselves on street corners, in front of wine shops and butchers, searching anyone they didn't recognize. They murdered two strangers found with a suspicious white powder. The powder later turned out to be chlorine meant to disinfect, but it didn't matter: the bodies of the alleged poisoners were torn apart and dragged through the streets by the mob.

Since the July Revolution, opposition to Louis-Philippe had struck a lighthearted note: fixating on the bulbous shape of the royal jowls, Charles Philipon, the editor of the journal *La Caricature*, drew the monarch's head as a pear. Soon images of the "pear king" proliferated in other satirical journals, engravings for sale, and scribbled graffiti on the walls of the city. However, everyone knew that the jest concealed real frustration with the regime. Cholera brought this to the surface.[10]

The rich blamed the poor for spreading the disease. The poor thought the rich were trying to kill them. And everyone blamed the government for not doing enough to halt the scourge. Realizing the danger he faced, Louis-Philippe decided to stay put in Paris during

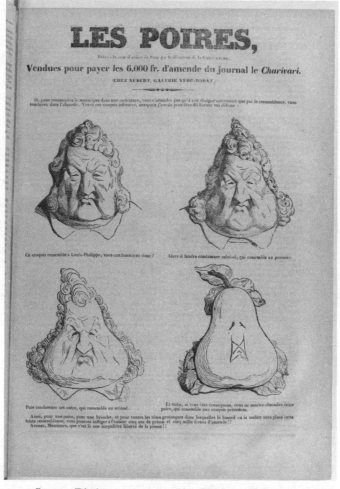

Louis-Philippe as a pear by Honoré Daumier
(*La Caricature*, 1831)

the epidemic, refusing to flee along with the rest of the upper classes. Queen Marie-Amélie sewed flannel belts with her own hands and distributed them to her servants. The couple's ten-year-old son handed out free soup. Their eldest son, Ferdinand Philippe, visited cholera patients at the Hôtel-Dieu and earned the effusive praise of the pro-regime press for his bravery. He was accompanied by the wary prime minister, Casimir-Pierre Périer, a man who viewed the

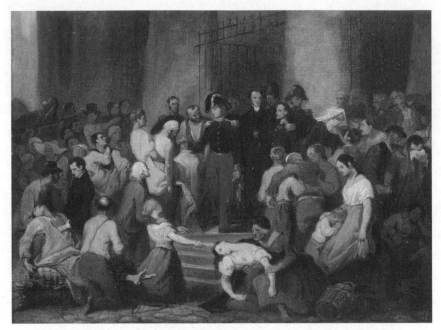

*The Duc d'Orléans Visiting the Sick at the Hôtel-Dieu
during the Cholera Epidemic* by Alfred Johannot (1832)

lower classes with suspicion and scorn. In a famous painting of the
visit by the artist Alfred Johannot, the prince reaches out toward
the sick while the prime minister looks on with an expression of
barely concealed repugnance. The next day, Périer came down with
the disease.

When the prime minister died on May 16, 1832, Louis-Philippe
gave him a huge state funeral. This outraged republicans, who saw
the tribute to a man they considered their enemy as one more indication of the July Monarchy's antidemocratic orientation. Yet it
was the government's failure to provide a state funeral for General
Lamarque, an opposition hero who died of cholera on June 1, that
nearly provoked another revolution. On June 5 enormous crowds followed the hearse carrying Lamarque's body as it made its way east
to the cemetery of Père Lachaise. Poor workers ducked out of their
shops to catch a glimpse of the coffin. Beggars elbowed housewives

as the procession passed. The crowd contained many committed republicans, a mix of workers and students, along with refugees from the failed revolutions in Poland and Italy, which Lamarque had supported. Aware of the danger of civil unrest, Prefect Gisquet deployed large numbers of police to follow the procession. Tensions mounted as the funeral cortège neared the Place de la Bastille, the symbolic heart of revolutionary Paris, the site of the infamous prison whose destruction had set off the first French Revolution and the center of the working-class Faubourg Saint-Antoine neighborhood. The people attacked a column of dragoons, and some of the soldiers on horseback rode into the crowd, injuring those in their path. Nearby, at the Austerlitz Bridge, some protesters tried to hijack the coffin and carry it to the Pantheon, where France traditionally buried its great men. The soldiers eventually recovered the body, but a revolt had begun.

Barricades went up almost instantly in the central and eastern districts of Paris: barrages composed of cobblestones, wagons, carriages, barrels, furniture thrown down from windows, anything that would block a street and give the revolutionaries some cover from the soldiers' bullets. The rebels numbered about three thousand. They were easily crushed by the twenty thousand National Guard troops and forty thousand regular soldiers, who by midnight regained control of the Left Bank and the area around Notre Dame. Louis-Philippe, who resolved not to flee as his Bourbon cousins had done in 1830, rode through the city the next morning to inspire confidence in his regime. The final barricades, in the Faubourg Saint-Antoine and the parish of Saint-Merri, fell soon after. Soldiers fired on the protesters, forcing the republicans to abandon their blockades. By the afternoon of June 6, it was over, and eight hundred people were dead.[11]

Victor Hugo would make this failed revolution the climax of *Les Misérables*, his epic novel about France's struggle for social justice in the nineteenth century. Despite the popularity of Hugo's novel, few today remember that the republican uprising was not the only threat that the regime of Louis-Philippe faced in the spring of 1832. By the time that the republican insurgents died on the barricades in Paris, the duchesse de Berry was already fighting her own right-wing revolt in the Vendée.

ALL THROUGH THE winter of 1831–1832, the duchess had hesitated, canceling several plans for insurrection as she weighed the chances for success and sought help from foreign powers. Although she received many letters urging her to remain cautious, others pleaded with her to launch her campaign immediately. One of the most urgent came from the legitimist lawyer Pierre-Antoine Berryer, whom she had appointed to her "secret government" in Paris along with Chateaubriand. In February 1832 Berryer won a highly publicized case defending a group of Vendéen peasants accused of conspiring against the government, and he wrote to her in Massa soon after, stating, "Madame would be shirking all her obligations to her son and to France if she delays any longer coming to place herself at the head of the populations that await her." In another missive, written in invisible ink—lemon juice—between the lines of a ship's navigation manual, which the duchess had to hold up to a candle flame to read, Berryer implored, "Hurry up, Madame, because if you don't, we will begin the action without you!" A letter from Charles-Athanase de Charette, baron de la Contrie, who had traveled to the Vendée and prepared a detailed plan for the duchess's military campaign, reiterated the sense of urgency by appealing to her maternal instincts: "Every day that you absent yourself from the homeland is a day you steal from the heritage of your son!"[12]

These letters pushed the duchess closer to launching her insurrection. On February 5 she issued a proclamation outlining the provisionary government that she would put in place once she regained control of France. All the legitimist leaders would have a role to play: those who surrounded her in Massa, her advisers in Paris, and the military commanders on the ground in France. On March 25 she held what would be the last formal meeting of her advisers. Bertier

made a special trip to Massa from France for the occasion and attempted to introduce a note of caution into the proceedings, warning
the duchess that her army risked getting crushed by the government's
superior forces. It was far better, he advised, to lie low and wait for
some event to turn public opinion against the regime. The vicomte
de Saint-Priest also raised some doubts from a military standpoint,
but he still thought that it was important for the honor of the Bourbons to have tried to win back their throne. The others brushed aside
all doubt: the comte de Mesnard, the duc des Cars, the comte de
Kergorlay, and especially the maréchal de Bourmont advocated immediate action. As commander of the duchess's forces in the Vendée,
Bourmont carried the most weight.[13]

It was cholera, however, that made the duchess think the time
had finally come. According to one contemporary observer, the legitimists saw cholera as "the dazzling sign of heaven's vengeance at
the impious city," God's punishment for fifty years of revolutionary
upheaval. They also saw it as a sign that God was on their side. Cholera provided the perfect opportunity for the legitimists to assume
the role of savior for the suffering capital. In late March the duchess
began receiving messages from her advisers in Paris describing the
deteriorating state of the city's health and of its political situation.
"Everything grows old quickly in France," Chateaubriand wrote to
her on April 12. "Every day brings with it new political opportunities." Although the legitimist writer privately referred to the duchess
as "that tightrope walker in Italy" and tried to make her understand
the perils of an insurrection, Chateaubriand came up with the idea
for a public-relations assault to precede the military one: the duchess
would offer twelve thousand francs to cholera victims in the capital.[14]

This put Louis-Philippe in the awkward position of refusing the
duchess's largesse, thereby lending credence to the perception that
the "citizen king" didn't care about his citizens' suffering. It also po-
sitioned the legitimists as a populist alternative to the republicans,
a party that would solve the social problem through the traditional
means of faith and charity rather than revolution. The right-wing

press trumpeted the "good and beautiful action of Madame," which "directed public attention toward that princess, and cast light on her many good works, the abundant generosity of her heart." In spite of this spin, astute observers at the time realized what the duchess was up to; the comtesse de Boigne notes in her memoirs that "the hope of profiting from the perturbation that cholera had provoked in the country and in the government determined madame la duchesse de Berry to hasten her enterprise."[15]

Convinced that the disease had—providentially—prepared the terrain for her return, the duchess finally made the decision that she had struggled with for so many months. She set a date for the insurrection to begin at dawn on April 30, 1832. This time there would be no more delays. She would time her landing in Marseille to coincide with the uprising. The duc des Cars headed to Marseille to supervise the military operation.

The duchess's thoughts now turned toward heaven. After all, the fate of France, as well as her own life, hung in the balance. A few days before setting off, she went to the church in Lucca to make a final confession. If she felt confident in the divine justice of her mission and in her son's God-given right to rule, she clearly also felt she could use an extra bit of help from on high. On April 20, four days before her departure, she wrote to her childhood friend: "Pray, my dear Suzette, and have the good souls of Naples pray for me as well. I am in great need of their prayers."[16]

Once the pressure of the decision making had been lifted, the duchess felt free to begin preparing for her voyage. She and her followers would set sail from Massa on the night of April 24. Under a false name, the vicomte de Saint-Priest purchased a small steamship called the *Carlo Alberto*. Meanwhile, the duchess drafted a solemn proclamation to the people of Marseille, to be issued on the eve of her arrival: "The granddaughter of Henri IV has come to ask your aid. . . . It is to your love and that of all good French people, and only French people, that Henri V desires to owe his crown. . . . Rally to the white flag [of the Bourbons]." To her commanders in the field, she wrote in secret code: "I will let it be known in Nantes, in Angers, in Rennes and in Lyon that I am in France. Prepare yourselves to take up arms as soon as you receive this message."[17]

On the evening of April 24 the duchess set out in a mail coach on the road to Florence in the company of Mesnard, Brissac, the marquise de Podenas, and the duchess's lady-in-waiting, twenty-six-year-old Mathilde Lebeschu. The duchess had taken care to secure a passport to Florence several days before. This was a diversionary tactic designed to fool the local authorities and French spies sent to monitor her activities, and at the first relay stop the duchess stealthily descended, along with Mlle Lebeschu and Mesnard, leaving the marquise de Podenas to continue the journey to Florence as a decoy.[18]

Disguised as Neapolitan sailors—the tiny duchess wore the uniform of a cabin boy—the three rebels made their way back to the beach at San Giuseppe near Livorno, where they met up with the rest of their party, which included Bourmont and his sons, the comte de Kergorlay and his son, Saint-Priest, and several other young French officers. They arrived before the ship was ready to lift anchor. No matter: the duchess wrapped herself in a heavy coat and tried to get some sleep on the beach. They woke her at 3 a.m. Under the cover of moonlight, the band stepped onto a small fisherman's boat and rowed silently out to sea to board the *Carlo Alberto*. The water was calm. The duchess said one final good-bye to Mme de Saint-Priest, who remained on shore, assuring her that the wind was blowing in the right direction and that God was on their side.[19]

The subterfuges employed by the duchess did not prevent her movements from being observed by the various spies sent to watch her. As she set out to sea, confident that she would surprise the world with her landing in Marseille, the Austrian Chancellor Klemens von Metternich noted in his journal, "The duchesse de Berry has left Massa. It seems she is headed to France with a considerable party and that her enterprise rests on solid foundations. It is possible that in a few days all of France will be up in arms." Nor was Metternich the only well-informed world leader. The French minister of the interior,

Camille de Montalivet, likewise cabled to the minister of the navy to announce that the *Carlo Alberto* had left Italy, officially bound for Barcelona but clearly headed for the coast of Provence: "We are threatened with a Carlist insurrection. The steamboat of the duchesse de Berry is expected at Marseille. Our sources say that she is aboard." The duchess had fooled nobody.

Montalivet gave the navy instructions to board the *Carlo Alberto*, arrest the duchess, and bring her to the port of Ajaccio in Corsica, whence she would be deported immediately to Scotland to join the rest of the Bourbons in exile. If this operation was carried out successfully, it might save the government the political difficulties—and negative publicity—involved in bringing the duchess to trial: once she touched French territory, she would be in violation of the edict forbidding members of the former Bourbon (or Bonaparte) royal families from entering France, and a trial would be unavoidable. Montalivet added that the navy should "have for Mme la duchesse de Berry all the consideration due to a person of her sex."[20]

After a few days plying the Tyrrhenian Sea, the crew realized that they lacked the necessary coal supplies to make it all the way to Marseille, so they stopped on April 27 to refuel in Nice, still a part of the kingdom of Piedmont-Sardinia. A description of the *Carlo Alberto* had now been made known to French officers in various ports. It was painted black, with a red stripe and a gold decoration on the stern, a coat of arms bearing a cross and topped by a crown. The interior was adorned with fleurs de lis, symbol of the French monarchy. Such a ship was not exactly camouflaged. Nevertheless, the French consul in Nice failed to signal its presence in the harbor to the authorities, and the *Carlo Alberto* resumed its journey.[21]

On the night of April 30 the sailors aboard the ship could see the lights of Marseille flickering in the distance. Not daring to approach any closer, they waited until a fishing boat, which had been dispatched to bring them ashore, made itself visible. The sea was extremely choppy, and the rebels had difficulty entering the smaller craft, which kept knocking violently against the side of the *Carlo Alberto*. As Mesnard would later remember, "The unfortunate boat did not have high enough sides to save Madame from the vi-olence of the waves, which drenched her, drenched all of us, in a continual torrent."[22]

Once ashore, the duchess and her companions had to climb a rocky path into the mountains in order to arrive at the refuge that des Cars had arranged for them. Her dress still sopping, the duchess followed close behind the guide during the perilous nocturnal hike through the woods, which lasted three hours. According to Mesnard, "There was a glacial wind and Madame must have suffered greatly, but not one complaint escaped from her." Finally, they reached a small hunting lodge. A messenger left immediately to inform des Cars that the duchess had arrived and that the insurrection could proceed as planned. He sent back a message: "Congratulations on the safe arrival. The Marseille uprising will take place tomorrow."[23]

Once she had dried herself, the duchess found the hunting lodge to her liking. Mesnard writes that "the humble abode pleased her more than the palace she inhabited in Massa, French soil being her dearest and almost her true homeland." As they settled in to wait for news of the uprising, they imagined that one victory would lead to another and that the army would rally to them as it had to Napoleon during the Hundred Days. At one point that morning, they saw the white flag of the Bourbons flying from the tower of the Church of Saint-Laurent. The kingdom, they thought, would soon be theirs.[24]

Then, around one in the afternoon, the duchess received a terse message from des Cars: "The movement has failed. You must leave France."

Everything, it seems, had gone wrong. The plan had been for the Marseille legitimists to assemble on the esplanade de la Tourette, overlooking the sea, at 4 a.m. They would ring the bell at the Church of Saint-Laurent as a sign that the revolt had begun, and crowds would join in the demonstration. But des Cars had been so careful to keep the operation a secret until the very last minute that word had not gotten out. They were expecting hundreds, but only about sixty legitimists showed up. As Mesnard would later lament, it was per-haps not very wise to stage an insurrection in the middle of the night, at a time when everyone was home asleep except for soldiers on patrol. To compound the ineptitude, when the legitimists arrived at the Church of Saint-Laurent, nobody could find the key to the belfry. Day had broken before they rang the bell and raised the white flag, by which time most people thought that the insurrection had been called off. Hoping to stir up enthusiasm, the rebels then marched through the Saint-Jean neighborhood of the city chanting, "Long live Henry V! Long live Religion! Long live the White Flag! Long live the Cross!" But by that point, the fishermen had all gone out to sea. Instead of taking to the streets, shopkeepers closed their boutiques and stayed inside until the disturbance ended.[25]

The duc des Cars tried to rally the remaining legitimists. But he was disguised as a peasant and had difficulty convincing the demonstrators that he was their leader. Eventually, around 8 a.m., des Cars managed to direct a small group of men to march on the Palais de Justice, where a division of the 13th Army Regiment was stationed. After a short fight, government troops subdued the legitimist rebels. Some men were arrested, but des Cars managed to escape and send his panicked message to the duchess. Several more small skirmishes took place at different locations in Marseille over the course of the morning. By 11 a.m., however, the army had restored calm. The tricolor flag replaced the white banner of the Bourbons on the tower of Saint-Laurent. The legitimists had just let their best chance of igniting a civil war slip away. "Never was so much devotion so poorly directed," commented a dejected Mesnard.[26]

According to Mesnard, when the duchess received the message from des Cars telling her to leave France, all the blood drained from her face. Without pausing to question the messenger, she turned to her coconspirators and declared, "Leave France! That remains to be seen. . . . But we must leave here without delay."[27]

The duchess now faced a moment of truth. The uprising she had counted on to launch her campaign had fizzled and with it the illusion that all of France would rally to her side. She had now officially become an outlaw: her presence in France risked sending her to jail or to the scaffold. Government agents had already begun to scour the countryside in the effort to arrest her, but she quickly determined she could not go back the way she came: the *Carlo Alberto* had already left the harbor. Her thoughts immediately turned to the region of the Vendée.

WHEN THE BOURBONS went into exile in July 1830, the Vendée had been ready to take up arms. Memories of the province's heroic and bloody resistance to the French Revolution were still fresh forty years later, even if some of the social factors that had led to the first Vendéen insurrection had dissipated. The transfer of land confiscated from nobles and the church to the rising middle class, along with the subsequent development of the local economy, had expanded the ranks of bourgeois liberals sympathetic to the July Monarchy, especially in urban centers such as Nantes. And priests no longer exerted the same level of ideological influence in an age of secularism and scientific progress. Nevertheless, there remained a core group of nobles and peasants fiercely loyal to the Bourbons and opposed to what they saw as a never-ending cycle of revolutionary upheaval.

Moreover, the July Monarchy's actions had roused a great deal of anger in western France. Knowing that the Vendée contained many Bourbon loyalists, Louis-Philippe had sent thousands of soldiers to the region, treating it almost as a conquered land. Not long after the July Revolution, the government ordered a general disarmament of the province and began raiding private homes to confiscate weapons. Veterans of the counterrevolutionary struggle were outraged to see their vintage shotguns from 1793—which had become trophies and precious family heirlooms—ripped from their place of honor on the wall over the fireplace. "Henceforth their tears were criminalized," wrote one legitimist historian, "their complaints were rendered seditious, and since they were sure to be arrested anyway, they left to join the neighboring band [of partisans]."[28]

Over the course of 1831, as the former royal family settled into their exile at Holyrood and the duchess took the waters in Bath, the legitimists began preparing for civil war. They divided France into military zones: the maréchal de Bourmont would command the Vendée while the duc de Bellune would take charge of the forces in the Midi. However, when the duchess left England for Italy instead of heading directly to France, enthusiasm for her enterprise began to wane. At a meeting of the Vendée's legitimist military leaders at the château of La Fetellière, held in September 1831, the most bellicose members of the assembly were outnumbered by more-prudent local leaders. The majority voted that they would take up arms if—and only if—the duchess had first staged a successful insurrection in the Midi. The critics of this wait-and-see approach would label the fair-weather partisans *pancaliers*, after a kind of local cabbage with abundant outer leaves but no heart.[29]

The La Fetellière resolution had been one of the prime reasons that the duchess decided to launch her campaign in Marseille. But now that the Midi uprising had failed, would the Vendée come to her aid? Could she count on the pancaliers in spite of their resolution? To do so meant taking an enormous leap of faith. It meant trusting that devotion to the Bourbons would trump prudence for these Vendéen nobles and their peasant armies. It meant wagering that the pancaliers had stout hearts after all.

Yet the Vendée had repeatedly proven its devotion to the Bourbons over the years. The province's leaders had specifically promised to come to her aid in the event of another revolution: "But if ever an abhorrent sect / Were again to break the sceptre of our kings, / Ah! Remember us, return to the Vendée / Bring Henri, we will defend his rights." All the duchess had to do was show herself to the population and, she was convinced, forty thousand men would take up arms.[30]

The duchess turned to her companions in the hunting lodge, whose faces no doubt registered desperation and a good bit of fear, and announced her decision: they would go to the Vendée.[31]

CHAPTER 8

Civil War

THE DUCHESS LEFT the hunting lodge that very night, instructing Mesnard to give their host the princely sum of twenty-five gold *louis* coins. The humble gamekeeper tried to refuse the money but eventually acquiesced and wept in gratitude as the mother of his king ventured into the night. The route out of Marseille presented even more dangers than the journey in, now that government agents were on the lookout for the duchess. Accompanied by Mesnard and Bourmont, she marched in the dark through the mountains, skirting rock faces and covering her tracks as she went. After five grueling hours, the band reached a tiny shepherd's hut and built a fire with brush from the mountainside. "Madame was broken with exhaustion," Mesnard tells us. Wrapped in a coat on the ground, she fell into a deep sleep. The next morning, they continued the perilous journey to the Vendée. The duchess refused a last appeal to save herself by slipping quietly out of the country. "I have burned my ships, gentlemen," she said with resolve. "I am in France and they won't get rid of me so easily."[1]

Over the course of the next month, the duchess made her way across the south and up the west coast of France, donning a series of outlandish disguises and sleeping in barns and haylofts on her way to fight a civil war against almost impossible odds. Some would accuse her of being a "high-class adventuress" and of having read one too many Walter Scott novels. But it was the very impracticality of her enterprise that constituted its appeal for the many young men who fought for her. According to the comtesse Dash, a novelist and memoirist from the period, most of the duchess's followers were probably more than a little in love with her: "She was admirable during that war. She radicalized all who approached her."[2]

In addition to seducing a generation of young nobles, the duchess's adventure in the Vendée would nourish the right-wing imagination in France for more than a century. All the worshipful biographies of the duchess give pride of place to her actions during the month of May 1832—to the journey to the Vendée and the war she fought there. Every act of self-sacrifice, every mark of courage, fueled the duchess's legend, her reputation as the royal who opposed the modernizing forces that were transforming France. In contrast to the petty calculations of a capitalist age, the duchess represented the traditional values of honor, devotion, generosity, and the *beau geste:* the glorious but futile act that is the hallmark of nobility. To follow the duchess to the Vendée is to witness the forging of a myth.

EVEN UNDER THE best of circumstances, traveling across France in 1832 was no easy feat. France's first railway line had opened that very year, but it stretched only a short distance, and horses pulled the cars at the agonizing pace of three miles per hour. Steamboats had begun to ply the nation's navigable rivers, but the duchess, perhaps the most recognizable woman in France thanks to the many portraits of her in circulation, could not risk so public a conveyance. She thus resorted to less modern means of transport: coaches, horseback, and sometimes walking, on poorly maintained roads, over more than five hundred miles.

On the first night of the journey, she sought refuge not with a devoted legitimist sympathizer but with a republican. Two versions of this surprising episode exist. According to Mesnard, she intended to spend the night at the manor house of a certain M. de Bonreceuil, a legitimist, but when he wasn't home, she asked for hospitality from his brother, a republican who lived nearby. Her companions advised her against it, but she simply asked whether the brother was an honest man. Told that he was, she had no qualms. "Let us go to him," she said. "I will tell him who I am and I am sure he will not betray me." When the republican Bonrecueil—whose name sounds very similar to *bon accueil*, meaning "good welcome"—learned that his guest was on the run from the government, he treated her with the utmost respect despite their differences of opinion. According to Mesnard, "Never was more useful or more loyal hospitality offered to the princess."[3]

In Dermoncourt's version the guide leading the duchess out of Marseille got lost. Seeing a house in the distance, the duchess learned that it belonged to the mayor of a nearby town, "a ferocious republican." At that point, she decided to separate from her companions to protect them, telling Mesnard to meet her in Montepellier and Bourmont in Nantes. Arriving with her guide at the home of the republican mayor, she announced plainly, "I am the duchesse de Berry and I seek asylum." When the mayor immediately agreed, she then asked for help procuring a passport before proceeding to bed. "Now, Monsieur," she said, "you will see how easily the duchesse de Berry sleeps under the roof of a republican."[4]

Like the parallel but different versions of Jesus's life contained in the gospels, these conflicting accounts from the time would not have caused true believers to doubt. On the contrary, to her supporters the variations enhanced the duchess's aura of divinity by showing it to transcend the contingency of events. The differing versions revealed how her fundamental essence remained the same even when facts and details of the situation changed. And both stories depict the duchess in a world in which honest people treat one another with generosity. It is clear from the tone of surprise that greets the duchess's decision to place herself at the mercy of the republican that the trust she both expects and extends is an anomaly in the world of July Monarchy France. By depicting her trusting nature, these accounts forge the image of a woman in revolt against modernity. They also serve a distinct political purpose by underlining the common value of honor linking legitimists and republicans, a key element of Bourbon propaganda at a time when the duchess was hoping to rally all enemies of Louis-Philippe to her cause, even those on the Left.

Although different accounts of the duchess's journey have her gracing almost every château between Marseille and Nantes with her presence—a bit like legends claiming "George Washington slept here" that developed after the American Revolution—it is nevertheless possible to establish her itinerary with a reasonable degree of certainty. On the night of May 3 the vicomte Alban de Villeneuve-Bargemon, a member of one of Provence's most important noble families and a former prefect who had resigned his post rather than swear loyalty to the July Monarchy, met her and Mesnard near the village of Lambesc with a carriage hitched to strong post-horses. The duchess decided that Bourmont would travel separately and meet them in Nantes so as not to "put all our eggs in one basket." Villeneuve had obtained passports for the group. Enveloped in a blue-and-black striped cloak, with a straw hat covering her signature blonde hair, the duchess assumed the identity of Villeneuve's wife. Mesnard played the role of her father, and the marquis de Lorges, their other travel companion, pretended to be the coachman. Although in constant fear of police patrols, the group traveled without alerting suspicion through the towns of Nîmes and Montpellier (May 4), Béziers and Narbonne (May 5), and Canson (May 6). According to Mesnard, they received reports along the way that the Vendée was full of government soldiers, but the duchess "was firmly resolved to brave everything." On May 7 they reached Plassac in the Southwest, where the duchess and Mesnard remained until May 16.[5]

If the police did not recognize the fugitive duchess, it was in part because they thought she had already been found. To the great amusement of the outlaws, the press announced her capture aboard the *Carlo*

Alberto. On May 8 the front page of *Le Moniteur universel*, the regime's official newspaper, reported that the naval ship *Le Sphinx* had accosted the *Carlo Alberto* in the harbor of Le Ciotat, near Marseille, on May 4. Government agents boarded the vessel, where they discovered a small woman hiding in a well-appointed stateroom. "Everything would seem to confirm that this is . . . the duchesse de Berry," the article declared, assuring the French public that the outlaw would be swiftly deported to Holyrood in Scotland, where she could reflect at her leisure and "in the bosom of her family upon the powerlessness of her party." In reality, the woman the government took for the duchess was none other than Mathilde Lebeschu, her lady-in-waiting, who imitated her mistress to perfection. (Mlle Lebeschu did not fool everyone, however. In her memoir, the ever-astute comtesse de Boigne says she immediately realized that the reports of the arrest were false because the physical description that they gave of the woman presumed to be the duchess made no reference to a wandering left eye.)[6]

Meanwhile, hiding out at Plassac, the duchess made plans for war. Over the course of the prior year, Bourmont, the commander of her forces in the West, had divided his army into three separate divisions. The comte d'Autichamp, a relic of the first Vendée uprising, had command of the Left Bank of the Loire, which included the region of the Vendée, and General Clouet had command of the Right Bank, which included Brittany. The marquis de Coislin took charge of a third, independent army in the region. On March 28, shortly before she left Massa, the duchess received a long report from d'Autichamp complaining of a lack of men and ammunition in the Vendée, as well as disagreement among the sub-commanders. His best-equipped division was the 3rd Corps, under the command of Charles-Athanase de Charette, the husband of one of the duc de Berry's daughters by Amy Brown. Charette's battalion counted ten thousand men and had a reasonable provision of rifles in working order. The rest of the divisions had only a few thousand men and not enough guns to go around.[7]

Before landing in Marseille, Bourmont had worked out a detailed plan for a coordinated attack throughout the West. On the night before the insurrection was to begin, the various divisional leaders would assemble their men into companies. At dawn, they would surprise the government's forces in all their encampments while also storming police barracks and disarming the National Guard units in the towns. They would seize the government's weapons and declare a general uprising of the local population of peasants. The second phase of the plan involved attacking the cities, including the significant military outposts in Nantes and Angers. D'Autichamp would direct his forces toward the towns of Saumur and La Rochelle, while Clouet concentrated on Brittany's capital, Rennes. They would then meet up with Coislin's army. The third phase of the plan involved putting into place a civil and military authority in the entire region while awaiting fresh shipments of arms from Holland or Portugal. Success depended on executing the plan in complete secrecy and with perfect coordination.[8]

Right from the start, however, the operation was jeopardized by poor communication. Because the duchess had ordered Bourmont to travel separately, she had to set the date for the insurrection to begin without consulting him. On May 15, with the help of Achille Guibourg, a verbally dexterous young lawyer who came to meet the duchess in Plassac, she drafted an order to take up arms in the early morning hours of May 24. At the same time, she had a stirring handbill printed and distributed in hundreds of copies throughout western France:

Proclamation of Madame, duchesse de Berry, Regent of France

Vendéens! Bretons! All you inhabitants of the loyal provinces of the West;

Having landed in the Midi, I had no fear of crossing France, amid danger, in order to fulfill a sacred promise: to join my brave friends and share their perils and their labors.

I am finally among this heroic people. Open yourselves to France's fortune; I place myself at your head, sure to vanquish with such men.

Henri V calls you; his mother, regent of France, devotes herself to your happiness; one day Henri V will be our brother-in-arms should the enemy ever threaten our loyal lands.

Let us repeat our cry both ancient and new:

Long live the king! Long live Henry V!

—Marie-Caroline

Her order to take up arms on May 24 caught her commanders by surprise: on the very day it was issued, d'Autichamp, Clouet, and Coislin together sent the duchess a letter imploring her to avoid undue haste and to wait until they had determined the readiness of the troops. The decision by the local chiefs made at La Fetellière the prior year had specifically stated that the West would take up arms only following a successful insurrection in the South, so the commanders worried that they would refuse to fight because the Marseille uprising had failed. When d'Autichamp received the duchess's order and realized that their letters had crossed, he resigned himself to the inevitable. "Madame has pronounced and I obey," he wrote in his return dispatch.[9]

Having made the fateful decision to begin the insurrection, the duchess and Mesnard now headed toward the battlefield, entering the territory of the Vendée on May 17. The voyagers were met by Charette, who led them to the château de La Preuille, a manor house on the road to Nantes near the town of Montaigu. To fool the government patrols, the party pretended to be British tourists; the duchess made a show of chatting in an approximate English mixed with heavy doses of Italian.

When they arrived at La Preuille, she undertook an even more dramatic self-transformation. Donning a black jacket adorned with metal buttons, a yellow vest, a peasant's shirt, and blue trousers made of the dense, heavily woven fabric known as *coutil*, she added a brown wig under a wool cap and blackened her eyebrows with charcoal. She assumed the identity of a Vendéen peasant boy and christened herself Petit-Pierre. She would remain in this disguise for the rest of the war. Only the ribbons on her dainty shoes—her feet were too small for men's boots and too delicate for anything but the most supple Moroccan leather—betrayed her true identity.[10]

This disguise was a bold move for a number of reasons. For one, it was technically illegal: a law of 1800 required French women to obtain a permit in order to wear men's clothing (although because the duchess was already an outlaw, committing this additional infraction could hardly have mattered to her). More significantly, cross-dressing was the kind of boundary-pushing gesture normally associated with women on the Left, such as the writer George Sand, who in the 1830s went around Paris dressed in men's trousers while writing novels that criticized patriarchal social structures. The duchess's politics could not have been more different from Sand's; the duchess was thumbing her nose at bourgeois standards of morality, but she did not seek to change traditional power relations in society. The duchess was merely claiming her prerogative as an exceptional being, as certain aristocratic women had done for centuries.

The duchess clearly delighted in her cross-dressing—in later years she would often sign her letters "Petit-Pierre" when reminiscing about her adventure in the Vendée. And the French public delighted in it as well. Because it symbolized the duchess's audacity, the Petit-Pierre disguise would live on in the right-wing imagination as the very embodiment of her ill-fated enterprise: "Too bad for those who would mock him!" wrote one author as late as 1946. "This little man, this Petit-Pierre, this Vendéen boy, is a heroic being . . . and should he fall, bringing down with him the old and tired body of the monarchy, it is because destiny could do no more."[11]

THE CRITICAL PHASE of the insurrection had now begun. In an effort to evade police patrols, the duchess started sleeping at a different hideout almost every night, often trekking through the woods for miles from one safe house to another. Crossing a river in the dark on the way to one of these redoubts, the duchess slipped and was plucked from the rushing water by Charette. The Petit-Pierre costume offered a distinct advantage on these journeys, as it was infinitely easier to walk in pants than in a long dress and petticoats.

At 3 a.m. on the night of May 18, shortly after she arrived weary, wet, and exhausted at Bellecour, the property of a legitimist gentleman, the duchess received the letter from the marquis de Coislin and the other military leaders. The commander of one of the three divisions of the legitimist army, Coislin had sent the duchess a plea to launch the insurrection while she was still in Massa. Now that she was in the Vendée, however, he saw things differently. "Armaments are hardly what they should be to conduct this war advantageously. . . . We lack gunpowder even more than rifles," Coislin and the other leaders warned. They begged the duchess to cancel her call to arms: "The day will perhaps come, if we have the patience to wait for it, when France can do everything on its own without help from abroad, which no doubt would be much better; but this day has not yet arrived." They concluded that she should wait either for a foreign invasion or a revolution in Paris to launch her insurrection. And they added this dire prognostication: "Taking up arms . . . in our current position, will inevitably lead to . . . the complete destruction of the royalist party."[12]

The duchess read this missive calmly, then sat down at her writing table and drafted the following scornful response:

I have reason to be aggrieved by the provisions contained in the note you sent me. You will remember, *Monsieur*, the contents of your [prior] dispatches; it was they, along with a sense of devotion that I consider sacred, which convinced me to entrust myself to the renowned loyalty of these provinces. If I gave the order to take up arms on the 24th of this month, it was because I counted on your participation. . . . I would consider my cause as forever lost if I were obliged to flee this land, and I will inevitably be forced to do so if arms are not taken up immediately. I will have no other recourse but to weep far from France for having counted too much on the promises of those for whom I braved everything. . . .

She furthermore declared that the order to take up arms on May 24 would remain in place and insisted Coislin ensure that instructions were given to all the divisional commanders. "Such are my firm desires," she concluded imperiously.[13]

Her disciples would approve her resolve. "If Madame refused to leave France," one right-wing historian at the end of the nineteenth century wrote, "it was because she understood better than all those who sought to give her advice . . . that agreeing to flee meant the ruin not only of her current hopes but those of the future as well." For the legitimist mythmakers, it was the duchess's boldness, her refusal to submit to the banal yoke of practicality, that set her apart from the cautious bourgeois mind-set of her century. "The French love and follow those who are imprudent," the same historian wrote. "Madame in 1830 and 1832 sought to hold fast until the end; it was the men who surrounded her who were not up to the task."[14]

The following evening the duchess received word that one of her couriers, charged with secret documents detailing her whereabouts, had been arrested by government agents. Fearing a raid, she immediately set off in the driving rain with Charette, Mesnard, and a local guide for a different hideout: a farm called La Chaimare, a mile outside the town of Montbert. Arriving after midnight, they were greeted by the farmer, who took the duchess in her Petit-Pierre costume for a young soldier. According to Mesnard's version, the farmer invited the "little gentleman" to take his bed, but the duchess refused. Holding the farmer's thick, coarse hands in her small, soft ones, she replied that she would sleep in the stable. Her companions looked on with admiration as the duchess threw herself onto a bale of straw and settled in for the night. Mesnard regretted not being able to cover her with his cloak: it was soaking wet. After being awakened the next morning at four when the farmer came to milk the cows, the duchess supposedly delighted in the simple black bread and cabbage soup she was offered before continuing on her way, a sign of her "simple" tastes. Even breakfast became part of her legend.

The next day, May 21, while staying at Les Mesliers, an isolated farmhouse, she learned that Bourmont had finally arrived in Nantes after a long journey through the countryside that had given him time to assess the readiness of the troops and reflect on the enterprise they were about to undertake. The maréchal held long discussions with local chiefs, the pancaliers who had voted to fight only following success in the Midi. They painted a grim portrait of their military prospects. Moreover, on May 22 the lawyer Pierre-Antoine Berryer arrived in Nantes bearing a letter composed by Chateaubriand on behalf of the duchess's "secret committee" in Paris advising against the insurrection. Recognizing how little chance they had of success and realizing that the July Monarchy was growing less popular by the day, the committee delegated Berryer to use his powers of persuasion to convince the duchess to postpone the war. Swayed by their pessimism, Bourmont made the fateful decision, without consulting the duchess, to issue a counterorder calling off the uprising.

Berryer now traveled to the farmhouse to deliver the letter and the news of the counterorder to the duchess in person. She received him dressed as Petit-Pierre, sitting on a rustic wooden bed and wrapped in a tartan plaid blanket. The irony of Berryer being the one to deliver such a message was not lost on the duchess, who remembered all too well how eagerly he had urged her to set sail from Massa just a few months before. "My friends in Paris cannot really know the state of this country," she objected when he presented the letter. "Believe me, monsieur Berryer, one cannot judge the chances for an uprising from 100 miles away."

Berryer spoke to her of all the difficulties she faced and presented the counterorder as a chance for her to slip out of France without compromising her associates any further or putting lives at risk. Worn down by his arguments and exhausted by her incessant nighttime peregrinations, the duchess had a moment of weakness—and in a sudden about-face, she agreed to leave France with a false passport supplied by Berryer. Ruefully, she spoke of taking her son to the mountains of Calabria, far away from those who sought to manipulate him for their political advantage or betray him out of weakness or greed. On his way out of the farmhouse, Berryer expressed his admiration for the duchess to Charette: "That princess has the head and heart of ten kings!"

The next day the duchess changed her mind.

After dispatching the counterorder to all the divisional chiefs, Charette headed to the next safe house, where he was to meet Berryer and the duchess. They were all to take separate routes: Berryer, who had a valid passport, traveling on the main road, and Charette and the duchess taking longer, less public routes. When the duchess did not arrive by late afternoon, Charette began to grow concerned. At 6 p.m. a peasant arrived bearing a letter from the duchess:

> My dear Charette,
>
> I will remain among you. I am writing to Berryer to express my determination. . . . I will remain because my presence has already compromised a great number of my devoted servants; it would be cowardice on my part to abandon them now. Moreover, I hope that, despite the unfortunate counterorder, God will grant us victory.
>
>   Farewell, my dear friend. Do not give your resignation because Petit-Pierre does not give his.
>
> —Marie-Caroline

Berryer and Charette were mute with shock as they read the letter. They knew they would have to carry out an insurrection that would not end well, especially since the counterorder had now gone out telling their troops the uprising had been postponed. But as devoted legitimists, who believed above all in the authority of the duchess as regent for her son, the two men had no other choice but to obey her command to fight.[15]

For the duchess and her followers, the meaning of legitimacy lay here, in the elevation of duty over self-interest. This was the very opposite of the spirit of modern capitalism that had begun to take hold in France. It was the opposite of the ethos epitomized by

Louis-Philippe, the "bourgeois king," and by his business-oriented ministers. The devotion to duty also lay at the heart of the duchess's decision to stay and fight: she claimed she did it for the sake of those who had compromised themselves for her cause. Later legitimist historians made this sense of duty the centerpiece of the myth they constructed around the duchess's image: "True daughter of a long line of kings . . . she bore within her the honor of her race which she wanted to transmit without stain or the trace of cowardice." It was not that the duchess did not understand the implications of her decision or that she overestimated her odds of success. She saw the difficulties she faced and chose to stay and fight despite them. According to legitimist historians, "These complications left her not indifferent, but calm." They displayed the true nature of her nobility.[16]

The duchess's decision to persevere in the Vendée was not entirely disinterested or delusional, however. From her incessant communications with her advisers in Paris, she knew that the republicans were planning an insurrection in the capital—the revolt that eventually broke out after Lamarque's funeral on June 5, the one described in Victor Hugo's *Les Misérables*—and she thought that the government would have a difficult time fighting on two fronts at once. She also realized that many in the Vendée had already compromised themselves legally in planning for her insurrection. The only way to save them now was through victory. This time, in consultation with Bourmont, she chose a new date for the uprising to begin: June 4. "God will help us to save our fatherland. No danger, no fatigue will discourage me," the duchess wrote in her official order declaring the revised call to arms. D'Autichamp and the other commanders immediately disseminated this new plan to their lieutenants in the field.[17]

But with so many contradictory instructions, the various brigades of legitimist fighters did not know what to think. "Order, counter-order, disorder" is a familiar military maxim, as one historian of the episode would aptly note. The situation was complicated by poor lines of communication and by the elaborate lengths that the duchess and her advisers went to in order to maintain secrecy and evade government spies: letters written in invisible ink and in a complicated code, carried by horseback. Many of them did not reach their destination. Some in the field never got the original counterorder and showed up to fight at dawn on May 24. Some commanders received the counterorder but not in time to inform their men, so they decided to proceed with the original plan. Chaos reigned.[18]

On the night of May 23, in the countryside of the Deux-Sèvres region, the legitimists hid white flags on which had been written *"Vive Henry V!"* Unaware of the counterorder, a band of the duchess's partisans encountered a detachment of the government's 64th Company and opened fire, forcing the Philippistes to retreat. Meanwhile, near the town of Bréal, the commander of a legitimist division did not receive the counterorder until his men had already assembled. He decided to hide them in the woods and succeeded in surprising a detachment of government troops. Attacking with bayonets, he was on the verge of winning the battle when two other government detachments arrived to reinforce their colleagues. The legitimist commander gave the order to disband. Some of his soldiers managed to get away, but many others were wounded or arrested.[19]

This spurt of guerrilla warfare alerted the government that a large insurrection was in the works. It also dispelled any lingering doubts that the duchess had made her way to the West. After realizing that they had captured the wrong woman aboard the *Carlo Alberto*, Louis-Philippe and his ministers at first thought the duchess had escaped to Spain, but they now realized that she remained in France. On June 2, 1832, the comte de Montalivet, the minister of the interior, telegraphed to his prefect in the West that "I have every reason to believe that the duchesse de Berry is in the Vendée. . . . She changes locations every day." Dermoncourt, the general in charge of the operation to put down the legitimist uprising, redoubled his efforts to hunt out the fugitive princess. Guessing that she intended to escape to England on a ship departing from one of the region's ports—which was, in fact, Berryer's plan for her—the minister of the navy increased surveillance along the western coast.[20]

The government also gained material proof of her presence during a raid on the château of La Charlière on May 27. Dermoncourt suspected the owner of the château, a colonel, of being one of the duchess's "most ardent and most devoted chiefs" and his château of being a center of legitimist operations. After searching the house and discovering the old colonel hiding in a closet clutching a pistol, the government agents made their way to the wine cellar, where they found dozens of empty bottles filled with paper. They had uncovered a secret cache of all the military plans for the insurrection. As one contemporary observer pointed out, the duchess should have known better than to hide her secrets in the wine cellar: it is the first place that thirsty soldiers would look.[21]

After learning of the raid, the duchess considered giving yet another counterorder to call off the uprising because the plans for the June 4 insurrection had been compromised, but she realized the impossibility of getting word out in time. The insurrection would proceed as scheduled even though the enemy was now expecting it. She spent the last days of May and the beginning of June moving incessantly through the countryside, meeting with various military commanders. Peasants would follow her to cover her tracks, for the duchess's feet were so small that the government's agents might be able to detect her whereabouts from the impression left by her tiny boots on the ground.[22]

At dawn on June 4, Dermoncourt received word that crowds of legitimist peasants had appeared near the towns of Louroux, Vallet, and Vertou. Bells rang out to signal the start of the uprising. At Saint-Philibert, 400 men marched under the command of the legitimist leader La Robrie. At Machecoul, 250 legitimists prepared for battle; at Montbert, 64 nobles assembled, joined by hundreds of peasants from the surrounding countryside. At Maisdon, 400 peasants and about 40 nobles attempted a surprise attack but were overcome by the government's 29th Company. Charette was chagrined when he learned of the defeat. The uprising at Maisdon was not supposed to happen until the following day; there had been another miscommunication. Further defeats followed for the legitimists. Overcoming a fever, Charette did his best to hold the line against the Philippistes but found his army outnumbered and outgunned on all fronts. Eventually, he signaled his troops to disband in order to avoid getting taken prisoner. "In the end valor gave way before the sustained and constantly replenished enemy fire," wrote Bertier.[23]

Over the course of the next few weeks, however, the legitimists managed to score several victories against the government's superior forces. One of the most sustained battles took place at Le Chêne-en-Vieillevigne. Charette, who left a detailed account of the battle in his journal, commanded the Nantaise company of legitimists. They took up a position behind a hedge overlooking a stream in the small village and waited for the arrival of the government's troops. At one point, an old man came running and said that the Philippistes were only a few minutes away. Wary of false messengers, Charette gave orders to shoot the man if the government's soldiers did not arrive. Offended, the old man said he had fought with Charette's uncle during the first war in the Vendée in 1793. At that moment, a column of Philippistes appeared, composed of two companies of the 44th Regiment of the line infantry and a detachment of National Guard troops. Charette had given orders not to shoot until the full army was in view, but the legitimists opened fire prematurely. Shooting lasted for a half hour without either side overtaking the other. Finally, Charette heroically decided to lead a charge. At the sound of his *"En avant!"* ("Forward!"), the legitimists attacked, hurling themselves across the stream with their guns carried over their heads in both hands. Terrified, the government soldiers broke ranks and fled, leaving the ground littered with the bodies of their dead and wounded.[24]

A report of the battle, written in invisible ink and found among the papers of the duchess after her capture, noted, "We only had two men killed, but a large number of wounded; the enemy must have lost forty men." In the margin, the duchess commented, "Anyone familiar with the adroit shooting of the Vendéens will not be surprised by that difference." The report went on to praise the duchess, "who gives the example of every kind of courage," beside which the duchess wrote that she herself was present at the battle and applied the first bandages to the wounded Vendéens. In a letter to Charette, she wrote, "My one regret is not having fought at Le Chêne. If I had been killed, it would have been with the assurance that you would avenge me, and I assure you that I am not one to retreat before danger." She signed the letter Petit-Pierre.[25]

Although the battle of Le Chêne represented the legitimists' biggest victory during the campaign, it was the heroic defeat at La Pénissière that became a symbol of their bravery in the face of impossible odds. On June 6 a group of forty-five legitimists, almost all young nobles from the surrounding region, convened at the château of La Pénissière, a mile from the town of Clisson. Led by two brothers, their plan was to attack a National Guard post nearby. However, the staff sergeant of the government's 29th Regiment got wind of the meeting and decided to surprise the legitimists. He was joined by several other detachments of government troops, and they greatly outnumbered the Vendéens. After firing a few shots, the legitimists retreated to the château and set up defensive positions, managing to repel several assaults by the Philippistes amid shouts of *"Vive Henry V!"*

After several hours of fighting, one of the government soldiers climbed a ladder and set fire to the attic of the château. As the smoke rose from the roof, the legitimists kept shooting. Next the government troops set the first floor ablaze, sending the legitimists hurrying up the staircase and pinning them between two layers of flames. Realizing they could not hold out much longer, the legitimists decided to make a break and delegated eight brave men to stay behind to offer fire cover while their comrades escaped out the back. The two brothers in charge said farewell, as one prepared to stay behind. Two of the legitimists were killed by musket fire, but the others managed to escape.

The situation of the eight who remained inside soon became critical. With the entire château about to collapse in a pile of flames, and smoke so thick that they could barely see or breathe, the final eight vowed to hold out until the last possible moment. Crouching in an enclosure, they continued shooting until they heard the roof collapse through the floor, sending flames darting everywhere. The legitimists thought that their enemies had been killed in the explosion and stopped shooting. This mistake saved them. When the government soldiers did not hear gunfire, they assumed in turn that their enemies had been crushed. This allowed the eight legitimist heroes to quietly make their way out the back, "gliding like shadows" along the garden wall and into the night. Dermoncourt, helped by Dumas, paints the scene after the battle ended in poetic terms: "There remained of this theater of combat, which had been so noisy and animated shortly before, only red and smouldering ruins, extinguishing themselves in silence, around which were strewn a few cadavers lit up by the last glimmers of the blaze."[26]

The battle at La Pénissière took place at the exact same time that the republicans staged their uprising in Paris during the funeral of General Lamarque. The day before, June 5, republican leaders had sent a delegation to the legitimists seeking their support. The duchess's "secret committee" debated whether to help their opponents on the Left bring down the government but ultimately decided against it. This was a strategic error: a successful republican revolution in Paris would surely have aided the legitimist cause. With Louis-Philippe out, the duchess would not have encountered resistance in the Vendée and might have pulled off her insurrection. Fresh from a victory in the West, she then might have been able to persuade the rest of the country to opt for the stability of the Bourbon monarchy instead of the chaos of another republic. For the duchess's myth-makers, this was yet another moment in which she was betrayed by the men advising her.[27]

Was the duchess wrong to have tried her chances in the Vendée? Should she have slipped out of the country after the defeat in Marseille? Or should she never have come to begin with? Just how "crazy" was her *folle équipée*, her crazy escapade? Many of her contemporaries, even those who disagreed with her politics, did not consider her plans for civil war so far-fetched. In his analysis of the events of 1832, the left-wing politician and historian Louis Blanc declared that all things considered, an insurrection in the Vendée was still possible when the duchess began the campaign. Surely, her plan was no crazier than Napoleon's decision to return from the island of Elba in the hope that the army would rally to him. If she had the success he did, subsequent historians would consider her a military and political genius.[28]

To her supporters, however, it was not the feasibility of her enterprise that mattered; it was the audacity. "Yes, there is courage at the heart of Madame's endeavor, whatever one thinks of it politically," wrote the right-wing journalist Alfred Nettement in *La Quotidienne* on May 9, 1832, after her uprising in Marseille had failed and she was secretly making her way to the Vendée. "It is this courage that seduces and subjugates French hearts." And he continued: "If the duchesse de Berry . . . is guilty of audacity, of fearlessness, of temerity, these are crimes that will find a great many accomplices in this heroic land." For the right-wing imagination, the duchess offered an idealized vision of a chivalric past that still resonated loudly, even in the debased world of July Monarchy France.[29]

On June 16 the duchess made the decision to go into hiding in the Breton city of Nantes, just north of the Vendée. With the war going badly, she needed time to weigh her options, perhaps finally to obtain aid from abroad. As she made her way into the western capital, she was accompanied by a lady-in-waiting, Eulalie de Kersabiec, whose father and brother had fought in the war. During the weeks of the campaign the duchess jokingly referred to Eulalie as Petit-Paul, the companion to Petit-Pierre. But now the duchess shed her masculine disguise and donned the garb of a peasant woman for the several-mile hike to Nantes. Unable to walk in the heavy shoes and coarse woolen stockings of her disguise, she removed them by the side of the road and decided to walk barefoot instead. When she realized that her legs and feet were too white for those of a peasant woman, she rubbed mud on them and continued on her way.[30]

In one of the most famous stories of the duchess's adventure, as they entered Nantes the duchess was approached by a real peasant woman heading to market. The old woman needed help lifting her heavy basket onto her head and offered the duchess and Eulalie an apple each if they would aid her. The mission accomplished, the woman set off on her way when the duchess stopped her and said, "Wait a minute, mother! What about my apple?" (*Dites-donc la mère! Et ma pomme!*) Starving after the long walk, the duchess devoured the fruit. Dermoncourt and others pause in retelling this story to marvel that the daughter and daughter-in-law of kings, whose feet were accustomed to the plushest Persian carpets and whose mouth had savored the richest delicacies, was now walking barefoot and eating apples by the side of the road. But the real purpose of the story is to highlight the eagerness with which the duchess embraced her new role: she had now truly become the "people's princess."

Once in Nantes, the band saw a poster declaring, in large block letters, "State of Siege." The duchess paused to peruse the document, which described the curfew put in place on June 3, and gave a description of the duchess to aid in her capture. "Age: 35 years—Height: 4 foot, 7 inches—Eyes: light blue, slightly misaligned and shifty." Mlle de Kersabiec pulled her away from the poster in alarm. They must not forget their disguise: a peasant woman would not know how to read.[31]

After they passed the Castle of the Dukes of Brittany, which looms over the banks of the Loire, they took the small street leading from the castle to the Cathedral of St. Pierre and St. Paul: the rue Haute-du-Château. They entered no. 8, the home of the Kersabiecs, without being seen. There they were led through a series of interior courtyards to a small apartment, part of the Psalette, a Gothic house from the fifteenth century belonging to the cathedral, on the deserted impasse Saint-Laurent. The remote apartment had a hidden panel in the duchess's room that would allow her to escape through the tunnels beneath the cathedral in case of a government raid. It was an ideal hiding place. However, the next day a messenger arrived from the cathedral's *curé* saying that she needed to find someplace else to stay; he had heard about the sacking of the Church of St. Germain-L'Auxerrois in Paris and did not want to provoke the wrath of the government or of the local liberals should the duchess be discovered.[32]

That night, the Kersabiecs found a different hiding place for their royal guest: the nearby home of their friends, the Du Guiny sisters, at no. 3, rue Haute-du-Château, just a few steps from the castle. It too had a secret panel and a place for the duchess to escape in case of a raid. She settled in to the attic with the ever-loyal Mesnard, who had arrived separately in Nantes, and a different Kersabiec sister with the unusual name of Stylite, who agreed to serve as her new lady-in-waiting. The sedentary life that was about to be hers constituted a radical change for the duchess, but not an entirely unwelcome one. After six weeks of constant motion and stress, after seeing men die for her cause but having nothing to show for it, the duchess needed rest.

PART FOUR

The Arrest

CHAPTER 9

Hiding

I N EARLY APRIL, Simon Deutz rode out of Massa, headed toward the port of Genoa, some sixty miles up the Ligurian coast. The rabbi's son, the Marais street urchin, the failed printer's apprentice was now Hyacinthe de Gonzague, plenipotentiary representative of the duchesse de Berry, entrusted with top-secret letters to the courts of Spain and Portugal. He would later state that as he boarded a ship bound for Barcelona in the company of a group of Jesuits, he was thinking not about how far he had come but already about betrayal.[1]

In both the testimony he gave immediately after the arrest and in his memoir from 1835, Deutz claimed that when he swore the oath of loyalty to the duchess in the olive grove outside of Massa—an oath that gave her supporters the right to take his life in case of treason—he was hiding a secret plan to turn her in to the government. "In taking this oath," he writes, "I was already thinking of how to save my country from the horrors of a civil war and a foreign invasion." By contrast, Morel and Dermoncourt assert that Deutz changed sides only later, once the legitimist insurrection in Marseille had failed and he realized he had more to gain from the July Monarchy government than from going down with the duchess's sinking ship. Although Deutz sought to portray himself as a patriot and as a crafty double agent with the best interests of France at heart, his critics made him out to be a venal traitor who sold out his benefactress when she needed his help the most.[2]

It's impossible to know Deutz's thought processes with certainty. However, we can follow his movements during the spring of 1832, as the duchess fought her civil war and he moved between the capitals of the Iberian peninsula as her emissary. We can chart his letters against events as they unfolded in order to establish a time line for his betrayal. Ultimately, a picture emerges of a man without fixed ties or loyalties, a man whose real secret may have been that he had no secrets, only a constantly shifting set of interests. It was this lack of center that made Deutz such a perfect emblem of the modern world and such an apt symbol for everything the duchess opposed.

As soon as he arrived in Barcelona, Deutz made contact with the small group of French legitimists who were hiding out in the Catalan capital, waiting to cross the border into France at the head of a Spanish army in support of the duchess. While in Barcelona, Deutz received a letter from Charles de Bourmont, one of the sons of the maréchal de Bourmont, whom Deutz had met in Massa and who had accompanied the duchess on the *Carlo Alberto*. The letter described the voyage from Massa and the duchess's secret disembarkation, under the cover of night and amid choppy waters, at the port of Marseille. Charles wrote the letter while waiting for news of the Marseille uprising—he stayed aboard the ship—fully expecting to see the white flag of the Bourbons flying from all the buildings when the *Carlo Alberto* next returned to Marseille. In the meantime he asked Deutz to communicate to Dom Miguel—the King of Portugal, from whom the duchess expected the most aid—the news of her arrival on the shores of France and the successful start of her insurrection. "You are acquainted, sir, with Madame's wishes," the young noble wrote. "It is up to you to make them known and to act according to the circumstances."[3]

Soon after receiving this optimistic letter, Deutz read an account of the failure of the uprising in Marseille. Although the details of the Marseille disaster remained murky, he immediately grasped that the nature of his mission had changed. It was one thing to solicit aid for an enterprise that had shown it could succeed. It was quite another to beg for help for a cause that already seemed lost. According to Dermoncourt, the failure in Marseille provoked in Deutz "some profound reflections during the voyage from Barcelona to Madrid." It was during this voyage, according to Dermoncourt, that Deutz suddenly began to appreciate the virtues of the July Monarchy and to see the legitimists as "enemies of liberty." Yet once he arrived in Madrid, he kept working actively on the duchess's behalf.[4]

His mission involved making contact with Don Carlos, the head of the Spanish apostolic party, which was fighting a political battle against an increasingly powerful liberal faction. In 1832 the Spanish monarchy was at the beginning of a succession crisis. The aged King Ferdinand VII had been persuaded by his third wife, Maria Christina of the Two Sicilies—a half sister of the duchess—to violate Salic law by appointing their infant daughter, Isabella II, as his successor over his brother, Don Carlos, who traditionally would have succeeded him because Ferdinand had no male heir. The archconservative Carlos believed that he was the rightful king and had begun plotting against Maria Christina, who allied with the liberals. The duchess saw Don Carlos and his supporters as her natural allies: they all upheld "legitimate" claims to their respective thrones and supported conservative, Catholic values. Deutz made overtures both to Don Carlos and to other right-wing Catholic intriguers who favored invading France in support of the duchess: the bishop of Léon, the counts of Spain and of Fournas, and Maria Teresa, the wife of Don Carlos, who was a sister of the Portuguese king, Dom Miguel.

The duchess also entrusted Deutz with a letter to her sister, Queen Maria Christina, requesting support for her campaign, which

Deutz—or Hyacinthe de Gonzague—had difficulty delivering. As a liberal sympathizer, the queen was little inclined to receive the odd French emissary with the vaguely Spanish name sent by her reactionary sister. Moreover, Deutz did not exactly possess the bearing of an ambassador, and he did not arrive in Madrid with the kind of retinue that would have made a favorable impression at the Spanish court. Nor did the fact that he was staying in a Jesuit residence further his cause with a queen who was engaged in a battle with the Catholics of the apostolic party. Without refusing him outright, Maria Christina offered an audience at such a far-removed date that Deutz could not take advantage of it.[5]

The fact that Deutz seems to have done his best to fulfill his mission for the duchess would seem to indicate that he had not yet definitively decided to switch sides. But even while cultivating the support of the right-wing Spaniards on the duchess's behalf, he did begin to hedge his bets (in the colorful French expression of Morel, *il se mit à ménager le choux et le chèvre*, which translates literally as "to tend both the cabbage and the goat"). In English we would say that he was attempting to play both sides against the middle.[6]

In his memoir Deutz says that when he learned that the duchess had begun her guerrilla war in the Vendée, he realized that he could, "without spilling a drop of blood, by having a woman arrested, prevent this upheaval and misery." He clearly wanted his readers to believe, after the fact, that he betrayed the duchess out of mercy, to save France from violence and civil war. In the testimony he gave right after the arrest, he said something similar: "I was acting not in the interest of . . . a party, an opinion, but in the sacred interest of humanity in general." It was patriotism alone that motivated him, according to Deutz: "France was my love, Louis-Philippe my Utopia." It is certainly possible that Deutz had some genuine reservations about the duchess's enterprise, but it is also worth remembering that he began to subvert her campaign only after its initial setbacks, once he realized that another Bourbon restoration would likely never come to pass.[7]

On June 1 Deutz drafted a letter to Montalivet, Louis-Philippe's minister of the interior, in which he offered his services to the July Monarchy government. He entrusted his letter to the French ambassador, Maximilien Gérard, comte de Rayneval. However, two days later Deutz wrote a letter to Drach, in which he made no reference to his shift in loyalties:

Madrid, June 3, 1832

My Dearest Brother, I am only writing you briefly so as to allay any fears you may have on my behalf. For I have little to report. I have been here for about a week, staying with the good fathers, the Jesuits of Saint-Esidro [*sic*]. I went to Aranjuez, where I had the honor to be presented to the royal family, who pleased me a great deal, especially the Portuguese princesses, sisters of D[om] Miguel, who deigned to grant me the most gracious welcome and who gave me letters for their august brother. I am extremely worried about the results of the skirmish [*échauffourée*] in Marseille. Give me as much reliable information as you can in your next letter. . . .

It is Morel who cites this letter, which might give reason to doubt its veracity, but this missive reads as vintage Deutz. It contains his signature blend of royal flattery—the agreeable Portuguese princesses and their august brother—and self-aggrandizing references to his familiarity with said highnesses (he doesn't mention that he was not able to gain access to the queen). It also reflects his penchant for availing himself of the generosity of the Jesuits whenever possible. Both Yiddish and French have colorful terms for this type of behavior, which must have occurred to the multilingual Drach when he read the letter: Deutz is both a classic *schnorrer*, or freeloader, and a *pique-assiette*, someone who eats off of someone else's plate.[8]

If we assume that this letter is genuine, it reveals that Deutz was still working actively on the duchess's behalf in early June, even while making overtures to the other side. It also shows that Deutz was aware of the duchess's failure in Marseille. By this point, the duchess's whole campaign—not just the uprising in Marseille but also the civil war in the Vendée—had already begun to seem like a lost cause: after the counterorder given by Bourmont, few legitimist soldiers showed up for battle on the date that the duchess had originally set, May 24, and the government was hot on her trail. There is little doubt that this turn of events motivated Deutz to offer his services to Montalivet, albeit without committing himself to anything definite lest the duchess still manage to pull off a surprise victory.

It seems clear, then, that Deutz's claim in his memoir that he was always working on behalf of Louis-Philippe even from the time he took the oath to the duchess is simply not true. If his goal from the beginning had been, as he claimed, to save France "from the horrors of civil war and foreign invasion," then he could have betrayed the duchess without traveling to Spain and Portugal and spending weeks cultivating allies on her behalf. On the contrary, Deutz seems to have kept tending both cabbage and goat until he knew definitively which side would prevail.[9]

Around June 8, Deutz traveled from Madrid to Lisbon, still working actively in support of the duchess. His mission in Portugal was to secure arms and a monetary loan from Dom Miguel. Portugal was embroiled in its own succession crisis, and Miguel was at the center of it. The third son of the Portuguese king, Miguel had followed his family to Brazil during the Napoleonic Wars, while Portugal was occupied by the French. When their father died, in 1826, his older brother Pedro chose to remain king of Brazil and abdicated the Portuguese throne in favor of his daughter Maria. The plan was for Miguel to eventually marry Maria, his niece, once she came of age and to rule the country jointly as her consort. Although Miguel at first seemed to accept the plan for succession and the constitution that underpinned it, in 1828 he and his absolutist allies staged a coup, which dissolved the parliament and placed Miguel on the throne. This set off the so-called "liberal wars," which were still raging in 1832.

Given Miguel's absolutist inclinations, the duchess had genuine hopes of securing a loan from him. Of all the reigning monarchs in

Europe, he was one of the most inclined to help her, so it is striking that she entrusted Deutz with this important negotiation. The letter from the duchess that he bore outlined her plan for obtaining both arms and a loan. Dom Miguel would have the guns and ammunition packed in many small containers. French sailors dispatched by the duchess would then transport the crates in secret from Lisbon to Brittany. The loan would be arranged through a network of false names so the French government would not be able to trace it; Deutz would then relay the secret names to the duchess in person in Nantes.[10]

No doubt Deutz realized that this plan offered the distinct advantage of necessitating a meeting between him and the duchess once he returned to France. This would give him the opportunity of leading the police to her hiding place if he decided to go through with the betrayal. In his memoir Deutz notes that the duchess also charged him with a mission of a more personal nature: he was to inquire about a possible match between Dom Miguel and Louise, the duchess's twelve-year-old daughter. This last element of his mission, Deutz could not refrain from noting, was "left to my discretion." Despite his supposed allegiance to liberal, democratic values, he displays more than a little self-satisfaction at playing a role in this dynastic intrigue.[11]

In Lisbon, Deutz stayed on a square in the center of the city, the *largo São Paolo*, where the Jesuits had their church. The sixteenth-century church's austere gray-stone edifice betrayed no sign of the elaborate baroque interior hidden within: an appropriate base of operations for a budding double agent. While waiting for an audience with Dom Miguel, Deutz set about making contact with the small community of French legitimist exiles in Lisbon, who had begun to receive dispiriting reports from France. Some of the leaders of the Vendée uprising had fled to Portugal to escape arrest, and they described to Deutz the battles of Le Chêne and La Pénissière as well as the duchess's decision to go into hiding in Nantes. According to Deutz's memoir, the defeats in the Vendée "sowed discord in their camp" and allowed conflicts among the exiled legitimists to rise to the surface. Deutz vowed to "profit from these internal divisions" in his effort to serve Louis-Philippe's government, which had yet to take him up on his offer to betray the duchess.[12]

After several weeks of waiting, Deutz finally obtained what he described as "multiple conferences" with Dom Miguel. Shortly after meeting the king, he received a letter from the king's minister, Fortunato de São Boaventura, the archbishop of Évora, containing a polite brush-off: the archbishop thanked Deutz for his devotion to the interests of his Very Christian Majesty but made only the vaguest promises of aid to the duchess. The prelate reported that Dom Miguel would "make every effort possible" to fulfill the first and second items requested by Deutz: the transfer of arms and the loan. However, the king was sorry to have to decline the third proposition—the marriage with Louise—for negotiations in that arena were already "well advanced in another European court." (In fact, Dom Miguel would not get married for nineteen more years.) The letter concluded with assurances of the king's respect for the duchesse de Berry, whom he called "the heroine of the century." As further proof of the king's admiration, the archbishop reported having seen a portrait of the duchess's son, young Henri, in the palace. "It is the portrait of Henri V," the king supposedly said, "because I cannot refer to him by any other name." The Portuguese were clearly quite adept at the game of royal flattery. They knew how to ease the sting of rejection by playing to the duchess's many vanities, including caressing the illusion that her son was already the reigning monarch in France.[13]

By late summer 1832, the duchess's uprising in the Vendée was effectively over. The support that the duchess had counted on from Portugal had failed to materialize. It was at this point that Deutz decided to commit himself fully to betrayal. He had not received a response to his initial letter to Montalivet, sent via M. de Rayneval, the French ambassador to Spain, so he drafted a second one in August in which he informed the minister of his negotiations on behalf of the duchess. "There is only one way to deliver France from anarchy and civil war," he wrote in the letter, "and that is the arrest of Madame." He concluded pompously: "There is only one man capable of bringing this about and I am that man."[14]

He entrusted this second letter to a French diplomat in Portugal to give to Rayneval. In late August, having still received no answer from Montalivet and suspecting that the duchess's spies had intercepted his letters, Deutz decided to return to Paris to meet with the minister in person. On his way back through Madrid, he wrote Drach another letter, this one in Yiddish and dated September 15, 1832. "My dear brother," he wrote, "Up until now everything has gone as well as could be expected. I was able to speak to Michel [Dom Miguel] only after much effort. . . ." He signed: "Your brother, Simon Deutz." Once again, he gave no sign that he had offered his services to the other side.[15]

Or almost no sign . . . Drach noticed that this was the first time since his conversion that his brother-in-law had signed with his birth name—Simon—instead of his baptismal name—Hyacinthe. To Drach, it seemed a clear indication that the volatile young man was once again in the midst of an identity crisis. "So much for the poor fellow's Catholicism," Drach lamented to Morel, although he could hardly have imagined the more dramatic reversals that would follow this initial lapse.[16]

Before leaving the Iberian peninsula, Deutz collected letters from the exiled French legitimists to give to the duchess. He was thinking ahead to his betrayal: the letters would furnish a further excuse for requesting a meeting with her in Nantes, which would allow him to lead the police to her hiding place. The journey back to Paris was not without "perils," Deutz tells us in his memoir. Surrounded by spies, his valise filled with compromising documents, he believed himself on the verge of being killed—by either agents of the government or the duchess—on at least twenty occasions. "But I had already braved so many dangers that I was not deterred," he states with retrospective equanimity.[17]

Did Deutz feel guilty as he outwardly went about securing aid for her enterprise while attempting to subvert it? Were all his efforts to justify his actions—by proclaiming his patriotism and humanitarian impulses—not just an attempt to convince his critics that he had acted morally but also an attempt to convince himself? Perhaps. But by this point, Deutz had grown extremely skilled at rationalizing the pain he caused those he admired. He had justified his conversion to his father by attributing it to a higher spiritual calling, and he did something similar with his betrayal of the duchess. Even if he was troubled by his actions, he did not let this trouble stand in his way.

WHILE DEUTZ TRAVELED through Spain and Portugal, the duchess settled into her hiding place in Nantes. The Kersabiec sisters had chosen the location well. Nothing about the house of the Du Guinys, at no. 3, rue Haute-du-Château, would attract the attention of a passerby. Located on a quiet street, just a few steps away from the imposing Castle of the Dukes of Brittany, beyond which stretched the Loire River, the house was stately and modest, like its owners.

Inside the house, a cloistral sobriety reigned. On the bottom three floors, the spinster sisters went about their daily routine, giving no outward indication that the most-wanted woman in France was hiding in their attic. Located under the eaves, with a sloping ceiling that trapped the heat in summer, the attic had two unadorned rooms. The duchess used the front room as an office during the day and at night placed a mattress on the tile floor for the comte de Mensard to sleep on. The duchess and Stylite de Kersabiec, her lady-in-waiting, slept in the back room, which had windows overlooking the courtyard.

The bedroom of the duchess and Stylite was decorated simply, with two narrow cots separated by a small night table and another table next to the door. A stark wooden crucifix presided over the plain white mantlepiece. To make the bare wooden walls less dreary, the duchess enlisted Mesnard to help her hang sheets of wallpaper with little blue, white, and black flowers against a gray background. It was the kind of wallpaper one could find in the dining room of a middle-class housewife in the provinces. Even if this bit of decoration relieved the drabness of the surroundings, the contrast with the grandeur of the duchess's former lodging at the Élysée Palace or with the Pavillon de Marsan in the Tuileries could not have been greater.[18]

Although nothing about the duchess's rustic bedroom seemed remarkable at first glance, an observant visitor might nevertheless have noticed that it did possess one curious architectural feature: instead of occupying the center of the wall, as is customary, the fireplace stood at an angle in the corner, which made the room trapezoidal. The reason for this anomaly was a secret closet. Constructed forty years before, during the Reign of Terror, when the guillotine threatened priests who would not swear oaths of loyalty to the French Revolution, the closet had already sheltered its share of outlaws. It would be the perfect refuge for the duchess and her accomplices should the government manage to track them down. The Du Guiny sisters had rigged a kind of alarm down below; in case of a raid, they would ring a bell, giving the renegades just enough time to squeeze through the tiny trapdoor in the fireplace before the government's agents could mount the stairs to the attic. They held several drills to practice.

The duchess spent five long months, the entire summer and fall of 1832, hiding in this attic. After weeks of almost constant motion and both physical and mental strain during the war—crossing the Vendéen countryside on foot and horseback, sleeping in a different place every night—the respite must have come at first as a relief.

For better or worse, the fighting had ceased, and she no longer had to worry for the safety of her men. The duchess could also take comfort from the devotion of her little coterie. Although she had less affection for the sharp-tongued Stylite than for her more docile sister Eulalie— the duchess's beloved Petit-Paul—she found in the resourcefulness of all the members of the Kersabiec family much to admire. Her hosts, the Du Guiny sisters, were every bit as devoted as the Kersabiecs, as were their two servants, Charlotte Moreau and Marie Boissy. Mesnard, who made up for in loyalty what he lacked in intelligence, stood ready to reassure her in moments of doubt. And when she felt cramped by her quarters, she could gaze out at the street below from the small windows of the attic's front room. In the distance she could see the moat and gardens of the castle, the banks of the Loire, and the meadows extending out to the countryside.[19]

But seclusion did not suit her. The duchess required distraction, if not for her body then at least for her mind. On the night she went into hiding, she wrote to Eulalie requesting—along with mundane personal necessities such as brushes, soap, buttons, and socks for "papa" (Mesnard)—books to help her pass the time. These included Catholic devotionals as well as the two latest Walter Scott novels to be translated into French, *Rob Roy* and *Kenilworth*. This mix of piety and adventure epitomized the twin poles of the duchess's character. She also devoured the output of the legitimist press while in hiding, and piles of *La Quotidienne* and other newspapers accumulated in the attic.[20]

From the start of her sequestration, she realized that they must take extreme precautions to keep her presence in Nantes a secret. Very few visitors gained entrance to the house at no. 3, rue Haute-du-Château. In order not to arouse the suspicion of the butcher or the baker, the Du Guiny sisters made sure that the orders they placed with all their local purveyors remained exactly as they had always been. It would be up to their devoted cook to figure out how to stretch supplies to feed the three additional mouths. The duchess herself never left the house, although rumors would later circulate that she had been spotted at various locations around Nantes—kneeling at church, accompanying the sisters on their social visits, or roaming the countryside. To make the time pass, she returned to some of the hobbies she had cultivated in her youth: flower painting and embroidery.[21]

Mostly, however, she wrote, from morning to night, letter after letter, as many as thirty missives a day, in a French strewn with spelling mistakes. She wrote to legitimists inside and outside France, and to foreign powers, to secure support for a new insurrection.[22] The letters were smuggled out by the house's occasional visitors, priests, and the few trusted friends of the Du Guinys. In order to deceive government agents who might intercept her correspondence, the duchess encrypted her writing using a complicated series of ciphers or codes. In one code the letters of the random phrase "lorsqu'il est du droit commun" ("when it is of common law") were matched against the twenty-four letters of the alphabet (without *w* and *z*):

I	I	I	IIIII	2 I 2
Lorsquil	est	du	droit	commun
abcdefgh	ijk	lm	nopqr	stuvxy

Letters that appear twice in the original sentence were marked with either a roman or Arabic numeral above them when used the second or third time. Sometimes she encrypted only the most sensitive parts of letters, but one can imagine the tedium of writing even a single word in this manner, let alone thirty letters each day. To further guarantee secrecy, the duchess's associates all possessed multiple noms de guerre: Bourmont was Laurent, Charette was Gaspard, etc. And in a final effort to ensure secrecy, the duchess wrote in invisible ink, which the French call *encre sympathique*—lemon juice that becomes visible when held up to the light.

This voluminous correspondence must have made the immobilized duchess feel less isolated. It also allowed her to feel like she was still waging a war, even though many of her chiefs had been arrested, were in hiding, or had retired to their own properties in frustration. She wrote to Charette daily, even as he was on the run from General Dermoncourt, who had advertised a reward for his capture. In one letter she sent Charette a letter of credit for four hundred francs to help another Vendéen chief in hiding. "Tell Bras-de-Fer [Iron Arm, the code name for another of her military leaders, Cadoudal] that being an outlaw myself, I must aid my brothers in arms." In another, she congratulated Charette on the birth of his son. Many of her missives attempted to boost morale, her own as much as that of her correspondents: "God will save us from the evil ones, my dear Ambroise," she wrote in one such letter, using Charette's code name and signing "Bernadin," one of her many noms de guerre.[23]

It is clear from her correspondence that the duchess had not given up the fight. "It is a pity that D . . . has not yet come!" she wrote in a letter to Charette, possibly referring to Deutz, who was supposed to bring her news of the arms shipment from Portugal and of the loan from Dom Miguel that would have enabled her to take up arms again. "I would really like us to be able to do some good work. With devoted men like you and with a bit of exertion, we will succeed. I am convinced that if *Babylon* [Paris] declares itself for Henri V, the *sheep* [the provinces] will follow." She followed her optimistic musings with plans for battle and for the administrative organization she would put in place once her son regained the throne.[24]

The hope of obtaining help from abroad in order to continue kept her in the attic all summer despite pleas from her associates to slip out of France before getting captured. And as the duchess saw things, the volatile European political situation—the tenor of revolutionary fervor, all the succession crises—made foreign aid a real possibility. In the summer of 1832, Belgium still threatened to pull France into a war: if Louis-Philippe decided to intervene to preserve Belgian independence from Holland or to annex the French-speaking region, then the other powers might take the opportunity to attack France. Although the duchess's letters make clear that she did not want her son to regain his crown thanks to an invasion, she had no qualms about using a war to further her own political goals. In Massa she had already imagined that if France were invaded from the east, she would rush to face the enemy. A grateful nation would then reward her with the return of her son's throne. Such, anyway, was the fantasy that she continued to nourish while hiding in the attic in Nantes.[25]

Along with sending Deutz to Spain and Portugal, the duchess had dispatched emissaries to Prussia, Russia, and Piedmont to request aid, and she held out special hope for a loan from King William of the Netherlands. In a series of letters exchanged between the duchess, her agents (especially Bourmont), and the prince of Orange, William's son, she devised a scheme to partner with William to overthrow Louis-Philippe and then to divide the Belgian territories and Luxembourg between them. "The idea of returning to France its natural limits [with the addition of Belgium] and its legitimate king, of contracting a kind of alliance that would be both offensive and defensive with a sovereign who is so remarkably courageous and generous, would strongly excite the attention of the wholly French mother [*la mère toute française*] of Henri V," she wrote in a letter to Bourmont, which he delivered to King William.[26]

Like all her foreign machinations, these plans came to nothing. The duchess faced a classic catch-22: she could not gain support from abroad while her prospects in France seemed so dim, but she could not improve her prospects at home without help from abroad. Realizing that she did not project an image of strength while hiding in an attic, the duchess's agents urged her to come to Holland to press her case in person. "All influence is lost if you remain in a position that proves your impotence," wrote one of her associates, Auguste de La Rochejacquelein, from The Hague. He begged her to slip out of France, if not to further negotiations then at least to avoid being arrested. "How do you not see," he wrote in language far plainer than most dared to use with the imperious duchess, "that you are using yourself up where you are, and that you are proving that you are incapable of doing anything?" Foreseeing her qualms about abandoning her troops, he added that "even in the event that another war breaks out, you would be more useful here [in Holland]."[27]

Charette visited the duchess in her attic, hoping that a face-to-face interview might convince his headstrong commander to escape. A ship was waiting, he told her, to carry her to Holland or England. The duchess refused categorically: "I have compromised too many people to abandon them now. I can't save my own head while those of my friends are in danger of falling." Moreover, her escape would not end the government's persecution of her associates. But her capture might. "If, on the contrary, I am arrested, then I would be a security guarantee and they would stop tormenting them," she reasoned. Besides, she had written to all the sovereigns of Europe asking for aid. How could she abandon France before receiving definitive answers?[28]

The duchess was aided in her tireless correspondence by her two companions in seclusion, Mesnard and Stylite, who disliked each other intensely. Mesnard was a military man of the old school. He had spent the years of emigration fighting in various counterrevolutionary armies. He was certainly not used to being the only man in a house full of women. Nor was he used to taking orders from them. And although he had fallen completely under the sway of the duchess—originally assigned to act as a stabilizing influence, he had become her subordinate, almost her lackey—Mesnard was not ready to be bossed around by her lady-in-waiting.

Nearly as headstrong as her mistress, Stylite was far more independent and voluble than her sister Eulalie. Mesnard does note with admiration that Stylite possessed a sharp mind and exerted a great deal of authority over the duchess, although his begrudging admiration ended there. With dark hair parted in the middle and pulled back from her oval face in a severe chignon, Stylite had handsome features and a resolute, clear-eyed gaze. "Madame Stylite de Kersabiec possesses elevation in thought and a mind that is quick to plan and to execute," noted Charette in his memoir. "She has the misfortune of being a *political woman* [*une femme politique*]," a designation that read as an oxymoron in the nineteenth century. "Men who no longer know how to be men complain that she has usurped their place. Most women don't or won't understand her," Charette explained. In his own memoirs, Mesnard comments that if he were to close his eyes while listening to Stylite, he wouldn't know if it were a man or woman speaking. This was not intended as a compliment.[29]

The government had captured the Kersabiecs' father during the war and now held him in prison. A trial loomed, and the sisters worried that the government would punish the old man in order to teach the legitimists a lesson: if the duchess had so far eluded their grasp, then they would go after her associates. And Kersabiec *père* was one of the highest-ranking legitimists in detention. Céleste de Kersabiec, the third sister, pleaded with the duchess to take the drastic step of writing to her aunt Marie-Amélie, the queen, to beg for his release.

This request put the duchess in a terrible position. She had loved her aunt growing up and had remained extremely close to her after they both moved to France, following her own marriage to the duc de Berry and her aunt's to Louis-Philippe, the duc d'Orléans. She had always tried to act as a bridge between the Bourbon royal family and their cousins, the Orléans, despite the rumors that Louis-Philippe coveted the crown for himself. Then the Revolution of 1830 proved the rumors right. Louis-Philippe usurped her son, and Marie-Amélie turned her niece out of house and home. Marie-Amélie reigned at the Tuileries, while the duchess was hounded, hiding in a miserable attic in Nantes. She was now being asked to request a favor from someone who had stolen everything from her.

"They are asking a very difficult thing of me," the duchess confided to Mesnard after a sleepless night. "But that family [the Kersabiecs] have stopped at nothing to second me. How can I refuse them this?" she asked. "And yet it costs me more than you can imagine." Mesnard refrained from responding that his own son was also in prison, yet he would never have dreamed of asking the duchess to compromise herself in this way. If the duchess had felt certain that her request would free M. Kersabiec from prison, that would have been one thing, but it was plain that her efforts were bound to fail. And yet the next day, she sat down at her desk and took up her quill. Devotion to her friends won out.[30]

Her letter did not grovel, however. On the contrary, it appealed to her aunt's sense of justice while planting fears for the future. The duchess tried to make the queen realize that what goes up can also come down, that revolutions are just that—reversals—and that doing this favor for someone who lacks power today might help her aunt tomorrow if the situation were to change. For if there is one thing that the previous forty years had taught her, it was that the wheel of fortune spins fast in France. "Despite the current difference in our situations," the duchess added, "there is also a volcano beneath your feet, Madame, and you know it." (Perhaps she thought a metaphor that drew on the geology of their mutual hometown—Mount Vesuvius, the volcano overlooking Naples—would have an effect on the queen.) The duchess signed off with a bit of flattery barely concealing an insult: "I wish you happiness. Because I have too high an opinion of you to believe that you can possibly be happy in your current situation." After sealing the envelope with hot wax and imprinting it with her stamp, the duchess gave the letter to one of her associates who had not yet compromised himself with the authorities to deliver to the Tuileries in person. She never received an answer, and her friends' father remained in prison.[31]

In recounting this painful episode, Mesnard notes that Stylite refrained from joining her sister Céleste in asking the duchess to intercede for their father: "I must say here that although I never much liked mademoiselle Stylite de Kersabiec, and she returned the favor, she sacrificed all her fears and all her affections to the duty that she held sacred of not compromising the dignity of Madame."[32]

Although her almost daily letters to Eulalie de Kersabiec (Petit-Paul) and Charette reveal her efforts to sound upbeat—the duchess describes the books she is reading and the dresses she wants to sew—the months of hiding took their toll on both body and mind. The heat of the summer caused her particular suffering. The duchess would spend hours at the window of the front room of the attic, which she used as an office: she could see the Loire below and might occasionally catch relief from a cool breeze. Sometimes, however, the view increased her misery. All through the spring and summer of 1832, cholera ravaged Nantes, and the duchess saw a procession of corpses being carried to the cemetery. At one point a stomach ailment made her think that she too had come down with the dreaded disease. By the time the epidemic subsided in August, 770 people had died in the city, but it had claimed nobody at no. 3, rue Haute-du-Château.[33]

August brought the duchess a different kind of distraction when Achille Guibourg took up residence in the attic. The thirty-two-year-old lawyer had the looks of a Romantic poet: a full head of wavy chestnut hair, wide-set blue eyes, and a noble, aquiline nose. He had advised the duchess during the heated days of the military campaign before being captured by the government in early June. On August 14 he managed to escape from prison and to make his way to the rue Haute-du-Château. Despite the cramped quarters and the constant presence of Stylite and Mesnard—Guibourg later claimed to have slept on the second floor of the house, separately from the other captives—it is likely that a romance developed between the duchess and the dashing new arrival as summer turned into fall.[34]

Surely the duchess needed relief from the claustrophobia and constant letter writing, and whatever tryst she had with Guibourg might have been one reason she refused to escape France when she had the chance. The very first lines of Guibourg's memoir, published immediately after her arrest, state that the duchess remained in France "because of serious concerns, for which she cannot be blamed," by which he certainly means her desire to relaunch the insurrection in the Vendée and to help her imprisoned associates. But it is difficult not to read in this curious disavowal a reference to their illicit affair, which many would soon see as deserving quite a bit of blame.[35]

The duchess kept resisting her friends' efforts to convince her of the danger of her situation, indignant at their attempts to defy her, to constrain her free will. "I will leave France when I want to," she told Mesnard. She was hopeful that the legislative elections in December might lead to a republican uprising in Paris or Lyon, which would force the government to withdraw its troops from the Vendée. This would give the legitimists an opportunity to relaunch their guerrilla war, but first they needed money and supplies, none of which were forthcoming.[36]

Meanwhile, the noose was tightening. Dermoncourt had redoubled his efforts to track her down and knew from intelligence reports that she was hiding somewhere in Nantes. He began raiding residences in the city near to where the duchess was staying. It was only a matter of time, the duchess and her supporters knew, before his agents would find their way to the house of the Du Guinys on the rue Haute-du-Château. She was running an enormous risk by staying in France, by continuing to believe, against all odds, that she could relaunch her war. The duchess understood the stakes and stayed anyway.[37]

CHAPTER 10

The Search

WHEN POLICE COMMISSIONER Louis Joly arrived in Nantes on June 5, 1832, tasked with tracking down the duchess, the legitimists could be excused for greeting the news with a touch of paranoia. They remembered Joly all too well from twelve years before, when he had been the police agent assigned to protect the duc de Berry on the night of his murder and was sitting at a nearby café when the assassin struck. Although Joly quickly arrested the perpetrator, legitimists never got over the suspicion that his inattention that fateful night had not been an accident.

Joly's origins remain something of a mystery. The legendary police chief Louis Canler informs us in his memoir that Joly began his career during the empire as a valet in the household of Napoleon's sister-in-law, Queen Hortense. With the fall of the empire in 1815, Joly joined the Paris police under the protection of Élie Decazes, who served as minister of police and then prime minister, and who helped push Louis XVIII's monarchy in a more liberal direction.[1]

The assassination of the duc de Berry in 1820 brought the downfall of Decazes: the *ultras* held the liberal minister responsible for the tragedy and forced him to resign. Chagrined to see his favorite go, Louis XVIII bestowed on him the title of duke and made him ambassador to England. Joly was not so fortunate. The cloud of suspicion that hung over Decazes after the assassination cast a shadow on his protégé for the remainder of the Restoration. Out of favor with the *ultras* and suspected of being a Bonapartist himself, Joly was fired from the police force. Once the Revolution of 1830 removed the Bourbons, however, Joly rejoined the police as a commissioner, a relatively high rank, and soon received the Legion of Honor. To those legitimists inclined toward conspiracy theories, Joly's arrival in Nantes in June 1832 seemed like an indication of the government's nefarious intentions, a sign that perhaps Louis-Philippe intended for the duchess to meet the same fate as her husband.[2]

The various documents that Joly left behind—including multiple letters to the minister of the interior, reporting on his progress in the hunt for the duchess, and a full narrative account of the events leading up to her arrest—give the impression of a no-nonsense, professional policeman. If he was involved in a secret plot against the Bourbons, there is no trace of it in these reports. He is all business, as if trying to make up for that night when he had been sipping a drink rather than guarding the duke.

In early June, while the duchess was still fighting her doomed civil war, the minister of the interior, Montalivet, faced intense pressure to capture her. The left-leaning opposition newspapers denounced the July Monarchy for its failure to locate the duchess, which provided the right-wing publications with an endless source of amusement. "She is everywhere and nowhere," mocked *La Mode*. "She is in Toulon, in Montpellier, in Lyon, in Brittany, in the Vendée. Who knows? She is everywhere at once. Perhaps she is even in Paris, in the church of Saint-Germain l'Auxerrois or in the residence of M. de Montalivet. Perhaps in the Tuileries where she attends the council of ministers incognito!" One can only imagine the duchess's bitter mirth as she read these accounts of her ubiquity while confined to her tiny attic bedroom on the rue Haute-du-Château.[3]

On June 2, 1832, Montalivet telegraphed all the prefects in the west of France that he had "every reason to believe that the duchesse de Berry is in the Vendée." The next day, he dispatched Joly to Nantes with "unlimited powers" to search the countryside and the towns of the West. But reports continued to arrive from across France that the duchess had been sighted wearing all sorts of fanciful disguises. Other reports indicated that she had embarked on a ship bound for England or Holland. Along with Joly, Montalivet charged the local police commissioner in Nantes with "determining positively if she is still in the country, or if not, when and how she left it."[4]

Upon arriving in Nantes—the sixth-largest city in France at the time and the fourth-largest port—Joly found that the local police had already put all foreigners under surveillance, as well as those locals known to have left the city recently. "That rigorously observed measure has furnished some useful information, although not directly linked to the specific object of our search," he reported in his first dispatch back to Montalivet. In addition, the army had begun a series of raids on nearby châteaus and their dependent farms, hoping to uncover the hiding place of the duchess. Not always performed with strict attention to legality, these raids had not yielded much more than a lot of broken doors and furniture. Indeed, the harsh tactics of the government threatened to push the local population—even those not inclined to legitimism—to sympathize with the fugitive duchess. Joly promised that henceforth these raids would be undertaken with greater respect for private property.[5]

By late summer, Joly's intelligence gathering had focused suspicion on the Convent of the Visitation, a seventeenth-century cloister located in the old center of Nantes, just a few streets away from the hiding place of the duchess on the rue Haute-du-Château. The strong-willed mother superior of the convent was from a distinguished Breton noble family with ties to the Bourbons: her brother had been one of the best friends of the duc de Berry and her sister-in-law one of the duchess's ladies-in-waiting. The mother superior made no secret of her legitimist sympathies but maintained that she had no idea where the duchess was hiding. In reality, she was an important intermediary between the duchess and the outside world, supplying her with information and helping to smuggle the duchess's letters to her many correspondents abroad. However, the government suspected the mother superior of more and thought she was harboring the royal fugitive in her convent.[6]

On July 31 the local police commissioner penned a secret report to Montalivet in which he described his unsuccessful attempts to bribe the mailman in the convent's neighborhood—"a passionate Carlist," which is to say a legitimist—and his plan to introduce a young shopgirl into the convent as a spy. In August the prefect of the Loire-Inférieure department, where Nantes was located, wrote to Montalivet that "even if the duchess is not at the convent, the latter nevertheless plays a big role in the affair. . . . I consider it [the convent] the clearing house for the correspondence of the duchess, not only with Paris but also with the South." The government also suspected that the mother superior was passing along copies of legitimist newspapers to the duchess in hiding.

On September 12, at 5 o'clock in the morning—two full hours before sunrise—the local police raided the Convent of the Visitation. Two companies of soldiers stood guard as twelve policemen searched the personal effects of the terrified nuns. Firemen were on hand to force open doors. They discovered several caches of suspicious letters but no duchess. The commissioner proceeded to interrogate the indignant mother superior, who denied having any knowledge of the duchess's whereabouts. "Were you not asked to provide asylum and a hiding place in your monastery to madame la duchesse de Berry and her associates?" the commissioner asked. "No, Monsieur," the mother superior replied. "Do you receive newspapers entitled *La Quotidienne* and *Le Revenant*?" "I do not receive either one," she responded. After the interrogation, the commissioner forced her to submit to a humiliating body search, which yielded no incriminating evidence.[7]

Despite these disappointing results, Montalivet remained convinced that the duchess was hiding either in this convent or in another one nearby. In a telegram to the local prefect, dated September 14, 1832, the minister commanded, "Continue the strict occupation of the Visitation as well as the convent of the Sisters of Charity. . . . Renew the searches of the interior. Interrogate the servants, promise rewards. Stop at nothing to attain favorable results."[8]

At this point, however, the end of the civil war had begun to make capturing the duchess less imperative. Indeed, *not* capturing her now began to seem advantageous to the king and his ministers. If the duchess were still on the loose in the West preparing to stir up another civil war, then Louis-Philippe could more plausibly avoid the Left's calls to get involved in a war over Belgium. Moreover, if the king did succeed in arresting the duchess, he would face the thorny question of what to do with her. The Left would push him to put her on trial, while the Right would turn her into a martyr for their cause. The king would outrage half the country no matter what he did. And could he really put his own niece on trial for treason? For a king who had carefully constructed his image as a family man—in contrast to his mostly childless Bourbon cousins—this violation of the bonds of kinship risked alienating even his own supporters.[9]

It was at this moment of political indecision that Deutz arrived back in Paris for the first time since 1828, when he had departed for Rome. Not having received any response to the two letters he sent to Montalivet from Spain and Portugal, the would-be double agent decided to present himself to the minister in person. According to Deutz's self-justifying memoir, published three years after the events, Montalivet claimed not to have received his letters but eagerly took him up on his offer to betray the duchess, promising any recompense for his services that Deutz might demand.

"I am acting out of conviction and not self-interest," Deutz supposedly responded with umbrage. "I want to save the country from civil war, but I will not sell myself." His vanity and grandiosity on full display, the convert professed shock at the insinuation that he wanted money in exchange for his services. "Be advised that if I wanted to sell myself, you would not be rich enough to buy me," he reports telling the minister. He then supposedly went on to stipulate that had he been tempted by honors or wealth, he would have remained in the "Carlist camp," where his fortune and future were assured. "Thus you see, this is not an affair of interest but of devotion." Of course, the duchess's fortunes had taken a decided turn for the worse at that point, and Deutz realized his own fortune was anything but assured if he remained in her service.[10]

According to the right-wing journalist Alfred Nettement, Montalivet was not very eager to take Deutz up on his offer of betraying the duchess, fearing the political difficulties that would ensue from the duchess's arrest. Not a skilled politician and aware of his own limitations, Montalivet did not want to risk making a bold move that might backfire. But on October 11, shortly after the meeting between Deutz and Montalivet, Louis-Philippe reshuffled his cabinet, and the liberal Adolphe Thiers became the new minister of the interior.[11]

Thiers saw the affair differently from his predecessor. He was eager to put an end to the troubles in the Vendée once and for all. And to do this, he needed to arrest the duchess. "It was necessary to find a traitor to deliver up Madame," Nettement writes in his retrospective account. "It must be said that to the honor of our loyal France, it was not a Frenchman who sank to the level of that infamous task. To find such a felon, whom they intoxicated with gold and shame, they had to go looking for a Jew"—his words offering more evidence of the kind of antisemitism that became commonplace in political discourse as a result of the betrayal of the duchess.[12]

Barely five feet tall, Thiers made up for in ambition what he lacked in stature. He had begun his career as a historian and journalist: his protests against Charles X's curtailment of press freedom helped spark the so-called "Three Glorious Days" of street fighting that brought Louis-Philippe to power. Buoyed by this success, Thiers won election to the Chamber of Deputies shortly after the July Revolution. But his first address to the assembly fell flat because of his lack of oratorical skills, his strong Provençal accent, and the fact that his head was barely visible above the lectern when he spoke. "The odious little dwarf," as Louis-Philippe's daughter Louise called him, hoped that the arrest of the duchess would raise his profile on the national stage, figuratively if not literally. Thiers immediately agreed to meet with Deutz.[13]

Deutz's plan for betrayal, which he had nurtured during his travels in Spain and Portugal, moved one step closer to reality when Montalivet put him in touch with Thiers. According to his memoir, Deutz made several stipulations to Thiers before agreeing to lead the police to the duchess: first, that the duchess would under no circumstances be put on trial; second, that no legitimists would be arrested in the operation; and third, that the maréchal de Bourmont would be allowed to leave France. His fourth and final condition was a poignant one and hints at a deeper—a Freudian would say "Oedipal"—dimension to his actions: that if he should be killed during the mission, the government would bury him next to his mother.[14]

Deutz's enemies would accuse him of cupidity, of having priced his services at a million francs. In his memoir he expresses outrage at the mere suggestion of such a sum: "In this whole affair, I was never guided by interest, never did a word about money cross my lips, never did the thought of turning this into a speculation enter my head, never did I see Madame as a woman for sale." Deutz may not technically be lying here; it is possible that he did not *ask* Thiers for money. But it seems likely that Thiers promised a hefty reward should he succeed in making the arrest.

JOLY KEPT UP his hunt for the duchess during the long, hot summer of 1832. Every night detachments of soldiers would scour the countryside around Nantes, raiding homes that intelligence reports indicated might be her hiding place. They searched the dwellings of Bourmont's aunt and of the Kersabiec family, whose liaisons with the duchess were well-known, along with the residences of dozens of other aristocrats. "But all these measures have not yet yielded satisfactory results," the discouraged Joly reported back to Paris after several weeks in the field. Joly and his men also kept a close watch on *L'Africain*, a ship docked at the nearby port of Paimboeuf, which they suspected the legitimists were planning to use for the duchess's escape.[15]

In early October, Joly received a summons to return to Paris immediately to receive new instructions for his search. When Joly arrived at the Ministry of the Interior, he was immediately escorted into the private office of Adolphe Thiers. According to Joly, the minister stressed "the importance of my mission" and the "confidence he placed in me." Thiers then left Joly alone in the presence of "an enormous dossier" and told him to take some time to absorb the background information it contained on Simon Deutz. An hour later, Thiers returned and asked Joly what he thought of the man who would become known, in official correspondence, as the "indicator."

Joly responded frankly that Deutz was "a great scoundrel who was going to sell out and deliver up a woman who had been his benefactress and that of his children." It is not clear whether the file that Joly read contained false information or whether he was simply a bad reader: Deutz had no children; it was his sister's children whom the duchess had perhaps helped to place in Catholic institutions after their kidnapping by her son's librarian, David Drach.

Thiers seems not to have noticed this error but rather focused on Joly's antipathy toward Deutz: "The minister, while applauding my philanthropic sentiments, responded that the safety of the country and that of the king were of higher consideration, and that whatever contact I was to have with this man, on this occasion, would not affect me and that in no way could I be held responsible for his crime." In this report filed immediately after the arrest of the duchess, Joly seems to have anticipated the wave of public revulsion that would surround Deutz when the details of his betrayal were made known and was eager to distance himself as much as possible from it.

Thiers dismissed Joly with the order to meet again that night at eight, at the home of an anonymous Monsieur F***, no. 6, rue Richepanse, between the Place de la Concorde and the Church of the Madeleine. Deutz attended this meeting as well, bringing with him twenty-two letters written in invisible ink that the banker Jauge had asked him to deliver to the duchess in Nantes. In his account of the meeting, Joly describes how he caught Deutz examining him while he pretended to study the letters. Later, Joly heard Deutz ask whether he could be trusted. Thiers replied in the affirmative, and Monsieur F*** added that "Joly is a man who is not for sale and who cannot be bought," an endorsement that seems calculated to rankle Deutz, who was at that very moment in the process of selling his own services to the minister.[16]

In his version, Deutz describes meeting Joly for the first time not on the rue Richepanse but in the office of Thiers, who presented the policeman as "a man who, like me, was devoted to the government of Louis-Philippe, and who had already had the opportunity to render more than one service to the new dynasty," which was perhaps a veiled reference to Joly's role in the duke's murder. Deutz does not mention any qualms he may have had about Joly's trustworthiness. On the contrary, he describes the policeman, who was wearing the red ribbon of the Legion of Honor in his buttonhole, as being well-spoken and polite, with "worldly manners." "It was he who, under the Restoration, had arrested the assassin of the duc de Berry," Deutz reminds his readers.[17]

Thiers supposedly then told Deutz not to travel with Joly to Nantes because it would put his life in jeopardy, and insisted that Deutz could direct the whole operation to arrest the duchess from Paris. However, Deutz maintains in his memoir that these concerns about his safety did not faze him. He had grown accustomed to "scorning danger, and walking with my head held high." He supposedly insisted to Thiers that he wanted to be present in Nantes to guarantee that no harm would come to the duchess after the arrest: "Because my goal was not only to have her arrested, but to have her arrested safe and sound, and without it costing a hair off her head, nor of the men of her party a drop of blood."

"I have taken upon myself, *monsieur le ministre*, a grave responsibility," Deutz supposedly told Thiers, "and I cannot entrust her safety to anyone other than myself." The convert said something similar in the testimony he gave immediately following the arrest, the document titled "Before God" ("Devant Dieu"). There he specifies that Thiers advised him to stay in Paris so that the legitimists would not know who had betrayed the duchess. "As for the dangers that could result for me," Deutz maintained with bravado, "I had long ago considered them coldly, and I scorn them." It was therefore decided that Deutz and Joly would set off for Nantes as soon as possible.[18]

AWARE THAT THINGS were about to heat up in Nantes, Thiers decided to replace the departmental prefect, a popular local aristocrat, with a political operative from the outside. Maurice Duval had been a bureaucrat during the empire, "one of those rude administrators formed by the imperial school, accustomed to executing, by any means necessary, the will of Napoleon," according to Nettement. With the fall of the Restoration, Duval was perfectly willing to offer his services to the July Monarchy, and he had gained a reputation as a ruthlessly efficient functionary in Grenoble. Thiers knew he would not hesitate to turn the region upside down in his quest to arrest the duchess.[19]

Angered by the change in leadership, the population of Nantes decided to greet their new prefect with a *charivari*. Known in English as "rough music," a charivari is an ancient French folk custom in which a crowd expresses disapproval of a member of the community through wild cacophony—from banging pots to discordant musical instruments—in a kind of mock serenade. When news of Duval's arrival spread through the city on October 20, a crowd formed outside the elegant Hôtel de France, on the Place Graslin, where the new prefect was planning to stay. According to General Dermoncourt, "People ran through the streets looking for bells, ripping them off the necks of cows that they happened to pass. . . . An army of cornetts assembled, more than six hundred people armed with that instrument, which as everyone knows, does not require any preparatory study." An enterprising whistle salesman stationed himself on the square and sold out his entire inventory within a few minutes.[20]

Warned as he entered Nantes of the reception that was waiting for him, Duval sent his empty carriage ahead and approached the hotel on foot. By this point, the square could not contain the number of musicians who had assembled. Noisy protesters spilled into all the surrounding streets in the center of Nantes, creating an enormous din. According to Dermoncourt, their number approached ten thousand. Duval cut a path through the crowd and tried to enter the hotel, but its doors were locked. He was forced to retreat into the mass of musicians and to pretend to protest against himself. The next day he took possession of the prefecture a few streets away, and the charivari followed him there. It lasted for two more days, until enthusiasm began to wane and the local police put an end to the protest.[21]

The discordant notes of the charivari, which could be heard clearly on the rue Haute-du-Château, were music to the duchess's ears. The noisy greeting given to the man sent to manage her arrest helped restore her spirits after the raid on the Convent of the Visitation, which was far too close for comfort. Despite her growing anxiety, the duchess strove to maintain an optimistic front: "If recent events pained my French and maternal heart, I at least have found noble consolation in the courage and loyalty of a great many of you," she wrote to her partisans that fall. "I have too much faith in French valor and in the old fidelity of the royalists to easily admit any contrary thought." Despite the fact that her partisans in the field showed no sign of returning to arms, the duchess remained confident of her ultimate victory, or at least wished to appear so: "Let all who have walked in the right path remain firmly planted there so that the others can rally to them. . . . It is perseverance that makes us strong; with it we will triumph. I act in the name of the people's interests, the will of kings, and my own determination, steadfast as the rule of law."[22]

All through the fall, the duchess refused to listen to her advisers, who begged her to slip out of France before getting captured. Despite her military defeats and the arrests of some of her most loyal supporters, she remained convinced that it was possible to rekindle the flame of civil war. All she needed was a bit of help from abroad, in the form of arms or a loan, and the loyalty of her partisans would do the rest.

She retained this hope despite a series of letters from advisers who shared their realistic assessment of her chances in no uncertain terms. One letter signed with the nom de guerre "Cheval d'Ami" warned her that the reports she had received about the possibility of rekindling an uprising in the Midi were unfounded: "There is in France a great moral degradation, and the most generous are themselves sometimes afflicted by it." The committee of her advisers, "full of admiration" for her "sublime character," must not feed any false hopes or maintain any illusions, her correspondent maintained.[23]

Another adviser was even more candid: "There is no longer any political faith in France; there are only interests. Before engaging themselves [on the duchess's behalf], everyone will want to know the chances of success." It was all too clear to this correspondent that these chances were not great: "Madame's character has grown through the audacious enterprise that she has attempted. But, the results having failed to live up to her noble courage . . . it is now necessary to listen to reason." The duchess refused to see it this way. If only she could hold out a bit longer, any number of events—from an uprising in Paris to a foreign war—could weaken the government and give her the chance she needed to strike again.[24]

In mid-October the duchess's spirits were buoyed somewhat by reports in the press of the trial of Pierre-Antoine Berryer, the lawyer who had journeyed from Paris the preceding May seeking to urge her, on behalf of her Parisian "committee" of advisers, to call off her plans for civil war. One of the highest-profile legitimists to be captured by the government, Berryer turned his trial into a platform for defending the principles of legitimism and the honor of the duchess. His oratorical skills on full display, Berryer recounted to a hushed courtroom, mostly full of women, that—despite the fact that the duchess was forced to move locations three or four times a week during the period of the civil war and that at least ten people knew where she was hiding—"not a single one had the thought to betray her!"[25]

The duchess was now relying on a similar kind of devotion from the small handful of people who knew she was ensconced on the rue

Haute-du-Château. She no doubt took comfort from false reports in the press that she had been seen in various locations throughout France: on October 19, for example, *Le Breton* noted that she was spotted fifteen miles from Paris, near Rosny, her old country house, dressed as a servant. Even if the police were keeping an eye on the nearby Convent of the Visitation, there was still enough doubt as to her location to allay any immediate fears of arrest.[26]

But as the warm summer months gradually gave way to fall, as the days grew shorter and a chill began to creep into the drafty attic, the duchess began to listen to her advisers. She still felt that it would be cowardly to escape while her many supporters faced danger of capture and imprisonment. "The captain of the vessel only abandons his ship once he has ensured the safety of his entire crew," she wrote to Bertier in early November. "The same obligation is imposed on me and I will only leave France when all those who compromised their existence for the cause that we are all serving no longer risk danger." She expressed special concern for Bourmont but said that he was now making plans to leave France and that if he did so, she would also go.[27]

Whether she feared that someone would betray her location or whether the attic was just getting too cold, for the first time she actively contemplated an exit from France. Achille Guibourg, the dashing lawyer with whom she was probably having an affair, arranged for a boat to take her to Holland or England or possibly to Spain. According to Mesnard, she decided to leave France on November 14. Just as she made this decision, however, she received word that Deutz had come to Nantes with letters he needed to show her. Perhaps the loan from Portugal had come through at last.[28]

DEUTZ AND JOLY had agreed that they would leave Paris separately and rendezvous at the Hôtel de France in Angers, about two-thirds of the way to Nantes, on the night of October 20, 1832. Deutz was traveling with an old passport under the name of Hyacinthe de Gonzagues, signed by Cardinal Bernetti during his days in Rome. In Angers they spent the morning of October 21 discussing their plans and then set off again separately to avoid arousing suspicion: Joly would travel by post chaise, a carriage driven by horses that were changed at prearranged stops in order to maximize speed, while Deutz would take a slower steamboat up the Loire River. What Deutz didn't realize is that two of Joly's undercover agents were accompanying him on his journey, both for his protection and to make sure their "indicator" did not attempt to double-cross them.[29]

Joly was watching as Deutz stepped onto the dock in Nantes. The policeman followed him to the Hôtel de France, on the Place Graslin, the same hotel where Maurice Duval had been met with a charivari a few days before. Considered to be one of the finest inns in France when it first opened in 1788, the five-story Hôtel Henri IV, which became the Hôtel de France after the French Revolution, had housed many important visitors to Nantes over the decades. It would now become Deutz's base for the next several weeks as he set about trying to gain access to the duchess.[30]

His plan, hatched months ago, was to befriend the local legitimists, gain their trust, and then reveal that he had important letters he needed to show to the duchess in person. Joly and his men would follow him to the rendezvous and make the arrest. Many legitimists exiled on the Iberian peninsula had in fact entrusted him with letters for the duchess; moreover, the duchess's Parisian banker, Jauge, had given him more letters, which he had shown to Thiers and Joly. These included missives from Charles X urging her to leave France as soon as possible and from the prince of Orange with vague promises of support. Therefore, Deutz was not lying when he claimed that the duchess would want to see the documents he had in his possession. But how to make the initial contact with her supporters?[31]

Deutz knew from Joly that the mother superior was suspected of hiding the duchess at the Convent of the Visitation, so he began with her. But after the raid on her convent, the mother superior was on the alert, and she gave the strange gentleman claiming to be the baron de Gonzagues a frosty reception. Deutz then paid a call on Mme

Piquetet, a relative of the banker Jauge. She was slightly more cordial, and Deutz felt hopeful she would help with further introductions to legitimist society.[32]

In the meantime, the convert resorted to a familiar tactic in his efforts to ingratiate himself with his aristocratic marks. Every day, he made sure to be seen taking communion at the chapel of the Church of the Visitation. Deutz had been practicing the part of the religious zealot for years and played his role to perfection: he knew how to arouse the sympathy of older religious ladies with the right combination of exaggerated piety and just a touch of romantic melancholy. Over the course of the next week, from October 23 to 30, Deutz alternated his very public daytime visits to church with secret nighttime assignations with the police. He would meet Joly at a prearranged location, and the policeman would escort him to Maurice Duval's office at the prefecture. They would enter through a side door along the quay so as not to be observed. Once inside the office, Deutz would go over that day's progress and make plans for the next one's operations. The meetings would often last late into the night. According to Joly, Deutz always insisted on being escorted back to his hotel, for he was afraid of "walking alone in the city at night"—so much for the boasts of fearlessness that Deutz had made to Thiers.[33]

During one of these meetings, Duval informed Joly and Deutz of a disturbing piece of intelligence gathered from Paris: someone had warned the banker Jauge that a traitor was headed to Nantes with the intention of betraying the duchess. Deutz himself had not been named, but they feared that his identity had been compromised. Because Jauge had just given Deutz letters for the duchess, Deutz would have been the obvious candidate.

The next day, Deutz trembled as he made his way to a meeting with the *curé* of the Cathedral of Saint-Pierre. His confidence was not restored by the "reserved greeting" and "sardonic conversation" of the clergyman, which Deutz took to be the attitude of someone on the lookout for a traitor. According to Joly's account, the convert began to panic when he heard a noise in the adjoining room and assumed that he was about to be ambushed. Only the thought that Joly's men were waiting outside, prepared to rush in at the slightest signal of distress, enabled Deutz to conclude the meeting with a semblance of calm.

The occupants of the attic on the rue Haute-du-Château were suspicious of this strange visitor claiming to be a Spanish nobleman with letters he needed to deliver to the duchess in person. Was it not odd, Mesnard asks in his memoir, that he seemed to spend all his time in churches and was so assiduously cultivating the mother superior, whose convent was under police surveillance? The legitimists therefore decided to have Deutz followed. It is surprising that they did not stumble across Joly's men: both the police and the legitimists were attempting to track Deutz's movements. Apparently, however, the legitimists did not follow him very closely. According to Mesnard, they did not detect that "Gonzagues" had had "any contact with the authorities" since arriving in Nantes and determined that he had gone out at night only on two occasions (they were wrong, of course).[34]

More trusting than her coterie, the duchess was convinced that the baron de Gonzagues must be Deutz, especially after she received a physical description of him. She was, after all, expecting to hear from her "plenipotentiary" again after his mission to Spain and Portugal. Moreover, she had not yet heard that the legitimist committee in Paris suspected a traitor and therefore had no reason to doubt his loyalty. She was inclined to grant the meeting.[35]

Meanwhile, Deutz was discouraged by his inability to gain the confidence of the local legitimists and had begun to despair of ever getting to see the duchess. He claims that Duval had already signed his passport to leave Nantes when he was accosted, in front of the hotel, by a mysterious lady who asked him if he was monsieur de Gonzagues. Deutz replied that he was. "God be praised! Mme Piquetet is waiting for you at this very moment. Go see her at once," the lady told him before hurrying away.

A few minutes later, Deutz was in Mme Piquetet's salon. This time his reception was much warmer. She handed him a letter from the mother superior in which she apologized on behalf of her associates for their coldness and informed him that the duchess had granted him an interview. He was to be waiting in the lobby of his hotel the following evening. A man would come to him with a note in the duchess's hand, and he was to follow the man to an undisclosed location, where the duchess would be waiting. Deutz went immediately to Joly's hotel and hashed out a plan to make the arrest.[36]

At 7 p.m. on October 31, night had descended on Nantes, and Joly and his men were watching the entrance to the Hôtel de France through the driving rain. At precisely 7:30 p.m. they saw Deutz exit the hotel, accompanied by a portly man of middle height who stumbled a bit, as if drunk. Deutz paused to light a match, the signal he had arranged with Joly to begin pursuit.[37]

Deutz's tipsy guide was Alexandre du Guiny, the brother of Pauline and Marie-Louise, the two women hiding the duchess. Although the walk from the Place Graslin to his sisters' house on the rue Haute-du-Château was short and direct, the escort led Deutz on a roundabout route, as if attempting to confuse anyone who might be following them. His feigned intoxication served as a cover for his meandering. They took the rue Crébillon, then the rues Grétry, Sauteuil, and Rousseau. They passed by the stock exchange before reaching the quay, at which point they doubled back, turning on the rue des États.

Joly and two of his agents did their best to keep the "indicator" in sight as they proceeded through the labyrinth of streets forming the old center of Nantes, but the darkness and the rain made their task difficult. Just as Deutz and Alexandre du Guiny turned onto the rue Haute-du-Château, a detachment of soldiers making their way to the castle barracks crossed in front of them, momentarily blocking the policemen's view. By the time the soldiers had passed, Deutz and his guide were nowhere to be seen.

Realizing that his "indicator" would no longer be able to indicate where the duchess was hiding, Joly decided to head back to the prefecture to get new orders from Maurice Duval. He stationed two of his men on the rue Haute-du-Château with instructions to watch all the houses for suspicious activity, especially the house at no. 1, which he suspected—wrongly—might be the one that harbored the duchess. Another agent, Dubois, stood at the corner so he could watch the other streets leading to the castle.

Deutz trembled as he entered the house at no. 3, believing that he was just moments away from making the arrest. He was led up to the attic, where Mesnard, whom he remembered from Massa, greeted him. Deutz asked to see Madame. At just that moment, the duchess emerged from behind a screen, dressed in a hat and coat that they had covered with dust in order to give the impression that she had traveled from the countryside for the meeting. "Here I am, dear Deutz!" she exclaimed with her characteristic warmth.[38]

Deutz almost fainted at the sound of her voice. "I felt myself grow weak," he says in his memoir. "A cloud passed in front of my eyes, and I felt ill." The fact that Deutz's memoir is filled with lies concerning his motivations, as he attempted retrospectively to convince his readers that he betrayed the duchess out of patriotic devotion rather than greed, makes him an unreliable source concerning his own state of mind, but this brief reference to nearly fainting in the duchess's presence would seem to indicate that he felt some pangs of conscience as he prepared to betray her. At the very least, he comprehended the importance of what he was about to do, and it left him feeling uneasy.

Seeing Deutz on the verge of collapse, the duchess quickly brought him a chair, the kind of spontaneous act of kindness that most royals would not deign to make toward a commoner. "Pull yourself together, my friend," she said. ("*Remettez-vous, mon ami.*") In the legend that grew up around the duchess following her arrest, it was this gesture of friendship extended toward Deutz that most scandalized her supporters. To them, it seemed almost an exact echo of the words spoken by Jesus to Judas in the Garden of Olives at the moment that the latter had come to betray him: "*Amice ad quid venisti?*" ("Friend, wherefore are thou come?") What kind of man, they asked, could betray a woman as good and kind and trusting as this?[39]

Deutz would claim that his resolution did indeed waver when confronted with the duchess's openhearted charm. "The sound of a woman's voice has always had a great deal of power over me," he wrote. But during their three-hour meeting, her talk of rekindling the civil war reminded him of his duty to save France from further suffering. Although Mesnard insists that the duchess had decided to leave France by the time she met with Deutz, it seems probable that she still harbored at least a residue of hope for continuing the struggle. If not, why would she have bothered to hear what Deutz had to say about the possibility of a loan and an arms shipment from Dom Miguel? According to Deutz, she spoke of waiting for the opening of the new session of the Chamber of Deputies a few weeks away, which she thought might lead to a general uprising of the French population against Louis-Philippe.[40]

"Madame, why do you persist in remaining in France? Are you not able to leave?" Deutz says he asked her. To which she replied testily, "No, no. I am here, and here I will remain. I will only leave France dead or as regent." The duchess's obstinacy once again supposedly made Deutz realize that she was an enemy of liberty and a danger to the country. "I regained my resolve," Deutz declares in his memoir, "and Madame would have been arrested immediately if M. Joly had not lost track of me amid the darkness of a cold and rainy night."[41]

According to Mesnard, once the duchess had received the letters from Jauge and the messages from the king of Portugal and her sister, the queen of Spain, she pretended to take her leave and asked Deutz to remain behind. Again, she intended to give the impression that she was not staying in the house. According to Mesnard, an agitated Deutz then threw himself at the duchess's feet, telling her to take precautions and begging her to accord him the title of baron. As Mesnard tells it, after the duchess's exit, Deutz collected himself and looked around the room carefully before making his way downstairs. Mesnard later surmised he was making notes about the layout of the house to help the police in their search. After the convert had vacated the premises, the duchess and Mesnard had a laugh over Deutz's thirst for nobility. "He is crazy!" the duchess said. "First he wants to be my plenipotentiary, now he wants to be a baron! All right, a baron it is. . . . Let us make him a baron!"[42]

At precisely 10:15 p.m., Deutz exited the house. Expecting to see Joly at the head of a division of soldiers ready to burst through the door, he was shocked at the quiet that reigned on the rue Haute-du-Château. Where were the men? Confused, Deutz headed in the direction of the cathedral. After twenty paces, the two policemen stationed by Joly emerged from the shadows and spoke the words they had agreed upon: "Monsieur, can you tell me what time it is?"

Visibly agitated, Deutz responded, "Ah! Here you are . . . thank goodness! The duchess is in there! Where is Monsieur Joly?" One of the men responded, "Very nearby."

"Go get him!" Deutz whispered, wild-eyed. And, grabbing the other man by the collar, he asked if he was armed. The policeman showed him his two pistols. With a tone that the two agents described as "diabolical," Deutz said that the duchess and Mesnard were still in the house but that they were about to leave at any moment. Then, in an effort to find Joly himself, or perhaps wanting to avoid being seen by the duchess as she emerged from the house, he asked the way to the prefecture. The policemen watched him head off in the wrong direction, talking to himself out loud and gesticulating wildly as he walked.[43]

Joly arrived back on the rue Haute-du-Château a few minutes later. The policemen explained what had happened and reported that they had seen nobody except Deutz come out of any of the houses on the street. Joly now dispatched the third policeman, Dubois, to the prefecture, where he found Deutz in Duval's office "in an almost frenetic state." Assuming that the duchess had managed to slip away, Duval gave the order to call off the operation at 11 p.m.

"The failure of that first attempt did not discourage me," Deutz reports in his memoir. The next day, he went to see Joly and apologized for his nerves on the previous evening, explaining that seeing the duchess again had rattled him. But nothing had been lost by their failed attempt, he insisted. On the contrary, they had gained precious details concerning what he assumed to be one of the duchess's many hideouts. Perhaps it had been a good thing that they had failed to raid the house, for the duchess and Mesnard most likely disappeared out a side door immediately after the interview.[44]

Deutz now returned to the mother superior and begged her to arrange another interview with the duchess, claiming that in his nervous state he had forgotten to pass along some key information. She promised to intercede once again on his behalf. After some deliberation, the duchess agreed to see Deutz a second time on November 6 at the house of the du Guinys. This time she supplied the address: no. 3, rue Haute-du-Château. In the meantime, Joly and his men maintained their surveillance on the street but did not notice anyone suspicious coming or going.

On November 5, the day before the second interview, Deutz went to see Mme Piquetet, who handed him two more letters from her relative, the banker Jauge, and a note, in English, saying, "Give the attached letters to our friend." Not knowing if the letters were for Deutz or the duchess, Mme Piquetet asked Deutz to look them over. Unable to decipher the letters, which were written in invisible ink, Deutz took them with him. That afternoon, he paid a call on Bourmont and asked him what to do with the letters. Bourmont told him to give them to the duchess the following day.

In an account of the arrest of the duchess from 1895 that brims with antisemitism, a nephew of the Kersabiecs relays a strange anecdote, recounted to him by his aunt, Stylite. For several nights before the arrest the duchess had dreamed she was being pursued by a terrifying monkey. The first two nights, she was able to elude the grasp of the beast, but this did not allay her fears. "To dream of monkeys is a bad sign," the superstitious duchess confided to Stylite de Kersabiec. Far more rational than her mistress, the lady-in-waiting refused to accord any credence to the dreams. But on the morning of November 6, the duchess reported that the monkey had attacked her in her dream the night before. Stylite attempted to calm her. "It is only a dream," she said, but she too was disturbed by this omen.

Joly and Duval could not afford to waste this second opportunity to arrest the duchess. They needed to find a way to surround the house on the rue Haute-du-Château so that the duchess could not escape, but to do so without alerting suspicion. They thus decided to stage a grand military parade near the castle on November 6, which would last until 5 p.m. Groups of soldiers would be heading back to their barracks when Deutz arrived at the house at 4:30 p.m. They would silently surround the street, blocking off any possible route of egress.

At his second interview, Deutz remained calm as he presented the duchess with the two new letters. "I have no secrets from you, M. Deutz," she said. "I will read them in your presence." After making the writing in invisible ink appear by holding it over a flame, the duchess skimmed through the first of the letters, an account of a negotiation for aid from the Spanish. The second letter was from Jauge, and she read it out loud; it warned her to "be on guard" because there was a traitor who had sold her out to Thiers for a million francs. Throwing this letter nonchalantly onto her work table, where it would be found a few hours later by Joly as he ransacked the house, the duchess looked Deutz squarely in the eye and asked him, with just a hint of amusement, if he was the traitor. "You heard me, monsieur Deutz. Is the traitor perhaps you?"

Deutz did his best to adopt the same bantering tone. "Possibly," he replied, meeting the duchess's penetrating stare. The duchess was reassured by his brazenness.

After conversing for an hour, Deutz took his leave. The duchess bid him a playful farewell. "*Adieu, monsieur le baron!*" she said, with a twinkle in her eye.[45]

On his way downstairs, Deutz paused on the landing of the second floor to notice that the table was set for dinner. This time, he realized, the duchess was not planning to leave the house after their interview—and Joly was waiting outside.[46]

CHAPTER 11

Into the Fire

THE GAS LAMPS on the rue Haute-du-Château had just been lit at 5:30 p.m. on November 6, and their flames cast a dim glow on the quiet cobblestone street. Nantes was deserted at the dinner hour, especially on this small residential street, bounded by the towers of the Cathedral of Saint-Pierre at one end and the moat of the Castle of the Dukes of Brittany on the other. Judging from the silence, nobody would have guessed that the government had twelve hundred troops waiting patiently nearby, ready to surround the house at no. 3 as soon as they received the signal.

Joly studied the house from the shadows. Built of gray stone, its exterior was dignified and plain, nearly identical to the houses on either side except for a small recess in the middle of the second floor in which a statue of the Virgin stood guard. The house had four floors, with three windows facing the street on every floor. Joly knew that behind one of these windows was the duchess.

Joly had watched Deutz enter the house for his second meeting less than an hour before. As the policeman kept his eye on the front door, which was halfway down an alley along one side of the house, he must have wondered whether the "indicator"—as he referred to Deutz in his reports—possessed the sangfroid necessary for the operation to succeed. Joly had enough experience of the convert's erratic behavior over the prior weeks to feel some doubt.

Joly had lost sight of Deutz on his way to the first interview and missed his initial opportunity to make the arrest, so this time he took no chances. He had devised a plan with the prefect, Maurice Duval, and with the generals, Dermoncourt and d'Erlon, who were leading the army's effort to suppress the revolt in the Vendée, to make sure that the duchess would not slip through their net a second time. As soon as Deutz confirmed that the duchess was in the house, Joly would give the signal for d'Erlon and Dermoncourt to surround it with the companies of soldiers who had amassed in the area after the military parade. Then Joly would begin the raid.

The son of a carpenter, the comte d'Erlon had risen up through the ranks in Napoleon's army, earning the Legion of Honor and a noble title thanks to his bravery and efficiency. Exiled by the Bourbons, he had been reduced to running a café in Germany during the Restoration and was only too happy to take up a military command once more after the Revolution of 1830. He had little sympathy for the legitimist cause and lent himself eagerly to the operation to arrest the duchess. Dermoncourt, on the other hand—although also a product of the Napoleonic war machine and a republican—was offended by this business of hunting down a woman. He thought it beneath the honor of a soldier. Although he would do what was required to make sure the area was secure so that the duchess could not escape, he left the actual searching of the house to the police.[1]

A few minutes after 5:30 p.m., Joly saw the door of the house open. By the faint glimmer of the gas jet, he identified the man who emerged as Deutz. The commissioner allowed him to get halfway down the street before making contact to avoid alerting anyone who might be watching from a window above.

"She's in there," Deutz confirmed as soon as he recognized Joly. "You can set your plan in motion. Everything is right this time. Old

Mesnard confided in me that the duchess is planning to have dinner in that house." And he added, his voice quivering with intensity, "It's all up to us!" Having already provided the commissioner with a description of the layout of the house after his last interview, Deutz told Joly that the duchess had received him again in the attic on the top floor. It was there that they were most likely to find her if they entered before dinner began.[2]

When Joly informed Deutz that it would take some time for the troops to assemble, the "indicator" offered to give the signal to the prefect himself, despite his fear of walking in the city alone at night. He wanted to be as far away as possible when the arrest took place.[3]

One of the policemen assigned to guard Deutz at the prefect's office while the operation was being carried out described his state of mind as one of extreme agitation and reported that he was "tormented with remorse."[4] This penitence contradicts the account given by Deutz in his memoir, in which he proudly explains that he betrayed the duchess out of patriotic duty and had no regrets. Whatever the state of his conscience, the convert would set off that very night for Paris in a post chaise. "My presence in Nantes was henceforth unnecessary and my mission was accomplished," he would write, as if to justify his hasty departure. Joly was surely glad to have him out of the way.[5]

While waiting for the troops to arrive, Joly and his men kept a close watch on no. 3 and its neighbors to make sure nobody entered or left. At precisely 5:50 p.m. the first soldiers of the 32nd and 56th Regiments turned the corner onto the rue Haute-du-Château and began their stealthy deployment. Row after row of men in blue uniforms, with red stripes down the trousers and red epaulettes on either side of their jackets, marched as quietly as they could in the darkness, taking care to muffle the sound of their boots hitting the ancient cobblestones. One column stretched along the moat of the castle. Another, led by General Dermoncourt, proceeded down from the cathedral along the Haute-Grande-Rue, behind the rue Haute-du-Château, encircling the house from behind. The third column came straight down from the cathedral on the rue Haute-du-Château and converged with the first two columns in front of the house at no. 3.[6]

Meanwhile, inside the house the duchess readied herself for dinner. Aided by Stylite, she straightened her simple dress of brown merino wool, smoothed her blonde hair, and made her way down the narrow wooden staircase to the dining room. The servant, Charlotte Moreau, had set the table with more care than usual: a white tablecloth and white flowers, the color of the Bourbon flag. The day before had been the duchess's thirty-fourth birthday, and tonight they were celebrating. The cook, Marie Boissy, had prepared *bouilli*, a stew with boiled vegetables and brisket of beef. This was the same humble dish that caused Madame Bovary, in Flaubert's novel, to despair over the monotony of her marriage. Tonight, however, one of the guests had brought a plum pudding, and the repast took on a festive air.[7]

The table was laid for eight. Pauline and Marie-Louise du Guiny, the hosts, had invited their friend and neighbor, Céleste de Kersabiec, the sister of Stylite, along with Louise de Charette, the wife of Charles de Charette (and daughter of the duc de Berry and Amy Brown), who also lived nearby. Mme de Charette had given birth to a son two months before. They were joined by the four rebels hiding in the attic: the duchess, Stylite, Mesnard, and the dashing Achille Guibourg.[8]

When the guests entered the dining room, everyone admired the stillness of the evening—too still perhaps, or so it would appear in retrospect. As Dermoncourt described the scene, "There are moments when nature seems so sweet and friendly that you can't believe, amid the calm, that any danger threatens." The duchess would later tell Dermoncourt that she felt her various worries recede as she approached the window: the failed campaign, the decision whether or not to escape from France, the warning of a traitor in her ranks in the letter she had received from the banker Jauge that very day. She was glad to celebrate her birthday with her closest supporters, whom months of confinement had turned into friends—or, in the case of Guibourg, more than friends. Gazing out, she remarked on the romantic tableau created by the silhouette of the castle set off against the purple night sky.[9]

When Guibourg drew up beside her at the window, however, he noted something else: the glint of the moon off a soldier's bayonet. "*Sauvez-vous, Madame!*" he exclaimed. "Make your escape!" With that single flash of light, there was not a moment to lose.

"Ready yourselves!" the duchess commanded, effortlessly slipping back into her role as military leader. "As we rehearsed!"[10]

The four rebels followed the plan they had gone over many times. In an instant they bounded up the staircase and entered the duchess's attic bedroom. Mesnard ran straight to the fireplace, in the center of which was the small iron door leading to their hiding place: a compartment tucked between the fireplace and the exterior of the house. The tiny closet formed a trapezoid, measuring only three and a half feet long at one end and just nine inches at the other. The roof sloped, so there was barely enough space for a man to hold himself upright at the tallest end.[11]

The duchess insisted that they enter according to size, with Mesnard, the biggest, getting the most space, followed by Guibourg, then Stylite, then the duchess herself at the cramped narrow end. The two men got down on their hands and knees and squeezed themselves, as fast as they could, through the small iron door, which measured only twelve inches wide. But when it came time for Stylite to enter, she tried to give the duchess precedence. The duchess refused. "My dear Stylite, according to proper strategy, when an army retreats, the commander takes up the rear," she supposedly said, pushing her companion in ahead and then closing the trapdoor behind her. Whether she really had the presence of mind to utter such a bon mot with twelve hundred soldiers lined up outside the house remains an open question.[12]

Out in the street, Joly pulled on the bell, a cloven deer's hoof dangling on a rope above the door. He heard the sound of feet on the staircase within and wondered whether they might encounter armed resistance, like at La Pénissière back in June, when a small company

The attic, with diagram
showing the hidden closet

of the duchess's guerrilla fighters—around fifty men—had held off
five battalions of government troops for an entire day. It had been
one of the few successes of the duchess's campaign. Was a similar
surprise in store for him here? Joly rang again. When nobody answered, he ordered his men to attack the door with axes. Finally,
the cook, Marie Boissy, opened the door, acting surprised as Joly
and his men poured into the house. They quickly dispersed to every
room, hoping to lay hold of the duchess before she had time to hide
or escape. Joly's men all carried weapons, and in the confusion of the
moment one officer shot off his gun, wounding himself in the hand.[13]

Instead of guerrilla fighters, they found four frightened aristocratic ladies pretending to sit down to dinner. Dubois, one of the
police officers, mistook Céleste de Kersabiec for the duchess because
of her blonde hair. Realizing his error, he held his gun to her head

and demanded, "Where is your lady?" Despite her terror, Céleste managed to reply that she did not have "the honor of accompanying Madame." Aware that every second these ladies stalled allowed the duchess and her accomplices more time to hide, Joly threatened them all with arrest if they didn't disclose the location of the outlaws. The women tried their best to feign innocence.[14]

Joly was having none of it. Looking at the table, set for eight, he noted that four dinner guests seemed to be missing. The Du Guiny sisters—proud women, with long straight noses, high cheekbones, and brown curls—responded that they were expecting other neighbors who must have been unable to enter the house because of all the soldiers blocking the entrance. Joly then pointed out the soup was already in the bowls and the meat had been cut. "I very much doubt," he added sarcastically, "that it is the custom in Nantes, any more than it is in Paris, to serve the food before all the guests have arrived." The aristocratic ladies maintained a haughty silence.[15]

Realizing that he would get nothing from these women, Joly began interrogating the servants. When they too would say nothing, he ordered them to be brought to the prefecture, hoping they would talk once they were out of earshot of their bosses. He was wrong. Their unwillingness to betray the duchess, even for huge sums of money (reportedly 100,000 francs), became a legend in legitimist circles. In the months that followed several sympathetic newspapers, such as the *Gazette du Languedoc*, would take up subscriptions for Marie Boissy and Charlotte Moreau, publishing the names of everyone who sent even a few francs to help the women. "I just did my duty," the modest cook declared in *La Quotidienne*.[16]

While the servants were being interrogated, Joly and his men began a systematic search of every room in the house as the prefect, Maurice Duval, and General Dermoncourt stood by. Outside, a row of soldiers formed a perimeter around the entire area to make sure that nobody could escape through a tunnel or a secret passageway through a neighboring house. Despite the late hour, another row of gaping onlookers surrounded the soldiers; it seemed like the whole town had come out to witness the arrest of the duchess.[17]

As Joly entered the attic, he recognized, from Deutz's description, the room in which the convert's two interviews with the duchess had taken place. The commissioner scanned the space, taking in the modest dimensions and simple furnishings, including the homely flowered wallpaper that the duchess had hung herself. "This must be the *reception room*, he commented, his ironic tone meant to underscore the contrast between the humble garret and the grand rooms at the Élysée and Tuileries Palaces where the duchess had formerly held court. As his agents searched under the beds, Joly seized the pile of letters addressed to the duchess lying on the work table. Some were stained and crumbling from being held up to a flame to reveal their invisible ink. Now the inspector had no doubt the duchess was hiding somewhere in the house.

On the other side of the thin partition, the outlaws tried not to make a sound. When she heard Joly's comment about the reception room, the duchess realized that it must have been Deutz who betrayed her: she had just met with him in that very spot.

Only a few hours before, she had jokingly asked Deutz whether he was the traitor mentioned in the letter from her supporters in Paris. But whatever suspicions she may have harbored were allayed when he responded in the same bantering tone, his dark eyes holding her gaze as he playfully refused to deny it. She had let herself be fooled, but she now realized her advisers had been right all along. The convert had betrayed her just as he had betrayed his family and his religion. "What bothers me the most," she would say a few days later, "is to have been betrayed, sold out, by a man to whom I had given so much . . . and whom I had trusted completely." The brazenness of Deutz's deception shocked her, but it was the realization that it was her own fault, that her instincts had failed her, which really enraged the duchess. She had been betrayed, yes, but she herself was to blame.[18]

There was only one consolation that the duchess allowed herself: the thought of Deutz's foreignness. "At least the wretch is not a Frenchman," she declared after the events, although some would

claim that she whispered this famous line at the very moment she realized she had been betrayed, while still hiding behind the fireplace.
The comment smacked of antisemitism. It implied that no matter
how hard he tried to assimilate, a Jew like Deutz could never really
become French. The duchess didn't say this explicitly—she never indulged in blatant antisemitism—but it was clear to her supporters
what she meant. Indeed, in a letter written just hours after the arrest,
Marie-Louise du Guiny made the subtext of the duchess's comment
plain when she declared, "The monster who delivered up the unhappy
princess is Jewish and not French: grace be to God!" Antisemites
would continue to repeat versions of the duchess's line for decades
to come.[19]

During those tense moments behind the fireplace, however, the
recognition that it was Deutz who had betrayed her had more immediate consequences for the duchess. It indicated that this was not
a random search: the police were clearly acting on real intelligence
about her whereabouts and therefore knew she was somewhere on
the premises. But it soon became apparent they did not know about
the secret compartment. After scouring her attic bedroom for what
must have seemed like an eternity, Joly moved on to the next room.
The duchess and her companions allowed themselves to breathe once
again. They began to hope that they might elude capture and perhaps
even get to eat some of their festive dinner, which had been left un-
touched on the table below.[20]

After their two guests were escorted home by the police, the Du
Guiny sisters kept up their mute resistance to the police interrogation. When told that their house would be torn apart if they did not
disclose the hiding place of the outlaws, Marie-Louise responded,
"All right then, be our guest." It was growing late, so they asked if the
guards were going to watch them all night, even while they attended
to the call of nature. "We will not try to escape out the window,"
they assured the police. Eventually, the two sisters were allowed to
sleep together in one of the bedrooms. A guard was stationed outside
their door.[21]

Meanwhile, on the first floor of the house the police started sounding the walls and tearing up floorboards. Joly sent for an architect, who went room by room, pointing to any wall that might harbor something behind it. The house was found to conceal numerous secret compartments with incriminating evidence. In one such space they uncovered a printing press and a pile of handbills, adorned with the Bourbon fleur-de-lys, proclaiming the duchess the regent of France and urging the local population to take up arms against Louis-Philippe's government. In several others they found bags of money, nearly 35,000 francs in total. Strangely, though, they failed to detect the secret compartment behind the fireplace in the attic, prompting Dermoncourt later to wonder whether the architect, like so many in France, was secretly a legitimist. The search dragged on for hours.[22]

Pressed up against each other in the dark closet, so close that one of them could not move a limb without silently obtaining the consent of all the others, the four fugitives began to suffer from both cold and hunger. Mesnard, the oldest of the four, found a few pieces of sugar in his pockets that he offered in tribute to the duchess, who insisted on sharing them. Other physical demands also made themselves felt. As the night wore on, it was Guibourg who solved the most pressing problem, offering his hat for use as a chamber pot. He would subsequently be known as *Guibourg-Chapeau* ("Guibourg-Hat") for this act of gallantry. "The situation was truly horrible, and we had to banish all ceremony," the duchess later reported. But with her characteristic insouciance, she added: "*A la guerre comme à la guerre!*" ("All's fair in love and war!")[23]

It seems likely that at least some of the outlaws were thinking of love as well as war during those long hours. Without ever admitting to the affair, Guibourg made plain the intensity of his feelings for the duchess in the book he wrote about that night. His body touching hers in the tiny closet, the heat of her breath mingling with his as they struggled not to move or make a sound, the lawyer transforms what could have been torture into an intensely erotic experience: "Who would have thought!" he wrote. "That horrible position was not without charms for Madame's three servants." He went on to evoke the exquisite pleasure he and the others derived from their extreme proximity to their royal leader: "To suffer with and for a princess for whom one's admiration grows the more one comes to know her, and to whom one has pledged oneself for all eternity . . . offered a satisfaction that soothed our burns and made us forget our hunger and exhaustion."[24]

It seems certain that the duchess shared his passion. Although she never confided her romantic feelings in any letter or diary that historians have been able to trace, it is evident from various eyewitness accounts that she was in love with somebody during the many months she spent in the attic in Nantes. And Guibourg is by far the most likely candidate. Perhaps, then, love helped her to endure the night's horrible conditions. But the duchess always had larger concerns.

She thought of surrender as a betrayal of her son, of the monarchy, and of the French nation. During the preceding months, as one after another distressing report of losses suffered by her partisans in the field made their way to her hiding place in Nantes, she had repeatedly urged her supporters not to give up hope. "It is perseverance that makes us strong: with it we shall triumph!" she had written. Now she faced the perfect test of her principles. If her son's throne depended on being able to stand all night in a miniscule closet without food or water, pressed up against three other people, shivering from the cold and damp, she would rise to the occasion. If her heroine Joan of Arc had been burned at the stake without lamenting her fate, she could as well. What, in the end, did individual suffering matter when the fate of the monarchy was on the line?[25]

After hours of fruitless searching in every corner of no. 3, a frustrated Joly eventually decided to move on to the neighboring houses, leaving two men behind in every room of the Du Guiny residence to stand guard. Before he left, he loudly announced that he would keep up the search for two weeks if necessary, intending to be heard by the outlaws, wherever they were hiding. Inside the cramped closet, the four rebels felt the first pangs of doubt.

November is a cold, damp month in Nantes. Wind blew in through holes in the roof of the house, stinging their skin and aching their bones. "But nobody dared complain," Dermoncourt asserts, "because Madame did not complain." The outlaws were not the only ones to feel the chill during that long, bitter night. The soldiers guarding the room also began to get cold, and one of them went down to the cellar for some peat, which he proceeded to burn in the fireplace. At first, the duchess and her accomplices felt relief as the warm air penetrated their cramped lair. But then the wall that contained the fireplace began to pulse with heat. Soon they couldn't touch the wall without burning their hands. As they struggled to breathe, they prayed for the torture to end.[26]

Just as the fire died down, they heard pounding next door. Joly and his men had begun searching the houses on either side. At one point, parts of the walls and roof rained down on the outlaws. "We wondered if, having resisted the flames, Madame was going to be crushed by stone," Guibourg wrote. "Ah, my poor children, we are going to be hacked to bits, it's all over!" the duchess whispered. Through the holes knocked in the wall, the fugitives could see the soldiers next door. They could also hear their foulmouthed oaths. According to Dermoncourt, who clearly admired how down-to-earth the duchess was despite her royal blood, she found the "bawdy military language" of the soldiers highly amusing.[27]

Fate seemed once more to be on her side. Just as the workers were going to break through the wall, they moved on to another part of the house. It became quiet once again. The guards in the room appeared to have fallen asleep. The duchess also drifted off into unconsciousness, allowing her eyes to close as her body slumped against those of her fellow outlaws. They were packed so tightly that she could stay upright without any effort on her part. She alone was able to sleep while standing up, and the others worried she had fainted.

The respite was short-lived. Toward morning, the soldiers guarding the attic again grew cold. Deciding that the peat didn't burn hot enough, they revived the fire, this time with pages of *La Quotidienne*, the legitimist newspaper, which they found in piles on the floor in the attic. The duchess had taken pleasure in reading this partisan daily during her months of seclusion, delighting in the paper's support for her cause and its descriptions of Louis-Philippe's failures. It now became the source of her torment.

Newspaper generates hot air in more ways than one: it burns much more quickly than peat and produces a great deal of smoke. Soon the hiding place turned suffocating. Gasping for air, Mesnard managed to dislodge a piece of the roof that Joly and his men had damaged during their search. The four outlaws took turns pressing their mouths to the small hole, careful not to make a sound as they maneuvered around one another in the tight space. The sixty-three-year-old Mesnard could no longer stand. Silently, the others had to make room for him as he crumpled to the floor.[28]

The burning-hot fireplace represented an even greater danger than the smoke. In the early 1830s, women's fashion dictated gigantic sleeves shaped like legs of mutton, full skirts down to the floor, and several layers of petticoats. Pressed against the trapdoor, the duchess's brown wool dress caught fire several times, forcing her companions to stamp it out as quickly as they could without alerting the guards on the other side of the thin wall. They also made use of the makeshift chamber pot, otherwise known as Guibourg's hat, dousing the fire with their own urine. "Finally the fireplace plate turned red," the duchess recounted. "My dress, which was touching it, was already burned in several spots and we were lucky to be able to prevent it from catching fire thanks to our handkerchiefs soaked in pee." Despite their resourcefulness, the outlaws wondered how much longer they could survive in this inferno. "It is on my account that you find yourselves in this awful position," the stricken duchess supposedly told her companions. By this point the ordeal had lasted for almost fifteen hours.[29]

The duchess weighed her options. If she waited any longer, they all might die. But if she gave up now, she would lose all she had fought and suffered for over the last six months.

She certainly did not want to see Deutz rewarded for his treason. Nor did she want to prove her many critics correct. These naysayers included first and foremost the exiled royal family—not only her sister-in-law, the duchesse d'Angoulême, but also her father-in-law, Charles X, who had given his official support to her plan for an invasion and civil war, all the while doubting that she could pull it off. Among the papers that were taken from her room after the arrest was a letter from Charles X, written a little over two months before (August 28, 1832) and delivered by Deutz, in which the ex-king instructs his daughter-in-law in no uncertain terms to leave France as soon as possible: "My dear child, I need to express the profound distress that I feel concerning your courageous but ill advised perseverance in an enterprise that is not only flawed in principle but that will no doubt prove as dangerous for you as it is deadly to the cause that we both serve." It must have occurred to the duchess that she had proved just how well-founded the king's doubts were.[30]

As if this shame were not humiliating enough, her arrest would also hand a monumental political victory to Louis-Philippe. What would the usurper do with her if he caught her? On the one hand, there would be pressure to put her on trial, especially from the left-wing advocates of a republic, who sought to erase the threat of another Bourbon restoration once and for all. She could face jail. Or the guillotine. Even if she had prepared for this outcome and had convinced herself she was not afraid to die, she must have worried what would happen to the effort to overthrow Louis-Philippe's government if she weren't there to lead the campaign. Would the Bourbons ever come back to power? Would her son ever be king?

On the other hand, Louis-Philippe and his ministers realized that punishing her risked enflaming her supporters. Jailed or dead, she would become a martyr for the legitimists, just as Marie Antoinette and Louis XVI had become martyrs during the French Revolution. Perhaps, then, Louis-Philippe would let her go free. But for the duchess, this outcome was worse than going to jail, worse even than the guillotine. It would be a humiliation for herself and her

party. "I know no outrage more violent than a pardon," Chateaubri-
and wrote in an open letter to the duchess published in *Le National*
on August 3, 1832, in an attempt to urge her to slip out of France
before getting caught. She had read Chateaubriand's letter, but she
had not listened.

If from the outset she had accepted the guillotine as a risk that she
was willing to take, her perilous situation also forced her to confront
what her death would mean for her family. "Ah, my poor children!"
her companions heard her exclaim quietly to herself as her dress smol-
dered. Although the duchess had left her children in the care of her
in-laws when she began plotting the campaign from Italy, she loved
them deeply, and they in turn felt a genuine bond with her. Some of
this affection comes through in the rather restrained letters they sent
to her while the duchess was in hiding, which were written under the
disapproving eye of the duchesse d'Angoulême. "My dear mother,"
eleven-year-old Henri wrote from Holyrood on August 10, 1832, in a
letter seized from the duchess's desk after her capture. "I think of you
all the time here and I regret not being able to console you. Every day
I pray from the bottom of my heart for heaven to protect you." The
twelve-year-old Louise added in a postscript: "Dear *Maman*, I am so
happy to have the chance to tell you again how much I love you. . . . I
will only be truly happy when we are together again." Reading her
children's plaintive letters, the duchess was no doubt comforted by
the knowledge that she was fighting to restore her son's crown. But
she surely also realized that because of her actions, she might never
see her children again.[31]

There was one other consideration that plagued the duchess during
those painful hours of hiding in the fireplace, a consideration even
more momentous than the others. It was a secret so dangerous that
if it became known, it would do far more damage to herself and the
cause of the legitimate monarchy than any threat that Louis-Philippe
and his ministers could muster. It was most likely the reason that
she had finally agreed, just days before, to leave France by boat the
following week.

The duchess had missed her last two periods. Henri had been dubbed the "miracle child" because he was born eight months after the assassination of the duke in 1820. But her husband had now been dead for twelve years, and if she had another baby, it would be seen by her supporters as anything but a miracle. Once it became known—and how gleefully Louis-Philippe and his ministers would make it known!—that the leader of the party devoted to traditional Catholicism and family values was about to bear a child out of wedlock, it would ruin her reputation and discredit her cause. It would cast the legitimacy of Henri's "miraculous" birth into doubt as well, thus undermining his claim to the throne, the very raison d'être of her whole enterprise. Her followers would abandon her, and she would be repudiated by the royal family. They would never let her see her children again.[32]

But despite her strong reasons for not wanting to get caught, she finally realized that they could not wait out Joly and his men. There wasn't time. Every breath she and her companions struggled to take seemed to be their last. They were all going to die. If they surrendered, arrest . . . humiliation . . . maybe execution. But if they didn't, they faced immediate death.

She gave the order to Mesnard to open the trapdoor to the fireplace.

The trapdoor was so hot that he couldn't get it to budge. Joly's men heard the sounds coming from behind the wall and thought there must be rats. They prepared to strike the vermin when they heard voices behind the wall: "Let us out. We are suffocating!" The soldiers quickly yelled for Joly to come upstairs. The commissioner arrived at 9:30 a.m., just as the soldiers managed to pry open the fireplace door. Out stumbled the duchess, followed by her three companions.[33]

As the guards looked on in shock, she declared, "I am the duchesse de Berry. You are French soldiers. I entrust myself to your honor."[34]

The duchess emerging from the fireplace

PART FIVE

The Scandal

CHAPTER 12

Surrender

WHEN THE DUCHESS emerged from the fireplace, she was pale and disheveled. Her brown wool dress was burned in several places, and her blonde hair was matted with sweat and grime. She had not eaten or had a sip of water for more than sixteen hours. Her voice brimming with emotion, she begged the soldiers not to harm her companions as she held her hands over her face to shield her eyes from the light. Joly thought she looked as if she were still trying to hide and wondered if she had gone insane.[1]

Seeing only the police commissioner and low-ranking subordinates, the duchess demanded to speak with the general in charge. When Dermoncourt entered the attic bedroom, she rushed toward him, practically into his arms.[2]

"General," she said, "I surrender to you and place myself at your mercy."

"Madame," he responded, "Your Highness is under the protection of French honor."

These words appeared to calm her. Despite being a republican who had participated in the storming of the Bastille and fought in the Revolutionary and Napoleonic Wars, Dermoncourt was willing to accord the duchess the respect due to her rank. Moreover, he was a gentleman of the old school and understood the value of gallantry. After helping her to a chair, he ordered the soldiers to bring her a glass of water. Dipping her fingers, the duchess wiped her brow with the cool liquid. The general then ordered another glass for her to drink. When it arrived, Dermoncourt carefully stirred in a piece of sugar before handing it to the duchess.

"General, I reproach myself with nothing," she said, as soon as she had recovered her equilibrium. "I was merely fulfilling a mother's duty by attempting to reclaim her son's birthright." The duchess was echoing a theme that her supporters had been using to justify her civil war for the past several months. Despite her virile military leadership, they had turned her into an icon of motherhood, a role that she fit into easily because the public already saw her as the woman who had saved the Bourbon line by giving birth to the "miracle child." *La Mode* had described the duchess as "at once man and woman, but always a mother" the previous July, after the failure of her military campaign. "Great and noble woman," the same publication declared following her arrest, "France understands all that is sublime in your maternity, superhuman in your sacrifice."[3]

Jo Burr Margadant has described how a sentimental image of motherhood, inspired by the writings of the Enlightenment philosopher Jean-Jacques Rousseau, overtook French society in the early nineteenth century. Along with this elevation of maternity came a cult of domesticity that sought to confine women to the home. On the surface at least, the duchess's cross-dressing military exploits ran directly counter to these conservative gender norms. But by emphasizing that the duchess acted not to gain power for herself, *but on behalf of her son*, her supporters attempted to soften her image and redeem it for their own political ends. According to Jeffrey B. Hobbs, the celebration of the duchess's maternal femininity—emphasizing instinct, devotion, and self-sacrifice—represented a calculated effort by the legitimists to offer a symbolic alternative to the discourse of the Left, which was based on appeals to masculine reason.[4]

As the duchess drank the sugared water given to her by General Dermoncourt, her eyes scanned the room, which was filled with soldiers and National Guard troops who had come to gape at the famous prisoner. She saw Mesnard and Stylite but not Guibourg, who had been requisitioned to help inventory the various articles that the government was preparing to seize from the house as evidence, including caches of printed handbills and 35,000 francs in gold. The lawyer's absence alarmed the duchess. "I do not wish to be separated from my companions in misfortune," she insisted to Dermoncourt, with agitation in her voice that would seem suspicious in retrospect, after her pregnancy had been revealed. The general promised to do everything in his power to keep the outlaws together.[5]

Every eyewitness of the aftermath of the arrest contrasted Dermoncourt's gallantry with the gruff manner of Maurice Duval, the prefect whose arrival in Nantes had occasioned the *charivari* in October. As he entered the attic bedroom, the unpopular bureaucrat committed a faux pas by failing to remove his hat in deference to the sex of his prisoner. Oblivious to manners, Duval rudely stared the duchess in the face for several long seconds, probably attempting to verify that she had a wandering eye, then declared, "Yes, it's her!" before proceeding to search the room for any incriminating evidence that remained.

"Who is that man?" the duchess asked Dermoncourt with evident disgust, once Duval had moved away. After learning his identity, she asked if he had served the Restoration government. Told that he had not, the duchess sniffed, "I am relieved on behalf of the Restoration."[6]

Duval demanded that the duchess hand over any papers that she might be concealing on her person. She replied that if they searched the secret compartment behind the fireplace, they would find a portfolio but asked that it be brought to her so she could hand over its contents herself. Along with several letters that she surrendered to the prefect, she also removed a small painted image of Saint Clement. The first-century martyr had been tied to an anchor and thrown into the sea for preaching to his fellow prisoners. He became the patron saint of sailors. Given her own captivity and the excruciating sea voyage she was about to take, the saint was an appropriate object for the duchess's devotion at that moment.

To all appearances the duchess was on the verge of collapse. But she clearly kept more of her wits about her than she let on. As she handed letters to Duval, the duchess surreptitiously slipped one to Stylite, who looked it over quickly before tearing it into little pieces. Joly witnessed this operation and retrieved the pieces, which he turned over to Duval. Nobody has ever discovered what that letter contained, but it surely involved something incriminating either for the duchess or for one of her associates. The government seized many letters that day—including some delivered to the duchess by Deutz—that would have compromised important aristocratic families and foreign powers by implicating them in the duchess's conspiracy. However, Adolphe Thiers chose to make certain of these letters disappear. The wily minister no doubt realized that holding back information can often be more profitable than revealing it.[7]

When Duval's men found 13,000 francs hidden behind the fireplace, the duchess asked which one of the soldiers had lit the fire in the room the previous night. She then made the kind of grand gesture she was famous for, insisting the money be given to the man who had smoked her out. (According to Alexandre Dumas, when the duchess later read Dermoncourt's account of the episode, she was outraged that the soldier had not been allowed to keep her gift and wrote a letter of protest to the government.) Meanwhile, as the government's agents ransacked the house, Simon Deutz sped to Paris, a journey that took around two days in a fast carriage. He reportedly left behind an unpaid bill for 100 francs at the Hôtel de France.[8]

Like myths of the duchess's generosity, Deutz's greed would become the stuff of legend. Jews, of course, had long been associated with money in the European imagination, but the stereotype took on new force with the development of the modern capitalist economy in the nineteenth century and the increased visibility of certain wealthy Jewish banking families in the French capital. Because many of these bankers, including the Rothschilds, supported Louis-Philippe, they became a target for critics on both the Far Left and Far Right of the political spectrum. To be sure, most of the bankers allied with the July Monarchy were not Jews, but the impression that Jews were the "kings of the age"—as the far-left journalist Alphonse Toussenel would label them in the 1840s—struck a chord. According to Toussenel, the Jews had laid hold of the nation's resources and were turning France into their feudal domain.[9]

Descriptions of Deutz were colored by these stereotypes. Immediately after the arrest of the duchess, rumors began to circulate that Adolphe Thiers had paid Deutz as much as a million francs as the price of his betrayal, although others said it was closer to a half million. Either way it was an enormous sum of money, given that a middle-class family could live comfortably on two thousand francs per year, and most French people earned much less than that. For the legitimists, this was Judas's thirty pieces of silver with compounding interest. And as in the Bible, the blood money turned the Jew who accepted it into a pariah. In one version that circulated after the arrest of the duchess, which Édouard Drumont relayed in *La France Juive* (1886), Thiers's secretary used a pair of pincers to hand Deutz the money so as not to have to contaminate his fingers with the dirty lucre.[10]

Other authors repeated the story of the pincers if only to deny its accuracy. But the terms of their dismissal say a great deal about the antisemitic lens through which the betrayal of the duchess was viewed in the nineteenth century. According to one contemporary, a viscount, "We don't believe the legend of the 500,000 francs handed over to Deutz with pincers. The functionaries of 1830 respected Jews and banknotes too much to treat them in such a cavalier manner." Another viscount, the nephew of Stylite, also discounted the legend, noting that Thiers and his minions had already sullied themselves to such a degree that no filth would have made them recoil.[11]

Deutz strenuously denied asking the government for money in exchange for his services. In his memoir he reports telling the minister of the interior that if he had wanted to sell out the duchess, the government would not have been rich enough to pay him. "In this entire affair, never did self-interest guide me, never did a word about money come out of my mouth, never did the thought enter my head to treat this as a speculation, never did I see Madame as a women to be sold." The comtesse de Boigne, a close confidante of Thiers, confirms that the minister claimed to her that "no salary had been either demanded or promised" in exchange for Deutz's betrayal.[12]

However, if Deutz denies *asking* for money, he notably does not deny *accepting* it. Likewise, Thiers denies having *promised* the money but not having *given* it. And indeed, conserved in a pile of the minister's papers at the Bibliothèque nationale is a receipt, dated November 17, 1832, and signed by Deutz, acknowledging that he received 500,000 francs from Adolphe Thiers. Deutz also admitted accepting the money later in a letter to Louis-Philippe. Even if we choose to believe that greed was not his primary motive in turning the duchess over to the government, there is no doubt that he profited handsomely from the betrayal.[13]

DEUTZ WOULD FEAR for his life once the news leaked to the press, but in the immediate aftermath of the arrest it was the duchess who was in greater danger. Once she had recovered a bit of her strength, the military authorities determined she needed to be moved to a more secure location. The comte d'Erlon confided in Dermoncourt that he feared a popular disturbance: crowds of people, many of them angry at the duchess for turning their region upside down with her civil war, had already gathered in front of the house on the rue Haute-du-Château. D'Erlon also feared that the legitimists might try to rescue their leader. The nearby Castle of the Dukes of Brittany seemed like the obvious choice for a temporary jail: it had ample rooms, thick walls, and a large moat to deter attack.[14]

Although the castle was just down the street, Stylite insisted that the government convey the duchess there in a carriage. Her royal highness should not have to go to jail on foot. However, the duchess understood the impracticality of riding such a short distance and agreed to walk, provided that Dermoncourt guarantee her safety. "Let us go, my friends!" she gamely declared. Two long rows of troops stretched between the house and the castle, forming a protected walkway for the duchess. Behind this human barrier, throngs of people pressed, ten rows thick, trying to catch a glimpse of the woman whose impetuous civil war had roiled their region over the prior six months.[15]

The duchess emerged from the house on the arm of the general, her head high. They were followed by Stylite, Guibourg, and Mesnard, who was practically carried by two policemen because he was too weak to walk. A murmur rose from the crowd at the sight of the prisoners, but when Dermoncourt gestured for quiet, the townspeople immediately fell silent.[16]

The distance they had to traverse was only some sixty feet, but it must have felt to the duchess like a marathon. Steeling herself and looking straight ahead, she showed no sign of emotion as she made her way past the gauntlet of soldiers, other than to grip Dermoncourt's arm a bit tighter. According to the reporter for the right-wing *Gazette de France*, "not a cry, not a murmur," escaped the onlookers as the duchess passed. "All eyes were lowered before the mother of the duc de Bordeaux, who displayed in the moment a sangfroid, a firm dignity that is assumed to be an attribute of the other sex." Dermoncourt did not breathe a sigh of relief until they had crossed the drawbridge and the door of the castle shut behind them.[17]

Built along the banks of the Loire, the waters of which fill the moat, the Castle of the Dukes of Brittany is really two castles in one. The side facing the city is a medieval fortress featuring four crenellated stone towers, squat and menacing, mostly constructed in the late 1400s. Facing the river is a sixteenth-century Renaissance palace, with flamboyant Gothic motifs decorating the windows of the main building, the *Grand Logis*, and tall, pointy spires presiding over a grand courtyard. Constructed as both a defensive bastion and a royal residence, the castle never really served either function, and by the early nineteenth century it was mainly used as a military barracks, an artillery factory, and a prison.

Once inside the castle, the duchess felt her legs buckle beneath her. The strain of the day's emotions had taken their toll, and Dermoncourt had to help her up the stairs to the rooms that the artillery colonel in command of the castle had made available. It was only then that the duchess realized how hungry she was. Joly arranged for a simple lunch—some soup and a bottle of Bordeaux—to be brought from a local caterer, and one of his men served the duchess, Stylite, and Guibourg. Mesnard was too exhausted to eat; carried to a room in a different wing of the castle, he collapsed fully clothed onto the bed. Dermoncourt left the other prisoners to attend to him.

After arranging for a doctor and ensuring that Mesnard was in no imminent danger, Dermoncourt returned to find the duchess enraged at having been separated from Mesnard despite the general's promise to do whatever was in his power to keep all the prisoners together. She demanded to be brought to him immediately. Dermoncourt reminded her that she was under arrest and could not give orders. "Ah! That is true," she sighed. "I thought I was in a castle but it is really a prison."[18]

As the duchess ate her meager lunch with Stylite and Guibourg, Joly spied on them from the adjoining room. He saw the duchess place a small note into the belt of the lawyer's pants. The police commissioner ordered his men to search Guibourg later that night, but his report states that he never learned the contents of the note. The comtesse de Boigne, better informed thanks to Thiers, says that the illicit communiqué contained the following message: "Whatever happens, insist on not being separated from me." According to Boigne, it was the story of this note that caused all of Paris to gossip about the romantic liaison between the duchess and Guibourg, and helped launch the rumor that he was the father of her unborn child. "I do not want to guarantee that there was nothing to it," Boigne says in her typical manner, at once distancing herself from the rumor and lending it credence.[19]

The duchess asked Dermoncourt whether she would be allowed to eat dinner with Guibourg that evening. The general responded, "I don't see why not, given how it will be the last time that he will have that honor." Dermoncourt had received word that the lawyer would be transferred to another jail later in the night. Guibourg had already been brought up on charges—and escaped from prison—so the government determined that he would be detained separately from the duchess, Mesnard, and Stylite.

The duchess apparently did not hear Dermoncourt's warning, because the next morning she was outraged to learn that Guibourg had departed. She accused the general of not being true to his word when he promised she would not be separated from her "companions in misfortune." When Dermoncourt tried to explain that it was really only Mesnard and Stylite who had shared all her trials and tribulations, not Guibourg, she accused him of resorting to a Jesuitical argument. "That insult was curious coming from the duchess," the general remarked of the woman who made such a show of her religious devotion. Stylite confirmed that Dermoncourt had in fact warned her of Guibourg's departure, and the duchess resigned herself to the separation.[20]

To pass the time as she waited to hear what the government would do with her, the duchess asked Dermoncourt if she could read some newspapers. As Dermoncourt relays the scene, he asked which papers she desired and was shocked that in addition to right-wing rags such as *La Quotidienne*, she also wanted left-leaning newspapers such as *Le Constitutionnel,* *Le Courrier Français*, and even *L'Ami de la Charte*. "Why, Your Highness . . . will become a Jacobin!" Dermoncourt teased. The duchess responded that she admired the way the left-wing journalists defended their opinions, even if she did not agree with them. She also admitted that she liked that the republican papers all called her "Caroline" rather than "her highness" or "Madame." Although she knew it was an insult for them to refer to her by her first name, it made her nostalgic for her youth. "My married name," she added wistfully, "has not brought me happiness."[21]

The newspapers that the duchess read in the days following her arrest were full of debates over her fate. The government now faced the dilemma that Louis-Philippe had dreaded since the summer. Should they put the duchess on trial for treason as the liberals were demanding? Or should they let her go free in order to avoid antagonizing the Bourbon loyalists? From a legal point of view, the duchess had committed treason by leading a civil war against the government and had to face judgment. The royal court of Poitiers ordered the duchess to stand trial, for part of her war had been conducted in its jurisdiction, and the Rennes court might have wanted to try her as well. According to those on the Left, political considerations had no bearing on the matter: the principles of the constitutional monarchy dictated that no individual could be above the law.

But was the duchess really just an individual? Legitimists claimed that attempting to put the duchess on trial would constitute lèse-majesté, the crime of insulting a monarch, akin to sacrilege and itself a form of treason. They remembered all too well the trial of Louis XVI, when Louis-Philippe's father voted for execution, which they considered the worst crime of the French Revolution. In private, however, some of the duchess's supporters admitted to wanting a trial because they assumed her popularity would lead to an acquittal, which would be an enormous triumph for their cause and a slap in the face of the government.[22]

The question of the duchess's fate, which cut to the heart of the ongoing debate over the legacy of the French Revolution, was a burning one not just in France but across Europe. As Louis-Philippe was only too aware, the crowned heads of neighboring countries, allies and in some cases close relatives of the duchess, were watching the affair closely. Threatened with their own revolutionary struggles, these monarchs would view any attempt to judge a royal personage as a provocation. Along with the increasingly volatile situation across the border in Belgium, the arrest of the duchess threatened to drag France into a European war.

Complicating matters still further for Louis-Philippe was the fact that the duchess was his wife's niece. Even if relations between them had chilled—frozen over might be the more accurate trope—since Louis-Philippe had seized power from the Bourbons in July of 1830, Marie-Amélie still viewed the duchesse de Berry as a member of her family. She had prayed that the duchess would slip out of France before getting arrested and was terrified that she would attempt something foolish to avoid going to prison. When the comtesse de Boigne went to the Tuileries on the day the arrest was announced in *Le Moniteur universel*, she found the queen in a state of nervous agitation. "You know that with Caroline's head there is much to fear!" Marie-Amélie told the countess and kept repeating: "She wanted this! She wanted this! It is not the king's fault." Boigne asked the queen whether they might simply deport the duchess to Naples or Trieste. A law passed on April 10, 1832, which banished the Bourbons from French territory, would have provided the legal cover for the government to expel her. "Ah, my dear," the queen said, "you can't imagine how much we would want this." But gone were the days when the king could act without consulting Parliament. "They won't allow it . . . they say it is impossible," the queen lamented before returning to her refrain. "If only she had taken advantage of those six months of patience to get out."[23]

The left-wing newspapers were adamant that the duchess stand trial. "There exists a legal order that obligates the duchess to appear before a criminal court," wrote *Le Constitutionnel*, "and we do not know of any power in France that can prevent the execution of such an order. The law has spoken and must follow its course." The journalists for *Le Temps* agreed that the duchess must stand trial even if they accepted that a pardon from Louis-Philippe might follow: "Nobody in France is above the law. The duchess should be judged. . . . Clemency can only come after justice is served."[24]

For the liberal *Journal du commerce*, it was fundamentally a matter of fairness, of applying the same law to all citizens. "Should ordinary laws, which are so strictly applied to commoners, be suspended, despite the Charter?" they asked. Royalty must not get a free pass when the lower classes were punished harshly for their crimes. But it was also vital not to let the right wing get the upper hand: "Should common law be vanquished by privilege and the France of July be humiliated in its hand-to-hand combat with legitimacy?" For liberals, bringing the duchess to trial was first and foremost a matter of principle, but it was also a matter of politics.[25]

Unsurprisingly, the right wing saw matters quite differently. *La Quotidienne* accused the government of using the arrest of the duchess to win points with the revolutionaries. The right-wing journalists also accused the government of arresting the duchess to avoid having to help the Belgians drive the remaining Dutch soldiers out of the fortress of Antwerp. "They [the government] found it both easier and more worthy of them to lay their hands on a woman than on a citadel." This kind of mockery had an effect, and Louis-Philippe ordered the army to lay siege to Antwerp the following week.[26]

After much hand-wringing, Louis-Philippe's Council of Ministers determined that the duchess would not stand trial, at least for now. Because anything pertaining to the Bourbons was a matter of state, they reasoned, the fate of the duchess should be decided by the Chamber of Deputies. Already on November 9, at the same time as it announced the arrest of the duchess, the government's official organ, *Le Moniteur universel*, published an ordinance signed by the king that would refer her case to the legislature: "Article 1. Proposed legislation concerning the status of the duchesse de Berry will be presented to the Chambers." An article in *Le Moniteur* on November 11 further explained that because the duchess was a Bourbon, she was beyond the reach of common law: "The members of families who reign, or who have reigned, are in a unique situation. Legislative resolutions [as opposed to common laws] determine their status, their fortune, their destiny." The minister François Guizot explained in his memoirs that the government considered this compromise "the only one allowed both by moral decency as well as politics, by fairness as well as good sense."[27]

But like so much about Louis-Philippe's regime, the compromise pleased nobody. The Left was outraged by the failure to put the duchess on trial, and the Right was outraged that the government had deferred to the Chamber of Deputies. "Everyone understands the goal of this expedient maneuver" was to shift blame "onto other shoulders," wrote *La Quotidienne.* The government's concern for the authority of the legislature was, to the right-wing journalists, little more than a smoke screen. "In pretending to pay homage to parliamentary authority, they are looking to provide themselves with shade," the same article claimed, "and their courtesy for the deputies is nothing but fear for themselves."[28]

The government's dilemma provided the journalists for the satirical newspaper *Le Corsaire* with a field day. Known for mocking both the Left and the Right, *Le Corsaire* poked ruthless fun at the minister of the interior. Shortly after the arrest of the duchess, it proclaimed, "Monsieur Thiers is now an immortal; he found the duchesse de Berri [*sic*] behind a fireplace, he will go to the Pantheon on the shoulders of a chimney sweep." The duchess's supporters also received their share of derision: "The legitimists were caught in a fireplace; they are going up in smoke."[29]

But it was the government's decision to place the duchess's case before the legislature that occasioned the satirists' most biting attack. On November 13 *Le Corsaire* mocked the government's proposed bill for violating the principle that laws should not target specific individuals: "Article 1. All duchesses of Berry are henceforth banished from the kingdom." "Article 2. All duchesses of Berry are declared incapable of holding any civil or military employment." "Article 4. All duchesses of Berry caught leading a civil war will henceforth be lodged, fed, clothed, heated, ironed, tailored, and entertained at the expense of the taxpayers in order to avenge the latter, and in order to deter future duchesses of Berry should any exist." It was clear that the government's decision had not provided it with shade after all.[30]

As they awaited the decision of the Chamber of Deputies concerning the fate of the duchess, the ministers determined that she and her companions should move to an even more secure location, far away from the angry liberal mobs, the reach of would-be rescuers, and the prying eyes of journalists. They were to be held at an isolated and remote military outpost farther down the Atlantic Coast: the Citadel of Blaye. Thiers gave orders to ready this forbidding edifice for its new royal resident.[31]

Out of a concern for their safety, Duval arranged for the transfer of the outlaws from the castle to take place under cover of darkness. On the afternoon of November 8, Duval and the comte d'Erlon instructed the duchess to be ready to leave that night. Stylite immediately began to pack the trunks that had been sent over for the duchess from the attic at no. 3. Joly informs us that unbeknownst to the duchess, he searched her luggage, and hidden with her regular outfits he found peasant costumes and other bizarre disguises. Perhaps the duchess believed they would come in handy if she made an escape.[32]

At 3 a.m. Joly knocked on the door of the room that the duchess shared with Stylite. The ladies did not make him wait, and at 3:30 a.m., illuminated only by the moon and a single torch, they and Mesnard entered a carriage in the courtyard, which conveyed them to the riverbank. The duchess wore an eccentric traveling outfit to protect her against the cold: a tulle bonnet, tied under her chin; a dress of puce and white stripes; a tartan shawl made of coarse wool; a scarf around her neck; and heavy laced boots over thick white stockings. As she exited the carriage, she donned a green wool coat with black flowers and a purple velvet hat adorned with matching purple ribbons. Her days as a fashion icon had definitively come to an end.[33]

Accompanied by a small delegation that included Duval, d'Erlon, and Joly, they boarded the Paimboeuf steamboat, which was waiting to take them to the nearby harbor of St. Nazaire, where a warship, the corvette *La Capricieuse*, was docked. Joly reports that during the transfer, the duchess was full of recognition for the soldiers and policemen who helped her. Once the duchess was settled in the captain's room on the steamboat, Duval and d'Erlon bid their prisoner good-bye. Joly stayed on; the man she held responsible for both her husband's murder and her own arrest would accompany the duchess to Blaye.

The duchess asked whether Guibourg would also be making the trip. Informed that he was staying behind to face trial, she quickly penned a note to the lawyer. "God will aid us and we will see each other again soon," she wrote the man who was very likely the father of her unborn child. "Give my regards to all our friends. May God keep them. Let us have courage and confidence in Him. We Bretons look to our patron Saint Anne." As the boat lifted anchor, she handed the note to one of the officers to deliver to Guibourg.[34]

She would never see him again; after his trial, Guibourg returned to private life and married someone else a few years later. For the duchess the pain of separation must have been intense, and it was compounded by her uncertainty about what lay in store. Her other companions—Stylite, Mesnard, and Mathilde Lebeschu, her attendant from Massa, who now joined her for the journey to Blaye—did what they could to alleviate her suffering.

The Atlantic is always choppy in November, but the weather on November 9 was so bad that the commander of *La Capricieuse* determined that they needed to wait for the sea to settle before leaving the harbor. The next morning, they spied another boat, *L'Africain*, approaching them. This was the same boat that Joly had ordered his men to keep an eye on that fall: he suspected it was waiting to help the duchess escape to England or Holland. Fearing a surprise attack, Joly told their captain they needed to set sail at once.

But his fears were misplaced. As *L'Africain* came within shouting distance, its captain doffed his hat to the duchess, who had come onto the deck of *La Capricieuse* to see what was happening. "Madame, these men do me the honor of thinking that I have come to save you," the captain said with the aid of a megaphone. "If only it pleased God to be so. I would much prefer to see you on my ship, whatever danger it would cause me, than to see you where you are now. Have courage, Madame, all is not lost!" The rest of his speech was drowned out by the movement aboard *La Capricieuse* as the sailors scrambled to prepare the ship. "*Au large!*" the captain cried. "Anchors aweigh!" But the weather remained stormy, and true to its fickle name, *La Capricieuse* was not ready to depart for another day.[35]

The corvette was built at the Bayonne shipyard between 1825 and 1828 and had served in the expedition to conquer Algeria in 1830.

Equipped with multiple cannons and designed for speed, it was not the most commodious vessel. "You will admit," the duchess would later complain to her doctor, "that the royal navy could have found something better to transport me." During the actual voyage, however, the duchess was too seasick to heed her surroundings. At a lull in the horrendous rolling of the ship, as the duchess took some air on the deck, she was forced to converse with her nemesis, Joly: she told him, only half-jokingly, that he would be in trouble with Dom Miguel, her ally, if the storm blew them all the way to Portugal. Joly responded that having done all he could to respect the duchess's misfortune, he would count on her to intercede on his behalf.[36]

A little later the police commissioner had an even more interesting conversation, this one with Stylite. After Joly shared his concern over the unhappy state of the duchess's stomach, Stylite mentioned that it was all the more concerning because her mistress had experienced "a suppression" for the prior two months. This was the era's euphemism of choice for a missed menstrual cycle. Stylite immediately appeared to regret the confidence, but it was too late to take it back. Joly let the matter drop. However, he and Stylite were not the only ones to realize that something besides the sea may have been making the duchess sick. D'Erlon remarked on the day they transported the duchess from the Château to the boat that "it seems to me that Madame is pregnant."[37]

After another day of horrible weather, they approached the mouth of the Gironde estuary on November 11, but it would take several more days to reach the port because of the contrary winds and high seas. Everyone aboard was violently ill. The duchess ate nothing except toast dipped in vinegar, some preserved sardines, a bit of tea, and mint pastilles to settle her stomach. Finally, on November 15, they were transferred to a steamboat, *Le Bordelais*, which would carry them up the estuary to the Citadel of Blaye. It was not a simple operation: one of the officers on board had to lift the duchess under her arms and hoist her from one boat to the other as the waves rocked the ships violently back and forth.[38]

In moments of calm aboard the various boats, the duchess devoured the coverage of her arrest in the press. It was on *Le Bordelais* that she learned that Deutz had received a huge reward for his treason and commented—or repeated—that at least it was not a Frenchman who had betrayed her.[39]

Included in the press coverage of her arrest was another item that would have displeased the duchess far more than the news of Deutz's sudden fortune, had she come upon it in *Le Corsaire* on November 12. It contained a snide innuendo about her pregnancy: "A Carlist journal assures us that since her arrest, the duchesse de Berri [*sic*] *has grown much more weighty*," a double entendre that referred to more than her importance. Her supporters would angrily denounce these rumors. Duels would soon be fought. But how long, the duchess must have wondered as she entered her new prison, would she be able to keep her secret?[40]

CHAPTER 13

The Illustrious Captive

THE CITADEL OF Blaye perches high atop a cliff overlooking the Gironde estuary, at the point where the Garonne and Dordogne Rivers converge on their way to the Atlantic. Constructed in the late 1600s by the military engineer Vauban on the site of a medieval castle, the fortress was designed to protect the port of Bordeaux, which lies just downstream, from a sea invasion. Stone ramparts rise up 150 feet from the water below, surrounding the fortress and cutting it off from the adjacent town of Blaye. Considered impregnable in its time, the citadel is a desolate place, especially in winter, when freezing winds blow in from the Atlantic.

It was nighttime when a small rowboat carried the duchess from the steamship to shore. Accompanied by her "companions in misfortune"—the comte de Mesnard, Stylite de Kersabiec, and Mathilde Lebeschu, her attendant—the duchess stepped into a waiting carriage to drive the short distance to the citadel. Torches lit the way as the carriage passed between a double row of soldiers shielding the prisoners from the curious gazes of the townspeople. Once inside the fortress gates, the duchess descended from the carriage and made the rest of the journey on foot.

She was joined by Colonel Martial Chousserie, who had sailed with her from Nantes and had now been appointed governor of the citadel. The duchess approved of this choice: the colonel had surprised her with his gallantry aboard the ship, as had his lieutenant, Ferdinand Petitpierre (with whom she developed a good rapport possibly because his family name recalled her disguise as a peasant boy during the war). They seemed sympathetic to her plight and perhaps also to her cause. Despite the sinister presence of the policeman Joly, whom the duchess now associated with the two worst tragedies in her life, she was still able to muster a bit of optimism.

The situation she faced was certainly dire. "The news of my misfortune will probably have reached you before this letter," she wrote to the duchesse d'Angoulême, shortly after setting foot in Blaye. "A man, a foreigner, who owed me more than his life, has trafficked in my liberty," she said, referring to Deutz. It was thanks to this "foreigner" that so many of her supporters had been arrested and that she herself now faced prison and perhaps execution. The duchess nevertheless expressed hope: "A clean conscience and my submission to the decrees of Providence will give me the strength I need to withstand these reversals of fortune. I will think of you, dear sister, and your example will teach me to suffer with patience."[1]

Of course, the duchess's conscience was not actually so clean. The press had already begun to make oblique references to her condition. Was this letter an attempt to warn her disapproving sister-in-law not to believe the rumors she would soon hear? At this point, legitimists still considered the duchesse de Berry the regent of France and the titular head of their party. She assumed that she would not remain so for long if her secret became known. Her only hope for continuing her struggle was to secure release from the citadel before the government learned of her pregnancy.

The duchess's arrest came at a particularly fraught political moment for Louis-Philippe. He had finally decided to intervene in Belgium:

the French army laid siege to the Citadel of Antwerp on November 15, 1832. The operation lasted until late December, when the Dutch finally withdrew. Meanwhile, the Chamber of Deputies had just opened its new session, and the government feared another round of republican agitation. It arrived on cue: on November 19 a radical republican journalist nearly assassinated Louis-Philippe as he crossed the Pont-Royal in the center of Paris. This was only one of eight assassination attempts from which the unpopular king managed to escape over the course of his eighteen-year reign. In December, Louis-Philippe shook up his cabinet yet again, replacing Thiers with Antoine d'Argout as minister of the interior, a move that must have pleased the duchess, given her loathing for the man who had overseen her arrest.[2]

By referring the duchess's case to the Chamber of Deputies, Louis-Philippe hoped to avoid bringing his niece before the court, which could only have disastrous consequences for his regime. "Nobody wants to see her brought to trial," the king told Guizot, his future prime minister. Given the duchess's popularity and the sympathy that was building for her after the dramatic details of her arrest were made known, there was a strong likelihood that she would be acquitted, but a conviction might prove even more politically dangerous, for it would outrage her supporters and anger neighboring monarchies.[3]

The Chamber of Deputies acquiesced to the king's wish, agreeing in a session on January 5, 1833, that the duchess would not stand trial. But neither would she go free. Louis-Philippe and his ministers decided to pursue a half measure of dubious legality: the duchess would remain interned at Blaye by executive order, for an unspecified amount of time, without having been judged. The only thing that explains the government's decision to keep the duchess at Blaye is suspicion of her pregnancy. We know that the comte d'Erlon guessed her condition in the days following the arrest and that Stylite had accidentally let slip a confirmation to Joly. Others, including Lieutenant Petitpierre, noticed the signs of pregnancy as well. The ministers thus decided to keep the duchess locked up so she could not end the pregnancy and until she could no longer hide it.[4]

A silent battle between the duchess and her captors now began: just as the duchess was determined to keep her condition hidden, so too was the government intent on exposing it. The stakes of this struggle could not have been higher for either side.

WHEN THE DUCHESS and her companions arrived in Blaye, the government had not yet finished the work of converting the citadel into a jail. Workers were still attaching iron bars to the windows of the house that the prisoners would occupy, which had formerly belonged to the commander of the fortress. Surrounded on all sides by soldiers' barracks, the house was rectangular, with two floors plus an attic. Soldiers occupied the ground floor and guarded the sole staircase leading to the six rooms occupied by the prisoners on the floor above.[5]

As the duchess made her way up the stairs, she took in the dwelling that would constitute her universe for the foreseeable future. It was the home of a mid-level provincial bureaucrat, respectable but

The house where the duchess was imprisoned in Blaye

devoid of style: chairs upholstered in yellow and blue striped velvet, a mahogany desk against the window, a screen adorned with green silk, a wool carpet, curtains of yellow and white calico, a small piano. There was a bedroom for her and a salon, as well as rooms for her companions. "The apartments of madame la duchesse de Berry were sufficiently large and decently furnished," the comtesse de Boigne tells us. "Aside from the only thing that she wanted, liberty, they met all her needs." Indeed, if the duchess felt depressed as she settled into Blaye, it was not only because of the stodgy decor. "It used to be that the slightest resistance to my desires exasperated me. I could not bear the idea of a prison," she told Mesnard. "Now my sufferings are no longer just ideas."[6]

During the early days of her stay in Blaye, the duchess took long walks along the citadel's windy ramparts. From that elevated position, she could look out at the harbor below, where *La Capricieuse* fired daily cannon shots to dissuade the "Carlists" from attempting a rescue. These walks also enabled the duchess to be seen by her many supporters who had flocked to Blaye to offer their moral support.

The inns were overflowing with aristocrats: even before her arrival on November 15, the population of the town had swelled in anticipation. *La Mode* sent a journalist to Blaye to report on the health of the prisoner, which everyone assumed must be suffering in the cold, damp coastal climate. Unable to gain access to the citadel, the journalist was reduced to filing weekly reports based on occasional long-distance sightings of the duchess wandering the ramparts. The *Gazette de France* printed its daily updates on the duchess's captivity in Blaye surrounded by a black border, as if anticipating her death.[7]

Of all the writers gripped by the betrayal of the duchess, it was the great Romantic novelist, essayist, and statesman Chateaubriand who most clearly expressed the heartbreak of the legitimists as well as their continued devotion to her cause. Born in 1768, Chateaubriand belonged to a generation—and a class, the provincial nobility—that had experienced the French Revolution firsthand. His brother had died on the guillotine, and his mother and sister spent time in a revolutionary prison. Chateaubriand would never get over the trauma of this period: both his literature and his politics would be marked by an abiding sense of melancholy and a devotion to lost causes. But even while remaining forever loyal to France's "legitimate" monarchy, he understood that the clock of liberty could not be set back, and he opposed the overreaching of the *ultras* during the reign of Charles X. After the Revolution of 1830 sent him into exile, he decried the usurpation of Louis-Philippe, as well as the petty materialism of his supporters, the egotistical capitalists of the *juste milieu*.

Chateaubriand saw in the heroic exploits of the duchesse de Berry an example of nobility—reflected in her willingness to sacrifice herself for the sake of a cause—that he thought had disappeared from modern France. This nobility became all the more sacred, and all the more interesting to Chateaubriand, once the duchess had failed in her attempt to recover the throne and when the extent of her sacrifice became plain. Upon learning of her arrest while he was in self-imposed exile in Switzerland, Chateaubriand immediately wrote to the government to request to serve as the duchess's lawyer. When he was denied, he published a *Memoir on the Captivity of the Duchesse de Berry* that, in the absence of a legal trial, sought to defend the duchess's actions before the court of public opinion.[8]

"Are all civil wars equally criminal?" Chateaubriand asked in his pamphlet, comparing the duchess to Napoleon and her campaign to the emperor's Hundred Days. Although as a member of her "secret committee" of advisers the writer had prudently counseled the duchess against launching her civil war, he now described her escapade in glowing terms: "I have nothing but admiration for the magnanimous devotion of a mother to the interests of her son," he wrote, raising the theme of maternity that had become such an important part of the duchess's image. For Chateaubriand, the flaws in execution of the duchess's campaign were excused by the boldness of the plan itself, which struck him as a gesture worthy of her noble ancestors. "We must not judge extraordinary deeds by common motives," he insisted. "Glory has its secret instincts, its hidden reasons, which seem like madness to more vulgar eyes."[9]

Although Chateaubriand considered the imprisonment of the duchess an outrage and called for her immediate release, he realized that the duchess was even more inspiring to her followers after her capture than before: "The arrest that we deplore . . . is an event that far from crushing the legitimist party has raised it up," he wrote, not yet realizing that the duchess harbored a secret that would soon place her defenders in an embarrassing position. He concluded the pamphlet with stirring words that would remain forever attached to the duchess and her adventure: "Illustrious captive of Blaye, Madame! Let your heroic presence in a land that is well known for heroes lead all of France to repeat that which my political independence has given me the right to say to you: *Your son is my king!*" These final five words would become the rallying cry of the legitimists in the aftermath of the duchess's arrest, expressing their continued allegiance to her cause and their faith in its eventual triumph.[10]

"M. de Chateaubriand said what the great majority of French people were thinking," wrote *La Mode* at the beginning of January 1833, a week after the pamphlet's publication. "Everyone in the kingdom of Saint-Louis who has retained a belief in law and a sympathy for honor will let the words of the admirable motto carry all the way to Blaye: '*Madame, your son is my king!*'"[11]

Meanwhile, within the walls of the citadel the mother of France's king settled into the dreary routine of prison life. Determined above all to resist the government's efforts to bring her pregnancy to light, she adamantly refused to submit to a doctor's visit. To explain away her telltale symptoms, she claimed to suffer from "rheumatism of the stomach." However, this mysterious abdominal affliction did not prevent her from indulging in copious meals during her time at Blaye. The chef of the Union Hotel served the prisoners lunch at 10 a.m., dinner at 6, and a snack in between. The files on the duchess at the French National Archives include the daily menus eaten by the captives along with the prices for the food: the duchess paid for her board from the money that was confiscated from the attic in Nantes. On December 2, an average day, she and her companions consumed the following at lunch:

Lamb chops: 2.50 francs
Andouille sausages: 1.50
Two partridges: 4
Butter and lemon: 1
Oysters: 1.25
Wine: 7
Coffee and liquors: 3.75
Chocolate: 2.50

They ate an even more elaborate dinner:

Noodle soup: 2.50
Bouilli (stewed meat): 4.50
Poulard (fattened chicken): 2.50
Pigeons with olives: 3.50
Sweetbreads with green peas: 4.50
Butter: .50
Truffled chicken: 12
Celery in sauce: 1.5
Gâteau anglaise (polenta pudding): 6.5
Salad: 1
Dessert: 5
Wine: 7
Tea with milk: 4
Bread: 1.25

Even by the indulgent standards of the day—it was not by chance that so many upper-class Victorians suffered from gout—the duchess consumed a rich array of delicacies while in prison. It was certainly not the regime of bread and water that the legitimists imagined had been inflicted on their leader. Supplementing the already sumptuous offerings, gifts of expensive foodstuffs, rare wines, and flowers from the duchess's supporters rained down on the citadel.[12]

The duchess also received other kinds of gifts that helped her pass the time. A spaniel puppy arrived one day with a note that read, "At least this one will be loyal." It was yet another reference to Deutz's treachery. She named the puppy Bewis and took it with her on her walks along the ramparts. An American living in Bordeaux sent two green parakeets, caged birds for an imprisoned princess, which the jailers allowed her to keep after determining they not been trained to deliver secret messages. The Bossange bookstore in Paris offered a case of books: classics by Voltaire, Rousseau, Racine, and Molière, along with some works for the duchess to read in her native Italian. One of her friends sent canvases, silk, and wool so that the duchess could create embroideries, which were then sold in the aristocratic precincts of Paris to raise money for charity.[13]

The duchess's main occupation, however, was dissimulating her pregnancy. In response to the right wing's concerns about her failing health and hoping to bring her condition to light, the government insisted that she see a doctor. The duchess eventually submitted to an examination on December 11, once she realized that the chosen practitioner, Dr. Gintrac of Bordeaux, was a legitimist.

Gintrac proved willing to play along with the duchess's charade. In his official report to the ministers, he noted a few symptoms that were consistent with pregnancy but refrained from drawing the obvious conclusions. In his journal, Lieutenant Petitpierre noted his surprise that Gintrac "failed to make an observation that I was able to make even without being a doctor, even though he saw her twice. How did he not notice that her stomach was very developed, that she walked on her heels with her back pushed in, like women do who are in an interesting position? Was it inattention on his part or was it discretion?" When questioned, the duchess and Stylite attributed her strange walk to hemorrhoids.[14]

Once the government realized that the duchess was not going to admit the pregnancy and that they had to wait until her condition became too obvious to deny, the new minister of the interior, d'Argout, decided it was time to find a stricter governor of the citadel than Colonel Chousserie. His replacement, Thomas Robert Bugeaud, marquis de la Piconnerie and duc d'Isly, was a career officer who had fought in Algeria and served every regime with equal fidelity: the Empire, the

Restoration, and now the July Monarchy. Irish on his mother's side, with disheveled white hair and a face ravaged by smallpox, Bugeaud was a large man who projected a fearsome image, although those who got to know him detected a frankness in his bright blue eyes.[15]

Accompanied to the citadel by his wife and two young daughters, Bugeaud attempted, as he put it, "to exploit the feminine character" of the duchess in order to trick her into revealing her pregnancy. On February 3, 1833, he reported to d'Argout that he had delayed meeting with the duchess after his arrival in Blaye, noting that acting aloof often induces devotion in beautiful women. However, the duchess proved immune to his charms and refused to admit anything.[16]

Aided by Joly, Bugeaud then instituted a harsh new regime of surveillance intended to forestall any communication between the prisoners and the outside world. To prevent the duchess from leaving messages in the latrines—and to stop her from provoking an abortion and secretly disposing of the fetus—they forced her to relieve herself in her bedroom, using a chair with a pierced seat, and sifted through the contents before disposing of them. To eavesdrop on the conversations of the prisoners, Bugeaud had holes drilled in the ceiling of the duchess's rooms and placed men in the attic to spy on what went on below. The captives noticed the holes and restricted their conversations accordingly. Joly reports searching the maids hired from the village as they entered and left the duchess's quarters to make sure that the captives had not attempted to pass any messages to their supporters on the outside.[17]

All letters to and from the citadel were opened and censored. Many were simply confiscated without being delivered. These restrictions infuriated the duchess. "I have a soft bed and a good dinner. But this is not sufficient," she complained to the minister of the interior. "I require a measure of liberty and the means of corresponding with my friends."[18]

But the duchess's righteous fury was a ruse; she had in fact begun communicating with the outside world through surreptitious means. Every day, a local priest came to celebrate mass in the duchess's salon.

He would fold messages intended for the duchess into a scapular: a little sachet that contains religious images or text, which was worn suspended from the shoulders as part of Catholic devotional practice. Upon entering the duchess's room, the priest would place a scapular containing incoming messages on a table. Without being observed by the guards, the duchess or her servant would then replace that scapular with a different one containing outgoing messages that the priest would carry away with him when he left. Through this channel the duchess was able to seek the counsel of her advisers and inform them of what was happening inside the citadel.[19]

The attempt to restrict her communications was not the only vexation the duchess faced over the course of the winter. In December she found herself deprived of her two loyal associates, Mesnard and Stylite, who had to face trial for their role in aiding her civil war (both were eventually acquitted). The departure of the two people who had shared her captivity for so long—first in Nantes, then in Blaye—upset the duchess a great deal. Her chagrin was exacerbated by the departure of Mlle Lebeschu a short time later. The government consented to allow replacements to keep the duchess company in Blaye, but the selection of these new companions provoked controversy.[20]

The queen at first suggested the duchesse de Reggio as a suitable new *dame d'honneur*, knowing that this tactful aristocrat would hold her impetuous niece in check. The duchesse de Berry surmised this as well and refused her, along with several other noble ladies who volunteered for duty. Finally, through the intermediary efforts of the comtesse de Boigne, the queen proposed Adèle de Maillé La Tour Landry, comtesse d'Hautefort, a noblewoman from Anjou who, despite her legitimist sympathies, solemnly swore not to take part in intrigue or engage in political correspondence with the outside world. Unable to find a reason to reject this worthy *grande dame*, the duchess consented to her presence at Blaye.[21]

Prosper Ménière, one of the doctors later sent to attend to the duchess, described the face of the comtesse d'Hautefort as "piquant and spiritual," a euphemism, one suspects, for haughty and mean.

"She had known some forty springs, mixed in with more than a few winters, and these latter . . . had left their traces," the doctor remarked. The comtesse d'Hautefort could play the piano but did not possess a talent for conversation. A melancholy woman, who complained often of her various ailments, she did little to lighten the mood in Blaye. Soon she was joined by the equally grand and equally stern comte de Brissac, the replacement for Mesnard, a forty-year-old former soldier who had suffered multiple wounds in the service of France. Although these two aristocrats, drawn from the highest nobility in the land, had come to Blaye of their own accord, they had to submit to the same harsh protocols as the actual prisoner.[22]

The government eventually allowed Madame Hansler, who had been the duchess's chambermaid at the Tuileries, to join her in Blaye as a substitute for Mlle Lebeschu. Plain and devoted, she was described by the duchess as a "brave woman," and she dissolved into tears upon being reunited with her mistress. The duchess's mournful new circle was complete.[23]

Frustrated by her confinement and by the strict new regime imposed by the government, the duchess directed her fury mainly at Joly, the man she held responsible both for her husband's assassination and her own arrest. According to Lieutenant Petitpierre, she "blamed the police commissioner for every disagreeable thing that happened to her" at Blaye. In his reports to the ministers Joly adopted a defensive tone, noting that the duchess "shows the greatest horror for everything that reminds her of the police" and that her repugnance went so far as to deny Joly access to the kitchen out of fear he would poison her. Eventually, the government bent to the will of the prisoner and removed Joly from the citadel. It was a small victory for the duchess, but a sweet one.[24]

As soon as he took control of Blaye, Bugeaud devoted himself to exposing the duchess's pregnancy. In his almost daily reports to d'Argout, he evaluated her every mood, expressing surprise whenever she seemed lighthearted given the heavy weight of the secret he was certain she concealed. He also noted every degree of expansion in her waistline. On February 6 he remarked that the various illnesses that the duchess claimed she suffered from to mask her condition—not only "rheumatism" but now also "hydropsy" (an edema or swelling of the limbs) and "engorgement of the viscera" (a protuberance of the stomach)—were inconsistent with her otherwise perfect health. "Everyone who sees her agrees that it's becoming more apparent every day," Bugeaud wrote, referring to her pregnancy. "In two or three months the problem will be resolved."[25]

Fearing that the legitimist supporters who gathered to catch a glimpse of her on the ramparts would discover the truth, the duchess insisted on wrapping herself in heavy garments on her walks and then stopped taking walks altogether. Her supporters grew worried that the harsh climate had caused the duchess to become seriously ill, and they pressed Dr. Gintrac to disclose particulars about the state of her health. Although he refused to reveal any details, word of the duchess's "interesting condition" began to spread.[26]

The legitimists vehemently denied what one right-wing newspaper referred to as "the vague rumors . . . concerning the enlargement of Madame." The reporter for La Mode began his January 28, 1833, dispatch from Blaye by addressing concerns over the duchess's health: "It now appears certain that the climate, and especially the air that Madame is forced to breathe on the rock of the citadel, is in no way suited to her temperament or to her delicate complexion." He then addressed the ever-expanding elephant in the ever-shrinking room, saying, "We have never dared to entertain the infamous rumors that are being spread here about that most noble and admirable of mothers, not wanting to lend our echo to that horrible calumny." The journalist insisted that the rumors must be false for the simple reason that the government wanted them to be true. He concluded by resorting to the time-honored tactic of turning the tables on the duchess's accusers: "We would never have thought that political hatreds would have led to the use of such execrable means to assure the triumph of such an unworthy cause."[27]

Unsurprisingly, self-righteous denials such as this did not succeed in halting the rumor mill. During this heyday of political journalism in France—when, as one scholar puts it, "published invective and satire reached a high-water mark"—the duchess's pregnancy became the topic of endless discussion. The only thing left for the legitimists to do was fight.[28]

On January 29 the satirical newspaper *Le Corsaire*—which had been among the first to allude to the duchess's condition—published an unmistakable reference to the pregnancy. The next day, a young nobleman presented himself at the newspaper's offices and challenged the author of the article, Eugène Briffault, to a duel. The encounter, with pistols, took place at dawn in a clearing in the Bois de Boulogne, the large park on the western edge of Paris. The legitimist officer was a better shot than the journalist. After wounding his adversary in the arm, the young nobleman supposedly remarked, "He won't be writing anything more for a while."[29]

But this did not stop others from saying what Briffault could not. On February 27 *Le Corsaire* punned, "The question of Carlism, which they take so seriously, is nothing but *child's play* [*enfantillage*]." On March 3 *Le Corsaire* upped the innuendo, writing of the duchess, "The Carlists were right to treat her like a divinity, she has just shown herself *in a saintly light* [*en-ceinte*]." This was a pun on the resemblance between the term for "in a saintly light," *en sainte*, and the term for pregnant, *enceinte*. The satirists clearly did not intend to back down.

More duels over the duchess followed that spring, both in Paris and in the provinces. "Everyone played at being characters in a historical novel," wrote the comtesse de Boigne of the legitimists' desire to defend the honor of their lady. "Walter Scott had brought chivalric actions into fashion, along with the mode for furniture from the Middle Ages. But both were little more than pathetic imitations of the original."[30]

After the legitimists accused their rivals of lying about the pregnancy, the left-leaning *Le National* demanded that they submit a list of twelve names so they could fight twelve duels over the allegations. On February 2, 1833, the first of these duels was fought by Armand Carrel, the director of *Le National*, against Roux Laborie of the legitimist newspaper *Le Revenant*. Carrel was gravely wounded, but the Left was undeterred. "On the field of honor, we did not emerge victorious," *Le Corsaire* wrote of its own lost duels. "But, in applying the first bandage to our wound, we kept repeating, 'She is still pregnant!'"[31]

It seems odd, in retrospect, that the legitimists would go so far out on a limb to deny something that was so obviously true. Some of the duchess's most ardent supporters no doubt genuinely believed that their leader could not possibly be guilty of such a moral lapse. Others adopted a more cynical strategy, hoping to provide cover for the duchess until she could find a way out of the situation, perhaps by getting released and then suppressing the pregnancy. Still others seem to have thought it was their duty to defend the duchess whatever the truth might be. Politics trumped veracity.

Frustrated by Dr. Gintrac's vague reports, the minister of the interior sent two new doctors, Orfila and Auvity, to Blaye in late January. But their report, which emphasized the insalubrity of the climate of Blaye, was also inconclusive concerning the question on everyone's mind. By this point, the duchess was almost five months' pregnant.

Before the invention of diagnostic imaging techniques, determination of pregnancy was not a straightforward matter. It often depended on the woman disclosing the date of her last period. Although experienced doctors could measure the distance from the pubic bone to the uterus (fundal height), it was theoretically possible to conceal a pregnancy until around 18–20 weeks, when the baby would begin to move and the heartbeat could be heard with a wooden stethoscope. That moment was fast approaching for the duchess.

In mid-February, d'Argout sent a new doctor to Blaye to serve as the duchess's regular physician in addition to the politically unreliable Gintrac. At the age of thirty-three, Prosper Ménière was on the cusp of a brilliant medical career. He was also a charming young man with a literary sensibility that comes through in the detailed journal he kept of his time in the citadel, later published by his son.

The minister of the interior instructed Ménière to ingratiate himself with the duchess in order to gain her trust. D'Argout did not spell out the real goal of his mission, nor did he need to: "The pregnancy question is on the top of the agenda," Ménière wrote in his journal, before setting forth from Paris. "The legitimist newspapers . . . have, it seems to me, indulged in some imprudent affirmations. The moral impossibilities they argue about will fall flat when confronted with physical realities," the clinician concluded. "We shall see."[32]

Ménière arrived in Blaye on February 18, 1833, but the duchess refused to meet him. The doctor therefore spent his first few days in the citadel observing his surroundings. He found Blaye to be "a rather sad dwelling place" and the climate to be atrocious. "The weather has been awful," he confided in his journal on February 20. "On the heights of the citadel, the wind blows strong enough to uproot carrots." He picked up this phrase from one of the guards. The conversation at Bugeaud's table, where Ménière was forced to take all his meals, was far less colorful, revolving as it did around battle plans from bygone military campaigns. The doctor complained of boredom.[33]

However, his time in Blaye did not remain dull for long. On February 22 the duchess shocked her captors, her defenders, and everyone else in France by announcing to General Bugeaud that she was married. The government's official paper, *Le Moniteur universel*, published the text of her declaration on February 26: "Pressed by circumstances and by the measures put in place by the government, and despite the fact that I have the most serious reasons for wanting to keep my marriage secret, I believe I owe it to myself, as well as to my children, to declare that I was married secretly during my stay in Italy." The duchess concocted the fake marriage announcement in desperation to lessen the scandal that the imminent revelation of her pregnancy would cause. She did not reveal the name of her supposed husband because she did not yet know it.[34]

But her plan backfired in a spectacular manner. When word of the announcement reached Paris, it caused eyebrows across the capital to raise, as the duchess's supporters finally realized that the rumors must really be true. "The public's modesty was offended," the comtesse de Boigne reports, "because everyone read pregnancy in the place of marriage."[35]

"It is an immense, irreparable misfortune!" the comte de Brissac fumed to Dr. Gintrac when he heard the news. Although Brissac and the comtesse d'Hautefort had come to Blaye to prevent the duchess from making precisely this kind of reckless move, she had kept them in the dark as she hatched her plan. Mesnard also was taken aback by the duchess's revelation and wrote from his prison cell to express dismay. As far as her advisers were concerned, she could not have done anything worse: not only did the declaration of marriage indirectly confirm her pregnancy, but it also disqualified her from acting as the head of the legitimist party. How could the duchess act as regent for her son if she were the wife of another man, and an Italian to boot? It was a disaster for her party, a legitimist Waterloo.[36]

The duchess had made an epic miscalculation. The comtesse de Boigne marvels that she so underestimated the consequences of her announcement: a servant girl would have thrown herself down a well rather than accept such public shame. But the duchess was not a servant girl. She was a princess, accustomed to playing by a different set of rules from the rest of society. According to Boigne, "she attached little price to chastity" and believed that by alluding to a husband, she had sufficiently deflected a scandal. Boigne adds that the duchess did not foresee the political problem her remarriage would pose. It was hard for her to understand what all the fuss was about.[37]

Indeed, when Gintrac rushed to see her upon hearing the news, the duchess appeared both perplexed and a little annoyed at the public outcry. "What do you want?" she supposedly said. "I thought this was my best option. I want to get out of this prison no matter what the cost." It appears the duchess thought that by inventing a story about her marriage, she would convince the government she was no longer a threat. Once the doors to the citadel had swung open, she would then be free to suppress the pregnancy and explain away the marriage declaration as a "wartime ruse." But the government saw through her plan and redoubled its determination to keep her locked up.[38]

When the reality of the situation sank in, the duchess began to lose hope for the first time. Following her military defeat, she believed she would eventually triumph. Even after her arrest, she thought she still had a chance. With perseverance and faith, she had written her commanders in the field, anything is possible. Now she began to sound defeated. On February 26 she wrote a letter to the duchesse d'Angoulême, which she had to present to her jailers for review, declaring, "I believe I have done enough for my son. I need rest. I tender my resignation."[39]

Left without options, the duchess understood she would have to submit to a full medical examination by Ménière and a team of doctors from Bordeaux. Perhaps if she admitted the pregnancy, she reasoned, they would let her go. The consultation finished, Ménière wrote a detailed report, finally providing medical evidence for what every eye could plainly see. Ménière was not without sympathy for the duchess's plight, however. He concluded his report with a plea for her release: "It is vital to procure for Madame la duchesse de Berry the ability to return as soon as possible to her native land [Italy], the climate of which appears to be essential to the reestablishment of her health."[40]

Ménière now became the unlikely ally of the duchess in her final battle with the government and worked hard to restore her liberty. Summoned to Paris, the doctor made the case to the government ministers that the duchess should be allowed to give birth in Naples or whichever other country would take her. He even had an audience with Louis-Philippe, proof that the duchess's pregnancy had become a matter of the highest state importance.

The citizen-king greeted the young doctor at his desk, wearing a black frock coat, like a banker or a businessman. Denying that he had known about Deutz and his betrayal, the king placed the blame for that sordid deal firmly on the shoulders of Thiers. And just as he claimed he had been powerless then to prevent her arrest, so too did he claim that only the legislature could now order her release. "My niece is not stupid," he said. "She knows a lot of things, but she does not yet understand what it is to be a constitutional monarch." The king explained—disingenuously—that his hands were tied by the Chamber of Deputies. After many expressions of sympathy for the plight of the duchess, and regrets that she had not seen fit to escape from France before getting arrested, the king made it clear that he intended his niece to give birth at Blaye.[41]

The duchess realized she had few choices left. Making the best of a very bad situation, she negotiated a deal with Bugeaud for her release after delivering the baby. It was contingent upon her written agreement to three conditions imposed by the government. First, she would alert the guards at the first sign of labor. Second, she would allow the medical authorities to enter her room during the delivery and certify her identity. Third, she would provide a written statement testifying that the baby she delivered was hers. It was a humiliating situation for the mother of a king, but she was now willing to do whatever it took to gain her freedom. Besides, she had given birth in public before. Modesty was not an issue for the duchess. She merely requested that Dr. Deneux, who had attended her prior births, be sent from Paris to supervise.[42]

During the night of May 10, the duchess felt a sharp pain and realized what it portended. Madame Hansler woke Doctors Ménière and Deneux, who for the prior few nights had been camped out in one of the rooms adjoining that of the duchess. Half asleep and more than a little frantic, Deneux could not get his belt fastened. "I beg Madame's pardon," he kept repeating at each failed attempt, with his pants falling to his knees. The duchess laughed at the distinguished practitioner's predicament. "I felt a sharp pain that I thought at first was indigestion," she told him with perfect calm. "I'm going to give birth soon, I'm certain of it."[43]

After a short labor, at precisely 3:20 a.m., the duchess produced a baby girl. The newborn was slightly premature and small, but healthy. At this point, the comtesse d'Hautefort arrived and offered her services to mother and child. Ménière detected a certain coldness in the noblewoman's manner; she had not been able to have any children of her own and envied the duchess this new baby, unwanted though it was. By the time Bugeaud entered, the duchesse de Berry had recovered sufficiently to present him with the child, saying, "General, you have two daughters. Here is a third!"[44]

Her ordeal was almost over. There was only one more formality remaining. "Let the gentlemen enter," she said. The president of the Tribunal of Blaye, accompanied by the sub-prefect, a justice of the peace, and several other dignitaries, stood in a solemn semicircle around the duchess's bed. "Is this Madame la duchesse de Berry to whom I have the honor of speaking?" the judge asked.

"Oui, Monsieur," she answered.

"Is Madame truly Marie-Caroline, princess royal of the Two Sicilies, duchesse de Berry?"

"Oui, Monsieur, it is truly I."

"The child that I see there, placed on your bed, is it your child?"

"Oui, Monsieur."

"What is its sex?"

"It is a girl."

Their dialogue complete, the gentlemen left the room. But if the formalities were over, the duchess had not yet finished. She still had one card up her sleeve or, rather, under her pillow. To the shock of everyone assembled, she said to Dr. Deneux, with calm poise but taking care to enunciate every word, "When you declare the birth, make sure to name the child's father. I want to make sure it is written on the birth certificate." And from under her bolster she removed a piece of paper that she handed to the doctor. It contained the name of the duchess's new husband: Count Ettore (Hector) Lucchesi-Palli, prince of Campo-Franco, gentleman of the chamber of the king of the Two Sicilies, domiciled in Palermo.[45]

It was a coup de théâtre to rival the revelation of her pregnancy after her first husband's assassination. She may have lost her war and given birth in prison, but her baby would have a legal father after all. Once again, even those closest to her—including the comte de Brissac and the comtesse d'Hautefort—had no idea what she had planned. It did not matter that nobody believed her story that she and Hector had known each other as children (in fact, he was eight years her junior), or her story that they had married secretly in Massa as she planned her campaign, or that she had slipped out of hiding in Nantes to pay him a clandestine visit in The Hague, where he was stationed as a diplomat and where the baby was supposedly conceived the prior August. She had saved at least a measure of face.[46]

The rush to find a husband before giving birth had preoccupied the duchess since the imprudent declaration of her marriage in February. It was not an easy task given the constraints on her communications with the outside world: messages carried to and from the citadel by the local priest. She managed to pull it off thanks to the diplomatic efforts of the beautiful Zoé Victoire Talon, comtesse du Cayla, the former "favorite" of Louis XVIII, an intriguer who was devoted to the Bourbons and who traveled between Naples and The Hague and made several offers of marriage on the duchess's behalf before turning up Hector. He was a handsome and genial Italian playboy: tall, dark, and badly in need of money as the third son in a family in which the oldest son inherited the title and the fortune. His reputation as a womanizer seemed to guarantee that there would be sufficient chemistry between them. Moreover, he had reportedly fathered a child with one of her cousins and seemed to like the Bourbon-Habsburg type. The Vatican even came through with a backdated marriage certificate to sanctify the union.[47]

Back in Paris, the salons were full of speculation over the identity of the real father of the "mysterious child of Blaye." Some said it was Mesnard. Others opted for his son-in-law "Ludovic," comte de Rosambo, who had accompanied the duchess on her journey into exile in 1830. Others said Charette or one of the sons of the maréchal de Bourmont. Still others ventured the outrageous suggestion that the father was Deutz. Despite his public role as the duchess's defender, Chateaubriand supposedly said to the comtesse de Boigne, when asked who could be the father of the duchess's child, "How can I tell you when she herself does not know?" One satirical ditty, sung to a popular tune from the day, mocked all the speculation:

> *Everyone is talking about the pregnancy*
> *Of the duchesse de Berry.*
> *The Carlists who call for clemency*
> *Are anything but merry.*

They say it is outrageous
The rumor about Mesnard.
But no woman who is sagacious
Gives birth to a bastard.

Historians still dispute the question, but evidence points to Achille Guibourg as the father. Unlike most of the candidates, he and the duchess were living together in the attic during the moment she conceived. Unlike Mesnard, he was young and attractive. And the duchess had been particularly determined to avoid a separation from Guibourg after her arrest. Nevertheless, the duchess now clearly realized that her future depended on acting as if Hector Lucchesi-Palli were the legitimate father.[48]

At first the duchess did not realize that her marriage to a nonroyal resulted in the derogation of her former title and the loss of her right to act as her son's regent. Nor did she realize that according to the law, by marrying an Italian she had ceased to be French. Although she sent Chateaubriand to plead her case in Prague, where her former in-laws were now in exile, Charles X and the duchesse d'Angoulême made it clear that the newly minted comtesse Lucchesi-Palli could play no further political role in France.

The duchess accepted this setback as she had come to accept the collapse of all her other dreams and ambitions over the preceding months. She confided in Dr. Ménière, who had now become a friend, that she was content to live in Palermo in "tranquil obscurity." After so much excitement, she welcomed rest. "Political agitations no longer suited her," the doctor wrote. "She needed to live from now on for those she loved and also for herself." At least that's what she told the doctor.[49]

The duchess spent the next several weeks recovering her strength and preparing to depart. Her half brother agreed to receive her—temporarily—in his kingdom. At first, she hoped that Hector might join her in the citadel so they could make the trip to Sicily together, but the "reunion" of the couple (who had never actually met) was deferred until she arrived in Palermo. She hired a peasant girl from Blaye to serve as a wet nurse to little Anna Maria Rosalia, whose welfare did not seem to occupy the forefront of her mother's consciousness during her final days in France.

On June 8, accompanied by General Bugeaud and Dr. Ménière, the duchess and her baby daughter boarded *L'Agathe* for the long journey around Spain to Sicily. Before leaving, she could not resist issuing one last proclamation to the people of France, a sign that perhaps political agitation still suited her after all: "Mother of Henri V, I came with only his misfortune and rights as my support, to put an end to France's calamities and reestablish legitimate authority, order, and peace, those gages necessary to the stability and peace of nations. . . . Held prisoner and long oppressed by people to whom I had offered nothing but kindness, I suffered their ingratitude and endured with resignation the evils they inflicted upon me. But I will never cease to protest against the usurpation of the rights of a child, which justice, the bonds of blood, honor, and sworn oaths obliged them to protect." It was a final jab at Louis-Philippe and Marie-Amélie and a farewell to her supporters, meant to show that even though she was retiring from the battlefield, she had not surrendered.[50]

And her supporters got the message. They remained devoted to the duchess despite her lies and humiliation, despite her defeat and departure. In fact, her legend only seemed to grow stronger in the months after she left France. "Let nobody be astonished to see us constantly repeat the name of MADAME," wrote *La Mode* in an article titled "Saint Caroline," published that fall. "If this name is more dear to royalist opinion than ever, do not be astonished," the journalist proclaimed, for the glory of the duchess "still lives among us. Whether she shows herself, or whether she speaks to us or writes to us, we follow her everywhere, we see her, we hear her." The duchess may have departed France, but her spirit remained.[51]

If Louis-Philippe and his ministers thought they had destroyed the reputation of the duchess by forcing her to have her baby in prison, they were wrong. In what would be the final twist of the drama of

Blaye, it turned out that the party devoted to the principle of "legitimacy" still revered the woman whom everyone knew had given birth to an illegitimate child. The loyal core of the duchess's supporters— what we would now call her *base*—accepted her lies because they believed she embodied a higher truth. She had fought a war on their behalf: a war against the government, a war against liberalism, a war against modernity. And in the eyes of the Far Right, this made her much more than the commander of an army or the leader of a party. It made her a saint.

CHAPTER 14

A Second Judas

B EGINNING IMMEDIATELY AFTER the arrest of the duchess, nearly every newspaper devoted breathless attention to the case, turning it into one of modern France's first "affairs." The scandal fascinated writers across the political spectrum, but it infuriated those on the Far Right, who saw the betrayal as an assault by the forces of modernity. As during the Dreyfus Affair of the 1890s, the right wing would turn this affair into an occasion to strike back: against revolution, against liberalism, against change in general. And as during that later affair, hatred of Jews would become one of their primary weapons.

The duchess captured the imagination of right-wing writers because she served as an ideal symbol of the old world they believed was disappearing: a world of chivalry and honor, faith and trust, rootedness and stability. "Everything that is poetry and elegance, everything that recalls the good old days . . . reminds us of . . . Madame," wrote one nostalgic journalist after the betrayal. "She was great, noble, and beautiful in the fields of the Vendée," another declared in a retrospective appreciation of her campaign, while many legitimist papers praised her "courage" and "noble misfortune." Heedless of her own safety, the duchess represented the last incarnation of an outmoded feudal ideal of sacrifice for the sake of a noble cause. "I did my duty," they imagined the duchess as saying to her captors as she emerged from the chimney in Nantes. "I welcome your blows!"[1]

The duchess appealed to all those who saw themselves as victims of modernity. To the fading aristocrats, hard-line Catholics, and disgruntled peasants who resented the French Revolution and the era it had inaugurated, her betrayal struck a chord because they felt similarly betrayed. "This woman, this mother, heard the frustrations of royalist France, of religious France, of rural France," one contemporary observer wrote, noting how the duchess served as the perfect vessel for discontent with the new economic and political order. Her suffering at the hands of Louis-Philippe stood in for the suffering of her followers and made it seem like part of a larger, grander struggle.[2]

In the right-wing narrative of the betrayal, the duchess's heroism and self-sacrifice signified in direct contrast to the greed-motivated betrayal of Deutz. He was "the Jew who had sold out his benefactress" for money, as *La Mode* made clear. And just as the duchess embodied the spirit of the age that had been lost, so too did Deutz perfectly epitomize the new world that was coming into being. It was a world of petty calculation, where cash was king and everything—even the head of a princess—had a price. In the right-wing coverage of the betrayal, Deutz became a stand-in for the post–Revolutionary era, but especially for the corrupt—and corrupting—monarchy of Louis-Philippe, the regime "that auctions off consciences and buys off everyone it can," as one of the duchess's resentful supporters put it.[3]

By associating Deutz's Jewishness with the evils of money, nineteenth-century antisemites were working within an ancient tradition. Early Christians had already labeled materialism as a specifically Jewish sin, one that they associated with the New Testament figure of Judas, the apostle who betrayed Jesus for thirty pieces of silver. In the centuries that followed, the association of Jews with a corrupting materialism would take on fresh significance as Jewish bankers and moneylenders came to fulfill an economic role denied to

Christians. With the rise of capitalism in the modern period, these existing stereotypes were once again pressed into service. The new form of modern antisemitism that emerged in the nineteenth century, though seemingly secular in focus, was built on deep theological foundations.[4]

Given this history, it comes as no surprise that Deutz would immediately be seen as the reincarnation of a Biblical model. "We have met a second Judas," pronounced *La Quotidienne* shortly after the duchess's arrest. Chateaubriand echoed the refrain: in the pamphlet he dedicated to the duchess during the early days of her imprisonment in Blaye, the Romantic writer called Deutz "the descendant of the great traitor . . . the Iscariot in whom Satan entered." Soon comparisons to the Jewish apostle became obligatory in legitimist writing about the affair. In the hate-filled harangue that he devoted to the case, the convert Morel went so far as to include a table with two columns comparing the treason of "Judas Iscariot" with that of "Simon Iscoblentz," Deutz's last name transformed to include the German town of his birth and to resemble that of Judas. The reference to the Biblical figure allowed the Far Right to understand their struggle with capitalist modernity as part of an ongoing battle against cosmic forces of evil, represented by Jews.[5]

If one piece of the modern ideology of antisemitism involved casting Jews as symbols of capitalist greed, another involved portraying them as rootless foreigners and enemies of the nation. Once again, the story of Deutz and the duchess seemed tailor-made for these associations. Deutz, the Jewish immigrant, provided the Far Right with a figure of otherness against which it could define its own cultural and political identity. He was everything that "real" French people were not. And his betrayal offered the perfect allegory to illustrate what the Right saw as the horrible mistake that the French Revolution had made by opening French citizenship to "alien" groups like the Jews. According to the terms of this allegory, the French (symbolized by the duchess) had welcomed the Jews (symbolized by Deutz) into their nation. They had given them citizenship, and the Jews had repaid this generosity with treachery.

The identification of the duchess with the French nation became a repeated refrain in right-wing accounts of her adventure. No matter that she was born in Italy, that she spoke French with an accent, or that she deliberately styled herself after the heroines of Walter Scott, the duchess seemed to her supporters to embody something essential about the French national character. "She came down from the mountains, she crossed the seas, Scottish yesterday, Italian today; always French," wrote one enthralled journalist. After her arrest, "that very French young woman" became even more closely identified with the nation she was fighting to regain. When a liberal minister called her citizenship into question in a speech before the Chamber of Deputies after her arrest, *La Mode* reacted with indignation, declaring that the nation had adopted her as its own.[6]

The Frenchness of the duchess was a matter of predilection, spirit, essence. In a long article devoted to the duchess published in *La Quotidienne* and excerpted as a pamphlet in May 1832, when she was still fighting her civil war against the government, the right-wing journalist Alfred Nettement admitted that perhaps she was "guilty of audacity" and displayed an excess of "zeal" but quickly added that these faults were typically French. He went on to contrast the French defects of the duchess with the un-French values of the July Monarchy regime, the overly cautious *juste milieu:* "A beautiful fault, a heroic fault is such temerity, and a hundred times more national than prudence," Nettement declared. For writers on the far right of the political spectrum, the qualities that made the duchess so French were paradoxically the very qualities that France itself no longer possessed: boldness, devotion to a cause, the spirit of self-sacrifice. These were Old Regime values that had vanished with the various revolutions, first 1789 and then 1830.[7]

The glorification of the Frenchness of the duchess went hand in hand with an emphasis on Deutz's foreignness. If right-wing journalists glossed over her Italian origins, they fixated obsessively on his German ones. Unlike the duchess, who was a descendant of the beloved King Henri IV and thus had Frenchness in her blood, Deutz was the kind of unassimilable outsider whom they thought could never be part of the nation. No matter how long he had spent in France, he remained an eternal wanderer. Indeed, shortly after the arrest the right-wing Catholic newspaper *L'Ami de la religion et du roi* printed a letter from David Drach referring to his former brother-in-law as a "modern Wandering Jew," a reference to the popular medieval legend of the ancient Jew who was forced to walk the Earth for eternity in punishment for having mocked Christ.[8]

Deutz's cosmopolitanism inspired disgust in the legitimists but also a sense of relief because it meant that it had not been a French person who bore the guilt of betrayal. On November 21, 1832, two weeks after her arrest, *Le Revenant,* another of the legitimist newspapers, reported approvingly that at the end of the previous night's performance of a play at the Palais-Royal theater, the actors sang the following song:

> *For the gold that was his,*
> *A traitor said: There she is.*
> *Who is this new Judas?*
> *Is he French? One of us?*
> *He ain't nothin',* [twice]
> *He ain't a fellow citizen;*
> *He ain't nothin',*
> *Our honor is safe then.*

The refrain concerning Deutz's foreignness echoed the comment that the duchess herself supposedly made while hiding behind the fireplace—"At least the wretch is not a Frenchman!"—which was repeated endlessly by her followers. It is not clear whether she was referring to Deutz's German birth or she simply believed that all Jews were by definition foreign. For the *Gazette du Languedoc,* it amounted to the same thing: "This traitor is not French, you said it, Madame, and all of France has rejoiced over it with you."[9]

All the legitimist newspapers contrasted Deutz's venality and treachery not only with the generous, heroic actions of the duchess but also with the naive loyalty of Marie Boissy, the servant in the house in

Nantes where the duchess hid who refused to betray her even after being offered a fortune by the government. "The Breton servant redeems the renegade Jew," *La Gazette du Languedoc* proclaimed. "This is good, noble girl! This is noble and beautiful! You honor us, you protect us, you reveal all at once the distance that separates Judas from Marie, the German Jew from the French Christian!" For the Far Right, the Jew was incapable, by his very nature, of the kind of devotion that the duchess required, a devotion that even the lowliest of Christians—an illiterate cook—displayed spontaneously. In the months following the arrest of the duchess, several of the legitimist newspapers would take up a collection for Marie Boissy and the other servant in the house, Charlotte Moreau, whose example of loyalty taught native-born French people that only their own could be trusted.[10]

What was it exactly about Jews that made them so untrustworthy, according to the Far Right? Was it a matter of religion? Or was it something deeper and more indelible? Because of his conversion, Deutz provided the ideal pretext for antisemites to reflect on this crucial question. The official position of the Catholic Church was that baptism sufficed to rid the Jew of all his negative characteristics: once he converted, the Jew ceased to be a Jew and hence was no longer a threat. In the right-wing response to the arrest of the duchess, though, we see a very different notion of Jewishness take shape.

For acolytes of the duchess, Deutz could no more cease to be Jewish than he could become French. When his identity became known several days after the arrest, *Le Revenant* began by referring to Deutz as a "Jew by birth" (November 13), in recognition of the fact that he had become Catholic, but then quickly dropped any reference to his conversion. Deutz became simply "a Jew" (November 21), "the Jew Deutz" (November 23), or even the "odious Jew" (November 17). *La Quotidienne* referred to his "apparent" conversion in order to underscore that he remained a Jew at heart. Only *L'Ami de la religion et du roi* refrained from labeling Deutz a Jew, no doubt because as a mouthpiece for the Catholic Church, it felt obligated to respect his conversion.[11]

For most of the legitimist writers, Deutz's Jewishness was a racial identity rather than just a religious one; it was in his blood and could not be washed away by baptismal waters. This was not an entirely new idea. Elements of race theory had been around for a long time even if racism did not become a so-called science until later in the nineteenth century. The Spanish imposed tests of *limpieza de sangre* (purity of the blood) after the Inquisition and continued to stigmatize Jews and Muslims who had converted. In the eighteenth century, natural scientists began using racial categorizations to describe observable physical differences among peoples, including Jews. By the early nineteenth century, French Jews themselves sometimes used the word *race* to describe what united them as a people in the absence of a shared set of religious beliefs. But it was during the affair that followed from the betrayal of the duchess that a racial conception of Jewishness became a key feature of antisemitic ideology in France.[12]

The physical descriptions of Deutz that appeared in various newspapers immediately after the arrest employed terms and tropes that the Nazis would later use in their antisemitic caricatures of Jews. Even left-leaning newspapers such as *Le Breton* and *Le Constitutionnel* called attention to Deutz's semitic features in a way that highlights their exotic, foreign nature: "Deutz is a man of medium height, with an olive complexion," we learn from their reports. "He has brown frizzy hair; his bright eyes are small and deeply set; he has a big mouth with extremely thick lips." Although they refer to Deutz's nose as "ordinary"—an indication that they saw his other features as *out of the ordinary*—these reports place unusual emphasis on a different appendage: "His hand is very beautiful," they tell us, "too beautiful perhaps for a man, and he shows it off with affectation." This gratuitous description shows how Deutz's Jewishness became a screen onto which was projected yet another fear about modernity: the way that it produced a breakdown in traditional boundaries between the sexes. It also anticipates the charge of effeminacy that would become common in antisemitic representations of Jewish men in the late nineteenth century.[13]

Visual representations of Deutz reinforced these racial stereotypes. The invention of the first practical photographic process—the
daguerreotype—was still six years away, so the few images we have of
Deutz are drawings, which are highly susceptible to the distortions
of antisemitic bias. In one image depicting the final meeting between
Deutz and the duchess in the attic in Nantes—part of a series produced in November 1832, right after the arrest—Deutz is depicted
with features that seem African, including very dark skin and tight,
curly hair. Although well dressed, he is bent in a subservient position,
hat in hand, as if begging for money. He is also depicted as extremely
small, out of scale with the comte de Mesnard and the duchess, who
herself stood only four foot seven. In this image, the Jew resembles
a "pygmy," the derisive name given to a tribe of very short Africans
whom nineteenth-century racists considered the most primitive form
of human being, the furthest extreme from the noble European.[14]

The other image we have of Deutz is a more conventional portrait.
Unlike the drawing of Deutz in the attic, there is nothing obviously

The final meeting between the duchess and Deutz

insulting about his posture in this image. He wears a stern expression but not an ignoble one. The artist has nevertheless taken his cues from those racialized descriptions of Deutz in the popular press: the curly black hair, dark complexion, and thick lips are very much in evidence, as are the spectacles that we know Deutz wore to correct his myopia. Is this an antisemitic portrait? Has the artist distorted his subject to reflect racial bias? Without comparison to the model, or to a photograph, it's hard to say. Deutz again looks almost African in this image, which would have placed him on the bottom of the racial hierarchies of the time. But he is also well dressed, wearing a frock coat and tie, which marks him as European and middle class, hence higher up the ladder. The fact that this image appeared on the frontispiece of Morel's viciously antisemitic book attacking Deutz perhaps indicates that it was intended to inspire revulsion in viewers at the time.

Portrait of Deutz as frontispiece of Morel's
The Truth about the Arrest of Madame

All of the elements of this emerging right-wing antisemitism come together in Victor Hugo's 1835 poem, "To the Man Who Betrayed a Woman to Her Foes" (*"A l'homme qui a livré une femme"*). Although not one of his more frequently read works today, this poem was, like everything Hugo wrote, a sensation in the nineteenth century. According to one scholar, it was "on everyone's lips" at the time, and Morel includes it in an appendix to his book attacking Deutz. The poem did not add anything new to the narrative of the betrayal; it treads very familiar ground by glorifying the duchess and demonizing Deutz. But it is noteworthy for the vehemence of its anti-Jewish rhetoric. Perhaps more than any other single work relating to the affair, this poem helped cement an image of Deutz—and of the Jew—in the popular imagination.[15]

Deutz, whom the poet does not deign to name, is described as both "the Jew" and "not even a Jew," the implication being that the only thing worse than a Jew is a Jew who has renounced his Judaism. "He is a disgusting pagan / A renegade, the world's disgrace and trash," the poem tells us. In addition to alluding to a modern racial conception of Jewishness that persists despite baptism, the poem also employs all the same Christian anti-Jewish tropes that were found in the press coverage of the affair. The concluding verses have Deutz walking the Earth in isolation like the Wandering Jew and make an explicit comparison between Deutz and Judas. In the dramatic image of the poem's final verse, not even Louvel, the assassin of the duc de Berry, will consent to shake hands with Deutz when he finally arrives in Hell.

To those accustomed to thinking of Hugo, the author of *Les Misérables*, as a liberal humanitarian, the antisemitism of this poem comes as something of a shock. So too does its politics: Hugo had started out as a legitimist, but by 1835, when he published this poem, he had already begun his political drift leftward. The explanation for the extreme right-wing stance of the poem can be found in the context of its composition. Hugo set pen to paper immediately following the publication of Deutz's *The Arrest of Madame* in July 1835. It seems that the disgust that Deutz's self-justifying memoir inspired in the poet was enough to reawaken his dormant reactionary tendencies. The success of the poem at the time certainly testifies to the outrage that many continued to feel about the betrayal three years after it had taken place.

Hugo, like the far-right journalists he echoed, saw the betrayal of the duchess not just as an ordinary political event but also as part of a cosmic struggle between good and evil. If the duchess became a kind of secular saint for these writers, it was because her heroic but doomed enterprise seemed to oppose the forces of modernity that were reshaping France. These forces were perfectly embodied by Deutz: the protean shape-shifting; the lack of fidelity to religion, country, or cause; and most of all the venality, the willingness to betray his God and his party for money. Deutz was not just a Jew; he became the emblem of everything that was bad about the new era that the revolutions of 1789 and especially 1830 had inaugurated. He was, in the words of a later legitimist writer, "the Jew of the nineteenth century, a worthy instrument of the new dynasty," meaning Louis-Philippe's July Monarchy.[16]

This reference to contemporary politics suggests that the antisemitism that surfaced during the affair functioned as what the historian Shulamit Volkov has called a "cultural code." According to Volkov, antisemitism serves as a kind of shorthand allowing Jew-haters to situate themselves in a cultural landscape and to signal their embrace or rejection of a set of political values and ideas. By the time of the Dreyfus Affair, at the end of the nineteenth century, antisemitism had come to signify opposition to all the values and institutions associated with modernity: capitalism, liberalism, parliamentary democracy, cosmopolitanism, etc. And although the roots of some of these antisemitic associations stretch back before the French Revolution, it was during the affair surrounding the betrayal of the duchess in 1832 that the cultural code of antisemitism really coalesced in France. The uproar over Deutz was the first time that hatred of the Jew would take on the full range of meanings that it would have for later antisemites.

The betrayal of the duchess set the tone for a century of antisemitism to come.[17]

Given that elements of the Far Left were just as opposed to the values of modernity—especially capitalism—as the Far Right, we might expect leftist writers also to have resorted to antisemitism in their discussion of the case. We know, for instance, that the utopian theorist Charles Fourier pioneered a virulent antisemitism that mixed a new socialist anticapitalism with an older form of Catholic Jew-hatred: in an 1808 tract he denounced "the Jew Iscariot" who arrives in France, fresh from a fraudulent bankruptcy, and proceeds to swindle unsuspecting Christians. And while the betrayal of the duchess is not mentioned in *Le Phalanstère*, the journal founded by Fourier at the very moment that the affair was unfolding in 1832, the early anarchist Pierre-Joseph Proudhon, who was strongly influenced by Fourier, includes Deutz in a list of notorious thieves in his famous anticapitalist pamphlet "What Is Property?" (1840). This suggests that the case did play a similar role for the two extreme ends of the political spectrum, allowing them to focus their hatred of capitalist modernity, despite the identification of the duchess with the specific political aspirations of the right-wing legitimists. The left-wing antisemitism of the early socialists, it should be noted, was no less dangerous than its right-wing variant: several years after denouncing Deutz, Proudhon would go on to call for the expulsion of the Jews from France and even for their extermination.[18]

If the betrayal of the duchess helped make antisemitism a form of resistance to capitalist modernity, then we might also expect centrist writers, those who approved of the economic and political changes that France had undergone, to describe the affair in very different terms from the Far Right and Far Left. And indeed, newspapers in the center or the center left of the political spectrum by and large avoided antisemitism in their coverage of the betrayal. This is not to say that they applauded Deutz or defended his actions. Even those opposed to her politics admired the duchess's courage, and nobody had a nice word to say about Deutz. But they mostly refrained from making the connection between his betrayal and his Jewishness.[19]

The popular novelist Alexandre Dumas is a case in point. As a young man, during the Restoration, Dumas had worked as a clerk for Louis-Philippe, and he was associated with the July Monarchy regime after his former boss took power in 1830. In his memoirs, Dumas congratulates himself on having ghostwritten one of the most popular accounts of the duchess's arrest, *The Vendée and Madame*, for General Dermoncourt, the general who had fought for the republic during the Revolution and been a friend of Dumas's father, also a revolutionary-era general. According to Dumas, the book sold three thousand copies in just eight days, and "everyone" in France read it, including the duchess herself, who was astonished to find "impartiality" in a work by her political opponents. As we might expect, given the moderate-left political orientation of its authors, *The Vendée and Madame* is free of antisemitism.[20]

It is true that Dumas also may have ghostwritten for Dermoncourt another book titled *Deutz or Deception, Ingratitude and Treason*, published, like Hugo's poem, in response to Deutz's memoir of 1835. This book contains much more animosity toward the Jewish "traitor." It repeatedly refers to Deutz as a "Jew" rather than employing the more polite term "Israelite" (or not referring to Deutz's race/religion at all). However, despite being a prolonged attack on Deutz, this book still largely avoids the kind of overt anti-Jewish tropes indulged in by Hugo and the right-wing journalists during the affair.[21]

The same can be said of the popular novel Dumas cowrote with Gaspard de Cherville titled *The Last Vendée, or the She-Wolves of Machecoul* (1858), which turns the duchess's civil war into a swashbuckling adventure tale along the lines of *The Three Musketeers*. Deutz appears only at the end of the novel, when he arrives in Nantes to betray the duchess. Referred to several times as "the Jew," he remains a shadowy presence: although his motivations are never explained in detail, he is shown at one point looking longingly at a wallet full of gold. But despite this rather obvious nod to the stereotype of Jewish greed, the novel refrains from the kind of sustained anti-Jewish rhetoric found in the right-wing press in the heyday of the affair. The Jewish character may be evil, but he is not a symbol for everything that is wrong with France, and Dumas does not generalize from Deutz to other Jews.[22]

These examples show that there were choices in how contemporaries told the story of Deutz and the duchess that correlated to the political positions of the storytellers, their attitudes for or against the July Monarchy regime, capitalism, and the forces of modernity more generally. Chateaubriand, Hugo, and the legitimist press chose to tell the story using anti-Jewish tropes, as did certain far-left writers such as Proudhon, while Dumas and the more moderate press made a different set of choices.[23]

UNLIKE THE DREYFUS Affair, which led to anti-Jewish riots across France and colonial Algeria, the controversy surrounding the arrest of the duchess remained largely a war of words. No actual physical violence threatened the Jews of France in the 1830s. Nevertheless, French Jews reacted with alarm to the events. They felt that their position in France was threatened by the sudden outpouring of antisemitism, and it is not hard to see why. In 1832 the Jews of France had been citizens for a mere forty years. And they were still among the only Jews in the world to have fully equal rights: the Jews of England could not sit in Parliament, the Jews of Rome were still locked in a ghetto, the Jews of Eastern Europe faced a multitude of restrictions and outright persecution, and the Jews of Muslim lands had second-class status. Even Jews in the United States envied the Jews of France: although American Jews had equality at the federal level, some religious restrictions existed at the state level until the beginning of the twentieth century. Equality for Jews was a rare and precarious thing in 1832.

Moreover, even in France, Jewish emancipation had not gone uncontested. During the Revolution of 1789, deputies to the Constituent Assembly from Alsace, where most of France's Jews still resided, argued vociferously against giving Jews citizenship, citing their moneylending as proof that they were unworthy. In the early 1800s aristocratic reactionaries like Louis de Bonald went so far as to call for revoking Jewish citizenship, and Napoleon imposed severe restrictions on Jewish moneylenders in Alsace in 1808, a clear violation of the revolutionary principle of equality of all people before the law. Although the Restoration government allowed these restrictions to lapse, it did reimpose Catholicism as a state religion.

When Louis-Philippe took power in 1830, French Jews were cautiously optimistic, believing that the liberal regime would be more inclined to promote religious equality. And Louis-Philippe did indeed take a big step in that direction by putting rabbis on the state payroll in 1831, right before the arrest of the duchess. French Jews no longer had to pay a special tax to maintain Jewish religious institutions, and the state began financing Jewish schools and the construction of synagogues. Before the official separation of church and state—which did not occur in France until 1905, as a result of the Dreyfus Affair—the July Monarchy's embrace of secularism, or what the French call *laïcité*, meant that the state would treat the three major religions—Catholicism, Protestantism, and Judaism—equally. Catholicism was no longer the only official state religion; it was now the religion "of the majority of French people." When Deutz stated in his testimony after the arrest that "France was my love, Louis-Philippe my Utopia," he was expressing the sentiment of many French Jews, even if he himself had until then professed support for the Bourbons. His statement certainly expressed the official position of the French Jewish community, which had genuine cause to feel gratitude to the July Monarchy.[24]

It is understandable, then, that French Jews felt panic when *La Quotidienne* announced on November 13, 1832, that the "second Judas" who had betrayed the duchesse de Berry was a Jew—and not just any Jew, but the son of the chief rabbi of France. That very day, Adolphe Crémieux paid a visit to Emmanuel Deutz, demanding to see Simon. A young Jewish lawyer from Nîmes, Crémieux had already begun to make a name for himself in liberal political circles. He would go on to become a great French statesman: he was first elected

Adolphe Crémieux, photo by Nadar

to the Chamber of Deputies in 1842 and would twice serve as minister of justice in republican governments. He was also a leader of the French Jewish community: he defended Jews accused of ritual murder during the Damascus Affair of 1840 and was one of the founders of the Alliance Israélite Universelle, the first Jewish international aid organization, in 1860. In 1870 he was instrumental in obtaining French citizenship for the Jews of colonial Algeria. He was a savvy choice for the delicate mission of confronting Deutz.

Emmanuel Deutz arranged a meeting between the lawyer and his son, who had just returned to Paris from Nantes and whom the rabbi had not seen since his conversion four years before. Afterward, the rabbi agreed to allow Crémieux to draft a statement on his behalf in which he officially denounced his son's actions. Such a statement, Crémieux believed, was necessary to shield the Jewish community from the anti-Jewish storm on the horizon. But when Simon pleaded with his father not to publish the statement, the rabbi told Crémieux that he had changed his mind, even though he risked angering the powerful lay leaders of the consistory, his bosses.

Crémieux did not issue the statement condemning the betrayal, but he made sure that the sentiments it expressed became known to the French public anyway. On November 23, *La Quotidienne* published a letter by Crémieux (whom they referred to as "the Israelite lawyer") to Simon Deutz. This cutting missive ostensibly contained Crémieux's refusal to help Deutz present his side of the story, but its real goal was to put as much distance as possible between the French Jewish community and the "traitor." "Sir," Crémieux began,

All relations between us must cease. I listened to you for two hours, that was enough. If you were called before a criminal tribunal and requested me as your lawyer, I would not refuse my services. All those accused of a crime have the right to such a request. But you are free, in all the splendor of your lucrative triumph, having fulfilled your fondest ambitions. I can do nothing for you. If your aim is to justify yourself before the public, France is deaf to the justifications of such cowardice. You must submit to shame when you commit treason. Moreover, I see nothing that excuses your crime, which I despise, and which places you only before the judge of public opinion. If you counted on me as your coreligionist, you were wrong to do so. You now belong to no religion. You have abjured the faith of your fathers and you are no longer Catholic. No religion wants you and you do not have the right to invoke any religion on your behalf, since Moses execrated those who commit crimes like yours and Jesus Christ, delivered up by the treason of his apostles, did so with equal eloquence in the eyes of the Christian faith.

In his letter, Crémieux strove to unite Judaism and Christianity in a common repugnance for the "treason" of Deutz. He furthermore dismissed the traditional charge of double loyalty leveled against Jews by demonstrating that Jewish devotion to France superseded the bond that Jews felt to one of their coreligionists. And he also let slip confirmation that Deutz had in fact received money for his betrayal, which all his critics alleged but which Deutz himself did not admit. Crémieux's letter anticipates in many ways the terms that Hugo would use to castigate Deutz, and the poet may have been influenced by it.[25]

The next day, Crémieux claimed in a letter to the editor of *Le Courrier Français* that he did not know how his communication with Deutz found its way to *La Quotidienne*. However, it is clear that the eloquent lawyer did not intend for his rhetorical gifts to be wasted on the convert's eyes alone and that he leaked the letter. Crémieux's biographer calls the maneuver a "great victory pulled off by the skilful lawyer and worthy statesman," which succeeded in at least partially deflecting the French public's rage over the betrayal away from the Jewish community.[26]

In the days following the duchess's arrest, other French Jews sought to distance themselves from Deutz as well. On November 18 the left-leaning *Le National* published a letter to the editor from "A French Israelite" taking offense at an article that referred to the "Israelites of Paris" as the "coreligionists" of Deutz. The anonymous Jewish letter writer pointed out that because Deutz had converted, he was now the coreligionist of the article's author, which is to say a Catholic.[27]

With the threat of an attack on the Jewish community averted by these efforts at damage control, the French Jews were free to turn on their own. Rabbi Emmanuel Deutz soon became the object of harassment by some of his congregants as well as by his bosses on the governing board of the consistory. On January 1, 1833, a delegation from the consistory was supposed to offer New Year's greetings to Louis-Philippe on behalf of the Jewish community, but the lay members withdrew rather than appear alongside Rabbi Deutz. A police report from September 1833 notes that "since Deutz the son renounced his religion and especially since he was identified as the person who turned in the duchesse de Berry, who had taken him into her service, most Israelites have viewed [the father] with scorn."[28]

Around that time a disturbance took place at the synagogue on the rue Notre-Dame de Nazareth when M. Alkan, one of the lay members of the consistory board, tried to stop the aged chief rabbi from delivering his sermon. The rabbi responded to Alkan, "You are nothing here!" and a physical altercation ensued. The police noted that the hostility to the chief rabbi did not indicate "Carlist" sentiments on the part of the Jewish community "since, in general, the Jews are appreciative of the advantages procured for them by the July government."[29]

Soon after, the lay consistory board members stopped inviting Emmanuel Deutz to their meetings. When Deutz protested that this violated consistory bylaws, the lay leaders—mostly wealthy bankers, businessmen, and professionals—told the rabbi that they would allow him to resume his functions provided that he no longer signed his name "Deutz" in order to erase all links to the traitor. When the rabbi refused, the lay leaders attempted to force him into retirement by suppressing the position of chief rabbi of France, proposing to the government that they assign his duties to the chief rabbi of Paris, who ranked below him in the official hierarchy.[30]

In a letter to the government minister in charge of religious affairs, which oversaw all Jewish religious matters, the lay consistory board members (including Adolphe Crémieux) tried to present the change as a cost-saving measure. They also complained that Emmanuel Deutz still gave his sermons in Yiddish rather than in French. No matter that the pious old man was beloved by the poor and humble among his congregants (who themselves spoke mainly Yiddish), he clearly did not fit the image of the modern, "regenerated" Judaism that the "enlightened" lay members of the consistory wanted to present to their fellow Frenchmen. For that, they needed a rabbi "whose knowledge of secular subjects is more in line with the progress of the times." But it was clear that the real motivation for pushing Deutz out was that he refused to renounce his treacherous son.[31]

The old rabbi did not give up without a fight. The consistory archives contain multiple letters by Emmanuel Deutz to the minister of religion, in which he justifies his actions and denounces his accusers, written in a bureaucratic French that he no doubt had help composing. Through these maneuvers, the rabbi managed to hold on to his position until his death in 1842. His obituary in the *Archives Israélites*, the newly founded French-Jewish newspaper, noted that even though the consistory forced him to deliver his sermons in French, he was still able to make himself understood to his congregants. It also noted that the "troubles" resulting from Simon's actions aged him greatly in the final decade of his life.[32]

The campaign against Emmanuel Deutz by the leaders of the French Jewish community reflects the great challenge that the betrayal presented for France's Jews. The antisemitism that circulated through the right-wing press, which was echoed by some of the era's most famous writers, provided a clear indication that the French Revolution had not put an end to the animosity that Jews had faced for millennia, as many had hoped it would. On the contrary, modernity had generated a new kind of hatred, the force of which would only become fully apparent in the century that followed the betrayal of the duchess.

CHAPTER 15

Aftershocks

O N THE MORNING of July 5, 1833, the duchess caught sight
of Palermo from the bridge of *L'Agathe* as the ship pulled
into the harbor. Her homecoming was certainly more bitter
than sweet. She had first come to Sicily as a baby fleeing revolution,
and now another revolution had forced her to return. She had risked
everything to reclaim her son's throne, and she had failed, utterly and
definitively. When she stepped onto shore, she would become once
again a subject of the king of the Two Sicilies. But she was not one
to dwell on defeat. As the local authorities readied to receive her, the
duchess prepared to begin a new chapter of her life. She was about to
meet her husband, probably for the first time.

"Her good humor and kindness always arise spontaneously, even
when heavy preoccupations would seem to justify a very different way
of acting. That is the secret of her influence on the people in her inner
circle," wrote Prosper Ménière in his journal that day. The doctor had
accompanied his royal patient on her journey from Blaye and now
regretted that he had to part from her. First, however, the French
government required him to issue an official statement certifying

that the duchess had arrived in Palermo in good health—in order to prevent her still-furious supporters from claiming otherwise. As Ménière signed the report, he could hear an excited commotion on shore: the fishermen were happy to see their princess again.[1]

Amid all the clamor, a small boat approached *L'Agathe*. It bore the official welcome party, officers in embroidered dress uniforms. Among them was Count Hector Lucchesi-Palli. Ménière describes him as "a tall, nice-looking young man, a bit English in style, with a chin-strap beard." He seemed embarrassed to be the focus of everyone's attention. Acting as the duchess's chamberlain, the comte de Mesnard, also in full dress uniform, officially welcomed the count into the duchess's quarters. "You could feel a kind of constraint that everyone tried to hide," wrote Ménière. "All eyes were fixed on the cabin containing the mysterious couple."[2]

The interview lasted no more than a half hour. When the door opened, the duchess emerged first, immediately followed by Hector, who offered his arm as they made their way across the deck. He continued to appear embarrassed. However, the duchess seemed perfectly at ease with all eyes upon her, laughing and chatting with the assembled group. As they prepared to go ashore, Ménière overheard the nurse remark that the count had not so much looked at baby Anna the whole time he was on board the ship. Rumor already had it that the Sicilians were referring to him as "Saint Joseph" because he was not actually the father of his own child.[3]

Although she had spent the whole winter in Blaye longing for the warmth of the Sicilian sun, the duchess did not stay there long. She had much to do if she wanted to restore her reputation and her place in the Bourbon royal family. On August 19 she journeyed to Rome, where Pope Gregory XVI received her in the throne room of the Vatican with all the dignity normally accorded to a royal highness. After a long conversation, the pontiff accompanied her to the door himself, proof that he still supported her cause and turned a blind eye to the irregularities surrounding her marriage. It was a slap in the face of Louis-Philippe and a signal to Charles X that he should forgive the duchess.[4]

Her former in-laws did not respond as hoped. The duchesse de Berry made known her desire to come to Prague, their current place of exile, for her son's thirteenth birthday on September 29, when according to French royal tradition Henri would assume his rights as king, even though French law now prevented him from setting foot in the country. She began the journey north, stopping in Livorno, where she left Anna with friends. However, Charles X made it clear that he would not receive his former daughter-in-law without first seeing her new marriage certificate.[5]

The duchess knew that the king and her sister-in-law, the duchesse d'Angoulême, had not wanted her to launch her "crazy escapade" in the Vendée. Its spectacular failure and her subsequent imprisonment and scandalous pregnancy had certainly not improved her standing with the Bourbons. Moreover, her former in-laws were surrounded by her enemies in Prague, especially the duc de Blacas, who, along with the baron de Damas and the duchesse d'Angoulême, oversaw her son's education. Still, the duchess might have expected that they would take her word about the marriage, or at least do her the favor of pretending to take it. To demand proof was a flagrant insult.

It was probably in response to this demand that one of her supporters inserted a falsified marriage certificate onto page 117 of the special register "in libro primo Matrimoniorum" at the Vatican. The duchess told M. de Montbel, an emissary of Charles X, that he was free to go to Rome to retrieve it. "M. de Montbel will have informed you that I have done all that you demanded," the duchess wrote to Charles X after he had received this apparent proof. "I now have only one desire, which is to be in Prague on September 29."[6]

Even after receiving the document stating that the duchess was married in the eyes of the church, Charles X was anything but eager for the duchess to come to Prague for the birthday celebration. Aside from his personal antipathy to the duchess and horror at the scandal she had created, he wanted to downplay Henri's majority. For although he and his son had abdicated in Henri's favor in 1830, Charles X wanted to retain his position as the head of the Bourbon royal family, a position that he rightly sensed the duchess wanted her son to assume. When the duchess failed to receive an invitation to Prague, she asked Chateaubriand, who had already acted as her intermediary with the royal family, to intercede once again.

Chateaubriand agreed to meet the duchess in Ferrara on September 18 at an inn called, appropriately, The Three Crowns. When the duchess's carriage approached the inn, a huge crowd formed to watch the woman who had made front pages around the world greet the famous writer. There were so many people that the duchess could barely descend from her carriage. Spotting Chateaubriand at the door to the inn, she called out to him, "My son is your king: so help me pass!" Wearing a simple gray dress, with a little hat that Chateaubriand thought made her look like a naughty schoolgirl, she seemed a bit thinner than before, but not too much the worse for her ordeal in Blaye. Hector followed her dutifully.[7]

Chateaubriand agreed to speak to the king on the duchess's behalf, but when he got to Prague, he found the ex-monarch angry and inflexible. Eventually, the writer was able to convince Charles X to see the duchess, but not in Prague. She would miss the birthday but at least be able to embrace her children again.[8]

The awkward meeting took place at the small Austrian town of Leoben on October 13, 1833. Henri and Louise were now teenagers and had not seen their mother in over two years. The duchess quickly perceived that the strict, old-fashioned upbringing overseen by Blacas and the duchesse d'Angoulême had not been calibrated to open their minds to the world. Henri might be able to mount a horse and wield a sword, but it was clear that he was not being prepared to lead a modern nation. When the duchess attempted to assert a bit of control over his education, the king reiterated his position that "Madame de Lucchesi"—as he persisted in calling the duchess, much to her annoyance—could have no say over the royal children of France. "I have exhausted all my resources of patience and sweetness," the discouraged duchess later confided in Chateaubriand about her dealings with her former in-laws.[9]

Shortly after this disappointing family reunion, the duchess learned of the death of baby Anna on November 18, 1833. The circumstances surrounding the death remain murky. According to the comtesse de Boigne, "This poor little child, essentially abandoned by everyone, died at the home of a business agent in Livorno, where she had been left like a highly inconvenient and compromising parcel." Although infant death was not a rare occurrence in the nineteenth century, the lack of parental attention could not have helped Anna's chances. It was a pitiful end for the baby whose birth had put one of the final nails in the coffin of the Bourbon monarchy. However, the duchess wasted little time in getting on with her life. She was pregnant again almost immediately, and although she lost this baby as well, she had four more children with Hector in rapid succession: Clementina in 1835, Francesca in 1836, Maria Isabella in 1838, and Adinolfo in 1840.[10]

Still unwilling to renounce her claims on Henri and Louise, the duchess decided to settle her new family in Austria, to be near the Bourbons. It was also one of the few countries that would take her. Her uncle, Francis I, the Austrian emperor, lent the duchess a series of castles, first in Brandeis and then in Graz, where he could easily keep an eye on his troublesome niece. The emperor also provided hospitality to the Bourbons at the Prague Castle from 1832 to 1836, but his death forced them to seek a new residence. They spent the summer of 1836 as the houseguests of various supporters in the Austrian countryside, eventually settling in Göritz, where Charles X succumbed to cholera on November 6, 1836. Every monarch in Europe wore mourning for the ex-king except Louis-Philippe.[11]

Charles X divided his estate of twelve million francs—huge by most standards but a fraction of what he once possessed as king— between the duc and duchesse d'Angoulême, Henri, and Louise. The duchesse de Berry received nothing. But she did get to see Henri and Louise more frequently after the ex-king's death. It helped that the duchesse de Berry gave up trying to have a say over her children's education, leaving them entirely to the care of the duchesse d'Angoulême.[12]

The children, in any event, were fast becoming adults. Louise married the future duke of Parma in 1845 and soon had a family of her own. When it came time to find a bride for Henri—who traded in the title duc de Bordeaux to become the comte de Chambord, after his most significant estate in France—the duchess hoped he would choose one of her relatives in Naples. Instead, the duchesse d'Angoulême steered him toward the Archduchess Maria-Theresa of Austria-Este, the melancholy and mostly deaf daughter of the duke of Modena.[13]

Although hope for the perpetuation of the Bourbon dynasty lay with them, Henri and his wife produced no children. They lived instead with the duchesse d'Angoulême—now a widow—at the austere Austrian castle of Frohsdorf, which they furnished with macabre relics salvaged from their days in France. The former "miracle child" grew into a stout middle-aged man, complete with a comb-over and a beard, waiting patiently for an opportunity to reclaim his throne. He had inherited his aunt's resignation rather than his mother's energy, and he did not attempt to bend history to his will. Instead, he

Henri, comte de Chambord

reproduced the routines of the French court on a pitifully reduced scale, surrounded by a circle of devoted aristocrats who made the pilgrimage from France to wait upon their "legitimate" king.[14]

While her former family moldered nearby, the duchesse de Berry decided to be, in the words of Chateaubriand, "the happy comtesse Lucchesi-Palli rather than the unfortunate mother of Henri V." She and Hector settled down in a rented house off the main square of Graz and devoted themselves to family life. With the proceeds from the sale of the contents of Rosny in 1836, she bought the castle of Brunnsee, located some thirty miles outside Graz in the Austrian countryside, where she spent summers with her large brood. A rather plain square building topped with a belfry, it lacked the gracious elegance of the duchess's French country estate, but had a large park surrounding it and a view of the mountains.[15]

In 1844 she purchased the truly grand Palazzo Vendramin in Austrian-controlled Venice for 160,000 Austrian lire. Constructed in the late fifteenth century, the ornate palace was one of the most beautiful on the Grand Canal. The composer Richard Wagner would die there later in the nineteenth century—a guest of the duchess's son Adinolfo—and it now houses Venice's municipal casino. The duchess enjoyed holding court at the palazzo, where she required guests to dress for lunch as well as dinner. She also required the men, including Hector, to carry their hats at all times to show they were not at home: only Madame was at home. It was there that she chose to hang the Thomas Lawrence portrait of her wearing the tartan beret.[16]

Hector—whom the duchess affectionately dubbed "the pacha" in letters to her friends—became a model husband, and by all accounts their impromptu union turned out to be a happy one. Despite his nickname, "the pacha" deferred to the duchess in public, always referring to her in the third person ("What does Madame desire?" "Does Madame wish to go out?") as one does with royalty. Between her two marriages and despite Henri's failure to produce heirs, the duchess had thirty-two grandchildren in total. After the highs and lows of her time in France, she found contentment in a quiet family life. She remained an inveterate correspondent, but in place of politics, her letters now spoke of everyday domestic concerns: her children's milestones, her hopes for marriages, sicknesses, and eventually deaths.[17]

Yet politics always had a way of drawing the duchess in. When the revolution that broke out in Paris in February 1848 toppled the July Monarchy, replacing it—briefly—with a republic, the duchess rejoiced in the downfall of Louis-Philippe and Marie-Amélie. However, she soon saw the spread of this new wave of revolution with alarm. In March 1848 a copycat revolution forced her daughter Louise's family into exile. Although he temporarily regained control of his throne, Louise's husband was assassinated in 1854. When the Duchy of Parma finally ceased to be an independent state in 1860 with the movement for Italian unification, Louise and her children came to live in Venice. "How many sad events happen every day," the duchess wrote to one of the duc de Berry's daughters with Amy Brown, the princesse de Lucinge. And to her childhood friend, the comtesse de Meffray, who counseled her not to read the newspapers: "You preach patience and resignation. Patience is fine, but you know that for me resignation is impossible!"[18]

A good-humored husband and devoted father, "the pacha" had one fault: lack of money. As a younger son, he inherited little and he was too much an aristocrat to think of making more. The duchess's finances were hardly on a better footing: her Parisian banker, Jauge, went bankrupt in 1839, taking a large part of her fortune with it, and she had difficulty collecting the proceeds from the sale of Rosny. This created a problem given her expensive tastes. For all her newfound devotion to the bourgeois ideal of a quiet domestic life, the duchess still entertained on a lavish scale. And although the Venetian palace came fully furnished with antiques and art, she kept acquiring more. She also gave liberally to charity, founding a school near Brunnsee along with other major philanthropic gestures.[19]

To finance this lifestyle, she did what all impoverished aristocrats do: she contracted debts. Eventually, the collectors began to harass her, and the duchess was forced to admit that she had no money left at all. Henri came to the rescue. By this point he had inherited not only from his grandfather, Charles X, but also from his aunt, the duchesse d'Angoulême, who had died in 1851. His yearly income reportedly equaled 1.5 million francs, which implies a fortune of at least 30 million. Still, the 6 million francs he paid to his mother's creditors did not go down easily. In exchange for settling her affairs, he forced the duchess to sell almost everything she had: paintings, furniture, jewelry, carriages, horses, country house. With an allowance of 100,000 francs a year, she was not exactly poor in her old age, but it was a bitter pill to swallow from a son for whom she had fought a civil war. Henri did buy the estate at Brunnsee and gave it to his half brother, Adinolfo.[20]

The duchess faced more than just financial woes in her later years. Her daughter Louise, chased out of Parma, died in Venice in 1864. "I am crazed with grief," the duchess wrote to a friend. The pacha died just a few months later. This was during the American Civil War, and in a photograph of the duchess from the period, she resembles war widows from across the Atlantic in the sour expression she offers to the camera as she flips the pages of an album. By this point, her eyesight had begun to fail, and she would have needed to use a magnifying glass to see the images it may have contained. Instead, she stares out into the middle distance, the space of memory, and is nearly swallowed up by the black silk dress she wore in mourning. She began to refer to herself in letters as "Carolina Vecchia," Italian for "Old Caroline."[21]

The world shrinks for everyone in old age as the senses dim and sorrows mount. But how very small indeed it must have seemed to the duchesse de Berry in her final years compared to the life she had led. This shrinking has a purpose, though. It prepares us for the end, which comes the same for royalty as for everyone else. In the spring of 1870 the duchess was suffering from her usual "rheumatisms." On April 16 she had pain in her stomach, which the doctors attributed to gout. Then she collapsed suddenly, probably from a stroke. She died that same day and was buried next to Hector in Mureck, near Brunnsee.[22]

Carolina Vecchia

Just a few months later, France once again plunged into political chaos. The Second Empire, which had replaced the short-lived
Second Republic, collapsed nearly overnight after the emperor
Napoleon III was taken prisoner at the Battle of Sedan during the
Franco-Prussian War. France's different political factions jockeyed
for primacy. On September 4, 1870, the Third Republic was declared
as a compromise measure. Adolphe Thiers, who had made his reputation thanks to the betrayal of the duchess, led the government after
the collapse of the Empire and became president of the republic in
1871. He famously declared that a republic was "the form of government that divides France the least."

But in a democracy, anything can happen. Parties opposed to democracy itself can get elected. In the elections of 1871 the royalists formed a majority in the National Assembly, and the nation seemed ready to replace the republic with a monarchy. Although the royalists remained divided between the two competing branches of monarchism—the legitimist supporters of the Bourbons and Orléanist supporters of the descendants of Louis-Philippe—the childless Henri managed to unite the two factions by naming the comte de Paris, a grandson of Louis-Philippe, as his successor. First Henri would rule, and then the throne would pass to his cousin and rival. It seemed like the "miracle child's" time had finally come: the moment his mother had dreamed of and that she had struggled so hard to bring about.

However, after being offered the throne, Henri fatally demurred. Raised according to the inflexible principles of the duchesse d'Angoulême, he insisted on replacing the tricolor revolutionary flag with the white banner of the Bourbons as his precondition for becoming king. The royalists knew they could never make the nation accept this symbolic change, but Henri would not accept any compromise with the forces of revolution. Instead, he preferred to remain at his ersatz court in Frohsdorf, where he finally died in 1883. He missed his chance, and France would never have another king.

Although she never admitted it, the duchess herself bore more than a little blame for the sad end of the Bourbon monarchy in France. Her adventure in the Vendée, brave though it was, suffered from poor planning and faulty execution. She hesitated when she should have acted and acted when she should have hesitated. She also trusted the wrong man. But Deutz's betrayal only sealed a verdict that had already been rendered by history. Ultimately, the duchess's failure had less to do with incompetence than with timing. What the duchess misunderstood in 1832—and never really understood—was that the time of the Old Regime had passed. No effort, no matter how heroic, would be great enough to bring it back. The revolutionary principle won—modernity won—and the world moved on. This last point, at least, the duchess grudgingly came to accept.

Whereas the duchess found a measure of happiness in a quiet domestic life after her release from Blaye, Simon Deutz stayed restless to the very end. Across countries and continents, he fled political opponents and his own demons, unable to remain with any single spouse, family, party, country, or religion for long. Always in motion, he remained the perfect emblem for the modern forces that the duchess had fought a losing battle to suppress.

Immediately upon his return to Paris after leading the police to the duchess's hiding place in Nantes, Deutz contacted his father in writing, after an absence of more than four years, to ask what he needed to do to become Jewish again. His Catholic faith had already begun to waver while he was still in Rome, he said, and he now wanted to make amends for the scandal he had caused the rabbi and the community. In reality, he must have hoped his former coreligionists would help protect him from the attacks he was about to face as a result of his betrayal of the duchess.[23]

Emmanuel Deutz had every reason to doubt his son's sincerity, given his history of turning toward whichever religion he thought might help him get ahead. But although he could have harbored few illusions about Simon, the rabbi seems to have felt an instinctive loyalty toward his son. He was also performing a religious duty by encouraging Simon to return "to the faith of his fathers." In a short unpublished manuscript that the rabbi wrote to defend himself for having taken Simon in after his betrayal of the duchess, he explained that the Jewish religion commands helping any Jew who has strayed from the faith to become Jewish again. It is all the more incumbent upon a father to help a son, the rabbi explained. He therefore told Simon that all he needed to do to reconvert was to tell a rabbi of his desire to return to Judaism. According to Emmanuel Deutz, Simon expressed this desire to the chief rabbi of Paris, Marchand Ennery, shortly after returning to Paris.[24]

His reconversion did not have the effect he desired. When Adolphe Crémieux, the lawyer who had assumed a leadership role in the French Jewish community, made it clear that the Jews wanted no part of the man who betrayed the duchesse de Berry, Simon Deutz realized that he had better leave town. As articles in the press began attacking the "odious Jew" on November 17, 1832, Deutz collected his 500,000 francs from Adolphe Thiers and headed to London that very day.[25]

Deutz already knew London from the time he spent there courting French aristocratic exiles in 1831. However, this time he seems to have elected to remain among the Jews. Deutz underwent a second reconversion in the handsome, light-filled, neoclassical Great Synagogue of London—perhaps to convince the English Jews of his sincerity. The historian Cecil Roth unearthed, in the London synagogue records, the Hebrew notice of Simon Deutz's readmission to Judaism on March 1, 1833 (the 11th of Adar 5593 according to the Jewish calendar). In the presence of several witnesses, he took the prescribed ritual bath and "rose from uncleanliness to purity." The chief rabbi of England, Solomon Hirschell, appended a note in the synagogue register expressing gratification at the event, which would no doubt soothe the mind of the penitent's father, his colleague Menachem Mendel (Emmanuel), chief rabbi of France.[26]

Whether because he fell out with members of the Jewish community or because he failed to find someone to marry, Deutz did not stay long in England. Sometime in late 1834 or early 1835, he returned to Paris with the aim of publishing a memoir. Although in the immediate aftermath of the duchess's arrest, when emotions were running very high, Crémieux had refused to help Deutz tell his story, he now put him in touch with a non-Jewish lawyer named Louis-Henri Moulin, who aided Deutz in turning his testimony into a publishable document, which Deutz hoped would convince the public that he had betrayed the duchess not for money but to save France from civil war.[27]

Deutz's memoir, titled *The Arrest of Madame*, appeared in bookstores on July 4, 1835, selling for 2.50 francs. The author presented a copy of the tome to Louis-Philippe the week before it was published, with a pompous profession of his undying devotion: "My arm and my head remain, as they were three years ago and as they will always be, at the disposition of Your Majesty's government." Given that the king wanted to downplay his government's role in arresting the duchess and to put the entire saga behind him, he could not have welcomed this attempt to reopen the case.[28]

But the memoir did not succeed in turning back the tide of hatred directed against Deutz. Indeed, it aggravated the situation considerably. Victor Hugo wrote his viciously antisemitic poem in response to Deutz's book. Several more extremely hostile works followed, including Morel's *The Truth about the Arrest of Madame, Duchesse de Berry, or the Lies of Deutz Revealed* (1836) and Dermoncourt's *Deutz or Deception, Ingratitude and Treason* (1836), both of which set out to show that Deutz was not only a traitor but a liar as well. Although Dermoncourt's volume was only mildly antisemitic, Morel's work went to ingenious lengths to pillory Deutz as a modern incarnation of the traitor Judas.

Deutz would never escape the infamy of his betrayal. Nor, it seems, would his family. In 1854 his brother Salomon, whom Édouard Drumont says made a fortune at the stock exchange, attempted to change his name to Adolphe Dumont. The nineteenth-century French equivalent of John Smith, it was a name designed to help its bearer blend into the crowd. Although name changes required the authorization of the Council of State and were not routinely granted, in this case the judge did not think twice: "The petitioner bases his request solely on the circumstance that he is the brother of that Jew who during the reign of Louis-Philippe betrayed and delivered up Madame the duchesse de Berry for money," the official wrote. "This reason appears to me sufficient to grant the request of Monsieur Deutz." Two decades after the arrest of the duchess, the name Deutz still connoted treachery.[29]

Simon's infamy caused him to be ostracized, including by his fellow Jews. An 1835 article in *L'Ami de la religion*, the conservative Catholic newspaper, reports that "it is in vain that he turns to his brothers, the Israelites, to ask for the hand of one of their daughters, they all have agreed to shun him." Although several historians suggest that Deutz got married during his stay in London, no records testify to this fact. According to Dumas, he managed to find a bride once he was back in France only because of the "enormous sum" that he had received from the government. Dumas also recounts how Deutz was unable to get the mayor of any of the twelve arrondissements of Paris to perform the ceremony. Their pretext was that he had not been a resident for the requisite six months, but in reality they did not want to oblige the man who had betrayed the duchess. Deutz supposedly crossed the city line to the small village of La Villette, where he produced papers saying that he had lived for six months in the home of one Pierre Delacour at no. 41, rue de Flandre. Dumas does not provide a source for this information, and no traces of the civil marriage certificate can be found. If she was French, Deutz's new wife was most likely not Jewish because there is no record of his marriage in the French synagogue.[30]

Nevertheless, a letter in Deutz's hand, to an unnamed friend, dated March 21, 1836, announces that he is married and "definitively established" in Paris. He gives his address as no. 21, rue de Lancry. This was still the Jewish neighborhood of the Marais, near the present-day Place de la République. The fact that Deutz had moved only a stone's throw away from his father and unmarried siblings, who lived on the rue de Meslay, would seem to indicate that he maintained good relations with his family after his return to Paris. His new residence was also very close to the main consistorial synagogue on the rue Notre Dame de Nazareth, a sign that he planned to stay Jewish.[31]

If Deutz kept this resolution, it was probably the only one. Within eight years, he had blown through the entire 500,000 francs he had received from the government. We know this from a letter he wrote to Louis-Philippe on June 28, 1840:

Sire,

I address myself to Your Majesty's heart.

It was almost eight years ago that, sacrificing my honor and my tranquility, I saved France from civil war. I did not hesitate to fulfill this duty to country, nor did I retreat before the ferocious reproaches of public opinion, or the dangers of the enterprise, or the threats and daggers of a party. . . .

In recognition of this service to which I blushed to put a price, your Majesty deigned to present me with 500,000 francs. I only accepted it because I had to help the unfortunate. I had a large family living in miserable circumstances, brothers to establish, children to raise. Perhaps I spread around the money too liberally, for today all that remains is the memory of your generosity. I am today, Sire, as I was eight years ago, full of devotion for your Majesty. I am 38 years old, not unintelligent and tirelessly energetic. I am requesting of you not charity but a position that will permit me to devote the rest of my life to your Majesty and that will free me from want. Moreover, Sire, I now have a wife and a child (named Bella Amélie after my late mother and Her Majesty the Queen of the French) and your Majesty cannot want us to perish in misery. This is my sole desire and I address myself to you, Sire, in the hope that you will deign to grant it. I am, most profoundly and respectfully, Sire, your Majesty's very humble, very obedient and determined servant and subject,

Simon Deutz

At once groveling and grandiose, this letter reiterates the claims that Deutz had made in *The Arrest of Madame* that he betrayed the duchess to save France from civil war. In his memoir he did not admit taking money in exchange for his betrayal, but here he very clearly acknowledges that he received 500,000 francs from the government. The letter is also notable for its mention of his wife and daughter. But just as no trace of the wife can be found, so too has Bella Amélie Deutz—Bella being the familiar name of Deutz's mother, Judith Bermann, and Amélie being the name of the queen—disappeared without a trace. She may very well have never existed, given all the other untruths Deutz packs into such a short message, including the suggestion that he spent his money taking care of his impoverished family.[32]

The letter concludes with a postscript informing the king that he attempted to contact Adolphe Thiers three times without success. This appeal to the monarch was equally unfruitful.

How did Deutz manage to squander 500,000 francs in such a short time? As any reader of Balzac's novels knows, July Monarchy Paris offered many opportunities for those with bad habits to waste their fortunes. Canler, the chief of police, says in his memoirs that although Deutz lived as a "pariah" in the capital, he devoted himself to gambling, debauchery, and strong liquor "with a kind of frenzy." He would not have had to go far to find outlets for his destructive passions. The Palais-Royal, just a short walk away from Deutz's new home at no. 20, rue des Marais, contained a plethora of cafés, restaurants, casinos, and prostitutes.[33]

The one thing we know for sure that Deutz purchased with his ephemeral fortune was a burial plot at Père Lachaise, the giant cemetery on the eastern edge of Paris, where his mother was interred. Although he had longed to be buried beside his mother, he did not get his wish. When his father died on February 2, 1842, the rabbi took the spot that his son had bought.[34]

The documents itemizing his father's small estate, prepared by a notary on February 16, 1842, list Simon Deutz as a "rentier," someone who lives off investments, residing in the rue des Marais. However, when the beneficiaries of the estate convened again in the notary's office on May 23, 1842, Simon was not present. His name is crossed out of the notary's record, and he did not sign the document along with his siblings (his sister Sara was also absent, as was David Drach, who was still her legal husband). It is possible that the notary prepared the document expecting Simon to be present and then crossed out his name when he did not appear. This suggests he may already have left Paris by late spring of 1842.[35]

According to Canler, Simon Deutz began regularly showing up at the Police Prefecture asking for a handout in recognition of the service he had rendered the government. Exasperated by his constantly renewed requests, the police eventually offered to give him a one-time sum of 3,000 francs provided he agree to leave France for good. The police bought him a new suit of clothes and a boat ticket to Australia: as far away as possible. They even accompanied him to the port of Le Havre and took care not to give him the money until the moment he stepped onto the ship. But Canler says he was back within the year, once again asking for a handout.[36]

Accounts differ as to what became of Deutz. Canler reports that the police took pity, giving him tiny sums to satisfy his insatiable need for "strong liquor" until he died in a squalid garret on the rue de Meslay, where his father had lived. Yet no death certificate corroborates this assertion, and neither Père Lachaise nor any of the other Paris cemeteries contains a record of his burial. According to Drumont's antisemitic screed *Jewish France*, Deutz did not die poor at all, but rather "the thirty pieces of silver . . . prospered in his hands." For antisemites, of course, Jews must always be rich and powerful. But the comtesse de Boigne, confidante of Thiers, maintains that Deutz went to America "to bury his sad secrets."[37]

Boigne seems to have been the best informed: Deutz did in fact try to reinvent himself in New Orleans.

Deutz probably arrived in the bustling, formerly French town sometime in 1842 or 1843. The *Journal des Débats* announced on October 1, 1842, that "Deutz has left France," bound for the United States, but no record of his entry into the port of New Orleans— or any other American port—has been found. He received a small monthly allowance from the French government, paid to him by the Delessert Bank through its representatives in New Orleans, the French-Jewish bankers Armand and Michel Heine, whose office was on the edge of the French Quarter, the Vieux Carré, with its grid of brightly colored houses and distinctive mix of people from different races, nations, and cultures.[38]

What Simon Deutz did in New Orleans remains a mystery. Perhaps he tried to launch a printing house or a bookshop as he had tried to do in New York. Or perhaps he tried to invest in one of the many small businesses that were sprouting up in the thriving port city. His name appears in no directory, however. And there is only one possible trace of him in city records. On April 8, 1842, a French-speaking notary drew up an agreement for a loan for sixty piastres (the French term at the time for dollars) made to one François Bon by a "Simon Deu," dwelling on rue Bacchus (now part of Baronne Street), outside the French Quarter in the area referred to as the American Sector. While the name on the document is Deu, the lender signed it Deutz. Given that his real name still carried negative associations because of his betrayal of the duchess, Simon might very well have sought to disguise it. However, the signature differs from that on other documents we know that Simon Deutz signed.

A series of letters in the French Diplomatic Archives in Nantes, recently discovered by the historian Philippe-E. Landau, reveal that by 1846, word had reached Deutz's family in Paris that he had died in New Orleans under the assumed name of Sylvain Delatour on July 1, 1844. Delatour is a suspiciously bland name—a bit like Dumont— perfect for using as a cover, although if spelled slightly differently (de La Tour) it could seem noble, which surely would have appealed to Deutz. As Landau points out, the initials matched his own, and the name resembles that of his supposed landlord in La Villette, Delacour.

Wanting proof that Simon had died, perhaps in order to claim his share of Emmanuel Deutz's small estate, the Deutz family turned to the minister of foreign affairs, who then wrote to the French consul in New Orleans requesting a death certificate for Sylvain Delatour. The consul reported that he could find no record of Delatour's death, either in church or governmental records. The Paris prefect of police, who presumably had been paying Deutz the small allowance via the Heine bank in New Orleans, then informed the consul that Delatour was really Deutz and told him to seek information either from the Heine brothers or from a Monsieur V. Weyl, with whom Deutz/ Delatour was supposedly lodging. Weyl (or Weil) was a very common Alsatian Jewish name and suggests that Simon associated himself with the small but growing Jewish community in New Orleans.[39]

The consul eventually supplied the requested information. Although he could not track down Monsieur V. Weyl, he did get the banker Armand Heine to certify that "Sylvain Delatour, a native of France, departed this life on the first of July, eighteen hundred and forty four at M. V. Weyl's domicile." On the basis of this vague (and not accurate because Simon was not a "native of France") affirmation, and without a coroner's report, the case was considered closed.

Landau suggests that Deutz may have died in one of the outbreaks of yellow fever that plagued New Orleans in this period. Another historian of New Orleans suggested it may have been one of the equally frequent bouts of cholera that carried Deutz away.[40]

But did Simon Deutz really depart the world on July 1, 1844, in New Orleans? The fact that there are no coroner's records of his death and that nobody was buried under the name Sylvain Delatour or Simon Deutz in either the Christian or Jewish cemeteries of New Orleans gives reason to pause. One of the main functions of the fledgling Gates of Mercy Synagogue in the 1840s was to bury itinerant Jews who happened to die in the city. A committee of synagogue members would prepare the bodies for burial according to the Jewish tradition and make arrangements for the service, all of which could cost up to $25, including the ritual shroud, the coffin, the hearse, and the opening of the grave. Careful records were kept, but none includes a name resembling Simon Deutz. Could Simon have been buried anonymously in a potter's field? Perhaps. Newspapers report that several men died of drowning and heatstroke in early July 1844. And coroner's records show that "the body of a white man" was buried in the Bayou St. John Cemetery at that time. But if Armand Heine knew that it was Simon Deutz who died that day, why didn't he have him buried either under his own name or the one he had chosen to hide behind?[41]

It seems possible that Deutz, who was already living under a false name, may have had his reasons for wanting people—including his family—to think he had died. He may have borrowed money to pay for his bad habits, either in Paris or New Orleans, and needed to escape the debt. Or perhaps he simply wanted to disappear once and for all, even if this meant giving up his small allowance from the French government. It had not been easy to be Simon Deutz. His reputation had certainly followed him to New Orleans. Perhaps he thought the time had come to start over.[42]

If someone really wanted to erase his past and adopt a new identity, that person could have picked a worse place to do it than New

Orleans in the 1840s. It was a city of immigrants from all over the world, a city of carnivals and masks, a city of hustlers on the make and bankers who would certify a death without asking too many questions. For those who wanted to escape, New Orleans—and America in general—offered the easy opportunity to surrender old ties and forge new ones. It seems possible, then, that Simon Deutz did not so much die as vanish in the New World, blending into the great American melting pot and taking his secrets with him.

CODA

Memory

W E TEND TO think of memory as something intimate and personal. It provides the context for our innermost fears and desires, defining who we are by connecting us with our prior selves. But memory can also be public and collective. Nations have memory, too. Events from the past have a way of surging up in the national consciousness, provoking jolts of yearning or anger, just as they do for individuals. And these collective memories help define national identity.[1]

The betrayal of the duchess provided the French with one such collective memory. For more than a century it kept returning to the national consciousness after stints of dormancy, a bit like cholera or yellow fever. But unlike diseases that arise organically, the memory of the betrayal was revived deliberately, often to debate the legacy of the French Revolution or the place of Jews and other immigrant minorities within the nation. Tracing the memory of the affair thus offers a unique perspective on some of the key battles in the ongoing war over what it means to be French.

"Twenty years ago, everyone would have known even the most minor details that we are about to recount. Today everyone has forgotten them. History moves so quickly in France!" lamented Alexandre Dumas when he set out to describe the betrayal—yet again—in an 1852 memoir. Thanks largely to him, France did not completely forget the case, although references to the betrayal in the popular press did indeed go through a lull in the middle of the nineteenth century. The reason can perhaps be traced to the fact that Jews were becoming more familiar as actors on the political, economic, and cultural stages during this period. The fact that the modernizing forces that Jews represented—especially industrial and finance capitalism—were also becoming more familiar might have led to a decline in interest in the case as well.[2]

This would change after the disaster of the Franco-Prussian War in 1870, which enflamed nationalist sentiment and helped create the climate of xenophobia and antisemitism that marked the fin-de-siècle. When Napoleon III was taken prisoner at the Battle of Sedan and the Second Empire collapsed nearly overnight, public sentiment turned on Émile Ollivier, a (non-Jewish) politician who had helped push France into the conflict. In a lithograph from the time, Ollivier is shown attempting to join "The Traitors' Club," presided over by Judas. Sitting three places to the left of Judas on the panel of judges that will rule on Ollivier's qualifications for membership is a figure identified in the legend as Deutz. However, this figure bears a striking resemblance not to the betrayer of the duchesse de Berry but to Adolphe Crémieux, the Jewish lawyer and politician who in 1870 helped secure French citizenship for the Jews of colonial Algeria (see the image of Crémieux in chapter 14). It is as if the sly caricaturist collapsed Deutz and his most prominent coreligionist into a single image of Jewish treachery.

After a slight uptick in the 1870s, references to the duchess's betrayal began to rise dramatically in the 1880s, reaching a peak between 1890 and 1910, when more than 250 articles about the case appeared in French newspapers. Not coincidentally, this was a period

The Traitors' Club

that also saw a dramatic rise in antisemitism in France. Historians of antisemitism cite many reasons for this: an economic downturn; an influx of poor, immigrant Jews from Eastern Europe, who competed for jobs with the working class; and a series of scandals—including the crash of a Catholic bank, the Union Générale, in 1882, and the Panama Canal scandal of 1892—which seemed to implicate Jews in financial corruption. By the 1880s, open hostility to Jews had become commonplace.[3]

Neighboring Germany also saw an increase in antisemitism in this period: the term *antisemitism* (*Antisemitismus*) was coined by a German, Wilhem Marr, in the late 1870s. But it was a Frenchman, Édouard Drumont, who penned the period's most significant attack on Jews. His thousand-page screed against the supposed Jewish takeover of the French nation, titled *La France Juive* (*Jewish France*), was published in 1886 and quickly became a sensation, selling 65,000 copies the first year and more than 100,000 by 1914. *Jewish France* was notable for combining the three distinct types of antisemitism— religious, economic, and racial—into one toxic brew that would provide a model for Hitler's *Mein Kampf*.[4]

The betrayal of the duchess occupies an important place in Drumont's foundational text. Before telling the story, however, Drumont pauses to savor its perfection: "Let me just say, in parenthesis, how charming I find this episode to be! How all the actors fit their roles!" What the godfather of French antisemitism means is that there is something *archetypal* about the characters of Deutz and the duchess. Although the betrayal took place in the 1830s, its two central figures already embodied all the characteristics that late-nineteenth-century antisemites, who had become enamored of the new racist pseudoscience, would attribute to the Jew and his racial opposite:

> Here is the descendant of the Bourbons, the knightly, intrepid Aryan, convinced that the whole world is like her, breathing through her finely wrought nostrils the odor of gunpowder. . . . Whom will she choose to trust? Will it be some artisan's son from the South of France . . . ? No. . . . It's the oily, viscous, creeping, thick-lipped Jew who seizes hold of that confidence. Are there no French people of good sense to say to the mother of their king: "What are you thinking, princess? The fathers of this wretch were persecuted, hunted, and burned by your august and royal ancestors; he hates you and he is right to do so."

For Drumont, the Jew is destined—because of both his race and his history—to bite the hand that feeds him, to betray the country that takes him in. If nobody was there to remind the duchess of this truth in 1832, then at least now Drumont himself would sound the alarm.[5]

And sound the alarm he did. In the daily newspaper that Drumont founded in 1892—titled *La Libre parole* (*Free Speech*)—he relentlessly denounced Jews who had become prominent in French national life. He was especially irate about Jews in the officer corps of the army, whom he saw as potential traitors lying in wait to betray the nation, just as Deutz had done. This constant demonization paved the way for the Dreyfus Affair. When the army discovered that a member of the French officer corps had sold military secrets to Germany in 1894, suspicion immediately fell on the Jewish officer because Dreyfus fit a familiar pattern, a lineage of treachery inaugurated by Judas and reactivated by Deutz. Thanks to this legacy, the traitor could be only a Jew, and the Jew could be only a traitor. History seemed to repeat itself during the Dreyfus Affair because it was overdetermined by the betrayal of the duchess.

Drumont admitted as much. Shortly after Dreyfus's arrest for treason, he gloated: "I predicted many times what has just happened. Not only did Dreyfus's treason not surprise me, it seemed to me quite natural. Dreyfus did what Judas did, what Deutz did." And a month later, as news of the arrest of the Jewish officer sent shock waves through the nation, another journalist for Drumont's newspaper wrote an article drawing parallels with Deutz: "Such is the Jew! Judas did not act any differently in delivering up his divine Master, and Dreyfus, who betrayed his adopted country, is not worth any more than Deutz and Judas." According to the antisemite's logic, the guilt of Dreyfus followed naturally from the guilt of Judas and Deutz: the first two traitors made the third a foregone conclusion. When angry crowds chanted "Death to Judas, death to the Jew!" at Dreyfus's public-degradation ceremony in 1895, it was as if they were reading from a script that Drumont had written.[6]

Drumont's fascination with the arrest of the duchess kept the case alive in the public imagination, helping to ensure that it would retain the power to determine how the French thought about the place of Jews within the nation. But Drumont was hardly the only one to draw the parallels between Deutz and Dreyfus. Some of the most famous right-leaning writers of the time followed his lead, including the novelists René Maizeroy, François Coppée, and Léon Daudet. Indeed, so strong was the connection between the two "traitors" that any retelling of Deutz's story was assumed to be about Dreyfus. When the Dreyfus Affair broke out shortly after a play titled *Simon Deutz* by Johannès Gravier had been planned by the Théâtre Libre in 1894, the producers decided to cancel the production rather than risk a "misunderstanding." Although Gravier drew on genuine historical research and presented the story in a straightforward manner that was not antisemitic, he later complained that the subject matter had doomed his play. There was no way that a play about Deutz could escape being seen through a political lens during the Dreyfus Affair.[7]

References to Deutz in the popular press subsided again between Dreyfus's official exoneration in 1906 and World War I, as the royalist Right retreated to a corner to lick its wounds. But then the case resurfaced in a major way during the late 1920s and 1930s, a period of economic instability that saw the rise to power of the Nazi Party in Germany and a huge influx of Jewish refugees to France. In 1936 Léon Blum became France's first Jewish (and first Socialist) prime minister, quickly igniting right-wing hatred. On February 13, shortly before taking power, Blum was dragged out of his car and beaten by members of the Camelots du Roi, a party that had transformed the old-fashioned royalism of the nineteenth century into something resembling fascism. Throughout Blum's time in office, the Far Right would constantly accuse him of selling out France to Jewish interests.[8]

The memory of Deutz reemerged to provide a historical precedent for these accusations. The main far-right newspaper in this period, *L'Action Française*, which under the directorship of Charles Maurras had revived royalism as a political force, repeatedly used the betrayal of the duchess as a reference point in its attacks on economic and social liberalism, parliamentary democracy, and Jews. In a series of articles for the newspaper titled "The Princess and the Traitor," for instance, Paul Mathiex lamented that the noble duchess had failed in her effort to restore the legitimate monarchy because of the "miserable traitor, the Jew Deutz." Such blatant antisemitism was considered a normal feature of French political discourse through World War II.[9]

During the war, as the Nazi occupants and their accomplices in Vichy France brought 150 years of Jewish emancipation in France to a brutal end, right-wing writers resurrected the story of Deutz and the duchess once again as a way of demonizing Jews. Writing in *Aujourd'hui* on January 12, 1942, the notorious Nazi collaborator René de Marmande described overcoming his disgust at discussing such an unsavory character as Deutz for the sake of the moral lesson his story provides: "However repugnant it may be, the figure of Simon Deutz, baptized Jew, remains curious and, in a certain way, exemplary." For this journalist the exemplarity of Deutz transcended even that of his Biblical predecessor: "the ignominious adventure of Simon Deutz, converted Israelite, inveterate traitor, more vile in his impudence and his satisfied crookedness than Judas the Iscariot." According to Marmande, Deutz's betrayal "spelled the end of the heroic times of the white flag [of the Bourbons], the beginning of the ministerial career of M. Thiers and the treason of a baptized Jew whom the most illustrious contemporaries, such as Chateaubriand, compared to that of Judas." If the betrayal of the duchess constituted a lost battle in the war against modernity, it was a loss that Marmande believed he was avenging.[10]

The following year, as France began deporting Jews to Auschwitz, another collaborationist newspaper, *Inter-France*, devoted a "special edition" to Deutz. The betrayal of the duchess became newly relevant during the Nazi occupation because the story so perfectly summarized all the grievances and resentments that National Socialism had pinned on the Jews. The French case played a role similar to that played in Germany by the "Jew Süss": the eighteenth-century court Jew whose trial and execution furnished the subject matter for a popular Nazi propaganda film. Recounting the story of the arrest yet again, the anonymous journalist for *Inter-France* predicted that "the name of the wretch is destined to traverse the centuries as a synonym to that of Judas, both of them odious beings who betrayed for money!"[11]

In fact, the legend of Deutz's betrayal would largely fade from French national memory after World War II. This disappearance was partly thanks to the Nazis, whose murderous rampage discredited antisemitism as a political ideology. The postwar period also saw the end of royalism as a political option. As France unified around a se- ries of national symbols that included two other female figures, Joan of Arc and Marianne, symbols of the Right and Left respectively, the duchesse de Berry did not form part of the nation's symbolic patri- mony. She was too polarizing, too identified with a politics of royalist resentment, for a postwar era focused on economic and other forms of modernization.

A small handful of more-or-less scholarly biographies of the duchess have been published in France since World War II, but they treat her betrayal by Deutz merely as a chapter in her life story, and they refrain from making moral judgments about the case. They are not antisemitic. The duchess herself continues to fascinate a cer- tain niche of the French population: nostalgic royalists or hard-core nineteenth-century-history buffs. Relics associated with her adven- ture appear occasionally at auction and find eager collectors. But it is safe to say that her story no longer galvanizes partisans against modernity or against the Jews.

By reviving the case, I am therefore taking a calculated risk. As the director of an academic program for the study of antisemitism, I am all too aware of the hazards of discussing the greed-motivated be- trayal by an immigrant Jew at a time when protesters on the streets of Paris turn against Jews in misguided populist anger, when marchers in Charlottesville shout "Jews will not replace us," when politicians on both the Left and the Right denounce the influence of Jewish money in politics, when activists with legitimate criticisms of Israel's policies indulge in paranoid fantasies of Jewish power, and when im- migrants are being demonized in both the US and Europe. Royalists may no longer pose a threat, but the forces they mobilized—the identification of Jews with the evils of modernity—still exert a dangerous influence.

I believe it is vital to revisit this case now, not in spite of resurgent antisemitism—but because of it. Analyzing the betrayal of the duchess enables us to understand how the various assumptions that continue to govern attitudes toward Jews first crystallized into a political ideology. Simon Deutz really did betray the duchesse de Berry, but the myth that took shape around the betrayal turned it into something much larger than a mere historical anecdote. The myth offered a way of channeling popular frustration with modernity. By revealing how this myth developed, we gain insight into the mechanism by which Jews and other minorities were demonized in the past and continue to be demonized today. We come to understand better what was at stake—and what continues to be at stake—when legitimate grievances find illegitimate targets. Only by examining our cultural myths in the bright light of history do we deprive them of their power.

Acknowledgments

I FIRST BECAME fascinated by the betrayal of the duchess almost fifteen years ago, while doing research for a different book. Since that time, I have been the beneficiary of extraordinary generosity from friends, colleagues, and institutions. The thanks I offer here cannot begin to repay my debts to everyone who helped me bring this project to fruition.

I was able to begin research on the book thanks to a fellowship from the John Simon Guggenheim Foundation in 2015–2016. The support of the Whitney and Betty MacMillan Center for International and Area Studies at Yale University allowed me to continue my research in France, Italy, and New Orleans. I finished writing the book thanks to a semester off from teaching in 2019, and I thank the Yale University administration for making this possible.

Many libraries and archives made their collections available: Sterling Memorial Library and the Beinecke Rare Book and Manuscript Library at Yale University, the Bibliothèque nationale de France, the Bibliothèque de l'Arsenal, the Archives nationales de France, the Centre des archives diplomatiques de Nantes, the Archivio Storico di

Propaganda Fide, the Archivio Segreto Vaticano, the Archivum Romanum Societatis Iesu, the Tulane University Archives, the Historic New Orleans Collection, and the New Orleans Notarial Archives Research Center. The librarians and archivists in all these places supplied much-needed advice. Numerous assistants helped me with this research: Isabella Iannuzzi in Rome, Erika Mandarino in New Orleans, and Walid Bouchakour in New Haven. Jennifer Carr patiently tracked down images and secured their rights. Charlotte Desprat and Talia Roth transcribed many long documents.

I am very fortunate to have colleagues and friends who are expert readers. David Geller, Alice Kaplan, Ghita Schwarz, David Sorkin, and Caroline Weber read the manuscript at various stages and were not afraid to tell me what was wrong with it. Their gentle but firm suggestions made it a much better book. Valerie Steiker, Gillian Thomas, Elliot Thomson, and Francesca Trivellato read parts of the book, and I benefited from their keen editorial eyes. Andrew Counter, Elisabeth Ladenson, and Nicholas White sharpened my insights in an article drawn from the book. Jann Matlock shared her thoughts on the duchess and helped me imagine different possibilities for Deutz's death. Edward Ball, Jason Berry, Pierre Birnbaum, Howard Bloch, Agnès Bolton, Dominique Brancher, Marc Caplan, Bruno Chaouat, Manuela Consonni, Carolyn Dean, Assi Berman Dyan, Elisabeth Franck, Susannah Jacobi, Jonathan Judaken, Julie Kalman, Lawrence Kritzman, Philippe Landau, Inessa Laskova, John Merriman, Joseph Peterson, Lawrence Powell, Jean-Marie Roulin, Jennifer Siegel, Jerome Singerman, Nanette Stahl, Peter Stallybrass, Eliyahu Stern, Edwige Tamalet, Laura van Straaten, Marina van Zuylen, Paul Vickrey, Liliane Weissberg, and Renée Zuckerbrot all lent their expertise in various ways. I also thank Patti Isaacs for designing the map and family tree that make this book easier to follow.

I am deeply grateful to the various colleagues who have invited me to deliver lectures on this material. I learned a tremendous amount from the discussions I had at Bard College; the Leo Baeck Institute London; Texas A&M University; Trinity College; the University of

California, Davis; the University of Pennsylvania; Oxford University; Princeton University; and Yale University, as well as at the annual Nineteenth-Century French Studies Colloquium.

My agent, Sarah Chalfant, helped me tell this story and pushed me to think about its meaning. She has been a steadfast supporter from the beginning. Leah Stecher, my first editor at Basic Books, guided me through the early stages. Claire Potter then shepherded the book through to completion. I could not have asked for a more intuitive, skilled, patient, responsive, and enthusiastic editor than Claire. My gratitude to her is boundless. I am also very grateful to Lara Heimert for her wit and wisdom throughout the editorial process, and to the dedicated team at Basic, including Melissa Veronesi, the production editor; Donald Pharr, the copy editor; Liz Wetzel, the publicity director; Melissa Raymond and Olivia Loperfido, the managing editors; Allison Finkel and Nancy Sheppard in marketing; and Chin-Yee Lai for her terrific jacket design.

As always, my family supported me in the most important ways. My father, Richard Samuels, was thrilled I was finally writing something that normal people might actually read. My stepmother, Barbara Samuels, and my cousins Elliot Samuels and Robyn Mortell have helped me in ways big and small. Last but not least, my thanks go to my friends, some but not all of whom are named above, for putting up with me through these years of researching, writing, and complaining. This book is dedicated to them.

Image Credits

Page 134   *Le duc d'Orléans visitant les malades de l'Hôtel-Dieu pendant l'épidémie de choléra, en 1832*, by Alfred Johannot, courtesy of the Musée Carnavalet/Roger-Viollet.

Page 216   *Intérieur et plan de la mansarde où S.A.R. Madame Duchesse de Berry a été arrêtée*, courtesy of the Bibliothèque nationale de France.

Page 227   *Arrestation de la Duchesse de Berry le 7 novembre 1832*, courtesy of the Bibliothèque nationale de France.

Page 252   *Maison où fut enfermée la Duchesse de Berry, dans la Citadelle de Blaye*, from *L'Illustration* (April 30, 1870), 310, courtesy of the Bibliothèque nationale de France.

Page 280   *Dernière entrevue de Madame avec Deutz*, courtesy of the Bibliothèque nationale de France.

Page 281   Portrait of Deutz, frontispiece to Ignace-Xavier Morel, *La vérité sur l'arrestation de Madame, duchesse de Berry, ou Les mensonges de Deutz dévoilés*, courtesy of the Bibliothèque nationale de France.

Page 288   Portrait of Adolphe Crémieux by Nadar, courtesy of the Bibliothèque nationale de France.

Page 298   *Henri, comte de Chambord*, courtesy of the Bibliothèque inter-universitaire Sainte-Geneviève, Paris.

Page 302   Photograph of the duchesse de Berry, from René de Monti de Rezé, *Souvenirs sur le comte de Chambord* (Paris: Émile-Paul frères, 1930), 190, courtesy of the Bibliothèque nationale de France.

Page 317   *Le Club des traîtres: Réception d'Emile Oliver* [*sic*], courtesy of the Bibliothèque nationale de France.

A Note on Sources

WHEN I BEGAN this book, my goal was to describe the betrayal of the duchesse de Berry with total objectivity. But the extreme biases of the sources made my task a difficult one. Why did so many in the nineteenth century seem to find the duchess so appealing? And why did they think that Deutz fit the role of the villain so perfectly? I struggled with these questions as I researched the book, hoping to discover the unvarnished eyewitness account that would set the record straight. Finally, though, I came to understand that the biases of the sources offered the most important clue to the story's deeper meaning. In a sense the biases *were* the story. I have therefore tried to peer behind the masks that were imposed on the historical actors while also examining the masks themselves: how they were created and why.

This is a work of nonfiction. Everything in it, every description of a person or place, is based on documents from the time. When the sources diverge over facts, I signal these discrepancies to the reader. I attribute speech to the historical actors only if their exact words were recorded in letters or by a firsthand witness.

Fortunately, many of those in the duchess's inner circle wrote
memoirs, which provide a valuable record of her reactions to events
as they occurred. One of the most widely read memoirs from the
time, *The Vendée and Madame* by General Dermoncourt, seemed to
me at first to be less trustworthy than the others because it was ghostwritten by the novelist Alexandre Dumas. However, because Dumas
relied on information supplied by Dermoncourt, I have decided to
treat it as an authentic firsthand source, especially for the events surrounding the arrest and its aftermath, in which Dermoncourt played
an important role.

I use contemporary accounts by nonparticipants selectively. Many
of these were written by passionate supporters of the duchess, such
as the journalist Alfred Nettement, and are mainly valuable for their
insights into the way that the Far Right viewed her campaign to regain the throne. One of the sources I turn to the most, the memoir of
the comtesse de Boigne, is no less colored by politics, but it provides
a useful balance to the pro-duchess works. Thanks to Boigne's association with the minister of the interior, Adolphe Thiers, her account
is a precious resource for understanding the way that the government
viewed events.

The sources pertaining to Deutz are even more biased than those
on the duchess. In his own memoir, *The Arrest of Madame*, Deutz
bends or ignores facts in order to clear his name. Because he is clearly
not to be trusted, I cross-reference any information I take from his
memoir with the accounts by his enemies, especially those by his
brother-in-law David Drach and the mysterious Ignace-Xavier Morel (who, as I explain in the Notes, may well have been an alter ego
created by Drach). In general, I do not view their narratives as more
truthful than Deutz's, but by comparing the conflicting accounts, I
believe I am able to provide an accurate picture of what took place.

This case coincided with the heyday of political journalism in
France, and dozens of newspapers covered it extensively. These
newspapers all had very explicit political points of view, so I was able
to identify how the betrayal was seen by observers from across the

ideological spectrum. Databases of newspapers allowed me to show the way the case was covered abroad and over time. Search engines also allowed me to chart the frequency with which certain words (such as *Jew* or *Judas*) appeared in press coverage of the affair.

In addition to printed materials, this book is grounded in archival research. The French National Archives yielded a wealth of documents, including police reports on Deutz, the report by Police Commissioner Joly describing the search for the duchess, the testimony given by Deutz immediately after the arrest, reports by the duchess's jailers at Blaye, and many of the letters confiscated from the attic in Nantes when she was arrested. The Vatican Secret Archives contain a great deal of information concerning Deutz's time in Rome, as do the Historical Archives of the Propaganda Fide, which house the personal papers of David Drach. The Archives of the French Ministry of Foreign Affairs in Nantes have a file that helped unlock the mystery of Deutz's last days, while the papers of Adolphe Thiers, at the Bibliothèque nationale de France, contain the receipt signed by Deutz acknowledging accepting money for the betrayal. Of course, archives are also subject to manipulation, and I discuss my qualms concerning the reliability and authenticity of certain documents in the Notes.

Several of the books published about the case in the late nineteenth century contain valuable information, especially the document collection of Hippolyte Thirria and the works by the historical sleuth Charles Nauroy. By and large, the many early- to mid-twentieth-century biographies of the duchess are lacking in historical rigor, but those by André Castelot and Jean Lucas-Dubreton offer useful information. Of the recent biographies of the duchess in French, the best are those by Jean-Joël Brégeon, Laure Hillerin, and Thérèse Rouchette. These works leave nineteenth-century biases behind and are discerning in their approach to the source material. I have learned a great deal from these biographies and cite them frequently.

In contrast to the duchess, who continues to inspire a fair amount of interest in France, Deutz has had very few recent biographers. Of the handful of mid-twentieth-century Jewish historians who wrote about the case, Zosa Szajkowski is notable for his misguided effort to claim that Deutz did not betray the duchess for money and for his failure to discuss key pieces of evidence. His article reads more as apology than history. Paul Klein also adopts a defensive tone, even if his work contains fewer inaccuracies. My account owes a debt to Philippe-Efraïm Landau, whose short article on Deutz relays significant archival discoveries. Jean-Claude Caron's *Simon Deutz, un Judas romantique*, the first full-length biography of Deutz since the nineteenth century, appeared after I finished drafting this book. I was able to supplement my account with several facts drawn from this work and have acknowledged in the Notes those instances where Caron uncovered material that I did not.

All the translations from the French in this book are my own, unless I indicate otherwise in the Notes.

Notes

Introduction

1. Eric Martone, "1832 in France—A Milestone Year," in *Royalists, Radicals, and* Les Misérables: *France in 1832*, ed. Eric Martone (Newcastle upon Tyne, UK: Cambridge Scholars Publishing, 2013), 4.

2. Unlike most historians, Léon Poliakov emphasizes that a modernization of "the old prejudice" took place as early as the first decades of the nineteenth century in France, and briefly mentions the case of Simon Deutz, in *Histoire de l'antisémitisme* (1955; Paris: Calmann-Lévy, 1981), 2:189–190.

3. Throughout this book, when I say "the French Revolution," I am referring to the Revolution of 1789. I refer to the revolution that brought Louis-Philippe to power as the Revolution of 1830 or the July Revolution.

4. Martone points out that the duchess cultivated a Joan of Arc image to contrast with Marianne, the republican goddess. Eric Martone, "The Last Vendée: The Duchesse de Berry, Propaganda, and Alexandre Dumas," in *Royalists, Radicals, and* Les Misérables: *France in 1832*, ed. Eric

Martone (Newcastle upon Tyne, UK: Cambridge Scholars Publishing, 2013), 30–33.

5. René Rémond describes how the French Right took shape after 1815 as a force opposed to the French Revolution. He distinguishes among several different branches of the Right in the nineteenth century, but when I use the terms *right-wing* and *far-right* in this book, I mean the branch of royalism that developed from the "ultras" during the Restoration and turned into the "legitimists" during the July Monarchy. As will become clear in this book, the betrayal of the duchess was a formative moment for the development of this branch of the French Right. See René Rémond, *The Right Wing in France: From 1815 to de Gaulle*, trans. James M. Laux (1963; Philadelphia: University of Pennsylvania Press, 1966), especially 23, 39.

6. David Nirenberg provides a magisterial overview of how Western culture has thought about Jews and Judaism from antiquity to modernity in *Anti-Judaism: The Western Tradition* (New York: W. W. Norton, 2013).

Chapter One: The Volcano's Edge

1. Although she was known as Marie-Caroline in France (and Caroline to her friends), her birth certificate contained no fewer than eleven first names. Her marriage certificate recorded her first names as Carolina-Ferdinanda-Luisa. Hippolyte Thirria, *La Duchesse de Berry* (Paris: Th. J. Plange, 1900), 4.

2. Harold Acton, *The Bourbons of Naples (1734–1825)* (London: Methuen, 1956), 121, 172.

3. Hugh Tours, *The Life and Letters of Emma Hamilton* (London: Victor Gollancz, 1963), 126.

4. Laure Hillerin, *La Duchesse de Berry: L'oiseau rebelle de Bourbons* (Paris: Flammarion, 2010), 18.

5. Tours, *Life and Letters*, 127.

6. Tours, 129.

7. Letter cited in Tours, 133. Jordan Lancaster, *In the Shadow of Vesuvius: A Cultural History of Naples* (London: I. B. Tauris, 2005), 172.

8. Tours, *Life and Letters*, 135.

9. Cited in Tours, 136–137. Hillerin, *La Duchesse de Berry*, 24.

10. Hillerin, 25.

11. Lancaster, *In the Shadow of Vesuvius*, 180.

12. Hillerin, *La Duchesse de Berry*, 26. Tony Henri Auguste, vicomte de Reiset, *Marie-Caroline duchesse de Berry 1816–1830* (Paris: Goupil, 1906), 12.

13. This judgment by the duchesse de Bourbon after Caroline arrived at the French court was typical: "Her face possesses every good quality without being pretty, her bearing without being affected; in a word, she is pretty enough to eat [*gentille à manger*]." Cited in Théodore Ducos, *La mère du Duc d'Enghien* (Paris: Plon, 1900), 408, and Thirria, *La Duchesse de Berry*, 8, 172.

14. *Manuel du voyageur en Italie* (Milan: Chez Jean-Pierre Giegler, 1826), 651.

15. Reiset, *Marie-Caroline*, 11.

16. Louis became Louis XVIII in deference to his nephew, the dauphin (prince), who had died in prison during the French Revolution. Royalists consider the dauphin to have reigned as Louis XVII.

17. "Learned nothing, forgotten nothing" is attributed to, among others, the prince de Talleyrand. Cited in Eugen Weber, "France," in *The European Right: A Historical Profile*, eds. Hans Rogger and Eugen Weber (Berkeley: University of California Press, 1966), 73.

18. On the Orléans' cultivation of the bourgeoisie, see Anne Martin-Fugier, *La vie élégante ou la formation du Tout-Paris, 1815–1848* (Paris: Fayard, 1990), 15–17. Michael Marrinan describes the appeal of the Palais-Royal in *Romantic Paris: Histories of a Cultural Landscape, 1800–1850* (Stanford, CA: Stanford University Press, 2009), 275–277.

19. *Histoire scandaleuse politique, anecdotique et bigote, des Duchesses d'Angouleme et de Berry; formant le complément indispensable de l'histoire scandaleuse de Charles X* (Paris: Chez les marchans de nouveautés, 1830), 174. Jean Lucas-Dubreton, *La Duchesse de Berry* (Paris: Flammarion, 1935), 8.

20. Lucas-Dubreton, *La Duchesse de Berry*, 8.

21. Reiset, *Marie-Caroline*, 8.

22. Comtesse de Boigne [Éléonore-Adèle d'Osmond], *Mémoires*, ed. Henri Rossi (1907; Paris: Honoré Champion, 2007), 594.

23. Both Charles Ferdinand and Caroline were descended from Louis XIV of France, one of whose grandsons fathered the French Bourbon line, and another became Philip IV of Spain and progenitor of the Bourbons of Naples. See Bourbon family tree.

24. Reiset, *Marie-Caroline*, 14; Lucas-Dubreton, *La Duchesse de Berry*, 8–9.

25. Reiset, *Marie-Caroline*, 17.

26. Cited in Reiset, 17.

27. Reiset, 18. Hillerin estimates the values from the time in today's money (*La Duchesse de Berry*, 459, note 65), although comparing historical values of currencies is notoriously difficult to do.

28. Duchesse de Gontaut-Biron [Joséphine de Montaut-Navailles], *Mémoires de madame la duchesse de Gontaut* (1855; Paris: Plon, 1909), 159.

29. Cited in Hillerin, *La Duchesse de Berry*, 42. Cited in Lucas-Dubreton, *La Duchesse de Berry*, 12.

30. Cited in Lucas-Dubreton, 13.

31. Gontaut, *Mémoires*, 162.

32. Lucas-Dubreton, *La Duchesse de Berry*, 14.

33. The description of the wedding is in Gontaut, *Mémoires*, 165. Martin-Fugier describes the ceremony of *le grand couvert* in *La vie élégante*, 27–29.

Chapter Two: A Parisian Education

1. Bernard Marchand discusses Parisian population growth in *Paris, histoire d'une ville: XIXe–XXe siécles* (Paris: Seuil, 1993), 12.

2. Archives nationales O/3/1881. Hillerin mentions these expenditures and points out that one franc at the time was worth about seven euros in today's money. This is the equivalent of between eight and ten dollars, depending on exchange rates. See Hillerin, *La Duchesse de Berry*, 61–62, 459, note 65.

3. On Marie Antoinette's fashion, including her taste for ostrich feathers, see Caroline Weber, *Queen of Fashion: What Marie Antoinette Wore to the Revolution* (New York: Henry Holt, 2006), 107.

4. Lucas-Dubreton, *La Duchesse de Berry*, 18.

5. Cited in Boigne, *Mémoires*, 726.

6. Andrew Counter, *The Amorous Restoration: Love, Sex, and Politics in Early Nineteenth-Century France* (Oxford: Oxford University Press, 2016).

7. Reiset, *Marie-Caroline*, 73. Susan Nagel, *Marie-Thérèse, Child of Terror: The Fate of Marie Antoinette's Daughter* (New York: Bloomsbury, 2008), 276.

8. Boigne, *Mémoires*, 679.

9. Reiset, *Marie-Caroline*, 70.

10. Nagel, *Marie-Thérèse, Child of Terror*, 279.

11. Nagel, 257. Boigne, *Mémoires*, 680.

12. Jean-Joël Brégeon, *La duchesse de Berry* (Paris: Tallandier, 2009), 74. On the slight of Louis-Philippe, see Munro Price, *The Perilous Crown: France Between Revolutions, 1814–1848* (New York: Macmillan, 2007), 115.

13. Price, *The Perilous Crown*, 72–74. The duchess is cited in Gontaut, *Mémoires*, 197.

14. Nagel, *Marie-Thérèse, Child of Terror*, 292.

15. On the factions within the French Right, see Rémond, *The Right Wing in France*. Grégoire is cited in Lucas-Dubreton, *La Duchesse de Berry*, 22.

16. Lucas-Dubreton, 22.

17. Lucas-Dubreton, 25–26.

18. Charles de Faucigny-Lucinge, *Souvenirs inédits du petit fils du Duc de Berry*, ed. André Castelot (1951; Paris: Perrin, 1971), 11–13.

19. *Histoire scandaleuse politique*, 202.

20. Cited in Reiset, *Marie-Caroline*, 104.

21. Reiset, 103.

22. Boigne, *Mémoires*, 892.

23. Gontaut, *Mémoires*, 217–218. Andrew Counter, "La naissance du duc de Bordeaux, ou la Restauration s'attendrit," *Romantisme* 159 (2013): 4.

24. Gontaut, *Mémoires*, 219–221.

25. Lucas-Dubreton, *La Duchesse de Berry*, 48.

26. Brégeon describes the "White Terror" that followed the duke's death (*La duchesse de Berry*, 26). Boigne, *Mémoires*, 899–900.

27. Martin-Fugier, *La vie élégante*, 15. Jo Burr Margadant also describes the duchess's negotiation of the conflict between court and city

in "The Duchesse de Berry and Royalist Political Culture in Postrev-olutionary France," in *The New Biography: Performing Femininity in Nineteenth-Century France*, ed. Jo Burr Margadant (Berkeley: University of California Press, 2000), 34–35.

28. Lucas-Dubreton, *La Duchesse de Berry*, 55. The comte de Mesnard reports that the duchess never rode on the omnibus but that she did make the bet. Charles de Mesnard, *Souvenirs intimes de M. le comte de Mesnard, premier écuyer et chevalier d'honneur de S.A.R. Madame la duch-esse de Berry* (Paris: L. de Potter, 1844), 1:158.

29. "Où est-elle?" *La Mode*, July 9, 1832, 186; Reiset, *Marie-Caroline*, 197.

30. Philip Mansel, "The Duchesse de Berry and the Aesthetics of Roy-alism: Dynastic Collecting in Nineteenth-Century France," in Susan Bracken, Andrea M. Galdy, and Adriana Turpin, eds., *Women Patrons and Collectors* (Newcastle upon Tyne, UK: Cambridge Scholars Publish-ing, 2012), 143–144. For the catalog of the sale of her art and antiques, see *Galerie de Mme la Duchesse de Berry, Objets d'art et curiosités* (Paris: Mannheim, 1865). The list of her books can be found in *Catalogue de la Riche Bibliothèque de Rosny* (Paris: Bossange, 1837).

31. Reiset, *Marie-Caroline*, 195–195. Brégeon, *La duchesse de Berry*, 151.

32. *Le Journal des dames et des modes* of March 10, 1829, provides a list of who dressed as which historical figure (105–107). As the March 15 issue declares, "These festivities, organized with an exquisite taste and executed with admirable precision, caused everyone to comment upon the beauty and elegance of many of the ladies" (114). Charles Baudelaire, who admired Lamy, wrote that he is "almost English in his love for aris-tocratic elegance." See "Le Peintre de la vie moderne," in *Oeuvres* (Paris: Gallimard, 1954), 885. On the ball, see also Reiset, *Marie-Caroline*, 199; and Boigne, *Mémoires*, 957.

Chapter Three: A Modern Jew

1. *Encyclopedia Judaica* (Jerusalem: Keter, 1974), 16:256–257.

2. Jay R. Berkowitz, *Rites and Passages: The Beginnings of Modern Jewish Culture in France, 1650–1860* (Philadelphia: University of Penn-sylvania Press, 2004). Paula E. Hyman, *The Jews of Modern France* (Berkeley: University of California Press, 1998).

3. Accounts of the deliberations over emancipation during the French Revolution can be found in Ronald Schechter, *Obstinate Hebrews: Representations of Jews in France, 1715–1815* (Berkeley: University of California Press, 2003), 150–193; and Maurice Samuels, *The Right to Difference: French Universalism and the Jews* (Chicago: University of Chicago Press, 2016), 17–49. The one exception to the complete legal equality of the Jews was a special oath, the More Judaico, that Jews had to swear in court until it was finally abolished (thanks to the persuasive arguments of the lawyer Adolphe Crémieux) in 1846. For an account that places the emancipation of French Jews in comparative context, see David Sorkin, *Jewish Emancipation: A History Across Five Centuries* (Princeton, NJ: Princeton University Press, 2019). It should be noted that the French revolutionaries also emancipated black slaves, but only after they had emancipated the Jews. Napoleon then reestablished slavery in the French colonies.

4. Napoleon had already reorganized the Catholic and Protestant churches in France with a similar goal in mind: to bring them under the control of the state. Hyman, *The Jews of Modern France*, 39–40.

5. Louis de Bonald, "Sur les Juifs," *Mercure de Franc*, February 8, 1806. Darrin M. McMahon places Bonald in a wider intellectual context in *Enemies of the Enlightenment: The French Counter-Enlightenment and the Making of Modernity* (Oxford: Oxford University Press, 2001). On Bonald and the Jewish response to antisemitism in this period, see Julie Kalman, *Rethinking Antisemitism in Nineteenth-Century France* (Cambridge: Cambridge University Press, 2010), 46–70; and Ari Joskowicz, *The Modernity of Others: Jewish Anti-Catholicism in Germany and France* (Stanford, CA: Stanford University Press, 2014), 99.

6. Simon Dubnov is one such Jewish nationalist historian; see his *History of the Jews*, vol. 5, trans. Moshe Spiegel (1925–1929; Cranbury, NJ: Thomas Yoseloff, 1971), 515. Simon Schwarzfuchs describes the work of the Grand Sanhedrin in *Napoleon, the Jews, and the Sanhedrin* (London: Routledge and Kegan Paul, 1979), 57.

7. Phyllis Cohen Albert discusses the structure of the consistory in *The Modernization of French Jewry: Consistory and Community in the Nineteenth Century* (Hanover, NH: Brandeis University Press, 1977), especially 45–46.

8. Christine Piette, *Les Juifs de Paris (1808–1840): La marche vers l'assimilation* (Québec: Les presses de l'universite Laval, 1983), 50. David

Caron, *My Father and I: The Marais and the Queerness of Community* (Ithaca, NY: Cornell University Press, 2009), 38.

9. Simon Deutz, *Arrestation de Madame* (Paris: Chez les libraires associés, 1835), 5. David Caron, *My Father and I*, 37.

10. Philippe-E. Landau, "Le cas étrange de Simon Deutz (1802–1844)," *Revue des études Juives* 164 (January-June 2005): 214.

11. Piette, *Les Juifs de Paris*, 51, 55.

12. Piette, 57–59.

13. Piette, 94–95.

14. Landau, "Le cas étrange," 214.

15. *Les Archives Israélites de France* (1842), 68.

16. *Dictionnaire de l'Académie française*, 6th ed. (Paris: Firmin Didot, 1835). Ben-Lévi, "Les Complices d'un adjectif," *Archives Israélites* (1842), 147. Phyllis Cohen Albert argues that the use of *Israélite* to denote someone who felt more French than Jewish came later, during the Dreyfus Affair. See Albert, "Israelite and Jew: How Did Nineteenth-Century French Jews Understand Assimilation?" in *Assimilation and Community: The Jews in Nineteenth-Century Europe*, eds. Jonathan Frankel and Steven J. Zipperstein (Cambridge: Cambridge University Press, 1992), 89.

17. *Archives Israélites* (1842), 68.

18. After Rabbi Deutz's death, the Paris consistory tried to raise money from the local consistories for a pension for his widow because the rabbi had left her almost nothing, but they received very little money. "It is painful to see the wife of the prime minister of the Israelite religion in France lead an existence that detracts from the dignity of our religion and which could cause our coreligionists to be criticized for lacking a sense of charity," the Parisian officials complained. Albert, *The Modernization of French Jewry*, 256–257.

19. Ignace-Xavier Morel, *La vérité sur l'arrestation de Madame la duchesse de Berry ou les mensonges de Deutz dévoilés* (Paris: Levasseur, 1836), 13, 16. The letter is cited in P. L. B. Drach, *Relation de la Conversion de M. Hyacinthe Deutz, baptisé à Rome le 3 février 1828, précédée de quelques considérations sur le retour d'Israël dans l'église de Dieu* (Paris: Chez l'auteur, 1828), 27. The authenticity of this letter is questionable because it is quoted (and translated into French from Hebrew or Yiddish) in the account given by his brother-in-law, David Drach, of Simon's conversion.

However, this account was published at a time when the brothers-in-law were on good terms, so I accept its veracity.

20. A police report from March 1825 states that in 1817 Samuel Deutz was officially exempted from conscription by a judge after displaying proof that he had been born outside France. The same report states that no record was found of Simon's exemption, but he also seems not to have served in the army (AN F/7/9430). See also Zosa Szajkowski, "Simon Deutz: Traitor or French Patriot: The Jewish Aspect of the Arrest of the Duchesse de Berry," *Journal of Jewish Studies* 16 (1965): 54, and Landau, "Le cas étrange," 215–217.

21. Drach, *Relation*, 12; Morel, *La vérité sur l'arrestation*, 19.

22. In a police report dated November 27, 1824, Drach refers to Simon as lacking an occupation after having been a jeweler's apprentice and a typesetter and "getting fired everywhere" (Archives nationales F/7/9430). On Simon's occupations, see also Paul Klein, "Mauvais Juif, mauvais chrétien," *Revue de la pensée Juive* 7 (April 1951): 99; Morel, *La vérité sur l'arrestation*, 21; and Jean-Claude Caron, *Simon Deutz, un Judas romantique* (Ceyzérieu, France: Champ Vallon, 2019), 32.

23. *Archives Israélites* (1842), 69; Landau, "Le cas étrange," 217.

24. Sigmund Freud, *Collected Papers*, ed. James Strachey (New York: Basic, 1959), 5:74–78.

25. Drach, *Relation*, 12.

26. Thomas Kselman also describes conversion as a symptom of an identity crisis facing nineteenth-century Jews in "Turbulent Souls in Modern France: Jewish Conversion and the Terquem Affair," *Historical Reflections/Réflexions historiques* 32, no. 1 (Spring 2006), 83–104; as does Kalman, *Rethinking Antisemitism*, 46–70.

Chapter Four: Apostasy

1. Deutz mentions the debts contracted "during my wood business" in a letter to Drach, cited in Morel, *La vérité sur l'arrestation*, 55.

2. Letter to his father cited in Drach (*Relation*, 27). Deutz's desire to get rich is cited in Morel, *La vérité sur l'arrestation*, 177. One such critic is Paul-Ferdinand-Stanislas Dermoncourt, *Deutz ou imposture, ingratitude et trahison* (Paris: Dentu, 1836), 6.

3. Drach, *Relation*, 12.

4. Paul Louis Bernard [David] Drach, *Lettre d'un rabbin converti, aux israélites, ses frères, sur les motifs de sa conversion* (Paris: imp. Beaucé-Rusand, 1825), 29. Kalman, *Rethinking Antisemitism*, 50. Philippe-E. Landau, "David-Paul Drach, à la recherche d'une harmonie religieuse," *Histoire, économie & société* 4 (2014): 46. Records concerning Drach's time as a teacher can be found in the Archivio Storico di Propaganda Fide, Paolo Drach, vol. 1.

5. Drach, *Lettre*, 49. Morel, *La vérité sur l'arrestation*, 6. Drach describes his experience of the "unyielding wall" separating religions in *De l'harmonie entre l'église et la synagogue ou perpetuité et catholicité de la religion chrétienne* (Paris: Paul Mellier, 1844), 1:36. In *Conscience and Conversion: Religious Liberty in Post-Revolutionary France* (New Haven, CT: Yale University Press, 2018), Thomas Kselman points to Drach's conflicts with the consistory as a reason for his conversion (*Conscience and Conversion*, 91). Klein argues that although Drach's professional setbacks did not alone convince him to convert, they contributed to his growing disenchantment with Judaism ("Mauvais Juif," 91). Kalman examines changes in the way that Drach refers to Judaism in his published texts prior to his conversion (*Rethinking Antisemitism*, 51). Landau points to other conflicts between Drach and his bosses ("David Paul Drach," 47–48). On Drach's conversion, see also Todd M. Endelman, *Leaving the Jewish Fold: Conversion and Radical Assimilation in Modern Jewish History* (Princeton, NJ: Princeton University Press, 2015), 229; and Jonathan Helfand, "Passports and Piety: Apostasy in Nineteenth-Century France," *Jewish History* 3, no. 2 (Fall 1988): 63–65.

6. Paul Catrice, "L'Harmonie entre l'église et le judaïsme d'après la vie et les oeuvres de Paul Drach, ancien Rabbin, Orientaliste Chrétien, 1791–1865" (Doctorate in Theology thesis, Faculté de Théologie de Lille, 1978), 232. Letters to and from the Paris police prefect concerning Drach are in Archives nationales F/7/9430.

7. Drach's letter to Rabbi Deutz appears only in Deutz's memoir, *Arrestation de Madame*, 65–66, so it may not be authentic. Klein, "Mauvais Juif," 95. The kidnapping episode is recounted in Roger Gougenot des Mousseaux, *Moeurs et pratiques des démons ou des esprits visiteurs du*

spiritisme ancien et moderne (Paris: Henri Plon, 1865), 276–277; and in Morel, *La vérité sur l'arrestation*, 47. Morel also describes the episode of the kidnapping in a pamphlet he wrote in support of Drach at the time, "Renseignements relatifs à la persecution dont M. Drach, rabbin converti a été l'objet," published in the *Mémorial Catholique* (March 1826) and separately as a pamphlet by the imprimerie de Gueffier (7–10). The Drach kidnapping foreshadows the Mortara Affair of the 1850s in Italy. See David I. Kertzer, *The Kidnapping of Edgardo Mortara* (New York: Vintage, 1998).

8. Report by Drach to the police, dated November 27, 1824. Archives nationales F/7/9430. Simon's threats are discussed in Landau, "Le cas étrange," 222.

9. Morel, *La vérité sur l'arrestation*, 51.

10. Letters cited in Morel, 50–51.

11. Landau, "David Paul Drach," 44. On conversion rates in France and the German states, see Endelman, *Leaving the Jewish Fold*, 73. Ratisbonne is cited in Endelman, 73. Kselman discusses conversion in relation to the questions raised by Jewish emancipation in *Conscience and Conversion* (80–121). Kselman also includes sections on the Ratisbonne brothers (95–105) and Notre-Dame de Sion (111–117).

12. Heine cited in Endelman, *Leaving the Jewish Fold*, 69.

13. Marie-Alphonse Ratisbonne, *Conversion de Monsieur M.-A. Ratisbonne, racontée par lui-même* (Le Mans: Gallienne, 1842). On the Ratisbonne brothers, see also Antoine Compagnon, *Connaissez-vous Brunetière? Enquête sur un antidrey fusard et ses amis* (Paris: Seuil, 1997); Kalman, *Rethinking Antisemitism*, 46; Helfand, "Passports and Piety," 63; and Thomas Kselman, "Social Reform and Religious Conversion in French Judaism," *Proceedings of the Western Society for French History* 28 (2000): 10–18.

14. Morel is clearly driven by animus against Deutz, and his opinions of the latter must be taken with a grain of salt. Landau makes the suggestion that Morel may really be a fictional persona created by Drach to voice particularly harsh opinions about Deutz, for Morel seems to have had access to all of Drach's private letters and innermost thoughts. Moreover, Morel provides only a few sketchy details about his own biography:

he says he was born in Mutzig, Alsace; that his given name (prior to converting) was Gumpel; that his father was named Yekl Montsich and his mother Hendla. Landau points out that neither Morel nor his parents appear in any official records under the names that Morel provides ("Le cas étrange," 216, note 11; Morel, *La vérité sur l'arrestation*, xiii). Strangely, though, Morel gets certain details about Drach's life wrong, including a reference to the death of his child, suggesting they were not in fact the same person (Klein, "Mauvais Juif," 94). Drach himself points to this discrepancy in Morel's account, which he says is otherwise accurate, in a letter published in the *Mémorial Catholique*, April 1826, 247–248. Therefore, the identity of Morel remains something of a mystery. However, I accept the letters by Deutz and Drach that Morel cites as authentic because they resemble very closely the style of both writers in documents they published elsewhere.

15. Drach, *Relation*, 13–14. Morel, *La vérité sur l'arrestation*, 51.

16. Deutz, *Arrestation*, 7.

17. Landau also questions the veracity of Deutz's explanation for his conversion ("Le cas étrange," 223).

18. At the start of his memoir, Deutz describes witnessing the fall of Napoleon as a child in 1814: "I had seen the empire crumble, then, on its ashes, rise the restoration under the tutelage of foreign bayonettes" (*Arrestation*, 6).

19. Drach, *Relation*, 15.

20. Deutz cited in Drach, *Relation*, 16.

21. Drach, *Relation*, 18. Both daughters did in fact become nuns, and Drach's son Auguste, who took the name Paul Augustin Drach after his conversion, became the canon of Notre Dame Cathedral.

22. Dermoncourt, *Deutz ou imposture*, 7. Deutz, *Arrestation*, 7.

23. Drach, *Relation*, 11.

24. *L'Ami de la religion*, 1828, tome 54, 342; tome 55, 172. Kalman discusses the publicity given to conversions in this newspaper (*Rethinking Antisemitism*, 34).

25. Archivio Storico di Propaganda Fide, Paolo Drach, vol. 1.

26. Dermoncourt, *Deutz ou imposture*, 6.

27. Letters cited in Morel, *Vérité sur l'arrestation*, 52–53.

28. Letter cited in Morel, 87.

29. Letter from Fortis dated October 25, 1827, Archivum Romanum Societatis Iesu (ARSI), Epistolae R.P.N. Al. Fortis, Lib. 5, 1827, 2261–2262. The order granting the allowance: Archivio Segreto Vaticano, Segreteria di Stato Esteri, 597, (minuta) Eccellentissimo Prefetto di Propaganda Fide, 21 novembre 1827, note 361187. Deutz says that he stayed at the "collège de Cordeliers" in Rome (*Arrestation*, 7). Catrice suggests this means he may have been expelled from the Holy Apostles ("L'Harmonie," 325), but I think that this is the same institution because the French sometimes refer to the Franciscans as Cordeliers.

30. Letters cited in Morel, *La vérité sur l'arrestation*, 88–89. Kalman discusses Lamennais's negative attitude toward Jews (*Rethinking Antisemitism*, 29–30).

31. Letter cited in Morel, *La vérité sur l'arrestation*, 92–93.

32. "Lettre 1597. Au R.P. Ventura," dated La Chenaie, March 1, 1830, in Félicité de Lamennais, *Correspondance générale*, ed. Louis Le Guillou (Paris: Armand Colin, 1973), tome 4, 253. Also cited in Landau, "Le cas étrange," 223, note 38; Catrice, "L'Harmonie," 328.

33. Letter cited in Morel, *La vérité sur l'arrestation*, 93.

34. Drach, *Relation*, 23. Dermoncourt, *Deutz ou imposture*, 9.

35. Letter cited in Morel, *La vérité sur l'arrestation*, 95; and Drach, 24.

36. On his baptismal name, see Catrice, "L'Harmonie," 330–331. Deutz sent the letter to Drach and asked him to transmit it to his father. Drach provided the translation from Hebrew to French (*Relation*, 27–28). It is of course possible that Drach edited or even invented the letter.

37. Drach, *Relation*, 31.

38. Letter dated 10/30/1828. Archivio Storico di Propaganda Fide, Paolo Drach, vol. 1.

39. Letters cited in Morel, *La vérité sur l'arrestation*, 99–101. Deutz, *Arrestation*, 9.

40. Morel, *La vérité sur l'arrestation*, 101–102.

41. David I. Kertzer, *The Popes Against the Jews: The Vatican's Role in the Rise of Modern Anti-Semitism* (New York: Vintage, 2001), 9, 27–29. Kenneth Stow, *Theater of Acculturation: The Roman Ghetto in the 16th Century* (Seattle: University of Washington Press), 2001. Ferdinand Gregorovius, *The Ghetto and the Jews of Rome* (New York: Schocken, 1966), 93–94.

42. Deutz, *Arrestation*, 9–10. Morel, *La vérité sur l'arrestation*, 103.

43. Deutz, *Arrestation*, 9. The letters concerning employment for Deutz at the Vatican printing office: Archivio Segreto Vaticano (ASV), Segreteria di Stato, Interni busta 764, 1830 (66), 12 aprile 1830, Sopra le premure dell'Eccellentissimo Cappellari a pro del Neofito Deutz; ASV, Segreteria di Stato, Interni busta 780, Monsignor Mai, Illustrissimo custode della Biblioteca Vaticana, 14 giugno 1830, Oggetto: Si propone di impiegare nella Stamperia Vaticana il neofito Deutz; ASV, Segreteria di Stato, Interni busta 780, Monsignor Tesoriere Generale, 9 giugno 1830, Oggetto: Si torna a raccomandare che in neofito Deutz sia occupato anche senza emolumento nella stamperia Camerale *Riservato*; ASV, Segreteria di Stato, Interni busta 780, Documento ufficiale del Tesoriere Generale al Cardinale della Segreteria di Stato, 12 giugno 1830, Sezione prima, *Riservato*.

44. Deutz, *Arrestation*, 12. Dermoncourt, *Deutz ou imposture*, 14–15.

Chapter Five: Exile

1. Duchesse de Maillé, *Souvenirs des deux Restaurations*, ed. Xavier de la Fournière (Paris: Perrin, 1984), 348.

2. Boigne, *Mémoires*, 1016. Brégeon, *La duchesse de Berry*, 159.

3. Hillerin, *La Duchesse de Berry*, 170.

4. Gontaut, *Mémoires*, 323, 337. Maillé, *Souvenirs*, 359.

5. Maillé, 352.

6. Maillé, 352. Gontaut, *Mémoires*, 354–355. Lucas-Dubreton, *La Duchesse de Berry*, 61.

7. François René de Chateaubriand, *Mémoires d'outre-tombe*, ed. Pierre Clarac (1849; Paris: Livre de Poche, 1973), 3:247–248. Gontaut, *Mémoires*, 355. Hillerin, *La Duchesse de Berry*, 189.

8. Chateaubriand, *Mémoires*, 248. Lucas-Dubreton, *La Duchesse de Berry*, 62.

9. Boigne, *Mémoires*, 1100. Hillerin, *La Duchesse de Berry*, 193. The name was also spelled "Rosanbo," but it appears as "Rosambo" in archival documents and in the memoirs of the comte de Mesnard. He is referred to as handsome in Artur-Léon Imbert de Saint-Amand, *La cour de Charles X* (Paris: E. Dentu, 1892), 204.

10. Lucas-Dubreton, *La Duchesse de Berry*, 62. Hillerin, *La Duchesse de Berry*, 195. Ange Hyacinthe Maxence Damas, *Mémoires du baron de Damas* (Paris: Plon, 1923), 2:192.

11. Gontaut, *Mémoires*, 347. Thérèse Rouchette, *La folle équipée de la duchesse de Berry* (La Roche-sur-Yon, France: Centre vendéen de recherches historiques, 2004), 45.

12. "Mais si jamais une secte abhorrée / Brisait encore le sceptre de nos rois, / Ah! Pense à nous, reviens dans la Vendée / Amène Henri, nous défendrons ses droits." The song is cited in full in Rouchette, *La folle équipée*, 41. See also Maillé, *Souvenirs*, 394; Jacques Crétineau-Joly, *Histoire de la Vendée militaire: La Cause des blancs* (1840; Paris: Editions du Trident, 2013), 375.

13. Maillé, *Souvenirs*, 396. Rouchette, *La folle équipée*, 50. André Castelot, *La Duchesse de Berry d'après des documents inédits* (1963; Paris: Perrin, 1996), 223.

14. Boigne, *Mémoires*, 1100–1101. Gontaut, *Mémoires*, 367. Mesnard, *Souvenirs intimes*, 1:231. Lucas-Dubreton, *La Duchesse de Berry*, 63.

15. Gontaut, *Mémoires*, 371. A widower, Weld lived in Paris during the Restoration and became a priest in 1821. He was elevated to cardinal on March 15, 1830.

16. Exchange between Charles X and the duchess cited in Mesnard, *Souvenirs intimes*, 1:244–245. Iron utensils and other hardships described by Gontaut, *Mémoires*, 371.

17. Financial difficulties described by Damas, *Mémoires*, 208. Duchess's travels described by Boigne, *Mémoires*, 1101. See also Hillerin, *La Duchesse de Berry*, 203–204.

18. Victor Hugo, "Le sept août, 1829" in *Les rayons et les ombres* (1840), cited in Hillerin, *La Duchesse de Berry*, 206. Faucigny-Lucinge relates his memories of Holyrood (*Souvenirs*, 30).

19. Chateaubriand quoted in Boigne, *Mémoires*, 1123. Damas, *Mémoires*, 212, 216–217.

20. Boigne, *Mémoires*, 1102. "Correspondance," *La Mode*, July 2, 1831, 4.

21. Price, *The Perilous Crown*, 224–261. The right-wing observer is Alfred Nettement; see his *Mémoires historiques de S.A.R. Madame, duchesse de Berri* [sic] (Paris: Allardin, 1837), 3:13.

22. Boigne, *Mémoires*, 1102.

23. Brégeon, *La duchesse de Berry*, 176.

24. Aurélien de Courson, *Le Dernier effort de la Vendée (1832)* (Paris: Emile-Paul, 1909), 25. Those legitimists who supported the duchess and her son (Henri V), as opposed to Charles X, also sometimes called themselves "henriquinquistes."

25. Price, *The Perilous Crown*, 226.

26. Boigne, *Mémoires*, 1106.

27. The avid pupil quotation is in Nettement, *Mémoires historiques*, 158. Ferdinand de Bertier remarked on her intelligence and frivolity, cited in Hugues de Changy, *Le soulèvement de la duchesse de Berry, 1830–1832: Les Royalistes dans la tourmente* (Paris: Albatros, 1986), 157. See also Hillerin, *La Duchesse de Berry*, 213.

28. Hillerin, 214.

29. On the conflict over the regency, see Damas (*Mémoires*, 221, 226) and Castelot (*La Duchesse de Berry*, 229–231).

30. Ferdinand de Bertier, *Souvenirs d'un ultra-royaliste (1815–1832)* (Paris: Jules Tallandier, 1993), 481–482. Francis Démier describes how Bertier assembled young, well-born men "animated by the Christian and monarchical ideal." Members in the lower ranks devoted themselves to charitable works. As one advanced to a higher level, however, the real mission of the Chevaliers de la Foi became clear: to fight for the Bourbons. See Francis Démier, *La France de la Restauration (1814–1830)* (Paris: Gallimard, 2012), 35–36. Bertier's letters are also cited in Guillaume de Bertier de Sauvigny, *Documents inédits sur la conspiration légitimiste de 1830 à 1832* (Paris: A. Hatier, 1951), 55, 73.

31. Hillerin, *La Duchesse de Berry*, 219.

32. Paul Ferdinand Stanislas Dermoncourt [Alexandre Dumas], *La Vendée et madame* (1833; Paris: Alphée, 2009), 64–65. Courson, *Le Dernier effort*, 27. Hillerin, *La Duchesse de Berry*, 218–219.

33. Dermoncourt, *La Vendée*, 65. Rouchette, *La folle équipée*, 94–95. Changy, *Le soulèvement*, 160.

34. "Vous concevez comme moi le plaisir que j'ai éprouvé en revoyant la patrie *sponde* et entendant la douce langue maternelle après seize ans de vicissitudes . . . je suis ici à parcourir la belle Italie, à respirer un air chaud et prendre des bains dont j'avais grand besoin après avoir respiré

tant d'air umide [*sic*] et froid. . . ." Letter cited in Lucas-Dubreton, *La Duchesse de Berry*, 232. Charles Nauroy provides a week-by-week itinerary of the duchess's travels in *La Duchesse de Berry* (Paris: F. Vieweg, 1889), 25.

35. Rouchette, *La folle équipée*, 96.

Chapter Six: The Meeting

1. Dermoncourt, *La Vendée*, 172. Morel cites a letter by Deutz to Drach: "The Jesuits of Georgetown had generously offered for me to stay with them as long as I would like in order to teach French to their students, and I thanked them for their kindness but I prefer to be less well off and more free, however without them I don't know what would have become of me" (*La Vérité sur l'arrestation*, 109). According to Susanne Klingenstein, in the 1830s no Jew had yet been appointed as an American college professor except to teach Semitic languages. See Klingenstein, *Jews in the American Academy: The Dynamics of Intellectual Assimilation* (Syracuse, NY: Syracuse University Press, 1998), 2. Jean-Claude Caron describes Deutz's itinerary in the United States (*Simon Deutz*, 47).

2. Kenneth T. Jackson, ed., *The Encyclopedia of New York City* (New Haven, CT: Yale University Press, 1995), 191.

3. Letters cited in Morel, *La Vérité sur l'arrestation*, 110–111. Also quoted by Landau, "Le cas étrange," 226. According to Morel, if Deutz was corresponding with his father, then he must have indicated he would reconvert to Judaism (*La Vérité sur l'arrestation*, 110).

4. Deutz, *Arrestation*, 14. Morel, *La Vérité sur l'arrestation*, 112–113. Jean-Claude Caron found an extraordinary document in the archives of the Saint Sulpice order in Montreal testifying to Deutz's stay there: "It is generally known that in 1832 the duchesse de Berry was betrayed by a Jew who had been converted in Rome a few years before. But what few people know is that this Jew lived in Montreal, and that during his rather long stay, he earned the estime and confidence of the leading citizens of the town. . . . The savages danced with him, made him an honorary citizen of their nation, the Superior [of the order] had an ox killed in his honor and gave a feast. As M. Deutz was soon returning to Europe and would go to Rome, we took advantage of the occasion to

encourage the savages to write to the Holy Pontiff. A diplomatic necklace was prepared by the Algonquins and the Nipissingues to be sent to His Holiness with a speech in French-Algonquin. . . . M. Deutz arrived in Rome carrying these letters and presents. Pope Gregory XVI who was then reigning expressed his great satisfaction in receiving them." See Jean-Claude Caron, *Simon Deutz*, 48–49.

5. Landau, "Le cas étrange," 226–227. Morel denies that Drach impregnated Sara during his stay in London, arguing that she suffered from a medical condition that would have prevented it (*La Vérité sur l'arrestation*, 68). However, as Landau points out, Morel also says that Drach can hardly be blamed for making his wife pregnant, which suggests that he may have been the father of Lionel after all ("Le cas étrange," 221). See also Klein, "Mauvais Juif," 96; Catrice, "L'Harmonie," 115.

6. Mary Cathcart-Boer, *The City of London—A History* (London: Constable, 1977), 219; and Laura Vaughn, "A Study of the Spatial Characteristics of the Jews in London, 1695 & 1895," Architecture master's thesis, University College London (September 1994), 12–13. Petra Laidlaw, "Jews in the British Isles in 1851: Birthplaces, Residence, and Migrations," *Journal of Jewish Sociology* 53 (2011): 29.

7. Kristy Carpenter, *Refugees of the French Revolution: Émigrés in London, 1789–1802* (New York: St. Martin's, 1999).

8. Bridget Cherry and Nikolaus Pevsner, *The Buildings of England: London 3, Northwest* (New Haven, CT: Yale University Press), 596.

9. Alexandre Dumas, *Mes mémoires (1802–1833)* (1852; Paris: Robert Laffont, 1989), 925. The comte de Falloux describes Montmorency's piety in *Memoirs of the Comte de Falloux*, ed. C. B. Pitman (London: Chapman and Hall, 1888), 1:95.

10. Hillerin, *La Duchesse de Berry*, 216. Deutz, *Arrestation*, 16.

11. Nettement, *Mémoires historiques*, 48–49. Nauroy describes the French government's spying on the duchess in Massa (*La Duchesse de Berry*, 34).

12. Nettement, *Mémoires historiques*, 47. The July Monarchy government gave the Bourbons a deadline to liquidate their properties, after which they would be auctioned off. The duchess sold Rosny to an English banker named Stone. Hillerin describes the complexity of the sale—the duchess would not see the money from the deal for years—and suggests that Stone may have been a straw man in a deal designed to allow the duchess to recover the property at a subsequent date (*La*

Duchesse de Berry, 222 and 281, note 96). On the duchess's struggles with her in-laws over the raising of her children, see, among others, Chateaubriand, *Mémoires*, 3:449–459.

13. Rumors of scandal cited in Boigne, *Mémoires*, 1123. Hillerin, *La Duchesse de Berry*, 221.

14. Bertier, *Souvenirs*, 481–482.

15. Hillerin, *La Duchesse de Berry*, 232. Mesnard, *Souvenirs intimes*, 2:32.

16. Caroline Weber, *Proust's Duchess: How Three Celebrated Women Captured the Imagination of Fin-de-siècle Paris* (New York: Knopf, 2018), 106.

17. Mesnard, *Souvenirs intimes*, 2:44.

18. Quotation by Nettement (*Mémoires historiques*, 21). Changy describes the loans (*Le soulèvement*, 161). See also Rouchette, *La folle équipée*, 98–99. Nauroy describes how Metternich manipulated the duchess, as well as her effort to gain the support of other European powers (*La Duchesse de Berry*, 27–28).

19. Price, *The Perilous Crown*, 220–223.

20. Changy, *Le soulèvement*, 155.

21. Citations in Bertier de Sauvigny, *Documents*, 78, 89, 92. Changy, *Le soulèvement*, 162–165.

22. The letter to the duchess, which was confiscated by the government and later published in the ministerial newspaper *Le Moniteur universel* on June 3, 1832, is cited in its entirety in Dermoncourt, *La Vendée*, 89–94. Dermoncourt dates the letter to May 17, after the duchess had already launched her invasion. Hillerin, following Crétineau-Joly, more plausibly dates it to December 1831 (*La Duchesse de Berry*, 482–483, note 114). The duchess's response is cited in Hillerin (234).

23. Chateaubriand, *Mémoires*, 3:299, 300, 305.

24. Cited in Hillerin, *La Duchesse de Berry*, 235–236. On the royal family's disapproval of her plans for insurrection, see Changy, *Le soulèvement*, 166.

25. Mesnard, *Souvenirs intimes*, 2:47. The duchess's comment about growing a mustache is cited in Lucas-Dubreton (*La Duchesse de Berry*, 69) and Hillerin (*La Duchesse de Berry*, 235), but I could not find it in any of the firsthand memoirs.

26. Dermoncourt, *La Vendée*, 68.

27. On the duchess's deliberations, see Courson, *Le Dernier effort*, 33–35, and Lucas-Dubreton, *La Duchesse de Berry*, 69. Mesnard writes that "she was beloved by the people, and the French people cannot resist courage and heroism, they understand all that is generous!" (*Souvenirs intimes*, 2:48).

28. Dermoncourt, *La Vendée*, 43. Crétineau-Joly, *Histoire de la Vendée militaire*, 394–396. Changy, *Le soulèvement*, 98.

29. Deutz, "Devant Dieu" [n.p.], Archives nationales F/7/12173. See also Deutz, *Arrestation*, 17.

30. Deutz, 17–18.

31. Deutz, 17. Mesnard, *Souvenirs intimes*, 2:41.

32. According to Morel, Deutz took advantage of the hospitality of the Jesuits, letting them pay for his carriages in Rome "as if the community owed him a car." And the morning of his departure, instead of leaving a tip, he took his nightcap with him (*La Vérité sur l'arrestation*, 209).

33. Deutz, *Arrestation*, 18–19.

34. Deutz, *Arrestation*, 19–20. Mesnard mentions Deutz's claim that he was traveling to Portugal in service of the Jesuits (*Souvenirs intimes*, 2:41).

35. Deutz, *Arrestation*, 20.

36. Deutz, "Devant Dieu" [n.p.].

37. Bertier, *Souvenirs*, 518.

38. Bourmont praise cited in Bertier, 518.

39. Courson, *Le Dernier effort*, 140–142. See also Rouchette, *La folle équipée*, 126–127; Hillerin, *La Duchesse de Berry*, 155.

40. Letter dated April 3, 1832. Archivio Storico di Propaganda Fide, Paolo Drach, vol. 1.

41. Deutz, *Arrestation*, 21. Dumas, *Mes Memoires*, 2:926.

42. Mesnard, *Souvenirs intimes*, 2:42.

43. Deutz, *Arrestation*, 26.

Chapter Seven: The Tightrope Walker

1. Peter Baldwin, *Contagion and the State in Europe, 1830–1930* (Cambridge: Cambridge University Press, 1999), 102–110.

2. Heinrich Heine, "French Affairs: Letters from Paris," in *The Works of Heinrich Heine*, trans. Charles Godfrey Leland (New York: E. P. Dutton, 1898), 7:167.

3. William P. Kladky cites twenty thousand cholera victims in "The 1832 Cholera Epidemic in Paris: The Disease That Changed France and Urbanity," in *Royalists, Radicals, and* Les Misérables: *France in 1832*, ed. Eric Martone (Newcastle upon Tyne, UK: Cambridge Scholars Publishing, 2013), 77, 81. Louis-René Villermé et al., *Rapport sur la marche et les effets du choléra-morbus dans Paris et le département de la Seine* (Paris: Imprimerie royale, 1834), 39. Boigne, *Mémoires*, 1119. Baldwin, *Contagion and the State in Europe*, 110.

4. *Traitement homéopoathique du choléra-morbus d'après plusieurs médecins du nord* (Lyon: Louis Perrin, 1832), 5–8.

5. Baldwin, *Contagion and the State in Europe*, 53–56.

6. Villermé, *Rapport sur la marche*, 18.

7. Heine, "French Affairs," 7:165.

8. Peter McPhee, *A Social History of France, 1789–1914*, 2nd ed. (New York: Palgrave, 2004), 144. Paul E. Corcoran, ed., *Before Marx: Socialism and Communism in France, 1830–48* (London: Macmillan, 1983).

9. Kladky, "The 1832 Cholera Epidemic," 89.

10. On the pear caricatures, see, among others, Robert Justin Goldstein, "Censorship of Caricature and the Theater in Nineteenth Century France: An Overview," *Yale French Studies* 122 (2012): 23; Sandy Petrey, *In the Court of the Pear King: French Culture and the Rise of Realism* (Ithaca, NY: Cornell University Press, 2005), 14.

11. On the uprising of 1832, see Jill Harsin, *Barricades: The War of the Streets in Revolutionary Paris, 1830–1848* (New York: Palgrave Macmillan, 2002), 57–60; Louis Blanc, *History of Ten Years, 1830–1840; or, France Under Louis Philippe*, trans. Walter K. Kelly (Philadelphia: Lea and Blanchard, 1848), 2:42–44.

12. Berryer letter cited in Hillerin, *La Duchesse de Berry*, 236. Charette letter in Mesnard, *Souvenirs intimes*, 2:46. Among the pessimistic voices was the former minister of war, Clermont-Tonnerre, who warned the duchess in a letter dated April 8, 1832, that it would be unwise to launch an insurrection at that moment (Changy, *Le soulèvement*, 172).

13. Bertier, *Souvenirs*, 515. Changy, *Le soulèvement*, 172–174.

14. Cholera quotation in Joseph Borély, *Acte d'accusation dressé par le procureur general J. Borély contre les inculpés dans le complot qui avait pour but le débarquement de la duchesse de Berry* [n.p., n.d.], 2. Chateaubriand, *Mémoires*, 3:307. Tightrope walker quotation in Boigne, *Mémoires*, 1123.

15. *La Quotidienne*, May 9, 1832, 1. Boigne, *Mémoires*, 1120.

16. Letter cited in Castelot, *La Duchesse de Berry*, 234.

17. Crétineau-Joly, *Histoire de la Vendée militaire*, 416. Castelot, *La Duchesse de Berry*, 235. Mesnard, *Souvenirs intimes*, 2:52.

18. I am translating *dame d'autour*, which is technically "lady of the bed-chamber," as "lady-in-waiting." Albert Maurin, *Histoire de la chute des Bourbons: Grandeur et décadence de la bourgeoisie* (Paris: Bureaux de la société des traveailleurs réunis, 1851), 5:81–85.

19. Lucas-Dubreton, *La Duchesse de Berry*, 70. Hillerin, *La Duchesse de Berry*, 240.

20. Metternich cited in Thirria, *La Duchesse de Berry*, 70. Montalivet letter from the Archive de la marine, cited in Nauroy, *La Duchesse de Berry*, 37.

21. Lucas-Dubreton, *La Duchesse de Berry*, 70–71.

22. Crétineau-Joly, *Histoire de la Vendée militaire*, 416. Mesnard, *Souvenirs intimes*, 2:53.

23. Mesnard, 2:55. Des Cars's message cited in Crétineau-Joly, *Histoire de la Vendée militaire*, 416.

24. Mesnard, *Souvenirs intimes*, 2:55–56.

25. Mesnard, 2:59. Borély, *Acte d'accusation*, 6.

26. The skirmish is described in Bertier, *Souvenirs*, 537; Borély, *Acte d'accusation*, 7–8; Mesnard, *Souvenirs intimes*, 2:61.

27. Mesnard, 2:58.

28. Auguste Johanet, *La Vendée à trois époques, de 1793 jusqu'à l'empire, 1815–1832* (Paris: Dentu, 1840), 2:145–148. Crétineau-Joly, *Histoire de la Vendée militaire*, 393.

29. Johanet, 163. Changy, *Le soulèvement*, 158. Nauroy, *La Duchesse de Berry*, 31.

30. The song is cited in full in Rouchette, *La folle équipée*, 41. The duchess's thought process is described in Mesnard, *Souvenirs intimes*, 2:66.

31. Mesnard, 2:61.

Chapter Eight: Civil War

1. Mesnard, *Souvenirs intimes*, 2:61–62, 71.

2. The Count Rodolphe Aponyi, an attaché at the Austro-Hungarian Embassy in Paris, referred to the duchess as *"une aventurière de*

bonne maison." Cited in Guy Antonetti, *Louis-Philippe* (Paris: Fayard, 1994), 703. La Comtesse Dash [Gabrielle Anne Cisterne de Courtiras], *Mémoires des autres: Souvenirs anecdotiques sur le règne de Louis-Philippe* (Paris: À la librairie illustrée, 1897), 27.

3. Mesnard, *Souvenirs intimes*, 2:64–65.

4. Dermoncourt, *La Vendée*, 78–79.

5. Accounts of the itinerary found in Courson, *Le Dernier effort*, 171–172; Mesnard, *Souvenirs intimes*, 2:70–71; Castelot, *La Duchesse de Berry*, 236–237. Her clothing described in Lucas-Dubreton, *La Duchesse de Berry*, 73. Her comment concerning Bourmont's travel cited in Courson, *Le Dernier effort*, 180.

6. Changy, *Le soulèvement*, 183. *Le Moniteur universel*, May 8, 1832, 2. Boigne, *Mémoires*, 1125.

7. Changy, *Le soulèvement*, 178–179.

8. Changy, 181–182.

9. Proclamation in Dermoncourt, *La Vendée*, 87. Letter cited in Changy, *Le soulèvement*, 182.

10. Castelot, *La Duchesse de Berry*, 238–239. Lucas-Dubreton, *La Duchesse de Berry*, 79.

11. Gilbert Dupé, *Chevauchée romantique* (1946), cited in Castelot, *La Duchesse de Berry*, 239.

12. Letter cited in Dermoncourt, *La Vendée*, 91–93.

13. Letter cited in Dermoncourt, 95–96.

14. Legitimist appreciation in Vicomte Édouard Sioc'han de Kersabiec, *Récits et souvenirs de famille, S.A.R. Madame, et ses amis* (Rennes: Vatar, 1895), 94–95.

15. Details of the meeting between Berryer and the duchess contained in Courson (*Le Dernier effort*, 185–188); Mesnard (*Souvenirs intimes*, 2:112–117); Dermoncourt, (*La Vendée*, 113–115); and Changy (*Le soulèvement*, 186).

16. On the significance of duty for the ethos of legitimacy, see Geoffrey Cubitt, "Legitimism and the Cult of Bourbon Royalty," in *The Right in France: From Revolution to Le Pen*, eds. Nicholas Atkin and Frank Tallett (London: I. B. Tauris, 2003), 63. The legitimist appreciation of the duchess's actions is contained in Kersabiec, *Récits et souvenirs*, 111.

17. Courson, *Le Dernier effort*, 192.

18. "Order, counter-order, disorder" cited in Changy, *Le soulèvement*, 188.

19. Courson, *Le Dernier effort*, 203–204. Changy, *Le soulèvement*, 190–191.

20. Telegram from Montalivet, dated June 2, 1832, in the Adolphe Thiers papers, Bibliothèque nationale, Manuscrits, Nouvelles acquisitions françaises, 20601, fol. 163. Dermoncourt, *La Vendée*, 116.

21. Dermoncourt spells it "Chaslière" in his account (*La Vendée*, 117–120).

22. Kersabiec, *Récits et souvenirs*, 137. Changy, *Le soulèvement*, 193–194. Mesnard, *Souvenirs intimes*, 2:189.

23. Dermoncourt, *La Vendée*, 133. Changy, *Le soulèvement*, 195–200. Bertier, *Souvenirs*, 540.

24. Charette's journal cited in Changy, *Le soulèvement*, 255–263.

25. Report cited in Thirria, *La Duchesse de Berry*, 62–63. Duchess's letter to Charette cited in Mesnard, *Souvenirs intimes*, 2:188.

26. Dermoncourt, *La Vendée*, 142–146.

27. Changy makes this case (*Le soulèvement*, 203–204). He draws on the *mémoire* drafted by the comte de Clermont-Tonnerre for the duchess's son, the comte de Chambord, in 1845. Archives nationales, Clermont-Tonnerre 359 AP 83.

28. Louis Blanc, *History of Ten Years, 1830–1840* (London: Chapman and Hall, 1845), 2:23–24.

29. Alfred Nettement, "Madame la duchesse de Berry, *La Quotidienne*, May 9, 1832, 1. Cited in Thirria, *La Duchesse de Berry*, 70–71.

30. Thirria, 71.

31. Dermoncourt, *La Vendée*, 164–167. Kersabiec, *Récits et souvenirs*, 165–167. Changy, *Le soulèvement*, 216. Lucas-Dubreton, *La Duchesse de Berry*, 93.

32. Kersabiec, *Récits et souvenirs*, 167–170.

Chapter Nine: Hiding

1. Deutz, "Devant Dieu" [n.p.].

2. Deutz, *Arrestation*, 26.

3. Deutz, 29–31.

4. Deutz, 26–27. Dermoncourt, *Deutz ou imposture*, 33.

5. Dermoncourt, 34. Deutz, *Arrestation*, 31.

6. Dermoncourt, *La Vendée*, 172. Morel, *La Vérité sur l'arrestation*, 151.

7. Deutz, "Devant Dieu" [n.p.].

8. Deutz, *Arrestation*, 32–33. Deutz letter cited in Morel (*La Vérité sur l'arrestation*, 152). San Isidro el Real is a Jesuit Baroque church in the center of Madrid, which served as the city's cathedral in the nineteenth century. Aranjuez is a royal estate to the south of Madrid.

9. Deutz, *Arrestation*, 33.

10. Courson, *Le Dernier effort*, 140–142. Also described in Rouchette, *La folle équipée*, 126–127.

11. Deutz, *Arrestation*, 34.

12. Dermoncourt, *Deutz ou imposture*, 39. Deutz, *Arrestation*, 37.

13. Deutz, 35–36.

14. Deutz, 38.

15. Deutz, 38. Morel reproduces the letter in French translation (*La Vérité sur l'arrestation*, 152–153).

16. Morel quotes Drach's response in *La Vérité sur l'arrestation*, 153.

17. Dermoncourt, *Deutz ou imposture*, 42. Deutz, *Arrestation*, 39.

18. A sample of this wallpaper is preserved in the collections of the Bibliothèque nationale de France. On the reverse, a note scrawled in pencil and signed Fossé Darcosse indicates that it was removed from the attic at no. 3, rue Haute-du-Château, on July 28, 1852. BNF Notice FRBNF41518375.

19. Nettement, *Mémoires historiques*, 3:240–241.

20. Hillerin, *La Duchesse de Berry*, 278.

21. Lucas-Dubreton, *La Duchesse de Berry*, 98. Dermoncourt, *La Vendée*, 168.

22. Kersabiec, *Récits et souvenirs*, 199.

23. Castelot, *La Duchesse de Berry*, 321. Kersabiec, *Récits et souvenirs*, 199. For the code and noms de guerre, see Dermoncourt, *Vendée*, 70, 86. Multiple letters were blackened when the recipient held the paper up to the flame of a candle to read it. The letters—and ashes—can be found in Archives nationales F/7/12172. Letter cited in Courson, *Le Dernier effort*, 299–300. Athanase Charles Marie de Charette, second baron de

La Contrie, was born on September 3, 1832, on the rue du Château, near the duchess's hiding place in Nantes, while his father was also in hiding. He became a career soldier, fighting in the Papal Zouaves and eventually for France in the Franco-Prussian War.

24. Letters cited in Courson, *Le Dernier effort*, 300–301.

25. Nettement, *Mémoires historiques*, 3:243.

26. Thirria describes her various diplomatic efforts (*La Duchesse de Berry*, 112–144). Letter cited in Thirria (97).

27. Letters cited in Hillerin (*La Duchesse de Berry*, 283) and Rouchette (*La folle équipée*, 370).

28. Letters cited in Kersabiec, *Récits et souvenirs*, 198.

29. Charette quoted in Kersabiec, 199–200. Mesnard, *Souvenirs intimes*, 2:305–306.

30. Mesnard, 2:307–308.

31. Hillerin reproduces the letter in its entirety (*La Duchesse de Berry*, 490, note 194).

32. Mesnard, *Souvenirs intimes*, 2:311.

33. Kersabiec reproduces many of these letters (*Récits et souvenirs*, 204–209). On the duchess in the attic, see Kersabiec, 202. Hillerin, *La Duchesse de Berry*, 285. On cholera in Nantes, see Michel Aussel, *Nantes sous la monarchie de juillet* (Nantes: Ouest, 2002), 28.

34. *Le Moniteur universel* reports Guibourg's arrest in Nantes on June 5, 1832. The details of the sleeping arrangement emerged at Guibourg's trial in March 1833. See Nauroy, *La Duchesse de Berry*, 66.

35. Achille Guibourg, *Relation fidèle et détaillée de l'arrestation de S.A.R. Madame, Duchesse de Berry* (Nantes: Merson, 1832), 3.

36. Mesnard, *Souvenirs intimes*, 2:336.

37. Dermoncourt, *La Vendée*, 169.

Chapter Ten: The Search

1. Hortense de Beauharnais (1783–1837), known as *la reine Hortense*, was Napoleon's stepdaughter: the daughter of his first wife, Joséphine de Beauharnais. In 1802 she married Napoleon's brother, Louis Bonaparte, who later became king of Holland. She was the mother of Louis Napoleon Bonaparte, subsequently Napoleon III. *La Gazette du Languedoc* describes Joly as having been a "valet" in the household of Queen Hortense

(November 23, 1832, 1). On Joly, see Pierre-Louis Canler, *Mémoires de Canler, ancien chef du service de sûreté 1797–1865*, ed. Jacques Brenner (Paris: Mercure de France, 1986), 140.

2. Boigne, *Mémoires*, 813. Brégeon, *La duchesse de Berry*, 85. All the royalist accounts of the affair are deeply suspicious of Joly. See, for example, Fortuné de Cholet, *Madame. Nantes, Blaye, Paris* (Paris: Hivert, 1833), 300, 315.

3. "Revue de la semaine," *La Mode*, April–July 1832, 158.

4. Montalivet, "Dépêche télégraphique du 2 juin 1832," in Adolphe Thiers Papers, Bibliothèque nationale, Manuscrits, Nouvelles acquisitions françaises, 20601, fol. 163. Louis Joly, *Extrait des divers rapports adressés à Mr. le Comte de Montalivet, Ministre de l'Intérieur*, Archives nationales F/7/12171. I will refer to this document subsequently as "Joly Report." See also Hillerin, *La Duchesse de Berry*, 286.

5. Aussel, *Nantes sous la monarchie de juillet*, 11. All subsequent references to Joly's narrative of the events can be found in the Joly Report [n.p.].

6. The mother superior was Marie-Antoinette de la Ferronnays, whose brother, Auguste-Pierre-Marie Ferron, comte de La Ferronnays, had been a close friend of the duc de Berry. Boigne, *Mémoires*, 723–727. Brégeon, *La duchesse de Berry*, 73.

7. Interrogation cited in Thirria, *La Duchesse de Berry*, 75–76.

8. "Dépêche télégraphique du 14 7bre [septembre], 1832," in Adolphe Thiers Papers, Bibliothèque nationale, Manuscrits, Nouvelles acquisitions françaises, 20601, fol. 163.

9. Dermoncourt, *La Vendée*, 173.

10. Deutz, *Arrestation*, 40–41.

11. Nettement, *Mémoires historiques*, 3:255–256.

12. Nettement, 3:250.

13. Pierre Guiral, *Adolphe Thiers ou de la nécessité en politique* (Paris: Fayard, 1986), 77. Dermoncourt, *La Vendée*, 174. "L'odieux petit nain" quoted in Hillerin, *La Duchesse de Berry*, 289.

14. Deutz, *Arrestation*, 42.

15. Thirria, *La Duchesse de Berry*, 74.

16. The street was named after Antoine Richepanse (1770–1802), a French general responsible for reestablishing slavery on the island of Guadaloupe during the empire. In 2001 the name of the street was

changed to rue du Chevalier-de-Saint-George after an advocate for the abolition of slavery.

17. Deutz, *Arrestation*, 44.

18. Deutz, 43–44. Deutz, "Devant Dieu" [n.p.].

19. Nettement, *Mémoires historiques*, 3:251–252.

20. Dermoncourt, *La Vendée*, 175.

21. Dermoncourt, 176.

22. Letter cited in Thirria, *La Duchesse de Berry*, 76–77.

23. Letter cited in Thirria, 85–86.

24. Letters cited in Thirria, 87, 92.

25. The trial is quoted extensively in *Le Journal du commerce*. This quotation appears on October 9, 1832, 3.

26. Cited in *Le Journal du Commerce*, October 22, 1832, 2.

27. Bertier, *Souvenirs*, 553.

28. In the same letter to Bertier quoted above, the duchess said that she would follow his advice to go see her sister Rose, which Berthier interpreted as a code for going to Spain (553). Mesnard, *Souvenirs intimes*, 2:336–341.

29. Deutz recounts the journey in *Arrestation* (45). Joly recounts it in his report to Thiers.

30. A plaque on the hotel informs today's passersby that the English economist Arthur Young considered the hotel to be one of the most beautiful in Europe and that the writer Stendhal, among other famous personages, stayed there.

31. Deutz, *Arrestation*, 45.

32. Deutz, 45–46. Joly Report [n.p.].

33. As Mesnard writes, "This baron de Gonzagues . . . does not go a day without visiting the chapel of the convent and taking communion, which served to greatly edify madame de La Ferronnays and contributed not a little, I believe, to convincing her to instruct Madame as to the nature of this foreigner's request" (*Souvenirs intimes*, 2:342–343).

34. Mesnard, 2:342–343.

35. Mesnard, 2:344.

36. There is some confusion over the date of Deutz's first meeting with the duchess in Nantes. In his report, Joly gives the date as October 31, which Dermoncourt confirms (*La Vendée*, 180). On the same page of his

memoir (*Arrestation*, 50), Deutz gives the date alternately as October 25 and October 28 but specifies that it was a Wednesday. On that week, Wednesday fell on the 31st, so I am inclined to believe Joly.

37. Deutz, *Arrestation*, 50.

38. Deutz, 51; Mesnard, *Souvenirs intimes*, 2:347.

39. Deutz, *Arrestation*, 51. Kersabiec, *Récits et souvenirs*, 219.

40. Deutz, *Arrestation*, 52.

41. Deutz, 52.

42. Mesnard, *Souvenirs intimes*, 2:351.

43. Joly Report [n.p.].

44. Deutz, *Arrestation*, 53. Deutz is referred to as "Herbault" in this section of Joly's report.

45. Deutz, 55.

46. Dermoncourt, *La Vendée*, 181.

Chapter Eleven: Into the Fire

1. Dermoncourt, *La Vendée*, 185.

2. Deutz cited in Joly Report [n.p.].

3. Joly Report [n.p.].

4. The brother-in-law of the Du Guinys reports hearing this account of Deutz's behavior that night from the policeman guarding him. "Lettre de M. Félix Chantelou à Madame de Chantelou, sa mère," November 16, 1832, published by J. Senot de la Londe, *Bulletin de la société archaeologique de Nantes et du Département de la Loire-Inférieure*, tome 46 (1905): 343. Rouchette cites this letter in *La folle équipée*, 312, note 51.

5. Deutz, *Arrestation*, 56.

6. Dermoncourt, *La Vendée*, 183. The current rue Saint-Pierre, leading down from the cathedral, was part of the Haute-Grande-Rue before 1867. The rue Haute-du-Château is now the rue Mathelin-Rodier. Édouard Pied, *Notice sur les rues de Nantes* (Nantes: A. Dugas, 1906), 135.

7. Kersabiec, *Récits et souvenirs*, 224.

8. In *La Vendée* Dermoncourt states that Deutz noticed, as he left the house, that the table was laid for seven. But eight dinner guests were present in the house that night, including the four outlaws (7). In his report, Joly confirms that he counted eight places laid at the

table during his search of the premises: "we arrived on the second floor where a sumptuously laid table in a chamber that served as a dining room caught my attention for a moment. Eight places were laid even though there were ostensibly only four people present in the house ..." [n.p.]. On this discrepancy in the sources, see also Rouchette, *La folle équipée*, 312.

9. Dermoncourt, *La Vendée*, 183. In his memoirs, Alexandre Dumas describes ghostwriting the first edition of Dermoncourt's account of the episode. When the duchesse de Berry read the work, she suggested several additions be made to a second edition, on which Dumas did not collaborate. Dumas, *Mes Mémoires, 1830–1833* (Paris: Robert Laffont, 1989), 2:784. The duchess's remark is cited in Guibourg (*Relation fidèle et détaillée*, 8).

10. Guibourg, 8. Kersabiec, *Récits et souvenirs*, 225.

11. Guibourg, *Relation fidèle et détaillée*, 9.

12. Dermoncourt, *La Vendée et Madame*, 2nd ed. (Paris: Canel, 1833), 356–357. Kersabiec, *Récits et souvenirs*, 225.

13. Joly Report [n.p.].

14. Kersabiec, *Récits et souvenirs*, 228.

15. Joly Report [n.p.].

16. Guibourg, *Relation fidèle et détaillée*, 13. *La Quotidienne*, November 25, 1832, 4.

17. "Procès-verbal de l'arrestation de la duchesse de Berri [*sic*]," cited in Cholet, *Madame*, 228.

18. Duchess cited in *Le Breton*, November 11, 1832, 2.

19. "Lettre de Mlle Marie-Louise du Guiny à Mme de Chantelou sa soeur à Rennes," *Bulletin de la société archaeologique de Nantes et du Département de la Loire-Inférieure* 46 (1905): 329. The letter is cited in Rouchette, *La folle équipée*, 312, note 51. Kersabiec claims the duchess uttered the line while hiding in the fireplace (*Récits et souvenirs*, 228).

20. Guibourg, *Relation fidèle et détaillée*, 13.

21. "Lettre de Mlle Marie-Louise du Guiny," 331–332.

22. In his report, Joly says that they found 34,074 francs and 10 centimes in the house [n.p.]. Dermoncourt, *La Vendée*, 2nd ed., 359.

23. Reference to Guibourg's hat in Hillerin (*La Duchesse de Berry*, 296, 492). The duchess recounted the episode later to her doctor, who cited her testimony in his published journals. See Prosper Ménière, *La*

captivité de Madame la duchesse de Berry à Blaye. 1833 (Paris: Calmann-Lévy, 1882), 1:435.

24. Guibourg, *Relation fidèle et détaillée*, 15–16.

25. Letter cited in Thirria, *La Duchesse de Berry*, 77.

26. Dermoncourt, *La Vendée*, 188. Despite Dumas's left-leaning sympathies and those of General Dermoncourt, the duchess emerges from their account virtually indistinguishable from the portrait painted in the legitimist press.

27. Demolition described in Dermoncourt, *La Vendée*, 189–190; and Dermoncourt, *La Vendée*, 2nd ed., 359–360. Guibourg, *Relation fidèle et détaillée*, 15. Duchess cited in Mesnard, *Souvenirs intimes*, 3:19.

28. Mesnard, 3:22.

29. Handkerchiefs description cited in Ménière (*La captivité de Madame*, 1:435). Duchess cited in Mesnard (*Souvenirs intimes*, 3:19).

30. Archives nationales F/7/12175. Cited in Thirria, *La Duchesse de Berry*, 83.

31. Duchess cited in Mesnard, *Souvenirs intimes*, 3:19. The letters from Henri and Louise are found, along with other letters seized that night in Nantes, in Archives nationales F/7/12175. Some of them are cited in Thirria, *La Duchesse de Berry*, 77–81. After her arrest the duchess would receive more letters of this sort from her children. She confided to her doctor that she realized that her children were not able to be completely honest or open in their letters because they knew they would be read by the duchesse d'Angoulême and others (Ménière, *La captivité de Madame*, 1:34–35).

32. See the discussion of the missed periods in the next chapter. See also Hillerin, *La Duchesse de Berry*, 492, note 214.

33. Cited in Cholet, *Madame*, 229.

34. This is how the viscount Kersabiec, nephew of Stylite, recounts the event, based on the remembrances of his aunt (*Récits et souvenirs*, 235). It is fairly close to what Mesnard quotes her as saying: "You are French and military men, I entrust myself to your honor" (*Souvenirs intimes*, 3:25). Other versions of the duchess's words upon emerging from the fireplace are similar if less poetic. According to Joly, she said, "We surrender, gendarmes, we are your prisoners, but don't call the army." According to Dermoncourt, she said, "It is I. I am the duchesse de Berry. Do not harm me!" (*La Vendée*, 192).

Chapter Twelve: Surrender

1. Joly Report [n.p.].

2. The following account comes from Dermoncourt, *La Vendée*, 193–195.

3. Dermoncourt, 193. Mesnard, *Souvenirs intimes*, 3:27. "Où est-elle," *La Mode*, July 1832, 186–188. "Revue de la semaine," *La Mode*, December 1832, 249.

4. Margadant, *The New Biography*, 33–71. Jeffrey B. Hobbs, "'Napoléon in a Skirt:' The Duchesse de Berry's Rebellion and the Politics of Emotional Representation in July Monarchy France," *French Historical Studies* 40, no. 4 (2017): 601. See also Martone, "The Last Vendée," 33.

5. Guibourg, *Relation fidèle et détaillée*, 22.

6. Dermoncourt, *La Vendée*, 195.

7. Joly Report [n.p.]. Boigne, *Mémoires*, 1163. As *Le Courrier Français* reported on November 13, 1832, "It is said that following the arrest of the duchesse de Berry and the discovery of papers in the Duguigny [*sic*] house, 800 people have been compromised" (2). Henri Gisquet, the prefect of police, writes in his memoirs that some of the papers were so compromising that the government chose to keep them secret (*Mémoires de M. Gisquet* [Paris: Marchant, 1840], 2:361). Charles Nauroy contends that some of the letters were burned by Thiers and some were returned to foreign kings: letters from Charles Albert, the king of Sardinia, to the duchess are now in the Turin Archives (*La Duchesse de Berry*, 78–79).

8. Dumas, *Mes Mémoires*, 2:939. Boigne, *Mémoires*, 1155, note 83.

9. Alphonse Toussenel, *Les Juifs rois de l'époque, histoire de la féodalité financière* (Nantes: Mlle Dauvin, 1846).

10. An article in *La Mode* commented that for the price of Deutz's betrayal, which the writer assumed to be 500,000 francs, 500 families could live for a year. The article began with an epigraph from Matthew 26 about Judas and the thirty pieces of silver. "Marie-Caroline, duchesse de Berry, prisonnière de son oncle Louis-Philippe," *La Mode*, November, 1832, 157. The origin of the pincers story is Alexandre Dumas *fils*, who claims to have heard it from the son of Thiers's secretary, who was one of his classmates at school. See Dumas *fils* letter to Charles

Nauroy, *Le Curieux*, October 15, 1883, 8–9. Drumont repeats the story in *La France Juive: Essai d'histoire contemporaine* (1886; Beyrouth, Lebanon: Edition Charlemagne, 1994), 1:46–47.

11. Courson, *Le Dernier effort*, 311. Kersabiec, *Récits et souvenirs*, 240–241.

12. Deutz, *Arrestation*, 42. Boigne's account contains a more genteel version of these antisemitic stereotypes. Describing Deutz's mission to secure a loan for the duchess from Miguel, she writes that "in renouncing the practices of his religion, [Deutz had not] forgotten the mercantile habits of his caste" (*Mémoires*, 1144).

13. Adolphe Thiers papers, Bibliothèque nationale, Manuscrits, Nouvelles acquisitions françaises, 20601, fol. 163. The receipt is also mentioned by Hugues de Changy, *Le soulèvement de la duchesse de Berry*, 211, note 609; Rouchette, *La folle équipée*, 317, note 59; and Landau, "Le cas étrange," 229, note 62. Jean-Claude Caron points out that the receipt is not on official ministerial letterhead and does not include the signature of Thiers, which might lead us to question its authenticity. A comparison of Deutz's signature with the very few other documents signed by him is difficult to make. However, Caron concludes the receipt is most likely authentic, pointing out that Thiers may have wanted such a receipt in case he were ever asked to account for the large sum of money given to Deutz. See Jean-Claude Caron, *Simon Deutz*, 149.

14. Dermoncourt, *La Vendée*, 196. On November 9, 1832, *Le Breton* referred to fears of a "chivalrous attempt, a last despairing effort" to rescue the duchess (1).

15. Dermoncourt, *La Vendée*, 197–198.

16. Boigne, *Mémoires*, 1158–1159.

17. *Gazette de France*, November 9, 1832, 1. Dermoncourt, *La Vendée*, 198–199.

18. Duchess cited in Dermoncourt, 202.

19. Joly [n.p.]. Boigne, *Mémoires*, 1159. The contents of this note remained the subject of intense speculation. Nauroy quotes a copy of a letter, dated February 14, 1833, from the comte d'Argout, who replaced Thiers as minister of the interior, to Joly, asking whether the latter could confirm that the duchess's note expressed a desire not to be separated from Guibourg. Written at the moment it had become clear that the

duchess was pregnant, the minister's letter was obviously trying to confirm the paternity of the child. Nauroy, *La Duchesse de Berry*, 80–81.

20. Dermoncourt, *La Vendée*, 206–207.

21. Duchess cited in Dermoncourt, 204–205. For example, on November 10, 1832, *L'Ami de la Charte* wrote that "the capture of Caroline Berry was, for all true patriots, a source of joy, because they hoped that event would put an end to the civil war."

22. Boigne, *Mémoires*, 1146. Hillerin, *La Duchesse de Berry*, 316.

23. Queen cited in Boigne, 1154–1155. François Guizot explains in his memoir that Louis-Philippe believed that the law of April 10, 1832, which banished the Bourbons but did not specify any punishment should they return to France, gave him the right simply to deport the duchess. However, the government believed that the political situation necessitated her imprisonment. François Guizot, *Mémoires pour servir à l'histoire de mon temps* (Paris: Michel Lévy frères, 1860), 3:47–48.

24. Both of these articles are quoted in the right-wing *La Gazette de France*, November 9, 1832, 1.

25. *Le Journal du commerce*, November 12, 1832, 1.

26. *La Quotidienne*, November 10, 1832, 1.

27. *Le Moniteur universel*, November 9, 11, 1832, 1. Guizot, *Mémoires*, 3:45–46.

28. *La Quotidienne*, November 10, 1832, 1.

29. *Le Corsaire*, November 10, 1832, 2, 3.

30. *Le Corsaire*, November 13, 1832, 2–3.

31. Boigne, *Mémoires*, 1147.

32. Joly Report [n.p.]. Also cited in Hillerin, *La Duchesse de Berry*, 308.

33. Ferdinand Petitpierre, *Journal de la captivité de la duchesse de Berry à Blaye* (Paris: Émile-Paul, 1904), 11. Also cited in Hillerin, who points out that Petitpierre's father had founded a factory that produced printed fabric, so he was an expert in textiles (*La Duchesse de Berry*, 309, 313).

34. Dermoncourt, *La Vendée*, 213.

35. Joly Report [n.p.].

36. Duchess's comment to her doctor cited in Ménière (*La captivité de Madame*, 1:80). Joly describes the conversation in his report. Cholet provides a different version of the same anecdote, in which the duchess says she would intercede with Dom Miguel on behalf of one of the guards but pointedly does not say she would help Joly (*Madame*, 93).

37. Stylite's comment cited in the Joly Report [n.p.]. D'Erlon comment cited in Ménière, *La captivité de Madame*, 1:30; and Nauroy, *La Duchesse de Berry*, 84.

38. Petitpierre, *Journal de la captivité*, 14–17.

39. Rouchette, *La folle équipée*, 322.

40. "Un journal carliste nous assure que depuis son arrestation, la duchesse de Berri est *beaucoup plus grande.*" *Le Corsaire*, November 12, 1832, 3; emphasis in the original.

Chapter Thirteen: The Illustrious Captive

1. Letter cited in Cholet, *Madame*, 356.

2. The king was saved by a young woman named Adèle Boury, the daughter of a postmaster, who was struggling to get a glimpse as the royal carriage passed by. When the would-be assassin stepped in front of her, rudely blocking her view, she pulled down on his arm just as he was aiming the gun. The bullet went astray, and the nineteen-year-old became a hero. "Miscellanies of the Month," *Lady's Magazine*, December 1832, 282.

3. Guizot, *Mémoires*, 3:48.

4. "Madame has the walk and the stomach of a woman who is five to six months pregnant," Petitpierre related in his journal on December 13, 1832 (*Journal de la captivité*, 87).

5. Petitpierre, 20.

6. Petitpierre, 29–30. Boigne, *Mémoires*, 1166. Mesnard, *Souvenirs intimes*, 3:53.

7. Cholet, *Madame*, 297–298. On January 2, 1833, a reporter noted that the duchess took a walk the prior Thursday but had not been seen since. "Revue de la semaine," *La Mode*, January 1833, 9.

8. Cubitt, "Legitimism," 63–64.

9. François René de Chateaubriand, *Mémoire sur la capitivité de Mme la duchesse de Berry* (1832; Paris: Editions Paleo, 2009), 43, 73–74.

10. Chateaubriand, *Mémoire sur la capitivité*, 77–78, 83.

11. "Madame, votre fils est mon roi!" *La Mode*, January 1833, 1.

12. Symptoms cited in Petitpierre, *Journal de la captivité*, 138. Menus found in Archives nationales F/7/12174. See also Hillerin, *La Duchesse de Berry*, 311.

13. Cholet, *Madame*, 318–319. Petitpierre, *Journal de la captivité*, 58. Hillerin, *La Duchesse de Berry*, 311.

14. Petitpierre, *Journal de la captivité*, 74, 82, 97.

15. Ménière, *La captivité de Madame*, 1:18.

16. Thirria, *La Duchesse de Berry*, 191.

17. Thirria, 188. Mesnard, *Souvenirs intimes*, 3:96. Joly Report [n.p.].

18. Thirria, *La Duchesse de Berry*, 192. Duchess's letter cited in Petit-pierre, *Journal de la captivité*, 44.

19. Thirria, *La Duchesse de Berry*, 192.

20. Cholet, *Madame*, 327.

21. Boigne, *Mémoires*, 1169.

22. Ménière, *La captivité de Madame*, 1:41–43. Arthur-Léon Imbert de Saint-Amand, *La duchesse de Berry en Vendée, à Nantes et à Blaye* (Paris: Dentu, 1893), 510–511.

23. Petitpierre, *Journal de la captivité*, 49.

24. Petitpierre, 39. Joly Report [n.p.]. Joly would later take up a post in the town of Blaye but not within the citadel.

25. Cited in Thirria, *La Duchesse de Berry*, 191.

26. Ménière, *La captivité de Madame*, 1:31.

27. *La Gazette du Languedoc*, March 25, 1833, 2. "Revue de la semaine," *La Mode*, February 1833, 106.

28. William M. Reddy, *The Invisible Code: Honor and Sentiment in Postrevolutionary France, 1814–1848* (Berkeley: University of California Press, 1997), 193.

29. Eugène Briffault, *Paris à table*, trans. J. Weintraub (Oxford: Oxford University Press, 2018), xvii. Alexandre Dumas also recounts this duel in *Mes Mémoires*, chapter 264.

30. Boigne, *Mémoires*, 1175.

31. *Le Corsaire*, May 12, 1833, 2. This duel is described in Elizabeth Wormeley Latimer, *France in the Nineteenth Century* (Chicago: A. C. McClurg, 1894), 47. See also Hillerin, *La Duchesse de Berry*, 327.

32. Ménière, *La captivité de Madame*, 1:12–13.

33. Ménière, 1:19–22.

34. *Le Moniteur universel*, February 26, 1833, 1.

35. Boigne, *Mémoires*, 1176.

36. Brissac cited in Ménière, *La captivité de Madame*, 1:28. Mesnard, *Souvenirs intimes*, 3:138–141.

37. Boigne, *Mémoires*, 1178.

38. Duchess cited in Ménière, *La captivité de Madame*, 1:29. Boigne, *Mémoires*, 1178.

39. Ménière was able to read the letter (1:38).

40. Ménière, 1:57–58.

41. Ménière, 1:182–185.

42. Ménière, 1:381.

43. Ménière, 1:404.

44. Ménière, 1:407.

45. Ménière, 1:408–414.

46. Castelot, *La Duchesse de Berry*, 265. Boigne writes that "even the most exalted partisans of the princess didn't take this supposed marriage seriously and nobody sought to invoke it as an excuse" (*Mémoires*, 1182).

47. Boigne, 1180. Reiset, the legitimist historian, reports finding a copy of the marriage certificate in the Vatican secret archives on page 177 of a special register marked "in libro primo Matrimoniorum." The certificate is marked Rome and bears the date December 14, 1831. Reiset also cites a letter he found in the private archive of the Lucchesi-Palli family in Brunnsée, Austria, written by Hector and mentioning the duchess's secret journey to meet him in The Hague, where she supposedly conceived the child. Reiset takes these two documents as proof of the duchess's version of events (*Marie-Caroline*, 204–205). Castelot disputes the authenticity of these documents, arguing that Mme du Cayla arranged for the forging of the certificate and pointing out that the duchess's dated correspondence from her period in hiding proves she did not leave Nantes in August 1832, when she conceived the child (*La Duchesse de Berry*, 265, 269). Castelot also cites a letter found in the archive of the prince de Beauveau, from the duchess to Hector, copied by Madame du Cayla, in which the duchess instructs Hector about how to lie concerning their prior acquaintance (264).

48. On the rumors about the baby's paternity, see Boigne, *Mémoires*, 1186–1187. Horace de Viel-Castel reports hearing secondhand that Bugeaud believed that the father of the baby was Deutz. Apparently, the duchess kept repeating in Blaye, "Him! . . . betrayed by him!" Viel-Castel says he personally thought the father was Mesnard. Horace de Viel-Castel, *Mémoires du comte Horace de Viel-Castel sur le règne de Napoléon III* (Paris: Chez tous les libraires, 1883), 2:128. The comtesse de

Boigne also includes a report from a French admiral saying that Bugeaud and others believed the father to be either Deutz or Guibourg (*Mémoires*, 1194). Hillerin includes an appendix to her biography on the question of the child's paternity. She weighs the evidence and decides the father must have been Ludovic de Rosambo because the duchess's love affair with him was the longest standing (*La Duchesse de Berry*, 427–436). The song reads in the original:

> Chacun parle de la grossesse
> De la duchesse de Berry.
> Les carlistes qu'elle intéresse
> Sur ses travers n'ont jamais ri,
> Ils disent qu'à tort on l'outrage
> Au sujet de monsieur Ménars,
> Pourtant aucune femme sage,
> N'a de batards.

"Couplet sur le prochain accouchement de la duchesse de Berry et sur sa captivité," sung to the tune of "Ça n'se peut pas" [*sic*]. Cited in Nauroy, *La Duchesse de Berry*, 436.

49. Ménière, *La captivité de Madame*, 1:422.

50. Cited in Thirria, *La Duchesse de Berry*, 226.

51. "Sainte-Caroline," *La Mode*, November 1833, 133–138.

Chapter Fourteen: A Second Judas

1. "A nos abonnés," *La Mode*, January 1834, 315 (note: this article appears in the volume dated October–January, 1833). "Marie-Caroline, duchesse de Berry, prisonnière de son oncle, Louis-Philippe, roi des Français," *La Mode*, October 1833, 158. *La Quotidienne*, November 19, 1832, 1. *La Gazette du Languedoc*, November 25, 1832, 1.

2. Narcisse-Achile de Salvandy, cited in Germain Sarrut, *Biographie de Marie-Caroline-Ferdinande-Louise de Bourbon, Duchesse de Berri* [*sic*] (Paris: Baudouin, 1841), 86.

3. "A nos abonnés," *La Mode*, December 1833, 314. Théodore Anne, *La prisonnière de Blaye* (Paris: Charpentier, 1832), 191.

4. See Nirenberg, *Anti-Judaism*, especially 121, 194–195. Francesca Trivellato describes the association of Jews with the rise of capitalism in the early modern period in *The Promise and Peril of Credit: What a*

Forgotten Legend About Jews and Finance Tells Us About the Making of European Commercial Society (Princeton, NJ: Princeton University Press, 2019). In *Socialism of Fools: Capitalism and Modern Anti-Semitism*, trans. Noor Mazhar and Isabella Vergnano (New York: Columbia University Press, 2016), Michele Battini argues that the tradition of anticapitalist antisemitism arose from the Catholic response to the French Revolution.

5. Chateaubriand cites the pamphlet in his *Mémoires d'outre tombe*, 3:392. Morel, *Vérité sur l'arrestation*, 156–157. Jean-Claude Caron provides an interesting discussion of the comparisons of Deutz to Judas in the light of nineteenth-century French political and religious history (see, especially, *Simon Deutz*, 166–167). Caron also remarks on Chateaubriand's antisemitism (181).

6. Chateaubriand refers to her Italian accent in *Mémoires d'outre-tombe* (3:610). "Arrestation de Madame la duchesse de Berry," *La Mode*, November 1832, 133. "Revue de la semaine," *La Mode*, January 1833, 36.

7. Alfred Nettement, "Madame la duchesse de Berry," extrait de la *Quotidienne* du 9 mai 1832, 3.

8. *L'Ami de la religion et du roi, journal ecclésiastique, politique et littéraire* (1832–1833), 74:303. In *Toward the Final Solution: A History of European Racism* (New York: Howard Fertig, 1978), George L. Mosse notes that the legend of the wandering Jew "reenforced the view of the Jew as the 'eternal foreigner'" (115).

9. *Le Revenant*, November 21, 1832, 2. *Gazette du Languedoc*, November 21, 1832, 1. The song reads in the original:

Pour de l'or qu'on lui donna,

Un traitre a dit: elle est là.

Quel est ce nouveau Judas,

Est-c' donc un Francais? non pas. [*sic*]

Ce n'est rien, (bis)

C'n'est pas un concitoyen; [*sic*]

Ce n'est rien,

Notre honneur se porte bien.

10. *Le Revenant*, November 17, 1832, 2. *La Gazette du Languedoc*, November 23, 1832, 1. Kalman notes the comparison to Judas and the contrast with Marie Boissy and discusses the quotation from *La Gazette du Languedoc* (*Rethinking Antisemitism*, 79).

11. *La Quotidienne*, November 13, 1832, 1.

12. Lisa Moses Leff discusses Jews' use of race theory in *Sacred Bonds of Solidarity: The Rise of Jewish Internationalism in Nineteenth-Century France* (Stanford, CA: Stanford University Press, 2006), 96–100; as does Mosse, *Toward the Final Solution*, 124–125. For an account of the eighteenth-century origins of European racism, see Mosse, 1–17; and Andrew S. Curran, *The Anatomy of Blackness: Science and Slavery in an Age of Enlightenment* (Baltimore: Johns Hopkins University Press, 2012).

13. *Le Constitutionnel*, November 14, 1832, 3. Sander Gilman, *The Jew's Body* (New York: Routledge, 1991), 96.

14. Although "pygmies" figured in Greek mythology, Europeans did not encounter actual Central African Forest Peoples until 1865. Christopher Kidd, "Inventing the 'Pygmy': Representing the 'Other,' Presenting the 'Self,'" *History and Anthropology* 20, no. 4 (December 2009): 395–418.

15. S. [Solomon] Posener, *Adolphe Crémieux, 1796–1880* (Paris: Félix Alcan, 1933), 170.

16. Kersabiec, *Récits et souvenirs*, 77.

17. Shulamit Volkov, "Antisemitism as a Cultural Code. Reflections on the History and Historiography of Antisemitism in Imperial Germany," *Yearbook of the Leo Baeck Institute* 23 (1978): 25–45.

18. The Fourier quotation is from the first part of his *Théorie des quatre mouvements et des destinées générales* and is cited in Poliakov, *Histoire de l'antisémitisme*, 2:201–202). The Proudhon quotation is from his *Qu'est-ce que la propriété? Recherches sur le principe du droit et du gouvernment* (1840; Paris: Lacroix, 1873), 206. In an unpublished journal entry devoted to Jewish bankers, dated December 26, 1847, Proudhon wrote, "Jews. Write an article against that race, which poisons everything. . . . Demand its expulsion from France, with the exception of a few individuals married to French women, abolish synagogues, do not admit them to any profession, pursue the abolition of their religion. . . . The Jews are the enemies of the human race. They should be sent back to Asia or exterminated." Jean-Claude Caron notes Proudhon's reference to Deutz (*Simon Deutz*, 212).

19. *Le Courrier Français*, November 14, 1832, 1.

20. Dumas, *Mes Mémoires*, 2:782. Not only is *La Vendée* free of antisemitic stereotypes, but Dermoncourt even sees Deutz's defection from

Judaism as prefiguring his later actions: "Thus, it was in betraying God that he learned to betray men" (*La Vendée*, 171).

21. One exception is when he refers to Drach as "still a bit of a Jew" because he does not want to lend Deutz more money (*Deutz ou imposture*, 6), which I refer to in chapter 4.

22. Alexandre Dumas [and Gaspard de Cherville], *Les Louves de Machecoul* (1858; Create Space Independent Publishing Platform, 2014), 559. Deutz is referred to as "the Jew," 560, 562. Poliakov notes that "only Alexandre Dumas treated Deutz in a more or less equitable manner" (*Histoire de l'antisémitisme*, 2:190).

23. The coverage of the affair in the English and American press of the time provides an instructive point of comparison. According to a search of databases, more than one thousand articles about the arrest of the duchess appeared in English-language publications between November 1832 and June 1834. Many of these referred to Deutz's Jewish background. Those published in the first months after the arrest tended to specify that Deutz was "educated in the Jewish religion," a direct translation from an article in the liberal *Courrier Français* (November 14, 1832, 2) and the least-antisemitic way of referring to Deutz's Jewishness. Later references became more pejorative, calling him "the Jew Deutz" (*The Times*, February 23, 1833), "a foreigner and a Jew" (*The London Standard*, February 28, 1833), or "the Jew Deutz who betrayed her" (*The Columbian Centinel*, April 17, 1833). It seems that all the Anglo-American papers began copying the same right-wing French sources (or one another) after February 1833. The fact that newspapers of very different political orientations used the same language to describe Deutz suggests that antisemitism did not function as a cultural code distinguishing Right and Left in the Anglo-American context. The databases I consulted include https://support.gale.com/tlist/additional, https://access.newspaperarchive.com, and https://infoweb.newsbank.com (all accessed January 25, 2019). Jean-Claude Caron notes that the case was covered eagerly by journalists in Italy and Austria as well (*Simon Deutz*, 132).

24. Deutz, "Devant Dieu" [n.p.].

25. *La Quotidienne*, November 23, 1832, 3.

26. *Le Courrier Français*, November 24, 1832, 4. Posener, *Adolphe Crémieux*, 172–173.

27. *Le National*, November 18, 1832, 3.

28. Posener, *Adolphe Crémieux*, 173. Police report dated September 1833. Archives nationales F/19/11038.

29. Police report dated September 1833.

30. Emmanuel Deutz, "Exposé," Archives nationales F/19/11038.

31. Letter from Consistoire des Israélites de France to Ministre de l'Intérieur et des Cultes, dated May 14, 1833. As Rabbi Deutz wrote in his response to the minister, "I believe it is my responsibility to respond to the reproach that has been made to me for having had relations with my son who abjured his religion five years ago." Both letters contained in Archives nationales F/19/11038. Phyllis Cohen Albert describes the conflict between Rabbi Deutz and the consistory in *The Modernization of French Jewry: Consistory and Community in the Nineteenth Century* (Hanover, NH: Brandeis University Press, 1977), 286–294; as does Landau, "Le cas étrange," 230.

32. *Les Archives Israélites de France* (1842), 67–71.

Chapter Fifteen: Aftershocks

1. Ménière, *La captivité de Madame*, 2:371, 375.

2. Ménière, 2:377.

3. Boigne reports on the nickname Saint-Joseph (*Mémoires*, 1191). Nickname also mentioned in Lucas-Dubreton, *La Duchesse de Berry*, 121.

4. Mesnard, *Souvenirs intimes*, 3:283. Thirria, *La Duchesse de Berry*, 242.

5. Thirria, 243.

6. Cited in Thirria, 250.

7. Chateaubriand, *Mémoires d'outre-tombe*, 3:606.

8. Chateaubriand, 3:645.

9. Boigne, *Mémoires*, 1189. Duchess's letter, dated February 1, 1835, appears in Chateaubriand, *Mémoires d'outre-tombe*, Maurice Levaillant, ed. (Paris: Flamman'on, 1982), 4:510. Also cited in Hillerin, *La Duchesse de Berry*, 378.

10. Thirria transcribes the death certificate (*La Duchesse de Berry*, 257). Boigne, *Mémoires*, 1186.

11. Hildegard Kremers, "L'Exil en Autriche," in Hildegarde Kremers, ed., *Marie Caroline de Berry: Naples, Paris, Graz, itineraire d'une princesse romantique* (Paris: Somogy editions d'art, 2002), 10. Thirria, *La Duchesse de Berry*, 275.

12. Thirria, 277, 281. According to the memoirs of the baron de Damas, Louis-Philippe did everything he could to keep Charles X from recovering the property he left behind in France. Some of the lawsuits continued until 1857 (Damas, *Mémoires*, 209).

13. Hillerin, *La Duchesse de Berry*, 383–384.

14. Caroline Weber provides a vivid description of the atmosphere of Frohsdorf later in the century in *Proust's Duchess*, 92–93.

15. Duchess cited in Maurice Levaillant, "Chateaubriand, Charles X et la duchesse de Berry (pages inédites des *Mémoires d'outre-tombe*)," *La Revue des Deux Mondes* 74, no. 2 (March 15, 1943): 203; Hillerin, *La Duchesse de Berry*, 389, 391. Kremers, "L'Exil en Autriche," 18.

16. Faucigny-Lucinge, *Souvenirs*, 79–80.

17. Faucigny-Lucinge, 72–75. Hillerin, *La Duchesse de Berry*, 390.

18. Castelot, *La Duchesse de Berry*, 318. Both letters cited in Castelot, 322.

19. Hillerin cites a letter from the duchess in which she complains of losing 430,000 francs in the Jauge bankruptcy (*La Duchesse de Berry*, 419). See also Hillerin, 393; Thirria, *La Duchesse de Berry*, 413.

20. Thirria gets the figure of his income from a private conversation with Prince Charles de Lucinge, who heard it directly from the Comte de Chambord (413, note 1). I am basing the amount of his investible assets on a 5 percent return, which was standard at the time. Castelot reports, based on information obtained from Maurice de Charette, that the agreement worked out between the duchess and the Bourbons in 1833 specified that her children by her first marriage (Henri and Louise) would inherit all her "immobile" property (real estate), while the Lucchesi-Palli children would inherit her personal property (art, antiques, jewels, etc.) (*La Duchesse de Berry*, 323). Hence, Henri was within his rights to force her to sell this personal property after paying her debts because otherwise it would pass to his half siblings. See also Thirria, *La Duchesse de Berry*, 415–416.

21. Cited in Castelot, *La Duchesse de Berry*, 324.

22. Thirria, *La Duchesse de Berry*, 439.

23. Emmanuel Deutz, "Exposé."

24. Emmanuel Deutz.

25. *Le Revenant* referred to Deutz as an "odious Jew" on November 17, 1832. The receipt that Deutz signed after receiving the money also bears that date. Bibliothèque nationale, Manuscrits, Nouvelles acquisitions françaises, 20601, fol. 163. Emmanuel Deutz ("Exposé") says that his son left for London on November 17.

26. Cecil Roth, "The Reconversion of Simon Deutz," *Journal of Jewish Studies* 17, nos. 1–2 (1966): 83–84.

27. At the end of his life, Moulin recalled what transpired: "This Jew was sent to me almost fifty years ago by M. Crémieux, his coreligionist, who asked me to hear him out, to examine the documents he supplied, and to defend him against the rumors that pursued him after the arrest of Madame." Moulin apparently believed Deutz's affirmation that he had not "made any request for money" in exchange for leading the police to the duchess's hiding place. Letter by Moulin to Charles Nauroy, cited in *Le Curieux* 15 (January 1885): 230. Jean-Claude Caron provides biographical details on Moulin (*Simon Deutz*, 139).

28. *Bibliographie de la France* (Paris: Pillet aîné, 1835), 418. Letter from Simon Deutz to Louis-Philippe, June 27, 1835, contained in Archives nationales 231/AP/3, Papiers du baron Fain. Also cited in Landau, "Le cas étrange," 231–232.

29. Drumont, *La France Juive*, 1:48. Archives nationales BB/11/646 (1), Changements de noms, dossier 2126. Also cited in Landau, "Le cas étrange," 229–230.

30. *L'Ami de la religion*, 1835, 84:293. Landau, "Le cas étrange," 232. Klein, "Mauvais Juif," 102. Zosa Szajkowski, "Simon Deutz: Traitor or French Patriot: The Jewish Aspect of the Arrest of the Duchesse de Berry," *Journal of Jewish Studies*, 16 (1965): 63. Dumas, *Mes Mémoires*, 2:946. Jean-Claude Caron describes how French newspapers offered conflicting reports on Deutz's marriage (*Simon Deutz*, 225).

31. Bibliothèque nationale FRBNF41518377.

32. Bibliothèque nationale, nouvelle acquisition française, no. 1309. Landau refers to this letter in "Le cas étrange," 232–233.

33. Canler, *Mémoires*, 141.

34. Deutz, *Arrestation*, 42. Landau found the receipt for the burial plot in the Archives du cimetière du Père-Lachaise (Paris), concession no. 400 P, purchased by Simon Deutz in July 1838. Landau, "Le cas étrange," 233, note 82.

35. Archives nationales, Minutier central, C1/1031, Etude de Me Morel d'Arleux, February 1842. Also cited in Landau, "Le cas étrange," 233. The purpose of the second meeting was for the brothers to waive the obligation of the married sisters to subtract their dowries from their share of the estate. It is possible that Simon's name is crossed off because he refused to do this rather than because he was absent.

36. Canler, *Mémoires*, 141.

37. Landau mentions various hypotheses ("Le cas étrange," 234). According to Nauroy, for instance, he became the father of the (Belgian) composer Magnus Deutz (*Le Curieux* 46 [January 1888]: 341). Szajkowski repeats the equally fanciful rumor that he remained in Paris and adopted a child who grew up to be the poet Catulle Mendès ("Simon Deutz," 63). Canler, *Mémoires*, 142. Nauroy, *Le Curieux* 15 (January 1885): 231. Drumont, *La France Juive*, 48. Boigne, *Mémoires*, 1146.

38. Jean-Claude Caron cites the *Journal des Débats* article (*Simon Deutz*, 234). References to the payments to Deutz can be found in letters contained at the Ministère des Affaires Étrangères, Centre des Archives diplomatiques de Nantes. La Nouvelle-Orléans, Consulat général, série D, article 5 (Sylvain Delatour—Simon Deutz). Landau discusses these letters in "Le cas étrange," 234.

39. There were only about 25 Jews living in New Orleans in 1820, but by 1860 there were more than 2,000 in a city of 168,000. See http://www.isjl.org/louisiana-new-orleans-encyclopedia.html, accessed on March 12, 2019.

40. I also could not find any trace of a V. Weyl in New Orleans directories or any government records from the time. There are multiple people with variant spellings of the last name (Weil, Veil, Vail, etc.) but none with the first initial V. For instance, the New Orleans city directory for 1844 lists a Frederick Weil who owned a piano store at 321 Royal St. According to immigration and naturalization records, about forty people with the last name Weil arrived in New Orleans before 1900.

Notarial Purchaser Indexes show that several of these Weils bought and sold slaves in the 1840s. The death certificate, written on December 3, 1846, now resides in the Louisiana State Archives. Index: New Orleans Health Department Death Certificates, Index to Records of Deaths 184a, v. 1 1843–47, 3. See also Landau, "Le cas étrange," 233–234. E-mail to author concerning diseases from Jason Berry, April 5, 2019.

41. Gates of Mercy burial services described by Bertram Wallace Korn, *The Early Jews of New Orleans* (Waltham, MA: American Jewish Historical Society, 1969), 238. An Aron Deitz, age thirty, died of consumption on June 27, 1846, and received a charity funeral at the Gates of Mercy, but he is too young to be Deutz (see Jones Hall at Tulane University Archives, manuscript 224 box. 1 v. 1—Touro Synagogue records [Gates of Mercy Records of Internment]). Death record of Aron Deitz also found in mf FF650 1846–9, New Orleans Health Department Death Certificates, v. 11. Drowning reported in *L'Abeille de la Nouvelle-Orléans*, July 6, 1844. Heatstroke death reported in *Times Picayune*, July 6, 1844. Bayou St. John Cemetery: recorded burials from 1835–1844. Mf LMC430 1835–1844—Mayor's Office Records (v. 1, Jan. 1, 1835–Dec. 31, 1844).

42. In suggesting that Deutz may have faked his death, I note that I differ from the two other historians who have examined the question, Philippe-E. Landau and Jean-Claude Caron, who both accept his death in New Orleans as a fact.

Coda: Memory

1. See Maurice Halbwachs, *On Collective Memory* (Chicago: University of Chicago Press, 1992); and Pierre Nora, ed., *Realms of Memory: Rethinking the French Past*, trans. Arthur Goldhammer, ed. Lawrence Kritzman (1992; New York: Columbia University Press, 1996).

2. Alexandre Dumas, *Mes Mémoires*, 2:780. The information contained in this chapter on mentions of the case in the French press comes from a database containing more than four hundred French-language newspapers (https://www.retronews.fr), accessed February 19, 2019.

3. Marc Angenot, *Ce que l'on dit des Juifs en 1889. Antisémitisme et discours social* (Vincennes: Presses universitaires de Vincennes, 1989). On the rise of antisemitism in France at the end of the nineteenth century, see

Léon Poliakov, *Histoire de l'antisémitisme* (1955; Paris: Calmann-Lévy, 1981), 2:284–307.

4. Elisabeth Parinet, *La librairie Flammarion, 1875–1914* (Paris: Imec, 1992), 256.

5. Drumont, *La France Juive*, 44–45.

6. "L'Affaire Dreyfus," *La Libre parole*, November 7, 1894, 1. A. de Boisandré, "Le traître Dreyfus," *La Libre parole*, December 23, 1894, 1. On the degradation ceremony, see Ruth Harris, *Dreyfus: Politics, Emotion, and the Scandal of the Century* (New York, Metropolitan, 2010), 1.

7. An article by René Maizeroy in *Le Gil Blas* on December 12, 1894, drew parallels between Judas, Deutz, and Dreyfus. An article by François Coppée in the *Indépendent Rémois* on December 24, 1894, referred to Deutz as a "hideous Jew" and compared his bargain with Thiers to the "thirty pieces of silver of the Iscariot." An article by Léon Daudet in *La Libre Parole* on August 21, 1904, stated that the Jewish race had been compromised since Judas and Deutz. As Gravier wrote about his play, "The name of the hero, the choice of the subject made such a supposition [that the play was really about Dreyfus] inevitable." Johannès Gravier, "Manifeste," in *Simon Deutz: drame historique en 8 tableaux* (Paris: Bibliothèque artistique et littéraire, 1896), 35. Gravier's play generally adopts an "Orléanist" point of view, suggesting that the arrest of the duchess was necessary for the safety of the country. It repeats many of the self-justifying claims made by Deutz in his memoir, including that he demanded that the duchess be kept safe after the arrest, etc. (47).

8. Pierre Birnbaum describes these antisemitic attacks in *Léon Blum: un portrait* (Paris: Seuil, 2016), especially 127–150.

9. Paul Mathiex, "La Princesse et le traître," *L'Action Française*, December 23, 1938, 4.

10. René de Marmande, "Hyacinthe-Simon Deutz, Juif baptisé," *Aujourd'hui*, January 12, 1942.

11. "Le 6 Novembre 1832 Le Juif Simon Deutz livrait la duchesse de Berry," *Inter-France*, Edition speciale, no. 431, November 6, 1943. The film *The Jew Süss* (1940) was directed by Veit Harlan. On the case and its repercussions in Germany, see Yair Mintzker, *The Many Deaths of Jew Süss: The Notorious Trial and Execution of an Eighteenth-Century Court Jew* (Princeton, NJ: Princeton University Press, 2017).

Index

Michael Marsland

Maurice Samuels is the Betty Jane Anlyan Professor of French at Yale University, chair of the Program in Judaic Studies, and founding director of the Yale Program for the Study of Anti-semitism. A recipient of the Guggenheim Fellowship, he is the author of three prizewinning books, *The Spectacular Past*, *Inventing the Israelite*, and *The Right to Difference*. He lives in New York and New Haven, Connecticut.